With this moving account of Theodore Roosevelt's post-presidential years and of his efforts to regain power after he left the White House, Joseph L. Gardner brings to life again one of the most intriguing figures in American history. Roosevelt was the youngest man ever to leave the White House, an ex-President at fifty, not a very congenial position for a man with his energies and his love of glory.

After hand-picking his successor, Taft, T.R. vowed to keep clear of Washington. He tried to occupy his time with his flamboyant and widely publicized travels — a safari to Africa and then a triumphal progression through Europe. But he found himself drawn more and more to politics. Despite his vow, by 1912 he was running for President again, against Taft and Wilson. In 1916 he again tried to get back to the center of power, but once more his attempts floundered. When World War I broke out, he maneuvered tenaciously to be sent over to France — to be a war hero again; but Wilson refused to allow it.

Gardner tells the poignant story with full attention to the historical processes operating; the book is the first to concentrate solely on Roosevelt's life after he left the White House. But he also manages to suggest strongly that personal drives — a need for action and glory — motivated Roosevelt as much as his political beliefs did; and that his failure to achieve any of his goals after 1908 brought personal tragedy in its train.

Departing Glory

The real problem that confronts you is whether you can be a sage at fifty. If you can, your permanent reputation seems to me certain. If you cannot, then the outlook is different.

Nicholas Murray Butler to Theodore Roosevelt
October, 1901

. . . when I am thru with anything I am thru with it, and am under no temptation to snatch at the fringes of departing glory. When I stop being President I will stop completely. . . .

Theodore Roosevelt to Henry Cabot Lodge
July 19, 1908

DEPARTING GLORY

*Theodore Roosevelt
as ex-President*

JOSEPH L. GARDNER

CHARLES SCRIBNER'S SONS
NEW YORK

Grateful acknowledgment is made to the publishers for the use of quotations from the following works:

The Letters of Theodore Roosevelt, Vols. 1–8. Edited by Elting E. Morison. Cambridge, Mass.: Harvard University Press. Copyright 1951, 1952, 1954 by the President and Fellows of Harvard College.

The Works of Theodore Roosevelt, Memorial Edition, Vols. I–XXIV. Edited by Hermann Hagedorn. Copyright 1923–26 by Charles Scribner's Sons.

The Autobiography of William Allen White by William Allen White. Copyright 1946 by The Macmillan Company.

Masks in a Pageant by William Allen White. Copyright 1928 by The Macmillan Company. Excerpts included by permission of William L. White.

The Letters of Archie Butt. Edited by Lawrence F. Abbott. Copyright 1924 by Doubleday & Company, Inc.

Taft and Roosevelt, the Intimate Letters of Archie Butt, 2 vols. Copyright 1930 by Doubleday & Company, Inc.

Printed in the United States of America
Library of Congress Catalog Card Number 72–11116
SBN 684–13300–8 (cloth)

FOR SADAKO

words are but empty thanks

Preface

Theodore Roosevelt's post-presidential career, the historian John Morton Blum has suggested, seems to prove the opposite of Lord Acton's famous dictum; in this instance, it was the lack of power that corrupted. As President, Blum writes in *The Republican Roosevelt,* T.R.'s performance was "noteworthy"; he "demonstrated perception, knowledge, principle of a kind, energy tempered with restraint." As a former Chief Executive, on the other hand, Roosevelt "exhibited the characteristics that least became him, prejudices of mind and traits of personality that he had subdued while he felt the responsibilities of office." The present writer, though strongly sympathetic to Roosevelt, can but sadly agree—at least in part—with Blum. Roosevelt could *not* be a sage at fifty; he *did* "snatch at the fringes of departing glory." Yet, it would be rash and perhaps unfair to doubt his sincerity.

Having installed William Howard Taft as his successor in the White House, T.R. removed himself from the political arena by going to Africa for a year. Upon his return, however, he could not resist becoming involved again in public affairs. Brilliant, restless, supremely self-righteous, he honestly thought himself a better man than either Taft or Woodrow Wilson and wanted to be back in office because he felt the times called for the sort of vigorous leadership only he could provide —or at least Roosevelt convinced himself of these things. And he was not a man accustomed to acknowledging mistakes or changing his mind. Such a rigid attitude, in the final decade of his life, led T.R. down some devious paths and ultimately proved fatal to any hope of an enduring high reputation. The admired, respected, even loved Theodore Roosevelt became, in time, the faintly ludicrous "Teddy." By dealing with these

vii

years in such depth—a period generally slighted by earlier biographers—I hope to restore somewhat a balance to our view of one of the nation's most fascinating historical figures.

Joseph L. Gardner

Acknowledgments

A number of people provided generous assistance in the preparation of this work. First, I must thank Theodore Roosevelt's two daughters. Alice Roosevelt Longworth welcomed me into her home and shared with me some typically lively and uninhibited memories of her father. Ethel Roosevelt Derby let me browse through the Pigskin Library and took me on a memorable behind-the-scenes tour of Sagamore Hill.

Throughout my labors Helen MacLachlan, Museum Curator of the Theodore Roosevelt Birthplace in New York, has always responded promptly and politely to my queries and shown the interest in this book that is the writer's best stimulus. To her and to Wallace Finley Dailey, Curator of the Theodore Roosevelt Collection at the Harvard College Library, I owe special thanks for supplying most of the photographs used here. Nicholas Roosevelt kindly lent me a typescript of his 1912 diary and allowed me to quote from it in Chapter 12. The book could not have been written without access to the enormous reservoir of the New York Public Library and the smaller but select collection at the Mercantile Library of New York.

I profited from brief but illuminating conversations with John Morton Blum of Yale, Arthur S. Link of Princeton, and Elting E. Morison of the Massachusetts Institute of Technology, scholars whose published works on this era have been a major inspiration. Melvin I. Urofsky of the State University of New York at Albany read the completed text and made a number of thoughtful suggestions for improvement. The responsibility for what follows, of course, is mine alone.

For their steadfast enthusiasm and encouragement I wish to thank Malcolm Reiss of Paul R. Reynolds, Inc., and Norman Kotker of Charles Scribner's Sons.

Contents

CONTENTS

Chronology

1858	Theodore Roosevelt born in New York City, October 27
1880	Graduates from Harvard in June; marries Alice Hathaway Lee, October 27
1881	First elected to New York State Assembly
1884	Deaths of mother and wife, February 14, following birth of daughter, Alice; attends G.O.P. convention in Chicago in June
1884–86	Ranching in Dakota Badlands
1886	Defeated for Mayor of New York in November; marries Edith Kermit Carow in London, December 2
1889–95	United States Civil Service Commissioner in Washington
1895–97	New York City Police Commissioner
1897–98	Assistant Secretary of the Navy

1898   Colonel of the Rough Riders in Cuban campaign of Spanish-American War; elected Governor of New York

1899–1900   Governor of New York

1900   Nominated and elected Vice President on McKinley ticket

1901   Inaugurated as Vice President, March 4; succeeds assassinated McKinley as President, September 14

1904   Elected President and renounces third term, November 8

1908   Fiftieth birthday, October 27; Taft, handpicked by Roosevelt as his successor, elected President, November 3

1909   Roosevelt leaves office, March 4; sails for Africa

1909–10   On safari in Africa

1910   Triumphal tour of Europe, April-June; returns to U.S. and reenters politics in fall congressional elections

1912   Defeated by Taft for G.O.P. nomination; enters presidential race as candidate of Progressive party; Wilson elected in three-way contest

1913–14   Traveling in South America; becomes seriously ill while exploring Brazilian river

1914–15   Leads campaign for U.S. preparedness and intervention on Allied side after war breaks out in Europe

1916   Refuses second nomination of Progressive party; returns to G.O.P. to support Charles Evans Hughes

1917   Request to lead volunteer division, after U.S. enters war, rejected by Wilson administration

1918   In hospital for operation, February-March; youngest of four sons serving in war killed, July; declines to run for Governor of New York; returns to hospital with inflammatory rheumatism, November-December

1919   Theodore Roosevelt dies in his sleep at Sagamore Hill, January 6, aged sixty

Departing Glory

⊷§ Chapter 1 §⊶

Hour of Triumph

The President arrived at Washington's railroad station nearly an hour before the scheduled departure of the midnight train to New York. He responded to the greetings of the small crowd gathered to see him off merely by raising his black slouch hat and saying "Good evening, gentlemen." Then, accompanied by two private secretaries, he boarded a special car—the "Sunset"—that had been sidetracked until the regular train was formed. Immediately upon entering the car, he dropped into a chair, picked up a book, and was soon absorbed in reading.

To reporters covering the presidential journey, Theodore Roosevelt seemed unusually reserved and calm. Only intimates knew of his nervous excitement that evening—Monday, November 7, 1904. It was Election Eve, and Roosevelt was going home to Oyster Bay, New York, to vote. The odds favoring the election to his own full term of the man who had succeeded to the Presidency upon the death of William McKinley three years earlier were overwhelming; most gamblers could not even get money on his colorless Democratic opponent, Judge Alton B. Parker of the New York Court of Appeals. Yet Roosevelt was tense, for this election was to be the climax of his career; winning it meant everything to him.

In the three years he had already been in the White House, Roosevelt's dynamic leadership had expanded the presidential office more than had any of his predecessors since Lincoln, bringing him both widespread praise and vociferous denunciation. Would he be rewarded with election in his own right in 1904? None of the four vice presidents who had previously succeeded to the Presidency upon the death of a predecessor had even been nominated for a full term of his own. Almost feverishly, T.R.

3

had worked for his own nomination in June, 1904, but turn-of-the-century convention decreed that a President did not actively seek re-election and so he had to watch the campaign more or less from the sidelines. The Democrats, however, had obliged him by naming Parker; and that reserved judicial character had further accommodated Roosevelt by refraining from making any public addresses until the week before the election.

Roosevelt should have been calmed and reassured by this knowledge as the train headed north on Election Eve, and perhaps he was. At any rate, he was still awake when the train stopped in Philadelphia at 3:15 A.M. He stepped out onto the rear platform of his special car to wave and bow to those gathered at the station; then he retired for the four-hour journey across New Jersey.

At 7:13 on Tuesday morning, November 8, the train from Washington—only five minutes late—pulled into Jersey City. A swarm of policemen gathered outside the presidential car and when Roosevelt emerged they formed a hollow square for his march down the platform. The President smiled, tipped his hat, and bowed to the railroad employees who cheered his arrival, and at the head of the train he paused and reached up to shake hands with the engineer and fireman in the locomotive. Still surrounded by police, he stepped into the baggage elevator and a few minutes later emerged on the lower pier at water level on the Hudson River. He waved at a few surprised early commuters to Manhattan and was not at all dismayed when a trucker proposed three cheers for Parker. He merely laughed and removed his hat for the tribute to his opponent. Nimbly he jumped across the three feet separating the pier from the deck of the tug *Lancaster* and joined the captain in the pilot house for the ride across New York harbor and into the East River.

A special two-car train was waiting for the presidential party when the tug reached Long Island City shortly before eight. Secret Service men and reporters clambered into the first, behind the locomotive; Roosevelt boarded the private car of the road's president at the rear. There was a delay of forty-five minutes before the train pulled out of Long Island City but en route it stopped only once, to pick up Roosevelt's old friend the reporter and social historian Jacob Riis, author of the President's 1904 campaign biography. At 9:50 A.M. the train pulled into Oyster Bay, where the President was taken in a carriage to the polling place, a hall over a Chinese laundry. After filling out his ballot and making sure it was properly deposited, he shook hands with the election officials and stepped back out onto the street. Friendly crowds followed his every movement.

After a short stop at his home, Sagamore Hill, Roosevelt returned to the railroad station, where nearly the entire village had gathered to give him a warm send-off for the return to Washington. Then, to the horror of the Secret Service, a man with a rifle suddenly materialized on the edge of the throng. Closing in on him, they discovered that he was merely a local hunter drawn to the station by the crowd. A small boy wearing an oversize slouch hat reminiscent of the Rough Rider headgear stepped forward to tell the President, "Teddy, we want four years more." Roosevelt smiled, responded to the cheers of his fellow townsfolk, and boarded the train for an 11 A.M. departure. From the rear platform he waved until the throng of admirers dwindled and disappeared in the receding distance.

At Mineola, where the presidential special stopped to take on water, another crowd had gathered. A grizzled workman stepped forward to say that, if his hands were not so dirty, he would like to shake hands with the President; he had voted for the first nominee of the Republican Party, John Charles Frémont, a half century before, in 1856. No honest hand was too dirty to shake, the President replied; he was more than willing to oblige so veteran a Republican. A delegation approached with a large portrait of T.R., and a young lady was bold enough to step forward and say, "You are my ideal President." As the train pulled out of Mineola, someone called out, "You will hear from Nassau!" From the rear platform Roosevelt answered, "I hope so."

Before noon Roosevelt was back in Long Island City for the return voyage across New York harbor to Jersey City, and at 12:30 P.M. he boarded the presidential car, at the end of the Washington train. A New York admirer came aboard with a four-foot-high floral tribute in the shape of a harp; it was, an inscription read, "emblematic of the immense vote of Erin's sons recorded for him this day (and will be again, Deo volente, in 1908)." Joining him for the first leg of his rail journey back to the capital was his younger sister Corinne, Mrs. Douglas Robinson. As the two sat alone in the drawing room of the private car, Roosevelt poured out his repressed longing to Corinne. He had never wanted anything in life quite so much as he now wanted to win the election, "the outward and visible sign of his country's approval of what he had done during the last three and a half years." Her brother's "every nerve was strained to the bursting point," Mrs. Robinson later recounted to a friend; "he could not stand it much longer. . . ." At Philadelphia Mrs. Robinson got off the train to return to her home in Orange, New Jersey, and the President—alone and thoughtful—continued south.

A carriage from the White House was waiting at the station when the New York train pulled into Washington at 6:18 P.M. The President was whisked away before a gathering crowd was even aware of his arrival; disappointed, most of them drifted off or walked up Pennsylvania Avenue to watch the election returns being posted on bulletin boards outside newspaper offices. At 6:30, when the carriage from the station drove up the circular drive to stop at the front entrance to the White House, the President stepped out and quickly mounted the stairs. Standing at the door to greet him was Edith Roosevelt.

At that moment, T.R. later in the evening wrote his sister, he suddenly realized that "no matter what the outcome of the election should prove to be, my *happiness* was assured . . . for my life with Edith and my children constitutes my *happiness*." To the First Lady, who asked if he had any news of the election, he replied that it no longer made any difference. "Nothing matters as long as we are well and content with each other." The beautiful moment was instantly shattered by seventeen-year-old Theodore Roosevelt, Jr., their eldest son Ted. A telegraph line had been installed in the Red Room and the first returns had just come clicking over it. Buffalo and Rochester had registered enormous pluralities for the G.O.P. ticket. Within twenty minutes other counts, from Chicago, Connecticut, Massachusetts, and additional New York precincts, made it clear that there was "a tremendous drift" to Roosevelt. At 7:30 P.M. the family retired to dinner "as unperturbed," a reporter noted, "as though nothing unusual were going on."

In the library of his home near Kingston, New York, Judge Parker was also receiving returns and, according to a newspaper of the following day, he "took his medicine like a scholar and a gentleman." At 8:30 P.M. he wired Roosevelt, "The people by their vote have emphatically approved your Administration, and I congratulate you." The news of Parker's concession reached T.R. at the dinner table and he tersely replied, "I thank you for your congratulations."

Not until the next day would the magnitude of Roosevelt's victory be known: a popular majority of 2,500,000 votes over Parker, the greatest up to that point in American history. Parker carried only the Solid South, minus traditionally Democratic Missouri. The electoral count was equally lopsided: 336 for Roosevelt; 140 for Parker. The little Dutch boy who kept his finger in the hole in the dyke had given humanity its greatest example of fortitude, a newspaper wit observed, until "Parker ran for the Presidency against Theodore Roosevelt and was defeated by acclamation."

Both houses of Congress would again be controlled by the Republicans; the G.O.P. majority in the House had swelled by forty-two—many of them Congressmen who rode T.R.'s coattails to victory. The novelist Owen Wister, Roosevelt's old friend and a man well accustomed to his periodic pessimism about the future, sent a cryptic telegram: "Richard Third Act one Scene one Lines one and two." Turning to their Shakespeare, the Roosevelts could read:

> Now is the winter of our discontent
> Made glorious summer by this sun of York.

After dinner the Roosevelt family returned to the Red Room, by then filling with members of the Cabinet and their wives and other political friends and well-wishers. Secretary of State John Hay crossed Lafayette Square in a drizzling rain and was greeted by an exuberant T.R. who told him it was all over. "I am glad to be President in my own right," he remarked to Hay. A younger son, Archibald—"plastered" with campaign badges—was running back and forth delivering the first telegrams of congratulations that were to build into an avalanche by the next day. The proud and happy Chief Executive entertained his guests by reading aloud from the messages.

At 10:15 P.M. the President excused himself and retired to his executive office to complete a duty to which he had pledged himself long before the election. For a few minutes he chatted amiably with the reporters he had summoned to his office, then he seated himself at his desk and asked the newsmen to gather in a semicircle in front of him. Slowly, deliberately—so the reporters could take notes if they wished—he dictated a statement to the private secretary at his side.

> I am deeply sensible of the honor done me by the American people in thus expressing their confidence in what I have done and tried to do. I appreciate to the full the solemn responsibility this confidence imposes upon me and I shall do all that in my power lies not to forfeit it.
>
> On the fourth of March next I shall have served

7

> three and a half years, and this three and a half years
> constitutes my first term. The wise custom which lim-
> its the President to two terms regards the substance
> and not the form. Under no circumstances will I be a
> candidate for or accept another nomination.

During the dictation of the announcement, it was so quiet in the presidential office that the attentive reporters could hear the ticking of the
clock on the mantle. When he was finished, the President dismissed
them so that they could get the statement on the wire to make the
morning editions of newspapers across the country. After stopping again
in the Red Room to receive additional congratulations, the President
went upstairs to retire at 11:30.

Second only to news of the Roosevelt landslide, in newspapers the
following day, was publication of and comment on this "no third term"
statement. Even so stern a critic as the New York *Sun* said that the renunciation of further ambition, "in his hour of triumph," would redound
to Roosevelt's everlasting honor. T.R.'s closest political confidant, Senator Henry Cabot Lodge of Massachusetts, wrote to compliment Roosevelt on the timing of his announcement, saying that "It was the moment
of all others" to make it. To a British journalist the next month
Roosevelt wrote a lengthy defense of his statement. The custom limiting
a President to two terms was a time-hallowed one, dating from George
Washington; it would affront the people to ignore it. A President was
much more powerful than a British prime minister and consequently
there could be a legitimate objection to one man exercising so much
power for so long. Finally, T.R. explained, after a President has been in
office seven or eight years, "he has inevitably contracted such animosities
and caused such discontents, and above all, has inevitably delivered his
'special message' so many times, as to become in the eyes of the public
stale. . . ." In this case, a new man dedicated to the same principles
could do more than the old leader to accomplish his goals. This was a
prime example of what Roosevelt's daughter Alice would call a "posterity letter"—not necessarily untrue, most certainly not the whole
truth, but nonetheless the truth as T.R. perceived it and as he wished
it recorded in history.

The Election Night statement of 1904 has been called Roosevelt's
"worst political blunder," one that was to cause him "poignant regret in
the years to come." There is strong evidence, however, that he had
planned his action at least a year earlier. In December, 1903, he had

written to Senator Francis E. Warren of Wyoming that even if he were nominated and elected in 1904 he would be leaving the Presidency on March 4, 1909. To a New York supporter he had written, only two weeks before the election, that "nothing would make me a candidate again," although he did not want to say this publicly until after the election. A family friend later related the unlikely story that Edith Roosevelt had never been consulted about the statement and that, if she had, she never would have permitted T.R. to make it. "Theodore has tied so many knots with his tongue that he can't undo with his teeth," Edith is supposed to have said. Perhaps Mrs. Roosevelt had objected, even strenuously, to the premature renunciation, but it is doubtful it came as a surprise to her. Roosevelt himself told another friend that every time he had gone against Edith's judgment he had later regretted it. And, whatever Edith Roosevelt's opinion on the matter, this was something Roosevelt later regretted, bitterly.

Once released, such a statement could never be recalled. And he kept his pledge: he did not seek renomination four years later in 1908 and left office on March 4, 1909, a few months after he had turned fifty. Too young to retire, too restless and ambitious to withdraw from public affairs, Theodore Roosevelt was left in the prime of his life with no legitimate goals to pursue, no practical worlds to conquer. Thus considered, the action of November 8, 1904, becomes the pivot of his later career, a major division between the crowded, triumphant years following 1901 in which he was "Mr. President" and the contentious, frustrating, and ultimately empty years in which he was merely "Colonel Roosevelt."

The Reluctant Candidate

In the spring of 1899 Vice President Garret A. Hobart went home to
New Jersey to die. A former state legislator and a wealthy lawyer
said to be connected with sixty corporations, Hobart was a leading Republican supporter of the gold standard—and thus a valued ally in
William McKinley's contest for the Presidency, three years earlier,
against that heretic of the free-silver movement, the Boy Orator of the
Platte, William Jennings Bryan. More than had most of his predecessors,
McKinley relied upon his Vice President for political support and often
consulted him on public affairs.

In Washington the Hobarts had leased a house on Lafayette
Square, diagonally across from the White House, and for two years their
home was frequently the setting for brilliant gatherings of Washington
society. President McKinley, the Major, came to rely almost equally
heavily, for personal and social support, on Mrs. Hobart.

The First Lady, his beloved Ida, refused to acknowledge that she
was an epileptic and insisted on appearing at state dinners and diplomatic receptions. At receptions, the President had perfected a system of
reaching to the left for a visitor's outstretched hands and swinging him
in a wide arc to the right—past Ida, in whose hands had been placed
a bouquet to indicate she would not shake hands—and thus into the
grasp of Jennie Hobart, next in line. In defiance of established protocol,
McKinley seated Ida to his immediate right at state dinners. When an
ominous hiss from Ida's pursed lips announced one of her "fainting
spells," he would flip his napkin over her face, usually without even interrupting his conversation, and signal for the First Lady's removal by a
prearranged route. Jennie Hobart, at his left, joined him in the elaborate

pretense that nothing had happened. And at other times Mrs. Hobart
—already a daily visitor to the White House—could always be
pressed into last-minute service when Ida McKinley was indisposed or
when the President needed moral support at a trying social function.
The two families even spent their first summer holiday together following the inauguration of 1897. Thus allied politically and socially,
McKinley and Hobart made a redoubtable team, and their renomination
by the Republican party in 1900 was virtually a foregone conclusion.

Early in 1899, however, it became known that the Vice President
had a serious heart ailment, and the doctors ordered a summer of rest.
The Hobarts went first to the Jersey shore and later joined the McKinleys at Lake Champlain. Seeking repose for his delicate wife, the President was trying to vacation as a private person, but there were too many
callers to receive, too many hands to shake—the curious were even
camping in tents on the hotel lawn. Hobart had thought he could relieve the President of some official functions at the lakeside resort; instead McKinley had to accompany his faithful but by then mortally ill
colleague back to New Jersey. Now only a forgotten face from America's past, Garret Hobart made his principal contribution to the destiny
of America by opportunely expiring on November 21.

The following morning, in New York City, Governor Theodore
Roosevelt breakfasted with Thomas Collier Platt, the senior U.S. Senator
from New York and Republican boss of the state. It is a reasonable assumption that among the topics discussed that morning was the Republican national ticket for the following year. McKinley was certain of renomination; but now, with Hobart gone, who would get the
vice-presidential bid?

For more than two decades Roosevelt—however subconsciously
—had been aiming for the Presidency. His approach to the highest office in the land had at first been slow and circuitous, and few outside the
inner circle of his family and close friends knew of his ambition. In
1881, a year out of Harvard, he had been elected to the New York State
Assembly and there, in his own words, "rose like a rocket." In his second
term, he was the unsuccessful Republican nominee for speaker. But in
February, 1884, a month after the start of T.R.'s third term, his young
wife, Alice Lee, died two days after giving birth to their daughter. His
mother died the same day, in the same house. Although Roosevelt returned to the Assembly and attended the Republican National Convention in Chicago the following June, he was devastated by the double

tragedy. That summer he retired to his newly purchased ranch in the Dakota Badlands and wrote a memorial to Alice Lee in which he claimed that with her death "the light went from my life forever." He was twenty-five years old.

Two and a half years later Roosevelt married his childhood friend, Edith Kermit Carow, and with her started a blissfully happy second life. Sagamore Hill, the large, unpretentious, but comfortable country home they built outside the village of Oyster Bay, overlooking Long Island Sound, was rapidly filled with the shouts and laughter of children: Alice, the daughter of Roosevelt's first marriage, and the four boys and a girl Edith gave him in the next eleven years. Roosevelt published several books, principally on Western life and history, during these years and in 1889 he re-entered public life.

His new post, United States Civil Service Commissioner charged with enforcing the new merit system in hiring and promoting employees of the federal government, was an unglamorous one; yet he made much of it. He stayed in Washington through the four-year administration of the Republican Benjamin Harrison and for two years into the term of Grover Cleveland, the Democrat who reappointed him. Later he served for two years as New York City Police Commissioner and for one year as Assistant Secretary of the Navy, back in Washington. The Spanish-American War of 1898, in which he served as colonel of a volunteer cavalry regiment, the Rough Riders, propelled Roosevelt into the national limelight. That year, backed by Senator Platt, he was elected Governor of New York.

Platt, a small, thin man, with deep-set eyes, a receding hairline, and a short, grizzled white beard, was a favorite with cartoonists who depicted him as a sinister manipulator, a political Svengali who had trained his Trilby, Roosevelt, to sing to his tune. Nonetheless, he had made the returning hero of San Juan Hill the successful Republican candidate for governor with some reservations. "But if he becomes Governor of New York," Platt had confided to a friend at the time, "sooner or later, with his personality, he will have to be President of the United States . . . and I am afraid to start that thing going." Once established in the executive mansion at Albany, T.R. proved far less pliant than Platt had imagined he would be. The two continued to confer regularly —at meetings like the breakfast of November 22—but Roosevelt was often unmoved by the gentle persuasions of the Easy Boss, the nickname Platt for once must have regretted.

Roosevelt was ambitious for the Presidency, that Platt knew—as did almost anyone else whose ear T.R. had—but he was aiming for 1904. In June, 1899, en route to and from the first annual reunion of the Rough Riders at Las Vegas, Nevada, the New York governor had been astonished, and frankly pleased, by the dense and enthusiastic throngs that had greeted him at every stop—"exactly as if I had been a presidential candidate." Back in the East, he had found it necessary to deny a boomlet for his nomination in 1900 and to declare his early support of McKinley's re-election. He hurried to Washington, spent the night at the White House, later visited the ailing Hobart in New Jersey, and finally conferred with both McKinley and Hobart at their Lake Champlain vacation spot. He also, however, listened thoughtfully to his friend Henry Cabot Lodge, when the Massachusetts senator proposed the Vice Presidency in 1900 as a stepping-stone to the Presidency in 1904.

The friendship of Lodge and Roosevelt—the austerely elegant Boston Brahmin and the exuberant former cowboy and war hero—was deep and enduring, and politically significant. Since their first political battle together—an alliance against the nomination of James G. Blaine for the G.O.P. nomination in 1884—the pair had thought and acted almost as one. Lodge had guided and actively maneuvered the political advancement of his younger friend through his successive positions up to the New York governorship. T.R.'s next step en route to the inevitable Presidency, Lodge strongly felt, was the vice-presidential nomination, a year away in 1900.

"Curiously enough Edith is against your view and I am inclined to be for it," Roosevelt wrote Lodge on July 1. His position as governor, T.R. feared, was "utterly unstable"; he could not be sure of another nomination or re-election at the end of his current two-year term. As for crowds on his trip west, "I have never known a hurrah to endure for five years. . . ." Yet, he continued to vacillate.

Already T.R. knew of Platt's displeasure with his performance as governor, and he knew too that Platt could easily block his nomination for re-election. Whether or not Platt urged the Vice Presidency on him at that breakfast following Hobart's death, Roosevelt had made up his mind by year's end that he did not want the second spot on the G.O.P. ticket. "I have told Cabot that I did not want, and would not take, the Vice Presidency; also Platt," he wrote his older sister Anna Cowles ("Bamie") on December 17.

Among the reasons he gave Lodge for avoiding the nomination was his inability to entertain as lavishly as had the Hobarts. Left a small income by his father, and supplementing it only by occasional writings, Roosevelt always found it difficult to live on the modest government salaries of the time and worried about money throughout his life. The salary of the Vice President in 1900 was $8,000 per year and "even to live simply as a Vice President would have to live would be a serious drain upon me, and would cause me continual anxiety about money," T.R. complained to his friend. Lodge, in his reply, attempted to be sympathetic. He pointed out that Adlai Stevenson, Hobart's predecessor, had lived in three rooms in a hotel and there must be a "reasonable medium which you could follow with perfect dignity and propriety without going beyond your income."

Platt, meanwhile, apparently refused to be deterred in his aim of kicking Roosevelt upstairs and replacing him as governor with someone more obliging. Early in the new year, on January 20, 1900, he made his first public statement in support of Roosevelt for the Vice Presidency. In the Senate about that time, Lodge rose to eulogize Hobart; he spoke— a historian has observed—not to his colleagues in the chamber but to his friend in the executive mansion at Albany. Under Hobart, Lodge stated, the Vice Presidency had been restored to its "true greatness." No longer could the office be considered a consolation prize, a political dead end; rather it should be the aim of "our most ambitious men . . . as a stepping stone to higher honors." McKinley, Lodge confidentially wrote to Roosevelt, was "perfectly content to have you on the ticket with him. . . ."

T.R. still thought it was within his power to resist the gentle promptings of his friend and the steady pressure of the Easy Boss; he was slow to grasp the simple fact that Platt wanted to get rid of him. ". . . I would a great deal rather be anything, say professor of history, than Vice President," he complained to Senator Platt early in February. Then, on February 12, Roosevelt issued a statement to the press: "It is proper for me to state definitely that under no circumstances could I or would I accept the nomination for the Vice-presidency. My duty is here in the state whose people chose me to be governor. I am happy to state that Senator Platt cordially acquiesces in my views in the matter." Whatever Roosevelt's impression, Platt had not given up. And talk of the Vice Presidency continued. "Teddy Roosevelt howls and yells that he won't be Vice-President," noted Henry Adams, that cynical but astute observer of the Washington scene.

Early in May Roosevelt went to Washington, again to deny his ambition for higher office. "Teddy has been here: have you heard of it?" wrote Secretary of State John Hay to a friend. "It was more fun than a goat. He came down with a sombre resolution thrown on his strenuous brow to let McKinley and [Senator Marcus A.] Hanna know once for all that he would not be Vice-President, and found to his stupefaction that nobody in Washington, except Platt, had ever dreamed of such a thing."

When Roosevelt called on him, McKinley did not even let T.R. launch into a full exposition of his argument for declining the Vice Presidency; the Major brusquely agreed that Roosevelt would be more valuable in New York. When Roosevelt started haranguing his old friend Secretary of War Elihu Root with his reasons for not wanting to be Vice President, Root smiled maliciously and said, "Of course not—you're not fit for it." "And so," concluded Hay, T.R. "went back quite eased in his mind, but considerably bruised in his *amour propre.*" To Roosevelt himself Hay remarked, "I think you are unduly alarmed. There is no instance of an election of a Vice-President by violence."

Root, the corporation lawyer turned public servant, was also a serious contender for the vice-presidential nomination. For a time Roosevelt entertained the hope that the secretary would move up so that he could succeed Root in the War Department. But Root soon took himself out of the running and urged Roosevelt to do likewise. The boundlessly energetic New York governor, he remarked to a newspaperman, would be "wretchedly unhappy" in the Vice Presidency, "the most necessary function of which is decorous and considerate inactivity."

The nomination for the Vice Presidency, of course, was not Platt's alone to offer. His chief opponent in the effort to maneuver Roosevelt out of Albany and down to Washington was balding, jug-eared Senator Marcus Alonzo Hanna of Ohio. It was Hanna who had engineered McKinley's rise from Civil War major to congressman to Governor of Ohio to President, and Hanna remained his protégé's closest confidant. As Chairman of the Republican National Committee, the Ohio senator firmly expected to have something to say about the Major's running mate in 1900—and the last man he would have chosen, Hanna made clear, was Theodore Roosevelt. The smooth, self-important senator from Ohio simply could not take Roosevelt—the ex-cowboy, Rough Rider, and parvenu governor—seriously. Between Platt and Hanna in the spring of that presidential year, a contemporary observer noted, there developed something like one of those card games in which you try to get an undesirable card into your opponent's hand. Each time the two met and parted, Hanna had to search his pockets to be sure Platt had not slipped Roosevelt into one of them.

There were other candidates for the office, but none of them struck sparks. Thus, as the spring lengthened, Hanna grew worried. It would have taken but a single word from the White House to assure, or block, the nomination of any man, but the Major remained serenely aloof from the speculation and the increasingly frantic political maneuvering.

In April Roosevelt accepted designation as a delegate-at-large to the G.O.P. convention, scheduled to open in Philadelphia on Tuesday, June 19. If T.R. went to the convention, Lodge warned, he would be nominated and, if nominated, would be unable to refuse. If he truly did not want the Vice Presidency, the Massachusetts senator advised his friend, he should at the last moment find himself too busy in New York to attend the convention and let an alternate take his place. But T.R. decided to ignore Lodge's advice and tempt fate by going to Philadelphia, and Edith Roosevelt was to join him there.

One evening at the Executive Mansion in Albany, a few days before the New York delegation was to depart, Mrs. Roosevelt found herself alone after dinner with one of their guests, Judge Alton B. Parker. She asked him whether she could expect to enjoy the convention sessions and if he thought her husband could avoid the vice-presidential nomination. In answering her, Parker described with astonishing foresight the governor's arrival at the hall: "And then—just a bit late—you will see your handsome husband come in and bedlam will break loose, and he will receive such a demonstration as no one else will receive. And being a devoted wife you will be very proud and happy. Then, some two or three days later, you will see your husband unanimously nominated for Vice-president of the United States."

2

Accompanied by Platt, Roosevelt boarded the train for Philadelphia on Saturday, June 16. That very afternoon the senator had broken a rib but, despite the considerable pain, he must have smiled broadly as he shepherded his rebellious young protégé—the reluctant candidate for the vice-presidential nomination—aboard the train. Upon reaching Philadelphia, Platt immediately went into a huddle with other politicians sympathetic to his cause.

Beginning Sunday morning, members of various delegations began calling on Roosevelt at the Hotel Walton. The chairmen of first the Pennsylvania then the California delegations pledged their support. The chairman of the Kansas delegation proclaimed that, like it or not, Roosevelt was going to get the votes of his group. Only T.R.'s name on the ticket, he claimed, would pull into office local G.O.P. candidates in the West. Other Western and even some Southern delegations fell into line. To all his callers Roosevelt flashed his famous smile and reiterated that he was not a candidate. Outside the hotel, an enterprising and farsighted souvenir salesman, "Buttons Bim" Bimberg, was pushing McKinley-Roosevelt buttons. "If it isn't Roosevelt," he said, "there will be a dent in the Delaware River caused by Bim commiting suicide."

On Monday a strong Roosevelt supporter, Henry C. Payne of Wisconsin, called on Hanna to ask the senator's advice. "Do whatever you damn please!" the thoroughly exasperated Hanna shouted at Payne. "I'm through! Everybody's gone crazy! What's the matter with all of you? Here's this convention going headlong for Roosevelt for Vice President. Don't any of you realize there's only one life between that madman and the Presidency?" Yet, Hanna was finding it difficult to fight somebody with nobody: none of the alternate candidates was strong enough to provide a rallying point for anti-Roosevelt sentiment.

Shortly after noon on Tuesday, June 19, Mark Hanna stood at the rostrum of the vast Convention Hall in West Philadelphia and signaled the opening of the Republican conclave with a somewhat listless thump of his gavel. A few minutes later a stout, militarily erect figure entered the hall and strode purposefully down the aisle to take his place in the New York delegation. On his head Theodore Roosevelt was wearing the same wide-brimmed, black felt hat—suspiciously like the headgear of the Rough Riders—that he had worn during his campaign for the governorship two years earlier. In that era and at that season, with most delegates wearing straw boaters, Roosevelt's hat was especially conspicuous. "Gentlemen," one delegate gleefully whispered to his neighbors, "that is an Acceptance Hat."

Only routine business was conducted on the first day, and that evening Hanna tried to secure the intervention of McKinley. To preserve the fiction of his complete isolation from the convention's proceedings, McKinley listened in on a White House extension as one of Hanna's colleagues pleaded with the President's secretary. The Major favored no particular candidate as a running mate, was the reply; the convention was free to choose whomever it wished.

A caucus of the New York delegation was held Tuesday night, but Platt—in pain from the broken rib—did not attend. Instead he sent his son Frank to bring Roosevelt to his room and there told him bluntly that he had better accept the vice-presidential nomination; he could not be renominated for governor. "I cannot be renominated?" the startled Roosevelt asked. "No," replied the Easy Boss, "your successor is in this room." And he pointed a finger at his henchman Benjamin Barker Odell. The senator then won a promise from T.R. that he would not formally decline the nomination of the convention, if it came.

Roosevelt—again wearing his Acceptance Hat—was greeted with a burst of applause when he entered Convention Hall on Wednesday for the second session of the G.O.P. conclave. Further applause greeted him as he helped escort Senator Lodge, chosen as permanent chairman, to the platform. "Our babe is in the manger," a Pennsylvania politician said of T.R.'s candidacy. "The kings have seen his star in the East and are come to worship him." As Indiana's Senator Charles W. Fairbanks began the tedious but obligatory reading of the convention platform, Thomas Platt slipped out of the hall and returned to his hotel to pack. There was no reason for him to stay for the actual nominations. "Roosevelt might as well stand under Niagara Falls and try to spit water back as to stop his nomination by this convention," Platt was reported to have said before leaving for New York to seek relief from the throbbing pain in his side.

"We want a candidate we can yell for," one of the Southern delegates had remarked early in the proceedings and on Thursday—following McKinley's unanimous endorsement—the Republicans got one. The Governor of New York was among those seconding McKinley's nomination. And when he rose to speak everyone knew that he was to be the vice-presidential candidate. Only with difficulty did Roosevelt stop the ovation that greeted his appearance. With the obviously pleased Lodge seated nearby on the platform, Roosevelt delivered a rousing address, ending in a vigorous metaphor: "Is America a weakling to shrink from the world-work to be done by the world powers?" he asked. "No! The young Giant of the West stands on a continent and clasps the crest of an ocean in either hand. Our nation, glorious in youth and strength, looks into the future with fearless and eager eyes, and rejoices as a

18

strong man to run a race." The delegates, roaring their approval of his muscular sentiment, accepted the statement as Roosevelt's own nominating speech.

The names of the other candidates for Vice President were withdrawn, Roosevelt's name was officially offered, and—with only his own vote as a New York delegate withheld—Roosevelt became the nominee of the G.O.P. convention. A band struck up the Spanish-American War song "There'll Be a Hot Time in the Old Town Tonight," as the delegates waving their state banners trooped by the New York delegation where Roosevelt sat expressionless. Above in the visitors' gallery, Edith Roosevelt beamed her approval.

In New York, recuperating in his suite at the Fifth Avenue Hotel, Senator Platt was asked by reporters to comment on the result of the convention. "I am glad that we had our way," he stated and then quickly added, "The people, I mean, had their way." From Washington McKinley sent Hanna a letter complimenting him on his leadership at the convention. In his reply, the senator noted that the proceedings in Philadelphia had not been exactly to his liking. "Your *duty* to the Country," he informed the Major, "is to live for four years from next March."

Among those who rushed to congratulate Roosevelt on his nomination was John Hay, who only the previous month had dismissed T.R.'s candidacy as unlikely and inappropriate. "Nothing can keep you from doing good work wherever you are—" the Secretary of State wrote, "nor from getting lots of fun out of it." Roosevelt was not entirely convinced that it was going to be such fun. "The thing could not be helped," he wrote his sister Bamie. But to Lodge, a few days later, he reported that he was "completely reconciled."

3

National political campaigns, in those leisurely and inhibited days, were conducted at a pace and on a scale vastly different than those of today —though things were beginning to change. To preserve the dignity of his high office, the President would conduct the classic "front-porch campaign" from his home in Canton, Ohio. One morning in July the notification committee—Henry Cabot Lodge, chairman—appeared on the lawn in front of McKinley's home. The Major stepped through the front door, listened attentively as Lodge gave him the unstartling news that he had been renominated for the Presidency, and then delivered himself of a speech. A month later, McKinley's formal letter of acceptance was published—and that about ended his participation in the campaign. "The President, being the President, can take but a slight part in the campaign," Lodge wrote Roosevelt. T.R., his friend predicted, would be the "central figure" in the G.O.P. effort.

The Democrats, meeting in Kansas City the first week in July, had again chosen as their standard bearer William Jennings Bryan. His running mate was to be former Vice President Stevenson. With Bryan heading the ticket, the free coinage of silver at a ratio to gold of 16 to 1 was a principal issue. Republicans at New York's Union League Club countered by offering odds of 16 to 1 on McKinley's re-election.

The Spanish-American War had lasted but a few months in 1898, but its aftereffects helped shape the politics of the next decade. The United States had emerged from its "splendid little war" as a major colonial power—with an "empire" stretching from its protectorate over Cuba and its actual possession of Puerto Rico, through the projected Isthmian canal at Panama, out to Hawaii, Guam, and the Philippine Islands. To convinced expansionists such as Lodge and Roosevelt, Kipling's urging to "take up the white man's burden" was far more than a topical poem; it was a very meaningful credo. Imperialism, with Bryan and most Democrats in opposition, was to be another major issue of the campaign of 1900.

A third major issue at the turn of the century was the largely unregulated power of the enormous business combines known as trusts. The Democratic platform pledged "unceasing warfare" against the trusts. But Theodore Roosevelt, in the campaign, was to blunt this issue with his frank condemnation of business excesses—without attempting to offer concrete reforms.

Not for Bryan was the sedate dignity of a "front-porch campaign"; he was committed to vigorous and extensive speaking tours in pursuit of the Presidency that had eluded him four years earlier. In 1896 the Great Commoner had set a record for presidential contenders by traveling 13,000 miles in fourteen weeks, speaking six hundred times in twenty-nine states. Bryan would make an equally vigorous canvass in 1900. To counter Bryan's anticipated effort, Hanna—at a conference with Roosevelt in Ohio early in July—arranged for the vice-presidential candidate to carry the brunt of the G.O.P. campaign effort.

Roosevelt even then was an accomplished campaigner. His race for the governorship of New York, only two years earlier, had been a colorful but effective circus. Issues were suppressed as the hero of San Juan Hill, accompanied by seven Rough Riders in uniform, toured New York State in a special train. At every stop, a bugler would sound the cavalry charge and the intense young candidate would step forward to speak. "You have heard the trumpet that sounded to bring you here," began one of Roosevelt's speeches. "I have heard it tear the tropic dawn when it summoned us to fight at Santiago." At one point in the tour, ex-Sergeant Buck Taylor was called upon to address the crowd at a station: "I want to talk to you about mah colonel," Taylor began. "He kept ev'y promise he made to us and he will to you. When he took us to Cuba he told us . . . we would have to lie out in the trenches with the rifle bullets climbing all over us, and we done it. . . . He told us we might meet wounds and death and we done it, but he was thar in the midst of us, and when it came to the great day he led us up San Juan Hill like sheep to slaughter and so he will lead you."

In 1900 T.R., while disdaining such obvious theatricals as being undignified at the national level, agreed to barnstorm about the country—though he was concerned about appearing to be a "second-class Bryan." At the outset, he told Hanna—in a characteristic phrase—that he was "strong as a bull moose." But, he warned, he would have to guard against throat trouble, a hazard for public speakers in those pre-microphone days, especially for those making frequent rear platform speeches at railroad stops. Roosevelt's first excursion as a vice-presidential nominee was a trip to Oklahoma City, ten days after the convention, to attend the second annual reunion of the Rough Riders. Later in July he made a quick trip to the Midwest, where—in a controversial speech at St. Paul, Minnesota—he accused the framers of the Democratic platform of standing for "lawlessness and disorder, for dishonesty and dishonor, for license and disaster at home and cowardly shrinking from duty abroad." Even Hanna thought he had gone too far, but T.R. stood by the charge, only making it clear that it was the Democratic leaders and not Democratic voters he was thus indicting.

Roosevelt's major effort was made in the fall, with a seven-week swing around the country that took him through the Midwest to Montana, Idaho, Utah, Wyoming, and Colorado, and back through the upper South to New York. On September 16 he stepped off the train at Medora, North Dakota. There, just seventeen years earlier, he had alighted from another train at the beginning of his great adventure as a cowboy and rancher. Now returning as a stouter and older politician seeking national office, T.R. was pleased to find so many people who recalled those bygone years on the vanished frontier. That afternoon he slipped away for a solitary ride across the prairie, keeping to himself whatever thoughts and memories it may have inspired.

The West was Bryan territory in 1900 and T.R. faced some unruly crowds during his campaign trip. At one gathering, where he had expected some heckling, he found the audience unusually attentive. At the end of the meeting he complimented the chairman on the fact that there had been no interruptions. "Interruption," exclaimed the chairman. "Well I guess not! Seth [a friend of Roosevelt's from ranching days who had been allowed to sit on the platform] had sent around word that if any son of a gun peeped he would kill him." But at most stops he was enthusiastically, even affectionately greeted as "Teddy"—a nickname, incidentally, he thoroughly disdained; no man who actually knew him ever called him Teddy to his face. T.R.'s gleaming, evenly spaced teeth came in for their first humorous mention in national politics. Entering a crowded hall on one occasion, with the route to the rostrum apparently blocked, the candidate flashed his famous grin—a wag remarked— "and bit his way to the stage."

The final two weeks of the campaign were spent in his home state, with frequent speeches from Buffalo to Long Island, a parade in New York City on November 3, and a reception on Election Eve at his hometown of Oyster Bay. His campaign was the most vigorous ever waged in American history, up to that date, and could only be compared to Bryan's effort of 1896. He had logged 18,000 miles and made 681 speeches in 24 states. "'Tis Teddy alone that's runnin'," the satirist Finley Peter Dunne had Mr. Dooley say, "and he ain't r'runnin', he's gallopin'."

On Election Day, November 6, McKinley and Roosevelt defeated Bryan and Stevenson by a popular plurality of 860,000 votes out of nearly 14,000,000 cast. The electoral count was McKinley, 292; Bryan, 155. Bryan had carried only the Solid South and four silver-mining states, losing even his native Nebraska. The rest of the country was a sweep for the Republican party. The victory, Roosevelt modestly noted, was due principally to McKinley and Hanna and, a poor third, to himself. But above all, he righteously added, credit was due Bryan for making the G.O.P. triumph inevitable.

Roosevelt's natural elation at victory was tempered with his uncertainty about the future. To one friend he confessed that he expected to go no further in politics; he had too many and too loudly expressed convictions. The possibility of the presidential nomination in 1904, he wrote to another, was that of "lightning striking."

With his gubernatorial term due to expire on December 31 and his inauguration as Vice President not scheduled until the following March 4, Roosevelt seized the opportunity for a typically strenuous vacation: a six-weeks' mountain-lion hunt in Colorado. He returned to Oyster Bay in mid-February and on March 2 left for Washington. Another traveler to the capital that week was Senator Platt. The Easy Boss had told his friends that he would not miss the inaugural for anything; he was especially eager "to see Theodore Roosevelt take the veil."

After the official ceremonies at the Capitol, Edith Roosevelt and the children repaired to rooms previously engaged over a manicure shop at 15th Street and Pennsylvania Avenue, from which they could view the inaugural parade. Looking down at the procession, Alice Roosevelt wondered what kind of "risk" McKinley was. She had resented her father's being shoved into the Vice Presidency and thought of the McKinleys as being "usurpers" of the positions her parents should occupy.

At his home across Lafayette Square from the White House, gloomy old Henry Adams sat penning a letter to a friend abroad. The morning had merely been threatening, he reported, but by afternoon the procession was marching in "a very heavy primeval deluge of rain." "Bad luck for the Major at the start!" Adams wrote. He remembered back to the evil omen of Grover Cleveland's second inaugural in 1893, an omen realized—in Adams' opinion—by the events of Cleveland's generally unsuccessful second term. "Perhaps the rain is too heavy to last. . . ." he concluded, in a rare attempt at optimism.

~§ *Chapter 3* §~

A Fateful Bullet

As one of the last acts of his expiring first term, McKinley had called a special session of Congress to deal with presidential appointments. It was to convene on March 5, 1901, the day following his second inaugural. The new Vice President, Theodore Roosevelt, thus had an early—but brief, for the session lasted only five days— opportunity to perform the only official function provided for him by the Constitution: presiding over the Senate.

Roosevelt's previous legislative service was limited to the three one-year terms he had served in the New York State Assembly, two decades earlier. Apparently unsure of himself now, he stationed a Senate clerk at his side as he rose that first day to preside over the elite body, most of whose members were senior to him in both age and experience. And, ever the partisan, he assumed that all Democrats by nature were opponents. "All in favor will say Aye," he called on an early motion— and turned expectantly to the Republican side of the chamber. "All those opposed say No," he said, nodding to the Democratic ranks.

Roosevelt lingered in Washington only a few days following the adjournment of Congress and then left for what was to be a nearly six-month-long vacation at Sagamore Hill. But before leaving, he paid a call on Supreme Court Justice Edward Douglass White. After his graduation from Harvard, and his early first marriage, Roosevelt had briefly studied law at Columbia. Now, qualified only for such uncertain professions as historical writer and politician, he wished to resume his legal studies. When he returned to the capital in the fall, he told White, there would be time enough to study law; his duties as Vice President were scarcely "onerous." (Only six weeks after the inaugural, he was writing a friend that the Vice Presidency was an office that "ought to be abolished.") The justice felt that it would be unseemly for the nation's second highest official to attend public law lectures. Instead, White offered to supply Roosevelt with books and quiz him on his readings every Saturday evening. This course of private instruction was to begin when Congress—reconvening in December—brought T.R. back to Washington. Later in the spring, he sought additional advice from Judge Alton B. Parker: Would service in a Washington law office qualify him for the New York bar? Apparently Parker reassured him on this point and Roosevelt began gathering law books—though whether or not he read any of them that summer is not in the record.

The summer of 1901, instead, seemed destined to be a golden idyll for Roosevelt and his family. The previous three summers he had spent as a soldier in Cuba, a hard-pressed Governor of New York, and a campaigner for the Vice Presidency. Indeed, for the first time since he had assumed office as United States Civil Service Commissioner twelve years earlier, T.R. had no real official cares.

All six children—ranging in age from seventeen-year-old Alice down to three-year-old Quentin—were still at home. The days at Oyster Bay would be filled with the riding, swimming, hiking, rowing, and fierce play that many family friends and visitors, obliged to join in, found so exhausting; and the evenings, with storytelling, indoor games, and provocative conversation. There were to be interruptions to this program of domestic relaxation, of course. But these would come later and were spaced generously far apart.

Meanwhile, McKinley faced a busy schedule. At the end of April the President left Washington on an ambitious speaking tour that was supposed to take him through the South to California and back through the Midwest to Buffalo. There, on June 12, McKinley was to speak at the newly opened Pan-American Exposition. The presidential party reached Los Angeles at fiesta time, the second week in May. Ida McKinley—despite the new complications of a bone inflammation on her forefinger and acute diarrhea—insisted on participating in the enthusiastic public reception granted her husband. But en route to San Francisco the First Lady collapsed, apparently after having had severe epileptic seizures.

All further public appearances were canceled as the special train speeded north. For a few days it appeared that the end was near for Mrs. McKinley, and curious but respectful crowds took up a deathwatch opposite the private home in the Bay City where the presidential couple was staying. But, almost miraculously, Ida passed out of danger and began to recover. The President, able at last to make one of his scheduled public appearances in San Francisco, spoke at the launching of a new battleship. "I am inexpressibly thankful," he emotionally began his speech, "to the Ruler of us all for His goodness and His mercy, which have made it possible for me to be with you here today." This one address completed, the President took his wife directly back to Washington. After a few weeks in the capital, the McKinleys left for their home in Canton, Ohio, on July 5. Their three-month-long vacation was to be interrupted only by a trip to Buffalo, for an appearance at the exposition, rescheduled now for the first week in September.

Roosevelt's lengthy vacation was also to be interrupted by public appearances far away from home. He was slated, on May 20, to open the Pan-American Exposition. "It will be a great occasion, one worthy of your attendance and speech," he wrote Lodge. "Do come. We shall then appear together, and our two speeches reverberate through time together!" The two friends duly appeared at Buffalo and their speeches on the Monroe Doctrine—at least in Lodge's opinion—"caused quite a sensation." From Washington, the President telegraphed his message of greeting at the opening of the exposition: "May there be no cloud on this grand festival of peace and commerce."

During June and July Roosevelt made a few local appearances, dedicating a sanitorium at Bedford, addressing the Long Island Bible Society, and holding a seminar at Sagamore Hill for Harvard and Yale students on "Applied Decency in Public Life." At the end of July he and six boys "of the hobbledehoy period"—his sons and two of his sister Corinne Robinson's—were guests of R. H. Post for a four-day yacht cruise on Long Island's Great South Bay.

The Vice President's next major foray was out to Colorado, where he was to speak August 2 at the celebrations marking the twenty-fifth anniversary of statehood. But there was a complication in this apparently nonpolitical event. The previous two summers T.R. had been an enthusiastic participant at Rough Rider reunions—in 1899 as the popular Governor of New York, hailed virtually as a presidential candidate; in 1900, as the G.O.P. nominee for Vice President, immediately after the Republican convention. By 1901, however, Roosevelt had come to fear that the reunions were perhaps getting out of hand, that his opponents would regard them as being held solely for his own glorification. He was frankly angered when the original reunion—which he would have been unable to attend—was rescheduled for the place and time of the Colorado quarter-centennial. Nevertheless, he journeyed out to Colorado, made his speeches, and then ducked out of sight for ten days of fishing and hunting coyotes and wolves in the Rockies.

Henry Cabot Lodge was spending his vacation abroad, traveling across Europe to Russia with cantankerous old Henry Adams. His one ambition for his young friend—the Vice Presidency—scarcely realized, Lodge was already dreaming of the next step, the presidential nomination in 1904. One thing he and Roosevelt did not have to fear: an unprecedented third term for the popular McKinley. Troubled by such talk following his return from California at the end of May, the Major had promptly and unequivocally taken himself out of the running for 1904. ". . . I not only am not and will not be a candidate for a third term," he told the press on June 11, "but would not accept a nomination for it, if it were tendered me." McKinley, his personal and political inclinations aside, had done the judicious thing. Already others were talking about the extraordinarily ambitious young man waiting in the wings. "I would not like to be in McKinley's shoes," a congressman remarked to a friend that summer. "He has a man of destiny behind him."

Yet, Roosevelt remained a pessimist as far as his political prospects were concerned. With no power base in his home state and, as Vice President, holding an office in which he could do nothing to shape policies, Roosevelt felt that his prospects were at best bleak. In a letter that July to his old friend William Howard Taft, then civil governor of the Philippines, he confided that "I should like to be President, and feel I could do the work well. . . ." But, "at the risk of seeming [to be] . . . the lady who doth protest too much," he went on to say that he had seen at too close quarters the suffering caused others by the presidential bee "ever to get it into my head." There were several others who would make admirable presidents, Roosevelt concluded, but above all these was Taft himself. If he ever had the chance of naming a President or a Chief Justice, T.R. declared, he would unhesitatingly choose Taft for either office. And sometime, he promised, he was going to say this in public.

A month later—apparently having talked to Platt in the interval—Roosevelt was in a slightly more optimistic frame of mind. The Easy Boss, he wrote to Lodge, had promised to support him in 1904, though T.R. did not take this pledge too seriously and also doubted that Platt would still be in a position to help him much by the time of the next convention. He reported that undoubtedly there was pro-Roosevelt sentiment in the Far West, from which he had just returned, in New England, and in those parts of the South where there was a genuine Republican party. Indeed, it seems that T.R. had already taken steps to build up a Southern following. First, he had agreed to visit, late in the year, Booker T. Washington's widely praised school for Negroes in Alabama, Tuskegee Institute. Washington, it was hinted, would help build a new Republican organization in the South, one dedicated to Roosevelt's candidacy. And, en route to Alabama, Roosevelt planned to make a pilgrimage to the Georgia plantation on which his mother had been born—thus somewhat ostentatiously calling attention to his Southern ancestry.

Roosevelt had one final political trip to make that summer, a journey out to Chicago, then on to Minneapolis, and back to Vermont. All along the way, he gleefully wrote to Lodge early in September, he was greeted with "wild enthusiasm" and Vermont's Senator Proctor, at a dinner in Rutland, had proceeded to nominate him for the Presidency. But Roosevelt's pessimism uncontrollably surged up: ". . . in the next three years all may change utterly," he complained to Lodge on September 9, "and indeed probably will change. . . ."

2

The McKinleys in Canton, on the other hand, were having one of their happiest summers in memory. The couple enjoyed a few drives in the country, went to a neighbor's home for a musicale, and even gave a small dinner party.

Years ago, at the outset of their marriage, they had owned a modest frame house on Canton's North Market Street. There they had been happiest, but there also their two daughters—one, an infant of five months; the other, a little girl nearly five—had died. And when the Major entered public life, they sold the house—to live the next twenty years in hotel rooms and rented houses, in Washington and Columbus. Never wealthy—indeed, in 1893, Hanna and others had to rescue the then Governor of Ohio from bankruptcy—the McKinleys had long dreamed of a retirement home. But not until the summer of 1899, two years after he became President, was the Major able to buy another house: with a cash payment of $14,500 he bought back their first home in Canton. An additional sum of $3,000 was spent on repairs and improvements, so that, during the relaxed summer of 1901, William McKinley could survey with inexpressible pride the cozy home he at last had provided for his adored Ida. (Theodore Roosevelt, after visiting the President in Canton, had unkindly compared the North Market Street house to one that might be suitable for a retired division superintendent of a railroad.)

Official business that summer in Canton was kept to a minimum, with a miniature executive office set up in the library of the McKinley home. The President's private secretary, George B. Cortelyou, handled routine correspondence, arranged the schedule of appointments, met visitors at the railroad station—and even joined the McKinleys in card games and played the piano for them evenings. And it was Cortelyou who made the final arrangements for the visit to Buffalo.

The theme of the Pan-American Exposition was hemispheric unity —an ideal heartily supported by McKinley; and the President decided that the visit would afford him an opportunity of making a speech in support of reciprocal trade agreements. A group of the promoters visited Canton in early August to discuss the program with McKinley and Cortelyou. Since the Major had promised to be in Cleveland for the national encampment of the Grand Army of the Republic the second week in September, his appearance at the fair was scheduled for Thursday, September 5—designated as President's Day.

At noon on that day, the President and Mrs. McKinley were to be driven to the fairgrounds. After delivering his speech, the Chief Executive would make a tour of the pavilions. That evening the presidential party would return to watch the turning on of the electrical illuminations that were the wonder of the fair and stay to see a fireworks display. On Friday, September 6, an excursion to nearby Niagara Falls was planned. The final event was to be a public reception in the exposition's Temple of Music, a ten-minute appearance in which the President would shake hands with any fairgoers prompt and patient enough to line up in advance. Cortelyou, for one, was worried about security arrangements at the Temple of Music. Twice he had the reception removed from the program; both times—at the President's insistence—it was put back. To his secretary's plea that he give up this last appearance, the Major calmly replied: "Why should I? No one would wish to hurt me."

The previous New Year's Day the President had given his wife a little pocket diary for the year 1901—a somewhat inappropriate gift, unfortunately, for one to whom the passage of days and weeks was so often slow and painful. Months went by in which Ida McKinley entered nothing in the diary or only such banalities as comments on the weather. The pages for the two months at Canton were mostly blank but on Sunday, September 1, she took up her pen. "I wish we were not going away from home," she wistfully commented. "My Precious and I had a very delightful ride today."

President's Day at the Pan-American Exposition, a city-wide holiday for Buffalo, turned out to be a triumph for William McKinley; a crowd estimated at 50,000 was on hand to greet the arrival of the presidential party at noon. A detachment of soldiers had formed up on the Triumphal Causeway and a military band was playing nearby as an open carriage carrying the McKinleys and John G. Milburn, president of the exposition, appeared. A hush fell over the enormous throng when the carriage paused and the President, his arm lifting and supporting Ida, stood to survey the grand scene. Escorted to the speakers' platform, McKinley acknowledged the wild ovation and then, waving for silence with the sheaf of papers containing his speech, launched into his address. The President and First Lady attended separate luncheons and met again only late in the afternoon, at the vine-covered Milburn mansion where they were staying. Friday evening, however, they returned for the electrical illuminations and the fireworks display.

Friday, September 6, was to be the President's "restful day"; and indeed the McKinleys seemed greatly to enjoy the morning excursion to Niagara Falls. The presidential party went out halfway onto the suspension bridge so that McKinley could view the Canadian falls—without actually leaving the territorial limits of the United States. But at last the heat and excitement proved too much for Ida. The First Lady was taken to a hotel to rest and after lunch, when the party got back on the train for the return to Buffalo, it was decided that she would be taken directly to the Milburn home while her husband kept his appointment at the Temple of Music.

Promptly at four o'clock McKinley strode into the Temple of Music—a large auditorium with galleries above—and took up a position on a dais along the east wall. Above hung a large American flag, while potted palms and two bay trees provided an attractive backdrop. The doors were opened, and a line of people entered to shake McKinley's hand.

At precisely seven minutes past four—with an aide already moving to close the doors—Leon Czolgosz stepped up to the dais. The Major, in his practiced manner, was reaching to the left for outstretched hands and swinging his well-wishers past him to the right. But the hand Czolgosz presented to the President was wrapped in a large white handkerchief—as if covering a cut or binding a sprain; and inside the cloth was a short-barreled revolver. Czolgosz, a demented anarchist who at least a week earlier had formulated his bold plan to assassinate the President, fired two shots at McKinley—one into his chest, the other into his abdomen. The assassin was immediately knocked down and pinned to the floor. McKinley, sagging into a chair, called out, "Don't let them hurt him." The President put a hand to his wounds and drew it away to see the oozing blood. To his private secretary, hovering nearby, he gasped: "My wife—be careful, Cortelyou, how you tell her—oh, be careful."

3

Some three hundred miles to the northeast of Buffalo, on Isle la Motte in Lake Champlain, Theodore Roosevelt—at the conclusion of his highly successful political tour of Vermont—was attending the annual outing of the state's Fish and Game League. Toward evening a reception for the Vice President was interrupted by a telephone call from Buffalo. Roosevelt was told that the President had been shot but that no one yet knew how serious were the wounds. Members of the Cabinet were being summoned to the Milburn house, where the President was resting, and Roosevelt was asked to join them. T.R. left immediately for the mainland, where a special train at Burlington awaited him. On the boat ride across the darkened lake, someone remarked that, if McKinley died, Roosevelt at that very moment might become President. The Vice President harshly rebuked his companion and said that they should all be thinking only of McKinley's recovery.

The next day, Saturday, September 7, Roosevelt was in Buffalo, by then a city in which all interest was focused on a second-floor room in the Milburn residence. Following the shooting, McKinley had first been taken to the exposition's emergency hospital, actually little more than a first-aid station. The first bullet had only grazed his ribs and, as the President was being prepared for surgery, fell from his undergarments. But the second bullet had pierced his stomach and remained lodged in his body. Although a version of the new X-ray machine was on exhibit at the fairgrounds, the doctors in attendance declined to use it and, after closing the lacerations in McKinley's stomach, sewed up the President and thereafter simply ignored the embedded bullet.

"The President is coming along splendidly," T.R. wrote to his sister Bamie the day he arrived in Buffalo. "When you receive this," he said in a handwritten postscript to another letter, "the President I am sure will be out of danger." Henry Cabot Lodge, in Paris, was frantic because he could get no news of the assassination attempt other than tardy and possibly inaccurate news bulletins. To his cabled query, Roosevelt replied on September 8 "Confident President will recover." Thus reassured, Lodge wrote to say that, whereas there was nothing he wanted so much as to see Roosevelt made President by vote of the people, "It wrung my heart to think of your coming to the great place through an assassination. . . ."

Among the Cabinet members who quickly assembled in Buffalo was John Hay. Met at the station by a military aide, the Secretary of State brushed off optimistic reports from the sickroom and gloomily predicted that the President would die. Before leaving the capital, Hay had cabled news of the shooting to Henry Adams. Having left the Lodges after their visit to Russia, Adams had continued his European tour alone, and the news reached him as he was breakfasting at a restaurant in Stockholm. "I think black, more than even I like to do. . . ." Adams wrote to Hay. "Then, curiously, behind all, in my mind, in all our minds, silent and awful like the Chicago express, flies the thought of Teddy's luck."

Buoyed by the continued optimism of McKinley's doctors, both Hay and Secretary of War Elihu Root left Buffalo for Washington on Wednesday, September 11. Before leaving the President's bedside, Hay had asked Cortelyou to send a medical bulletin the following day, stating whether or not the doctors could gurantee that McKinley would recover. The doctors so affirmed and Cortelyou sent the message to Hay on Thursday. Hay was preparing a statement for circular release to all the embassies abroad, in answer to the hundreds of queries that were being received from around the world. But after he had written the reassuring message, Hay later wrote, "the black cloud of foreboding, which is just over my head, settled down and enveloped me, and I dared not send it." An aide walked in and remarked that he distrusted the eighth day—

32

and Friday would be the seventh following the shooting. Hay decided to wait another day before sending his circular.

The Vice President had also left Buffalo, on Tuesday. He had gone first to Oyster Bay and then, the following day, to the Adirondacks, where he joined his vacationing family at the Tahawus Club at the foot of Mount Marcy. Roosevelt had left instructions as to where he could be reached with his friend Ansley Wilcox, the man at whose home he had briefly stayed in Buffalo.

Early in the week the President had regained consciousness and Cortelyou was admitted to the sickroom. "It's mighty lonesome in here," the Major sighed. By Thursday the doctors agreed to allow the President a light breakfast of toast, coffee, and chicken broth. It did not seem to agree with him, however, and he was given purgatives and digitalis for his heart. That evening the doctors retired as usual. Shortly after midnight on Friday morning, Ansley Wilcox was awakened by a messenger from the Milburn mansion. The President had suffered a collapse; although the doctors could not have known it, gangrene had infected the President's stomach, pancreas, and one kidney. All the Cabinet members were again being assembled in Buffalo. Where was the Vice President?

A phone call was placed to Albany, and a courier left immediately for the Tahawus Club. But Roosevelt had arisen early that morning for an ascent of 5,344-foot-high Mount Marcy, New York State's highest peak, and could not be reached.

Halfway up Mount Marcy is Lake Tear in the Clouds, the source of the Hudson River. The Roosevelt party had reached it early in the day and sat somewhat disconsolately contemplating the heavy mists that shrouded the forests. Edith Roosevelt and the younger children had already turned back. Now Roosevelt, perched on a fallen log, speculated that the bald peak above might be piercing through the clouds into sunshine. He called for a resumption of the climb. But the top of Mount Marcy, that gloomy Friday the thirteenth, proved no brighter or warmer and the Vice President's party returned to timberline to spread a lunch on the grass. Their idle chatter was suddenly interrupted by an alien sound: the snap of a twig breaking under a man's swift footstep. Across the clearing appeared a stranger, waving a yellow envelope in his hand. "I felt at once that he had bad news," Roosevelt later recalled.

"The President's condition has changed for the worse— Cortelyou." Roosevelt studied the message carefully and then turned to

33

his fellow mountain climbers and softly said, "I must go back at once."

By dusk Roosevelt and his party had reached a small cottage near the foot of the mountain. There was no further news, and he stopped to change his damp clothing and rest—meanwhile sending a message on to the lower clubhouse, ten miles farther down the trail, that he was coming.

William Loeb, the Vice President's private secretary, had been trying frantically to reach his chief. He had requisitioned a special train and brought it to North Creek, the nearest railhead but still some forty miles from the Tahawus Club. He telephoned an urgent plea: "Come at once." Loeb's message reached Roosevelt about midnight but the Vice President had not yet gone to sleep. Riding in an open buckboard and accompanied only by the driver, Roosevelt set out down the murky, twisting dirt roads. Several times the driver turned to express his concern for the risks they were taking—at any moment the wheels might become lodged in a rut or strike a rock, and the wagon, team, and two passengers be hurtled into a mountain abyss. Wrapped in his own thoughts, T.R. merely said: "Go on—go right ahead!" They stopped only twice during the forty-mile ride, to change horses, and as dawn was breaking on Saturday, September 14, the buckboard pulled up at North Creek station. William Loeb stepped forward and removed his hat: "The worst has happened," he told Roosevelt. "The President is dead."

The special train waiting at North Creek to take Roosevelt to Buffalo had been kept at full steam for hours; now, with the Vice President behind the closed doors of a private compartment, it left for the long journey across New York State. At all the stops en route—Albany, Amsterdam, Utica, Rome, Syracuse—reporters clambered aboard and asked for a statement; Roosevelt remained silent. Disdaining a military escort that greeted him at Buffalo upon his arrival at 1:30 Saturday afternoon, T.R. went to the Milburn mansion to pay his respects to the departed President's inconsolable widow. Then, he retired to the Wilcox residence, a large attractive house with a wide front veranda behind imposing, two-story-high pillars. Six of the eight-member McKinley Cabinet, summoned once more to Buffalo, called upon Roosevelt later in the afternoon. The senior member and spokesman for the group was Secretary of War Root.

In another September, exactly twenty years earlier, Elihu Root had participated in a drama strikingly similar to the one now unfolding. A prominent New York corporation lawyer, Root had formed a close political association with Chester Alan Arthur, the unremarked Collector of the Port of New York inexplicably catapulted into the Vice Presidency in the election of 1880. The following July, only four months after his inaugural, President James A. Garfield was shot in the Washington railroad station by a disappointed office seeker. For months Garfield lingered on but finally the end drew near. On the evening of September 19, 1881, Root was among several friends visiting Vice President Arthur at his home on Manhattan's Lexington Avenue when a telegram arrived from Washington. Secretary of State Blaine announced that Garfield had died and urged Arthur to take the oath of office as soon as possible, to avoid a vacancy in the office of Chief Executive. It was past one o'clock the following morning before a judge could be rounded up and the oath administered in Arthur's living room with a small circle of friends—including Root—as witnesses.

Root now felt it "vastly important" that the same procedures established at the Arthur swearing-in be followed at Buffalo. Stepping forward toward Roosevelt, he recited—as best he could remember them—the words of Blaine's telegram to the earlier Vice President. A local judge was summoned and, late in the afternoon of September 14, in the library of the Wilcox residence, Theodore Roosevelt took the oath of office to become the twenty-sixth President of the United States. Six weeks short of his forty-third birthday, he was the youngest man ever to hold the position.

It must have been with special poignancy that Root watched the oath being administered. In that same autumn of Garfield's death twenty years earlier, he had been among the New York Republican leaders who had signed a petition urging the candidacy for his first public office—state assemblyman—of Theodore Roosevelt. Still looking to the elder man for guidance, Roosevelt now asked Root if there was anything that need be added to the oath. Root said there was and whispered something into the new President's ear. T.R. nodded and then made a short speech, ending with the statement: "I wish to say that it shall be my aim to continue, absolutely unbroken, the policy of President McKinley for the peace, the prosperity, and the honor of our country." After asking all the members of McKinley's Cabinet to stay in office, Roosevelt drew Root out of the house for a short stroll in the September twilight.

Early in the evening, after Roosevelt had returned from his walk, a carriage drove up to the Wilcox residence and out stepped Mark Hanna, his face drawn, leaning heavily on his cane. Prostrate at the death of his best friend and political protégé, Hanna had come to wish well the man whose nomination to the Vice Presidency he had so desperately tried to block only a year earlier. Not waiting upon custom, Roosevelt darted from the house with hands outstretched to greet the Ohio senator. Hanna swept off his hat and said, "Mr. President, I wish you success and a prosperous administration. I trust that you will command me if I can be of any service." And the two men walked into the house together.

Sunday was a trying day for the new President: a memorial service for McKinley; conferences with Root, other Cabinet members, and local politicians; a flurry of correspondence; visitors to receive; and finally arrangements for the departure, the next day, for Washington. To his friend Owen Wister, who had sent a cable of condolences and good wishes, Roosevelt replied in a handwritten scrawl: "I can't know that I have the ability, but I do know that I have the will to carry out the task that has fallen me."

In Washington John Hay composed an overwrought letter to the young man whom he had taken so lightly and who was now his chief. The familiar "Theodore" not quite yet "Mr. President," Hay stiffly addressed his letter to "My dear Roosevelt." "With your youth, your ability, your health and strength, the courage God has given you to do right, there are no bounds to the good you can accomplish for your country and the name you will leave in its annals." His official life was at an end, he concluded, and he did not expect to live long after leaving office; "and so, in the dawn of what I am sure will be a great and splendid future, I venture to give you the heartfelt benediction of the past."

4

The funeral train left Buffalo at 8:30 on Monday morning, with McKinley's coffin, his widow, and her entourage riding in one section; Roosevelt and members of his circle, in another; Cabinet members and other politicians shuttling uncertainly back and forth between the two poles. Chicago newspaper publisher H. H. Kohlsaat nominated himself to act as intermediary between Roosevelt and Hanna who—despite the friendly gestures of Saturday evening—were clearly going to be wary rivals. "I told William McKinley it was a mistake to nominate that wild man at Philadelphia," Hanna grumbled to Kohlsaat upon boarding the train. "I asked him if he realized what would happen if he should die. Now look, that damned cowboy is President of the United States."

T.R. reluctantly agreed to Kohlsaat's proposal that he invite Hanna to a private dinner on the train, complaining only that "Hanna treats me like a boy. He calls me 'Teddy.' " Despite their reservations about one another, the two did dine together that day and apparently achieved some sort of modus vivendi. Hanna candidly said that he could not commit himself, that early, to Roosevelt's nomination to a full term in 1904, but he agreed to support the new President as long as he followed McKinley's policies. And, in return for a more dignified form of address from the Ohio senator, Roosevelt promised to stop calling Hanna, even affectionately, "Old Man."

It took the train thirteen hours to reach Washington. Nearly every station platform was lined with mourners, generally delegations of schoolchildren chanting the words of the hymn "Nearer My God to Thee"—McKinley's favorite and the words reportedly last on his lips. For days afterward, Kohlsaat wrote, awake or asleep he heard echoes of that mournful dirge.

Hay was waiting in the Washington railroad station when the train pulled in. Roosevelt stepped from the cars and greeted the Secretary of State with the demand that he stay in office, forbidding him to decline or even consider doing so. "Well, he is here in the saddle again," Hay wryly noted in his next letter to Henry Adams. "So Teddy is President!" Adams wrote a few days later from Norway. "Is not that stupendous! Before such a career as that, I have no observations to make." To him and Hay at sixty-three, Roosevelt at forty-three "could not be taken seriously in his old character, and could not be recovered in his new one."

After having been reassured by Roosevelt that McKinley would recover, Senator Lodge—still in Paris—was all the more shocked at the President's sudden death. "Dear Old Theo!" a mutual friend had written him. "He is too good a man to win on a foul." To Lodge, Roosevelt now confided: "It is a dreadful thing to come into the Presidency this way; but it would be a far worse thing to be morbid about it. Here is the task, and I have got to do it to the best of my ability; and that is all there is about it." Unable to book an earlier return passage, the Massachusetts senator sailed for home as scheduled on October 5 but immediately upon his arrival in the United States went to Washington to confer with the new President. Meanwhile, Roosevelt had journeyed out to Canton to attend McKinley's funeral and by the end of September had moved into the White House.

Edith Roosevelt had returned to Sagamore Hill, to supervise the packing and moving of the family's belongings to Washington. The new President, however, was unwilling to dine alone his first night in the White House, so he invited his two sisters and their husbands, Mr. and Mrs. Douglas Robinson and Captain and Mrs. William Cowles, to join him. As they sat around the table, he suddenly asked the two ladies if they remembered that the date, September 22, was their father's birthday. The thought had come to him as he signed papers all that day, and it seemed a good omen. "I feel as if my father's hand were on my shoulder, and as if there were a special blessing over the life I am to lead here." It was then a White House custom to pass with the coffee a boutonnière to each gentleman present; the flower handed to Roosevelt that evening was a yellow saffronia rose. Mrs. Robinson later recalled that the President's face flushed at the sight. "Is it not strange!" he remarked. "This is the rose we all connect with my father." The two ladies concurred; they both remembered their father pruning a bush of yellow saffronia roses with special care and could still see him picking one of the flowers for his own buttonhole. "I think there is a blessing connected with this," T.R. solemnly remarked.

Another friend Roosevelt had been most eager to see following his assumption of office was Nicholas Murray Butler—"Nicholas Miraculous"—the young, brilliant, energetic, and highly self-esteemed educator who was then at the outset of a forty-four-year career as president of Columbia University. The week following McKinley's funeral Butler arrived in Washington and accepted a dinner invitation at the home of T.R.'s elder sister, Anna Cowles, with whom the President was temporarily staying. In the evening gloom before dinner, the two went for a brisk walk of about two miles, with Roosevelt "in a great state of emotional excitement" doing most of the talking at first. He seemed concerned about the men in government about him, and Butler spoke of the "generations in politics." He warned T.R. of working with men of an older generation, officials who would not be likely to work well with a man their junior.

Roosevelt next confessed his own sense of inadequacy and expressed fears that his administration would be unsuccessful. Butler firmly reassured him. Roosevelt, he was convinced, would be an enormous success as President; with his vitality and youth, he would captivate the American people; and he was certain of election in 1904, so he would most probably serve seven and one half years in the office, very nearly the two-term limit set by Washington's precedent. Roosevelt's major concern, Butler concluded, lay in the distant future. He would be leaving the Presidency while he was still in the prime of life. "The real problem that confronts you is whether you can be a sage at fifty," Butler affirmed. "If you can, your permanent reputation seems to me certain. If you cannot, then the outlook is different." The two friends talked of numerous things during that evening walk, before returning to dinner at Mrs. Cowles'. But three decades later the warning about the post-presidential years is what remained clearest in Butler's mind.

~§ Chapter 4 §~

Serving McKinley's Term

The Fifty-seventh Congress—elected in 1900 along with McKinley and Roosevelt—assembled in Washington on December 2, 1901, to hold its first session. With Roosevelt not yet three months in his new office, there was far more than the usual curiosity about the annual message, scheduled for delivery the following day. Almost immediately after his unexpected accession to the Presidency, T.R. had begun work on the message—soliciting advice from friends and relatives, sending drafts to members of both houses of Congress for their suggestions, discussing it at great length with members of the McKinley Cabinet he had retained. The Major customarily had asked his Cabinet members to draft sections of the message pertaining to their departments and these drafts apparently had been incorporated wholesale into the presidential reports. Roosevelt's first message to Congress, according to John Hay, was every word his own, "the most individual message since Lincoln."

Ignoring the precedent set by his two predecessors, Thomas Jefferson did not go in person to the Capitol to deliver his annual messages to Congress, and for a century presidents had followed his example. With clerks reading the messages to each house, all possibility of drama was removed from those periodic reports required by the Constitution. It was not unusual during the reading of a presidential message for members of Congress to wander in and out of the two chambers, chatting with colleagues they may not have seen for a year, greeting constituents and other visitors. The clerk droning the presidential words from the rostrum could scarcely be considered a compelling figure; everyone would later have a chance to read the printed message in the Congressional Record. But Roosevelt's address of December 3, 1901, proved the exception. "I

40

have never seen an annual Message followed with so much interest and attention in the Senate," Lodge wrote the President later that same day, "and I am told it was even more marked in the House." At the end of the lengthy recital—the message was 20,000 words long—no more than a dozen of the ninety senators had left their seats. Several times the message had been interrupted by applause; at the end of the reading there was an enthusiastic demonstration on the Republican side of the aisle.

Roosevelt's message opened with a long and obviously sincere tribute to his murdered predecessor. Then the President ranged over the entire field of domestic and foreign issues confronting turn-of-the-century America. He discussed the perennially controversial tariff and endorsed the reciprocity treaties advanced by McKinley; he paid tribute to the gold standard and spoke in favor of forest protection and water conservation. He called the projected canal across the isthmus of Central America the greatest remaining material work to be undertaken by the American people, and he announced that he would shortly be laying before the Senate the second Hay-Pauncefote Treaty with Great Britain. In this treaty Britain renounced her joint rights to a canal and gave the United States the exclusive right to build, control, and fortify the proposed interoceanic waterway. The President mentioned the special problems associated with the nation's new role, following the Spanish-American War, as a colonial power, and he reaffirmed the Monroe Doctrine, by which the United States stoutly opposed European interference in the affairs of the Western Hemisphere.

During the weeks of shaping his annual message, Roosevelt had confessed to one correspondent that he had more difficulty with the currency section than anything else. Yet it is likely that he spent an equal if not greater amount of time agonizing over what to say about the giant business combines known as trusts.

The Sherman Antitrust Act of 1890 had made combinations in the restraint of trade illegal and punishable by fines and jail terms. The act was vaguely worded, however, and its effectiveness rested on the willingness of the Department of Justice to institute proceedings against guilty corporations. While the number of industrial giants rose into the hundreds, the attorneys general under three presidents—Harrison, Cleveland, and McKinley—brought suit against exactly eighteen firms. Meanwhile, in a tortured decision of 1895, the Supreme Court held that a monopoly of manufacturing was not a monopoly of com-

merce and thus most trusts were put beyond the reach of the law. At the
same time several labor leaders were successfully prosecuted on the
grounds that the fledgling unions of the era could be considered combinations in restraint of trade.

As Governor of New York, Theodore Roosevelt had pondered the
abuses of monopoly and suggested at least some basic regulation of big
business. In his letter accepting the vice-presidential nomination in
1900, he had warned against "wrong-headed attacks" on the industrial
system and declared that no good could come of "indiscriminate denunciation of corporations." Abuses existed, he continued, and remedies for
them should be sought. Among his recommendations were full publicity
as to capitalization and profits and more effective taxation of corporations. Yet, he concluded, only when the states declined to act should the
federal government intervene. For advocating such mild reforms as these
Roosevelt had been condemned by Mark Hanna and feared as a dangerous radical by other members of the G.O.P. Old Guard.

Shortly after T.R. was sworn in as President, Hanna had written
urging him to "go slow," and Roosevelt replied that he would do nothing without consulting the party chairman. The statement regarding the
regulation of big business that Roosevelt finally incorporated into his
first annual message was quite unexceptionable and gave little hint of
the importance this issue was to play in his administration. Listening to
the message being read that day, few if any of the senators or congressmen would have been able to predict for Theodore Roosevelt a reputation in history as a trustbuster.

The perfect characterization of Roosevelt's stance was that of Mr.
Dooley, the creation of humorist Finley Peter Dunne: "Th' trusts," says
he [Roosevelt], "are heejous monsthers built up be th' enlightened in-
therprise iv th' men that have done so much to advance progress in our
beloved country," he says. "On wan hand I wud stamp thim undher fut;
on th' other hand not so fast." The country chuckled, along with Mr.
Dooley, at the new President's cautious daring, but the occasion for
mirth—as far as some big businessmen were concerned—was to be
short-lived.

On November 13, 1901, as Roosevelt was polishing the annual
message that he hoped would set the tone for his entire administration,
E. H. Harriman, James J. Hill, and J. P. Morgan had formed the
Northern Securities Company. The first important holding company,
Northern Securities was in effect a combination of the Great Northern,

Northern Pacific, and Burlington railways. Together with Harriman's Union Pacific and Southern Pacific lines to the south, it created a vast rail network that could control travel and transport in the entire western half of the continent. In his message to Congress three weeks after the creation of the new monopoly Roosevelt did not mention Northern Securities, nor any other corporation, by name. But he must already have been thinking of action to take against the giant combine.

For a man used to seeking the advice of such a wide circle of friends and associates, Roosevelt now acted with unusual secrecy. In planning his attack on the Northern Securities Company, the President consulted only one man, Attorney General Philander C. Knox, the Pennsylvania "country lawyer" he had inherited from McKinley. Late in the afternoon of Wednesday, February 19, 1902—shortly after the stock market in New York had closed for the day—a news bulletin arrived from Washington. In a very short time, Attorney General Knox had announced, the federal government would institute proceedings under the Sherman Antitrust Act to dissolve the Northern Securities Company. To his guests at a dinner party that evening Morgan complained that Roosevelt, in not giving him any advance warning, was not acting like a gentleman. Hill blustered to a friend that it was unfair "that we should be compelled to fight for our lives against the political adventurers who have never done anything but pose and draw a salary."

The day following Knox's announcement the stock market suffered its worst setback since the assassination of McKinley. "Wall Street is paralyzed at the thought that a President of the United States would sink so low as to try to enforce the law," one newspaper commented.

Both Hill and Morgan, as well as a variety of lesser representatives of the business community, were among the callers at the White House in the next few days. "It was a social call," a senator accompanying Morgan said as the pair emerged from the executive office; the Northern Securities case had not even been discussed. Apparently Morgan returned later that same day, however, and this time he definitely mentioned Northern Securities.

"If we have done anything wrong," Morgan loftily said to the President, "send your man [nodding in Knox's direction] to my man [and he named one of his lawyers] and they can fix it up." Perhaps a bit awed by the imposing financier—whose direct, burning gaze was said to make even the stouthearted tremble—but far from deterred, T.R. replied, "That can't be done." It was the government's intention, Knox

43

explained, to stop illegal combinations, not to fix them up. "Are you going to attack my other interests, the Steel Trust and the others?" Morgan asked; an even more important Morgan creation of 1901 had been United States Steel, the world's first billion-dollar corporation. No, Roosevelt responded, he would not move against U.S. Steel or the other Morgan firms "unless we find out they have done something we regard as wrong." After Morgan left, the President told Knox that they had just been privileged to witness a fine example of "the Wall Street point of view." Morgan, T.R. said, could not help but view the President as a "big rival operator, who either intended to ruin all his interests or else could be induced to come to an agreement to ruin none." In his typically succinct manner, Roosevelt had expressed a dilemma of turn-of-the-century America. The nation's enormous economic growth after the Civil War had not been matched by an equal enlargement of governmental authority—though T.R. would be doing much to extend the nation's power during his Presidency. In 1902, however, the federal government would still have seemed no more than a "rival operator" to a man of Morgan's economic stature.

The case dragged through the lower courts and not until March, 1904, did the Supreme Court—in a five-to-four decision—uphold the legality of the government's suit. The Northern Securities Company was ruled to be an illegal combination in restraint of trade; the Sherman Antitrust Act had been resurrected. Thus armed, Roosevelt subsequently brought action against the meat and tobacco trusts. In 1905 he offered Elbert H. Gary, chairman of U.S. Steel, a compromise. If Gary would cooperate with a government investigation of his firm, Roosevelt would bring to his attention any malpractices uncovered and give the steel executive a chance to correct them—without threat of prosecution. A similar arrangement was made with International Harvester, but when Standard Oil backed away after agreeing to cooperate, the Justice Department sought—and won after Roosevelt had left office—the dissolution of the oil combine.

2

In his conversation and correspondence Roosevelt was fond of quoting what he called an old West African proverb: "Speak softly and carry a big stick." And it is this image of T.R. that has endured: the exaggerated, slightly ludicrous cartoon figure in Rough Rider uniform, teeth bared and eyeglasses flashing, on the prowl with an enormous club. "It is very curious," Roosevelt once lamented to a friendly newspaperman. "Ever since I have been in the Presidency I have been pictured constantly as . . . a blustering, roaring swashbuckler type of ruffian, and yet all the time I have been growing in popularity. I don't understand it." Eventually, of course, he became resigned to the simplistic characterization but, he insisted, there was more to his methods than outright bludgeoning. When he came to write his *Autobiography* in 1913, Roosevelt called the chapter dealing with the regulation of industry "The Big Stick and the Square Deal." He may have used the big stick against the Northern Securities Company, but it was as the impartial dispenser of a square deal that Roosevelt preferred to be remembered. He saw an opportunity to earn such a lofty reputation as he entered his second year in office.

Hard, anthracite coal, found mainly in a 500-square-mile triangle of northeastern Pennsylvania, was the principal fuel of the eastern seaboard at the turn of the century. Thus, when the anthracite miners went out on strike in the fall of 1900 a fuel crisis in the approaching winter was predicted for most of the nation's major cities. Such a crisis, Mark Hanna had reasoned, would threaten William McKinley's re-election chances in November. The Republican chairman had put pressure on his Wall Street friends to grant the miners a 10 per cent wage increase, and the strike happily ended before Election Day. The mine owners, however, had not met other strikers' demands—a shorter work day, honest weighing of coal mined, standard wage scales—and they had most certainly not been willing to grant recognition to the struggling United Mine Workers of America. Thus, it was no real surprise when the miners walked out again in May, 1902.

Up to this point in American history, no President had intervened impartially in a labor dispute; indeed, it was considered government's obligation to protect the citizenry against those dangerous conspiracies in restraint of trade, the unions. Roosevelt, it now became evident, held a different view of matters. It was his theory, he later wrote, "that the executive power was limited only by specific restrictions and prohibitions appearing in the Constitution or imposed by the Congress under its Constitutional powers." He refused to follow the line of reasoning that the President must find specific authorization for his every action. If something needed to be done, and there was no constitutional prohibition nor any law *against* doing it, then Roosevelt would act. This became T.R.'s justification for stepping into the middle of the coal strike of 1902.

The principal antagonists in the strike were John Mitchell, the youthful, almost evangelical leader of the United Mine Workers, and George F. Baer, the haughty president of the Reading Railway Company, which controlled a number of mines. When a high clergyman had offered to mediate, Baer had sanctimoniously replied that mining was "a business . . . not a religious, sentimental, or academic proposition." Baer took the final step to the plateau of smug self-righteousness when he responded in mid-July to a plea that he take the initiative in settling the strike. "The rights and interests of the laboring man will be protected and cared for," Baer wrote, "—not by the labor agitators, but by the Christian men to whom God in his infinite wisdom has given the control of the property interests in this country."

A month later, on August 21, Roosevelt sought advice from Attorney General Knox on whether the coal and railroad companies—standing fast together against the strikers—could not be considered an illegal monopoly under terms of the Sherman Act. Knox doubted that they could and advised against prosecution. The next day T.R. left on a tour of New England, where he learned of the shortages that were already pushing up coal prices. Spending the night with the Lodges at their summer home in Nahant, Massachusetts, the President was told that schools in New England and New York might have to close in October for want of fuel and that this was bound to have grave consequences for the Republicans in the coming congressional elections. The President went on to Maine, New Hampshire, and Vermont, but returned to Massachusetts on September 1.

After spending the night at the home of Governor Murray Crane in Dalton, Roosevelt was en route to Pittsfield on the morning of September 3 when an accident came close to cutting short his Presidency after one year. The carriage in which he and the governor were riding was hit by a trolley. A Secret Service man was killed instantly, but Roosevelt and Crane were thrown clear of the vehicle. Although his face was badly bruised and he walked with a limp, the President insisted on completing his engagements that day and returning in the evening to Oyster Bay. Two days later he left for a five-day tour through West Virginia, Tennessee, and North Carolina, and on September 19 he departed for another and longer trip that was to have taken him to the Far West. He got only as far as Indianapolis.

The injury to Roosevelt's leg was finally discovered to be serious and, faced with the threat of blood poisoning, the President submitted to an operation in which the abcess was opened and the bone scraped. That evening, September 23, the presidential party set out for the return to Washington and five days later a second operation was performed in the capital. The injury healed slowly and for a time the President was confined to a wheelchair. Meanwhile, Roosevelt had hit upon a possible solution to the coal strike: a Washington conference between the operators and the miners—at which the President himself would preside. On October 1, telegrams went out to Mitchell and to several of the operators to meet with him two days later.

Shortly before eleven on the morning of October 3, the conferees appeared on the doorstep of Blair House. (With the White House undergoing extensive renovation, the Roosevelts had temporarily moved across Lafayette Square). The two groups were shown to a second-floor conference room and, with no attempt to mix socially, repaired to opposite ends of the room to await the President. Rolled in on his wheelchair, the President promptly opened the conference with an appeal to the patriotism of both groups to resume mining operations. John Mitchell was asked to speak first, and the intense union leader immediately won over the President with his obvious sincerity and his generous offer to accept the ruling of a presidentially appointed tribunal "even if it be against our claims."

When George Baer rose to speak—that afternoon, after a break for lunch—he did not even address himself to the issues. Instead he spoke of the "crimes" of the union leader and lectured the President on his constitutional duties to break the strike. Roosevelt was livid. There was "only one man in that conference who behaved like a gentleman," T.R. later admitted, "and that man was not I." As for Baer: "If it wasn't for the high office I hold, I would have taken him by the seat of the breeches and the nape of the neck and chucked him out that window." The acrimonious meeting broke up in failure at 5 P.M. Called upon for a comment as he left Blair House, Baer said "We object to being called here to meet a criminal, even by the President of the United States."

Such high-handedness, especially in the face of Mitchell's offer to accept arbitration, irrevocably turned the tide against the operators. Even so basic a conservative as ex-President Grover Cleveland wrote Roosevelt in defense of some sort of federal action to bring the operators into line. Quietly, this time working behind the scene, Roosevelt formed a plan. First, he maneuvered to get Pennsylvania's governor to request federal troops for the restoration of order in the mine areas. The army would seize the mines and, calling back the strikers, operate them as a receivership. Knox and Root both raised legal objections to the President's plan but reluctantly agreed to go along with him. "Theodore was a bit of a bluffer occasionally," Root later wrote, "and at the same time he had nerve to go on—to take a chance his statements would have the deciding effect and, if not, to go on and trust the country would back him up."

The Secretary of War, acting this time as a private citizen—but one of course with official inside information—went to New York to lay the President's plan before Morgan. The Wizard of Wall Street was horrified. Although he was emphatically unsympathetic toward the strikers, he felt the owners had gone far enough. George Baer was summoned to New York on Sunday, October 12. The next day Morgan himself journeyed to Washington, where he reported that the operators had at last agreed to accept a presidential commission—the very proposal they had so peremptorily dismissed when it had been made by Mitchell at the Blair House conference. Thus began the final act of what T.R. later was to call a "ludicrous comedy."

The mine operators would abide by the decisions of the tribunal, Morgan declared, only if that tribunal contained no members representing the laboring man's viewpoint. Baer and his cohorts specified exactly the type of commissioners they would accept, including someone "of pronounced eminence as a sociologist." Roosevelt had already drawn up the list of men he wanted on the five-man commission, but the operators refused to accept Roosevelt's panel.

The climax was reached on Wednesday, October 15. Two Morgan partners, Robert Bacon and George W. Perkins, called on the President after dinner. For several hours the pair argued with Roosevelt, occasionally breaking off to telephone Morgan for additional advice. Suddenly a light switched on in the President's mind. All at once he grasped the fact that the mine owners "would heroically submit to anarchy rather than have Tweedledum, yet if I would call it Tweedledee they would accept it with rapture. . . ." He would name the panel as directed by the operators, but he would interpret the categories they wished represented in his own way.

Four positions were filled entirely to the satisfaction of the owners; to the fifth position, that of the "sociologist," Roosevelt named E. E. Clark, Grand Chief of the Order of Railway Conductors, "a man who has thought and studied deeply on social questions and had practically applied his knowledge." On his own authority, T.R. added the Catholic bishop of Peoria, Illinois, a man known to be sympathetic to the strikers, and as recorder—and later full member—United States Labor Commissioner Carroll Wright. Somehow the operators swallowed their pride and accepted the commission; the miners went back to work almost immediately; and five months later—after extensive hearings— an award was made that granted many of the strikers' major demands but denied recognition to their union.

Of equal if not greater importance to Roosevelt, the Republicans won a decisive victory in the November elections, gaining a plurality of the total congressional vote in every state outside the Solid South except Nevada. In the next Congress the G.O.P. would have increased majorities in both houses.

3

For centuries, ever since Balboa had hacked his way through Panama's jungles to stand gazing at the untroubled blue expanse of the Great South Sea, men had dreamed of a canal across Central America to link the Atlantic and Pacific oceans. Fresh from his triumph of constructing the Suez Canal, Ferdinand de Lesseps undertook the task in 1881. Five years and $260,000,000 later—defeated by yellow fever and engineering difficulties—de Lesseps withdrew from Panama in disgrace. But the dream did not die. A decade later the need for an Isthmian canal was clearly demonstrated to Americans by the two-month-long voyage of the battleship *Oregon* around Cape Horn—a thrilling race against time—to reach the United States battle fleet off Cuba for the climactic naval engagement of the Spanish-American War.

Since 1850 the United States had been bound by a treaty with Great Britain not to undertake alone the construction or fortification of a Central American canal. In February, 1900, Secretary of State Hay signed a new pact with Lord Pauncefote, the British minister in Washington, by which England renounced her joint rights to a canal in return for an American pledge to maintain the neutrality of the waterway the United States would then be free to build. A week later the impetuous young Governor of New York, Theodore Roosevelt, issued a statement to the press in which he expressed his hope that the Senate would reject the treaty unless it were amended so as to allow the United States to fortify the canal and deny its route to enemies in wartime. "Cannot you leave a few things to the President and the Senate, who are charged with them by the Constitution?" a hurt and angry Hay wrote to his longtime friend. But when the Hay-Pauncefote Treaty came before the Senate, Henry Cabot Lodge succeeded in having it amended along the lines suggested by Roosevelt.

The amendments proved unacceptable to Britain and the original treaty died. But Hay and Pauncefote negotiated a second agreement in November, 1901, which did give the United States those rights Roosevelt—by then President—had earlier demanded. The new President, in his first annual message to Congress, urged ratification. Thirteen days later, on December 16, the Senate obliged him—and the United States at last had a green light to build a canal. The question remained: where?

Panama, of course, offered the shortest route, about fifty miles. But the de Lesseps disaster had shown its terrain to be difficult and inhospitable. An alternate route—four times longer but much of it along natural waterways—lay through neighboring Nicaragua. Roosevelt himself seems to have favored this second route, but he did not count on the very effective backstage manipulations of a French engineer named Philippe Bunau-Varilla, and the New York attorney William Nelson Cromwell. Bunau-Varilla, who had served with de Lesseps in Panama, had helped organize the New Panama Canal Company to take over the assets of the bankrupt French firm in an attempt to sell them to the American government for $109,000,000. Cromwell was retained as a lobbyist for the venture. The attorney later took credit for a change in the 1900 G.O.P. platform whereby the words "Isthmian Canal" were substituted for "Nicaragua Canal" in the plank favoring an interoceanic waterway. Thereupon Cromwell had donated $60,000 to the McKinley-Roosevelt campaign fund.

After his re-election, McKinley appointed a commission to study the route. But its report, issued in December, 1901, after the President's death, stated that the Panama assets were worth no more than $40,-000,000 and that the Nicaragua route should thus be designated. Bunau-Varilla panicked—and quickly lowered his price to meet the commission's estimate. And when the Senate met in June, 1902, to make a final choice of the route, he had two powerful allies: Mark Hanna and Mother Nature.

On June 5 the Ohio senator rose to make what was later considered the most important speech of his career. In his hand were two small sheets of paper filled with page references to a stack of books behind him. At his call, a secretary handed him in turn each volume, so he could read facts and statistics that built a slow but impressive case for the Panama route. Hanna's speech had to be continued the following day and when he was through one senator—previously pro-Nicaragua—said that he would now be voting "not for a Panama but for a Hannama Canal."

Nicaragua's Mt. Momotombo provided the final necessary boost to Panama's fortunes by a timely eruption just as the senators were opening their debate on the issue. Bunau-Varilla scurried around Washington purchasing every issue he could find of a graphic Nicaraguan stamp that showed the volcano, smoke drifting from its summit in a picturesque stream. The next morning each of the ninety senators found on his desk one of the stamps with an inscription: "An official witness of the volcanic activity of Nicaragua." Three days later, on a critical motion, Panama won by forty-two to thirty-four votes.

With the route selected, the next step for the administration was to negotiate with Colombia—of which Panama was then still a part—for a right-of-way across the Isthmus. In January, 1903, Hay concluded an agreement with the Colombian chargé in Washington, Tomás Herrán, to pay Colombia $10,000,000 and an annual subsidy of $250,000 for permission to build the canal. The big winner, however, would still be the New Panama Canal Company, which would be awarded the $40,000,000 it sought. At this point, Colombia balked.

Roosevelt was convinced that the "contemptible little creatures in Bogota" were merely greedy for more money. Money aside, the Colombians were understandably reluctant to surrender all sovereignty over a strip of land three miles wide on each side of the canal, as the Hay-Herrán agreement specified. "History will say of me," the unhappy dictator of Colombia, José Manuel Marroquin, lamented, "that I ruined the Isthmus and all Colombia, by not permitting the opening of the Panama Canal, or that I permitted it to be done, scandalously injuring the rights of my country." Called into an extraordinary session by Marroquin, the Colombian Senate rejected the treaty on August 12, 1903. "I do not think," T.R. exploded, "that the Bogota lot of jack rabbits should be allowed permanently to bar one of the future highways of civilization." In this and in equally deplorable comments about Latin Americans made at the time, the President was giving vent to the blatantly racist sentiments that he shared with all too many of his fellow citizens, including most policy makers of the first two decades of the century.

Fortunately for Roosevelt's desires, Bunau-Varilla and Cromwell did not allow the Colombian rebuff to halt their efforts in behalf of a Panama canal. Through the fall the two plotted a revolution that would overthrow Colombian rule of the Isthmus and declare Panama an independent state. As the new republic's George Washington, they picked Dr. Manuel Amador de Guerrero. In mid-October Dr. Amador was summoned to Bunau-Varilla's room in New York's old Waldorf-Astoria Hotel, where he was given $100,000 to stage the revolt, drafts of a declaration of independence and a constitution, and a design for a Panamanian flag. The revolution was scheduled for November 3.

Back in Panama, Dr. Amador found to his dismay that Colombia was sending reinforcements to the Isthmus on November 2; he cabled New York that the plans would have to be abandoned. Bunau-Varilla replied with a pledge that, by the time the flag of revolt was raised, American warships would have appeared on the scene to protect the freedom of transit across the Isthmus—a right the United States claimed under terms of an old treaty. Roosevelt later claimed that Bunau-Varilla had made such assurances to the revolutionists merely as a result of a "shrewd guess." The President knew nothing of it. "I did not lift my finger to incite the revolutionists," T.R. stated in his *Autobiography*. ". . . I simply ceased to stamp out the different revolutionary fuses that were already burning." At any rate, the U.S.S. *Nashville* appeared off Colon on November 2, the nearly bloodless revolution went off on schedule the next day, American marines landed at Colon on November 4, and two days later—ninety minutes after news of the successful revolt reached Washington—the United States recognized the infant republic. "Free sons of Panama I salute you!" Dr. Amador proclaimed in his first presidential oration. "Long live the Republic of Panama! Long live President Roosevelt!"

Roosevelt spent a good deal of time in later weeks and years defending his actions in Panama. As for charges that he had failed to deal fairly with the government of Colombia: "You could no more make an agreement with the Colombian rulers," he explained, "than you could nail currant jelly to a wall." Nonetheless, Roosevelt refused to admit that there had been any wrongdoings on his part. "We conducted the negotiations for its construction," he said in reference to the canal when he accepted the Republican nomination the following year, "with the nicest and most scrupulous honor, and in a spirit of the largest generosity toward those through whose territory it was to run."

At a Cabinet meeting shortly after the inspired revolt, he started to give a lengthy legal analysis of American rights in the Isthmus. "Oh, Mr. President," Attorney General Knox interrupted, "do not let so great an achievement suffer from any taint of legality." T.R. persisted, and when he was finished, he asked the Cabinet if he had answered all the charges, if he had successfully defended himself. "You certainly have, Mr. President," Elihu Root remarked. "You have shown that you were accused of seduction and you have conclusively proved that you were guilty of rape."

On November 18, John Hay signed a new canal treaty with the minister plenipotentiary of the Republic of Panama, none other than Philippe Bunau-Varilla. Panama got the money earmarked for Colombia; the New Panama Canal Company got its $40,000,000. It took two more years before a lock canal rather than a water-level one was decided upon, but in the meantime yellow fever had been conquered. In November, 1906, Theodore Roosevelt boarded a warship and steamed to Panama—there to inspect the work in progress and, clad in white suit and straw hat, pose in the cabin of a big steam shovel gouging away at the Culebra Cut. He thus became the first President to go abroad while in office—though on the warship, and in the Canal Zone, and on a return stop at Puerto Rico, he was still technically on American soil.

"I am interested in the Panama Canal because I started it," T.R. said two years after he had left the Presidency. "If I had followed traditional, conservative methods . . . the debate would have been going on yet. But I took the Canal Zone, and let Congress debate, and while the debate goes on the canal does also." The Panama Canal was the proudest achievement of Roosevelt's first term and inevitably one that he would stress in his campaign for election, to his own term, in 1904.

4

It is safe to assume that Roosevelt began thinking about election to his own term as soon as he recovered from the shock of McKinley's assassination. When Mark Hanna, traveling with the new President on the train from Buffalo to Washington, remarked that he could not commit himself that early to T.R.'s nomination in 1904, he must have been responding to an implied if not an actually stated request for support. ". . . Hanna says we must support the President," Henry Adams wrote to a friend early in 1902, "and the President is always at him for a pledge to support his nomination in 1904. . . ." According to Adams, Hanna would reply on such occasions that there was only one man who could defeat the President in the next election, and that was Roosevelt himself.

An incumbent seeking re-election has an enormous advantage in presidential contests. There is something about the Presidency that turns a politician into a statesman. And T.R., only a year earlier regarded by many in his party as a ridiculous if not dangerous cowboy, achieved instant dignity with his accession to the high office. His assurance that he would continue McKinley's policies and his retention of McKinley's Cabinet calmed a jittery stock market. The annual message to Congress was considered to be firm and dignified. To some, of course, the prosecution of the Northern Securities Company seemed not so much a surprising departure as it did a reversion to form. Yet this alone did not alienate the Old Guard in the Republican party. And T.R.'s popularity with the public continued to soar.

In June, 1902, Roosevelt and Secretary of State Hay went to Cambridge to receive honorary degrees from Harvard. As T.R. concluded his remarks, President Charles William Eliot of Harvard turned to Hay and whispered "What a man! Genius, force, and courage, and such evident honesty!" Back in Washington, Hay could not resist telling Roosevelt of Eliot's remark—and adding some flattery of his own: "And another thought was in everybody's mind also. 'He is so young and he will be with us for many a day to come.' We are all glad of that—even the old fellows, who are passing." The settlement of the coal strike the following autumn further boosted the President's popularity. "There never was the least doubt about your nomination," Lodge wrote to T.R. at the end of October, "but I consider that your success in this settlement has made your calling and election equally sure."

Even though presidents in those days did not campaign for re-election, T.R. on April 1, 1903, left Washington for a nine-week-long swing through the Midwest and Far West that can only be described as a 1904 campaign trip—a year early. In a letter to his sister Corinne Robinson on the eve of his departure, he confided that it would be "as hard a trip as I have ever undertaken, with the sole exception of the canvass of 1900." From Washington the presidential special the first week passed through Maryland and Pennsylvania and sped on to Illinois, Wisconsin, Minnesota, and the Dakotas. At Medora, North Dakota, where he had once ranched, it seemed as if the entire population of the Badlands "down to the smallest baby" had gathered to meet Roosevelt. Then came a two-week break for a camping trip in Yellowstone National Park, Wyoming, with naturalist John Burroughs.

Emerging from the park, Roosevelt went up through Montana, where he received an especially warm welcome. The mayor of Butte, overcome by the honor of presiding at a presidential banquet, literally swept T.R. off the floor, tucked him under one arm, and carried him into the hall—"so that I felt like one of those limp dolls with dangling legs carried around by small children." Hammering the table with his knife handle, the mayor opened the proceedings with an imperious command, "Waiter, bring on the feed!" Then, recollecting that there was an over-flow crowd outside that could not be admitted to the dinner, the mayor asked the waiters to pull up the shades and "let the people see the President eat!"—a display to which Roosevelt quietly but firmly objected. From Montana, Roosevelt backtracked to Nebraska, South Dakota, and Illinois and then headed south to open the Louisiana Purchase Exposition in St. Louis—the fair that gave America the tune "Meet Me in St. Louis, Louis." Heading west again, the President's train went through Kansas, Colorado, and New Mexico en route to California.

There should have been no doubt by then that Roosevelt was campaigning. In dozens of speeches—scheduled addresses in great halls as well as rear-platform remarks at whistle stops—he expounded on the achievements of his administration. He received additional honorary degrees, posed in front of the Grand Canyon, visited a miners' camp, went to admire the redwoods with John Muir, broke ground for a McKinley statue in San Francisco's Golden Gate Park, dedicated a Lewis and Clark monument in Portland, Oregon, and inspected a naval yard outside Seattle. From Tacoma, Washington, on May 22, T.R. wrote to Lodge that his voice had stood the strain well and that he did not think he had made any slip—"although I was rather exasperated at the apparently general acceptance of the outrageous lie that I had been kissing babies." During the following four days, while continuing through Washington State, Roosevelt scored the biggest political coup of the year—one that had nothing to do with his trip, however.

Mark Hanna, the adroit strategist who had engineered McKinley's first election to the Presidency and had been generally regarded as the power behind the throne from 1897 to 1901, was also undergoing a transformation from politician to statesman. To the great surprise of many, Hanna had continued to play the role of presidential confidant and adviser under Theodore Roosevelt. He was still Chairman of the Republican National Committee and, although still in his first term, was a commanding figure in the Senate. It is probable that Hanna himself had no higher ambition, preferring instead his unchallenged position as party leader; but from 1902 on, the senator began to be mentioned with increasing frequency as a presidential contender. In April Hanna sent Roosevelt a clipping of a *Saturday Evening Post* article that claimed he had no presidential ambitions. The author, Hanna added, saw things as they were "outside the area of smoke." Yet when the Ohio State Republican Convention met the next month, delegates buzzed with talk of a Hanna candidacy in two years. Stumping the state that fall in behalf of congressional candidates, the party chairman was often greeted with shouts of "Hanna in 1904!"

Hanna's rival in Ohio politics was the state's senior senator, Joseph B. Foraker. Eventually destroyed by revelations of his questionable connections with Standard Oil, Foraker in 1903 was a man—one historian has remarked—who when he shaved in the morning saw in the mirror the Republican presidential nominee of 1908. Essential to Foraker's rising ambition was the nomination and election of T.R. in 1904—events to be brought about by Foraker's maneuvering so as to win the President's gratitude and eventual designation as his successor. To get his own engine moving, he first had to derail Hanna. The time and place he chose to do this was at the Ohio G.O.P. convention, scheduled to meet in June, 1903, to endorse candidates for the coming state elections. Foraker's method was the classic gambit of stating opposition to something that was only a rumor he himself had caused to be started.

On May 23 Foraker called reporters to his Senate office in Washington. He was disturbed by reports from Ohio that the convention would decline to endorse Roosevelt for the G.O.P. nomination in 1904, and this would be a mistake. He knew little of the controversy, Foraker claimed, other than the fact that it had been precipitated by Hanna supporters. Outraged, Hanna denied the entire story later that same day. Yet, he told the Associated Press, as national chairman he must remain aloof from presidential politics. Furthermore, the Ohio convention had no right in 1903 to attempt settling an issue that only the national Republican convention the following year was entitled to resolve. To the President he wired that the issue had been forced on him in a way that made it necessary for him to oppose any pro-Roosevelt resolution.

"When you know the facts I am sure you will approve my course," he concluded.

With gleeful alacrity, Roosevelt seized his opportunity. The time had come to "stop shilly-shallying," he wrote Lodge on May 25, and let Hanna know that he did not intend to become a suppliant to whom the party chairman might give the nomination as a boon. T.R. carefully composed a reply to Hanna's telegram and gave it out to the press: ". . . I have not asked any man for his support. I have had nothing whatever to do with raising this issue. Inasmuch as it has been raised of course those who favor my administration and my nomination will favor endorsing both and those who do not will oppose." Hanna was trapped. That same day he replied to the President that he would no longer oppose the resolution of endorsement to be placed before the Ohio convention. "I thank you for your telegram and appreciate your action," Roosevelt tersely replied.

Across the country, people were soon laughing at Hanna's "back-action-double-spring-feat." A New York newspaper joked that "Senator Hanna, with really marvelous agility, considering his years and his rheumatic afflictions, stepped to his seat on the Roosevelt bandwagon yesterday. . . ." He would have done so earlier, the article continued, if only "he had known that the band was about to begin to play and the procession to move." Lodge snorted over Hanna's "stupid blunder" in opposing the Ohio resolution just long enough to make it clear to the public that his eventual assent to it involved a defeat. The exchange, T.R. confided to his best friend, had revived him. "I was feeling jaded and tired. . . . But this last business gave me a new and vivid interest in life."

Even before the exchange of telegrams with Hanna, Roosevelt's renomination had seemed to Lodge "as safe as political future can be." Earlier in the trip Roosevelt had encountered ex-President Grover Cleveland, six years out of office and then in his sixty-seventh year. Despite the fact that he liked the "old fellow," T.R. immediately wrote to Lodge that he feared Cleveland still had "the presidential bee in his bonnet" and might prove a formidable opponent should the Democrats turn to him again. Almost exasperated at his friend's nervousness, Lodge replied that he did not think Cleveland would be nominated, that he would be easy to beat, and that Roosevelt need have "no earthly fear of him."

By June 5, the President was back in Washington, where he found Edith and four of their children—"all five in their best clothes, and

Edith in a dress she knew I liked"—waiting at a window in the East Room of the White House. A few days later Roosevelt was a guest at the wedding in Cleveland of Hanna's daughter. T.R.'s humiliation of Hanna apparently had not cooled their friendship—nor stifled talk of Hanna's chances for higher office. As the throng gathered under a tent on the lawn of the Hanna home, one guest raised a champagne glass in a whispered toast: "To the next President—whichever one it is!" At the end of the month the Roosevelts withdrew from the capital for their customary three-month-long vacation at Sagamore Hill. A summer White House office was set up in the nearby village of Oyster Bay, and the President entertained a steady stream of visitors—when he was not horseback riding, rowing on Long Island Sound, or taking the children on marathon point-to-point walks.

Hanna's triumph in the Ohio elections that fall brought renewed talk of his availability for the 1904 presidential nomination—and renewed activity on the part of T.R. to line up delegates committed to his own candidacy. It was whispered that he would invite any sort of local politician for lunch or dinner at the White House, if it meant a vote in the convention. Early in December the national committee met in Washington to choose a convention site—Chicago—and its members were nearly unanimous for Roosevelt. H. H. Kohlsaat reported this a few days later to the President but warned that, if he did not stop politicking so shamelessly for the nomination, he would make a fool of himself and lose it. Chagrined, Roosevelt pledged to stop discussing delegates with anyone who would listen. The fact remained that T.R. enjoyed being President enormously, enjoyed especially the potential for power the office held and which he was only beginning to exploit. He was, as Kohlsaat perceived, anxious to continue in office to the point of obsession. It was a characteristic that embarrassed even his friends and was, much later, to have tragic consequences.

At the end of the year Senator N. B. Scott of West Virginia wrote Hanna asking him to sit down and pray with himself for an hour and a half and then ask himself if he would not be doing the country a service by running against Roosevelt. Rumors reached the Ohio senator that there was going to be a knock-down-and-drag-out fight over the nomination between T.R. and Wall Street's champion, Hanna. "I'm the person who's going to be dragged out," Hanna snorted. "Don't those fools in New York know I'm sixty-six years old?" There was a conspiracy to nominate him over his protests, Hanna was told. "Conspiracy is the right word for it!" Hanna complained. "They want to kill me!"

Although exhausted by the Ohio campaign, Hanna had returned to Washington for the opening of Congress on December 7. Then, despite an attack of grippe, he went to New York the following week for a meeting of the National Civic Federation, an organization to promote better labor-management relations. From New York Hanna returned home to Cleveland to spend the Christmas–New Year holidays, and on January 12, 1904, he was at Columbus for his formal election to the Senate by the state legislature. Two days later he was back in Washington, but when he appeared in the Senate he complained to friends that he somehow no longer felt "up to the work." Soon he took to his bed at the Arlington Hotel; on February 3 a specialist from New York diagnosed Hanna's complaint as typhoid fever.

The President paid an unprecedented call on Hanna at the Arlington on February 5 but found the senator too ill to receive visitors. Told that Roosevelt had waited below to see him, Hanna roused himself to scrawl a brief note: "You touched a tender spot, old man, when you called personally, to inquire after [me] this A.M. I may be worse, before I can be better, but all the same such 'drops of kindness' are good for a fellow." Crowds began gathering outside the hotel for news of Hanna's condition; in the Senate, his colleagues sat mournfully around waiting for news of his death. On Sunday, February 14, Roosevelt called twice —once in the morning, once in the afternoon—at the Arlington, but by evening Hanna had already slipped into a coma. The end came at 6:40 P.M. the following day. On Wednesday, February 17, both houses of Congress assembled at noon in the Senate chamber, where they were joined by the President, members of his Cabinet, and the Supreme Court for a funeral service.

The New York *Sun* the day of the funeral combined its eulogy of Hanna with an attack upon the President. The Ohio senator, the newspaper claimed, was the only Republican who had "the strength of will and the force of character, the unselfishness and the patriotism, to act as an effective brake against [Roosevelt's] headlong course." T.R., the *Sun* complained, "had forgotten all about the promise so dramatically and so effectively entered at Buffalo and had no thought but to convert the whole power of his great office to securing his own nomination. . . ."

5

The *Sun* might as well have conserved its ink and newsprint. Whatever doubt there may have been about Roosevelt's nomination in 1904 evaporated with the death of Hanna. When the Republican delegates assembled at Chicago four months later, that same newspaper unhappily remarked that the President's nomination was "as certain as that Theodore Roosevelt was alive and Mark Hanna dead."

Of course, Roosevelt himself had not given up the fight, even though there was no longer an opponent. Henry Adams had returned from a White House dinner in March to complain that "Theodore has stopped talking cowboy and San Juan. Every idea centers now on the election, and he talks about that with all the fluency and *naiveté* of a school-boy." To the irascible Adams, T.R. was still "a bore as big as a buffalo. . . ." About this time Lodge wrote asking the President to say a few words for a phonograph record to be played at a Boston political rally. Despite his anxiety to be elected, Roosevelt had his dignity to maintain. "Did you write this when entirely sober?" he asked Lodge. "Besides talking into the phonograph would you not like me to dance a little before a kinetoscope."

In spite of—or perhaps because of—Roosevelt's efforts to choreograph every last movement of the 1904 Republican convention, the Chicago conclave was the dullest within memory. There were no cheering throngs, no street parades, and only one band, reported the embittered *Sun.* The opening session, on Tuesday, June 21, lasted exactly one hour and twenty-two minutes; the first mention of Roosevelt's name brought a burst of applause lasting a full twenty-seven seconds. At this rate, concluded the *Sun,* the convention would "sit to empty benches" at the Thursday nominating session. Once the formality of naming T.R. had been observed, the delegates would "break for the train out of town," leaving no one to pick a vice-presidential candidate.

The benches on Thursday were not quite as empty as the *Sun* had predicted they would be, but so monotonous was the roll call that, when it reached New Jersey, a move was made to stop and declare Roosevelt nominated by acclamation. Enough delegates objected to the suspension of the roll call, however, so that the clerk was required to continue until he had the unanimous tally of 994 votes for Roosevelt.

As its vice-presidential choice, the convention turned to Indiana's senior senator, Charles W. Fairbanks—"a bald-headed man without the courage of his baldness," a reporter called him, because of the three long locks of hair carefully combed up over and plastered down upon his bare crown. To Fairbanks, for whom he had never before expressed any enthusiasm, Roosevelt sent a telegram of warm congratulations. When the Cabinet met in Washington the next day, John Hay noted in his diary, the President appeared as not particularly elated by his nomination—"it was too clear a walk-over."

Two weeks later the Democrats gathered at St. Louis to open a convention that, in both temperature and politics, was to be hotter than the G.O.P. conclave. The party was sharply divided between the old conservative eastern wing—called the Cleveland or Gold Democrats, though the ex-President was no longer a contender—and the western free-silver Democrats, whose Peerless Leader, William Jennings Bryan, had twice been defeated by McKinley. The candidate of the Gold Democrats, and clearly the convention leader, was Judge Alton B. Parker of the New York Court of Appeals.

Less organized than the Republicans, the Democrats tended to hold sessions that dragged on through the nights and left much of the drama to the early hours of morning. At daybreak on Saturday, July 9, Bryan rose to second the nomination of Missouri's Senator Francis Marion Cockrell, a man even Bryan must have known was not a viable candidate but was nevertheless someone to oppose Parker. The heat in the hall was intense, reported Nicholas Murray Butler, who was attending the convention as a special observer for Roosevelt. The weak light of dawn was mingling with the glare from electric bulbs to create an eerie effect. "Bryan himself was white," Butler later recalled, "his face was drawn and he was visibly greatly fatigued." He had had no sleep for two nights and his voice was almost gone, but the faded Boy Orator of the Platte still knew how to hold an audience. Eight years ago, he reminded his listeners, he had been commissioned as the standard-bearer of his party; four years later that commission had been renewed. Tonight, Bryan said, he was returning that commission. "You may dispute whether I have fought a good fight, you may dispute whether I have finished my course, but you cannot deny that I have kept the faith." As one, the vast audience jumped to its feet in a tremendous demonstration of the party's enduring affection for Bryan. But there was to be no stampede to the Nebraskan nor to his candidate. The tumult calmed,

Bryan finished his speech, and two hours later—at 6:45 A.M.—Parker was nominated on the first ballot.

The *Sun* groped at an explanation for Parker's selection. It was not because of "his commanding personality or popularity, for he was largely unknown to voters." It could not be "for the virtue of his opinions, because these he had kept to himself." How much he had kept his views to himself, the exhausted delegates at St. Louis were soon to find out. Parker was a reserved and regulated gentleman, who every morning was known to walk from his home near Kingston, New York, to take a plunge in the Hudson River. Promptly at 10 P.M. on Friday, while the nominations were just beginning in St. Louis, the judge had gone to bed with strict instructions not to be disturbed until 7 the next morning. Shortly after rising on Saturday morning he received news by wire that he was the choice of the Democratic convention. And only then did Parker break his silence.

Noting that the party's platform was silent on the matter of the gold standard, Parker sent a telegram to St. Louis saying that he regarded the gold standard as "firmly and irrevocably established." If the convention took exception to this opinion of his, then it must turn to another nominee. Had he or had he not accepted? For twenty-four hours St. Louis was in an uproar. As word of Parker's message spread Saturday morning, the delegates—many of whom had just turned in after the all-night session—poured through hotel corridors and down into the lobbies. Many Southern and Western delegates had grown up regarding free silver as gospel dogma and still believed unreservedly in Bryan's admonition against "the Cross of Gold." Now they angrily tore Parker badges from their lapels. The Governor of Missouri sarcastically suggested that Parker take another jump in the Hudson.

Saturday evening the convention opened its final meeting, one even more tumultuous than the nominating session the night before. This evening Parker did not retire, but instead stayed up until he was notified, at 1:30 A.M. Sunday that the convention had accepted him on his own terms. Nothing in the platform was to be construed as a denial of the gold standard. Parker went to bed, and the overwrought delegates went on to select a vice-presidential candidate. Their unlikely choice was Henry G. Davis, an eighty-two-year-old ex-senator from West Virginia, said to be worth $40,000,000. Obviously, the convention hoped that the surprised octogenarian—he had come to the convention to support a friend's nomination—would dispense some of his millions in the

Democratic crusade. He never did, but it is unlikely that anything short of $40,000,000 could have purchased the election of Alton B. Parker.

"I think Parker will be as handy for us to beat as anyone, and more so than some," Lodge wrote to Roosevelt the day of the nomination. "We shall do him up early I believe." A few days later, Lodge wrote again to complain that by his maneuver on the gold standard Parker had converted himself from a nobody to a somebody, and "we have more therefore to reckon with." By mid-August, however, even the habitually pessimistic Roosevelt was acknowledging—but only to such confidants as Lodge—a strong feeling that he would be victorious. And by early September he was calling the states that he expected to find in the Republican column—including a chance in traditionally Democratic Missouri.

To his new Secretary of War, William Howard Taft, who was scheduled to make campaign appearances in his behalf, he wrote later that month: "Attack Parker." In no speech should the administration appear to be on the defensive; there was nothing to apologize for, and it should be clear that—if retained in office—he would continue precisely as before. By early October, for some reason, T.R. was less sanguine. In another letter, this time to his old comrade from the Rough Rider campaign Leonard Wood, he called only 216 electoral votes as certain, with 239 needed to win. Nevertheless, he thought the Republicans would win by a small majority—though they might lose, or even win by a large majority. To Lodge all such agonized speculation was plainly unnecessary. ". . . you are going to receive in my opinion the largest electoral majority ever given," he wrote on October 26. Two days later, remembering T.R.'s birthday on the twenty-seventh, Elihu Root, no doubt also amused by the President's undue concern, wrote "I congratulate you on attaining the respectable age of 46. You have made a good start in life and your friends have great hopes for you when you grow up."

As early as the second week in August, the New York *Sun*—always critical of Roosevelt—had conceded the President's election in a five-word editorial: "Theodore! with all thy faults—" Later the paper had explained its reasons for giving T.R. such grudging support: "We prefer the impulsive candidate of the party of conservatism to the conservative candidate of the party which the business interests regard as permanently and dangerously impulsive."

For his part, Parker was proving to be an utterly lackluster candidate. "The people need a judicial chief magistrate," observed Joseph Pulitzer in the New York *World*, "but not too judicial a candidate. . . . It is the part of a leader to lead." Inexplicably, Parker did not take to the stump until the last two weeks of the campaign. And when he did at last speak out, it was with the sensational charge that the Chairman of the Republican National Committee, George B. Cortelyou, had taken advantage of his previous position as Secretary of Commerce and Labor to demand and win large contributions from corporations—apparently in return for immunity from antitrust prosecution.

Roosevelt naturally was outraged. To his son Kermit he wrote that remaining silent in the face of such charges was as agonizing as "lying still under shell fire . . . at Santiago." Parker was laying himself wide open with such statements, he continued, "and I could cut him into ribbons if I could get at him in the open." But a President could not go on the stump, and he would just have to "sit still and abide the result." The problem he faced in the campaign, T.R. concluded, was that he was a very positive character and Parker, a negative one. He had both attracted supporters and made enemies in ways Parker never could. The Democratic nominee could be "painted any color to please any audience; but it is impossible to make two different pictures of any side of my character."

With Parker belatedly stepping out along the campaign trail, "Cortelyouism"—the secret financing of the trustbuster's campaign by the trusts—became a last-minute issue. On October 26 T.R. wrote the party chairman directing him to return to Standard Oil the $100,-000 donation about which he had just heard. When Parker persisted in claiming that the big corporations were bankrolling the President's campaign, Roosevelt at last replied. On November 4—four days before the election—he denounced Parker's accusations as "slanderous," "monstrous," "a wicked falsehood," "unqualifiedly and atrociously false," and containing "not one particle of truth." As far as Roosevelt knew, Parker *was* fabricating his charges—but T.R. himself did not know the whole truth. It later came out that large corporations had indeed supplied most of the $2,195,000 in the G.O.P. campaign chest that year. And Cortelyou, or rather the party treasurer who served under him, Cornelius N. Bliss, seems to have ignored the President's demand to return the Standard Oil contribution. But Parker could offer no proof for his claims about the financing of the campaign, and the two candidates reached the finish line—one, appearing to be an inept and desperate politician making wild charges; the other, an honest President viciously maligned. Lodge's prediction that Roosevelt would receive the largest majority in history was triumphantly fulfilled on November 8.

To his friend the Massachusetts senator, T.R. wrote two days later, "You were right about the election, and I was mistaken. I had no idea that there would be such a sweep." Indiana's Senator Albert J. Beveridge had an apt summary: The country, he noted, had "gone Rooseveltian, not Republican."

Chapter 5

In His Own Right

On the eve of the 1905 inaugural Secretary of State John Hay sent Roosevelt the gift of a curious ring, accompanied by a touching note. "The hair in this ring," Hay wrote, "is from the head of Abraham Lincoln. Dr. Taft cut it off the night of the assassination, and I got it from his son—a brief pedigree." The secretary asked his chief to wear it the next day, since the President was "one of the men who most thoroughly understand and appreciate Lincoln. . . ." T.R. sat down immediately to pen a reply: "Surely no other President, on the eve of his inauguration, has ever received such a gift from such a friend. I am wearing the ring now; I shall think of it and you as I take the oath tomorrow."

The Lincoln ring was the only somber note in an otherwise joyously festive inauguration. The weather was menacing early on Saturday morning, March 4, but after a light rain, the skies cleared by the hour slated for the procession of the presidential party from the White House to the Capitol. Congress had finished its business and taken a recess to kill time until the inauguration of the Vice President, Senator Fairbanks, shortly after eleven. Another cloud appeared in the north but blew away as the inaugural party moved out to the east front of the Capitol at noon. The skies were clear, with a brisk wind sweeping across the plaza, as Theodore Roosevelt—his left hand on an open Bible—raised his right hand and faced Chief Justice Melville W. Fuller to repeat the oath of office. The inaugural address, in Lodge's words, was "simple and solemn." The President's voice—thin and high-pitched, often inclined to crack on high notes—carried well in spite of the wind that forced him to speak louder and more slowly than usual.

Thirty Rough Riders—well lubricated by three days of preparatory celebrations and thus resigned, or oblivious, to the indignity of riding artillery rather than cavalry mounts—formed an honor guard to and from the Capitol. At the outset of the march T.R., red-faced and shouting, had stood in his open carriage, in an effort to get his old comrades in arms properly lined up.

After the oath-taking, he had retired to the reviewing stand to watch a parade that contained—in addition to the Rough Riders—detachments from the Regular Army, the Navy, and the National Guard, a delegation of coal miners bearing a banner citing his settlement of the anthracite strike in 1902, Puerto Ricans and Philippine scouts, mounted Indians in war paint under trailing war bonnets and carrying spears and tomahawks, a younger, more sedate generation of Indian youths studying at special schools, cowboys recalling T.R.'s ranching days, a hundred and fifty Harvard fellows in black gowns, and members of civic organizations, farmers clubs, mechanics clubs—"everybody and everything," Roosevelt happily wrote to an English friend a few days later.

Roosevelt himself presented a picture of ebullient animation—chatting with his guests on the reviewing stand, jumping to his feet to wave and applaud at each new group passing by, swaying blissfully to the rhythm of "There'll Be a Hot Time in the Old Town Tonight," the Spanish-American War song that the marching bands one by one picked up as they approached. To be perfect, thought Alice Roosevelt, the procession needed only Judge Parker with other prominent Democrats "marching in chains."

Receiving visitors at the White House the previous day, Roosevelt is supposed to have remarked: "Tomorrow I shall come into my office in my own right. Then watch out for me!" Now, joking about critics who complained of his innovations in office, even in his first term, he turned to a friend on the reviewing stand and said: "I really shuddered today as I swore to obey the Constitution." Indeed, that crisp March day in 1905 marked a new, more aggressive, and self-confident phase in the career of Theodore Roosevelt. It was the beginning of what one of his biographers has called "the imperial years."

2

Roosevelt, however, had not waited until the beginning of his own elective term to put an individual stamp on the Presidency. As soon as the shock and grief of McKinley's death had worn off, T.R. hurled himself into the myriad affairs of his high office. "Every day, almost every hour, I have to decide very big as well as very little questions. . . ." he wrote to a friend a year later. "It has been very wearing, but I have thoroughly enjoyed it, for it is fine to feel one's hand guiding great machinery, with at least the purpose, and I hope the effect, of guiding it for the best interests of the nation as a whole." Enjoy was a word he frequently thereafter used to describe his attitude toward the Presidency; indeed, none of T.R.'s predecessors or successors ever displayed quite such an uninhibited relish for the high office.

The transition from the austere Major McKinley to the irrepressible Colonel Roosevelt was as marked as it was sudden. The Executive Mansion officially became the White House, the informal name by which it had long been known. And invitations to dine there—a dread obligation in the days of McKinley—were eagerly anticipated. In place of the tragic and embarrassingly ill Ida McKinley there now was Edith Roosevelt—handsome, intelligent, ever charming and gracious. "I do not think my eyes are blinded by affection," the President wrote of his wife in 1902, "when I say that she has combined to a degree I have never seen in any other woman the power of being the best of wives and mothers, the wisest manager of the household, and at the same time the ideal great lady and mistress of the White House." Most people who fell within her orbit would have agreed; no one ever faulted Edith Roosevelt's performance during her husband's term in office. Not the least of her talents, guests were delighted to discover, was her ability subtly but firmly to check Theodore's rash impulses and humorously but kindly to challenge his most outlandish statements. "Oh, Ed-ie!" he would sheepishly protest at some put-down but he never contradicted her generally valid objections.

In place of the ghosts of the McKinley daughters, the White House now had the six rambunctious Roosevelt children. The lovely Alice— child of Roosevelt's first marriage—was seventeen when her father became President, and with her impudent wit and often unconventional manners she soon became a national celebrity. Asked why he did not keep a tighter rein on his firstborn, T.R. was said to have complained that he could either be President or be a more watchful guardian of Alice—he could not be both at the same time. On February 17, 1906, five days after her twenty-second birthday, she was married in a White

House ceremony to Nicholas Longworth, a member of the House of Representatives from Ohio, a man fourteen years her senior.

Theodore, Jr. (Ted), and Kermit, fourteen and twelve at the time the family moved into the White House, were soon away at school, but the three youngest children—Ethel, Archie, and Quentin—filled the White House with laughter and gaiety. Ethel and Archie liked to startle visitors by stalking the stately rooms and corridors on stilts. The long hallways seemed designed for foot races and the mansion was unexcelled as a place in which to play hide-and-seek. Quentin had to be roused from bed one night and severely reprimanded for placing spitballs on the portraits of some of his father's distinguished predecessors. Stopping by the children's rooms en route to an official dinner, T.R. occasionally became so absorbed in storytelling that he had to delay his entrance. Worse yet, a pillow fight would sometimes necessitate another change of clothes before the President went downstairs.

A number of pets made their home at the White House during the Roosevelt years, including Ted's macaw. Against all regulations and precedents a pony was once smuggled up to the second floor in an elevator to visit a sick youngster. A congressman waiting to see the President one day was disconcerted to have Quentin ask him for help in retrieving a snake that had gotten lost up one of his sleeves. Yet, it was a wild animal, not a domestic pet, that came to be most enduringly linked with Roosevelt's name. On a hunting trip to Mississippi in 1902, the President had refused to shoot a small bear brought into camp. The incident was celebrated by a cartoonist, toy makers hastened to take advantage of the publicity, and across the country woolly lambs were displaced as favorite stuffed animals by "Teddy bears."

Ever the exponent of the strenuous life, Roosevelt loved long horseback rides and took almost fiendish delight in point-to-point walks through Washington's Rock Creek Park. His helpless companions on these vigorous outings—be they congressmen, Cabinet officers, or foreign diplomats—followed him as he scrambled up rock faces or plunged into icy streams for unscheduled swims. Turning back meant an irretrievable loss of face. An energetic if erratic tennis player, T.R. soon had a Tennis Cabinet of unofficial advisers who somehow mixed play with breathless discussion of public affairs. Roosevelt had boxed on the college team at Harvard and as Governor of New York he had wrestled with professionals up to the time he damaged two ribs and shoved a shoulder blade out of place. He continued to box in the White House, until in 1904 he received a blow that later caused him to lose the sight in his left eye. Thereafter, he wrote with unconscious humor in his *Autobiography*, "I thought it better to acknowledge that I had become an elderly man and would have to stop boxing. I then took up jiu-jitsu for a year or two."

Roosevelt threw himself full force into every activity. The Lodges kept a special rocking chair for his visits to their home, but they must have had to clear space around it for he was wont to rock so vigorously that the chair sometimes was propelled clear across the room. He once borrowed a book from the French ambassador and read it "with such thoroughness and assiduity that at the end it was dangling out of the covers," and he had to have it rebound before returning it. The English essayist John Morley told a newspaperman that the two most extraordinary things he had faced in America were Niagara Falls and the President—"both great wonders of nature!"

Unkind critics described T.R. as a supreme egoist, who wanted to be the bride at every wedding and the corpse at every funeral—and it is true that the President outshone the bride he gave away when his niece Eleanor (orphaned daughter of his only brother, Elliott) married a distant cousin, Franklin Delano Roosevelt, early in 1905. A contemporary magazine tried to sum up Theodore Roosevelt. "The Scrapes He Gets Into, the Scrapes He Gets Out of; the Things He Attempts, the Things He Accomplishes; His Appointments and His Disappointments; the Rebukes that He Administers and Those He Receives; His Assumptions, Presumptions, Omnisciencies and Deficiencies, Make Up a Daily Tale Which Those of Us Who Survive His Tenure of the Presidential Office Will Doubtless Miss, as We Might Miss Some Property of the Atmosphere We Breathe."

Not content with pushing his domestic reforms and wielding the big stick in his foreign policies, Roosevelt as President engaged in a number of extracurricular activities that surprised and delighted, and sometimes angered, his fellow Americans. He contributed articles to national magazines on hunting and the outdoor life, reviewed poetry, wrote a scholarly appreciation of the ancient Irish sagas, and preached against birth control as race suicide—the White House, he was fond of saying, was a "bully pulpit."

As President, he got into a long, public argument with what he called "nature fakers," men who wrote inaccurately and sentimentally about wildlife. And he shocked many when he had the sculptor Augustus Saint-Gaudens redesign the nation's gold pieces, leaving out the traditional phrase "In God We Trust." He argued that the legend had only been permitted—not required—by an act of 1866 and that he felt that thus linking God and mammon was not religious but sacrilegious. An even bigger tempest in an even smaller teapot was caused by his advocacy of simplified spelling.

For some years scholars had been advocating a reform of erratic and outmoded spelling in the English language. In 1906 Andrew Carnegie gave his first annual grant of $10,000 to the Spelling Reform Association, and that summer the President ordered the public printer to use the simplified spelling of three hundred common words, as recommended by the board. Most of the changes were not extreme and indeed were already becoming sanctioned by common usage: dropping the "u" from honour, labour, colour and unpronounced final letters from programme and catalogue; reversing the final letters in centre and theatre; eliminating double letters in waggon, woollen, skillful, and even mamma; changing cheque to check and hiccough to hiccup; and banishing the ligatures in such words as mediæval and archæology. But the public was not prepared to go all the way and balked at accepting such oddities as wisht, lookt, dropt. And finally America was not ready for tho, thoro, and thru.

Congress, confronted with that year's annual message in the new spelling, was outraged and ordered the printer to return to conventional spelling. The newspapers exalted in the President's discomfort. "Nuthing escapes Mr. Rucevelt," wrote the Louisville *Courier-Journal*. "No subject is tu hi fr him to takl, nor tu lo for him to notis. He makes tretis without the consent of the Senit. He inforces such laws as meet his approval, and fales to se those that du not soot him. He now assales the English langgwidg, constitutes himself a sort of French Academy, and will reform the spelling in a way to soot himself." By year's end T.R. admitted a rare defeat, though he stated that henceforth he would use the simplified spelling in private correspondence—a promise he kept, when he or his secretaries remembered to do so. "I am glad the new spelling is dead," William Howard Taft confided to a friend, " 'for it grated on me rite thru.' "

It was always difficult for Roosevelt to accept defeat—even in such an inconsequential matter as simplified spelling—for he was a supremely self-righteous man. "Right is right," he once wrote Lodge, "and wrong is wrong, and it is a sign of weakness and not of generosity to confuse them." His brilliant, restless mind cut through the most complicated issues, almost too quickly, to find the right and wrong and he stubbornly refused to deviate from a decision as to which was which, never allowing for shadings of gray between the white and black. He was unstinting in warm appreciation of those who agreed with him and relentlessly hostile to those who opposed him. Dissenters were relegated to his Ananias Club, named after a biblical figure who was struck dead for lying.

Maine's Republican Senator Eugene Hale disagreed with T.R. about the necessity of building a big navy; indeed Hale was generally opposed to America's imperial course after the Spanish-American War. Hale's opposition in the President's eyes, became cowardice, the consequence of having a "shriveled soul." In a private letter T.R. was to accuse the stern and upright senator of being "a conscienceless voluptuary." It troubled Roosevelt to have to cross swords with members of his own party; he usually reserved his venom for the Democrats. Young Quentin at breakfast one morning heard his father exclaim over a newspaper report of a football game: "Oh Lord! it's too bad that Pensy won." Unfamiliar with the nickname for the University of Pennsylvania, Quentin remarked, in a meditative aside, "I suppose 'Pensy' is a Democrat."

"There is an impression that we are to elect a President next November," the highly critical New York *World* had warned during the campaign of 1904. "It is a mistake. . . . we are to elect a czar." Roosevelt must have been angered by the charge. He disliked titles and refused to be called "Excellency"; it was an unsuitable form of address—and besides one that every third-rate German potentate claimed. Henry Adams returned from a White House dinner early in 1905 to pick up his pen, dip it in acid, and write: "The twelfth century still rages wildly here in the shape of the fiend with tusks and eye-glasses across the way. The Boar of Cubia! I love him. He is almost sane beside his German and Russian cousins [Kaiser Wilhelm II and Czar Nicholas II], but he is mad enough to suit me." The comparison with the European monarchs was more than just casual and was soon to be even more pertinent as Roosevelt assumed another role for the President of the United States: international mediator. It was in this guise, as 1905 lengthened, that he was to share the stage of international power politics with kaiser, czar, and mikado.

3

Shortly after the inauguration, John Hay departed for Europe, complaining—as he had been for the past few years—of failing health. Everyone expressed polite concern for the Secretary of State's delicate constitution but few took his complaints seriously. It was almost impossible to imagine government proceeding without Hay, a Washington fixture since Lincoln's arrival in the capital. The President was at first encouraged by the reports of doctors at the German spa where Hay first went and kept in touch as his secretary traveled through Italy that spring. In June, Hay returned to Washington but Roosevelt insisted that he take the summer off at his home in New Hampshire. It was a genuine shock to T.R., as well as to the public, when news arrived on July 1 that John Hay had died in his sixty-seventh year.

Roosevelt would later charge that Hay had not been a great Secretary of State, and only a few days after his death was complaining that critics gave Hay credit for everything they approved while blaming him for all they did not. The simple truth is that Roosevelt was his own Secretary of State. Hay's absence, or his presence, would have made no difference whatsoever, for instance, in the President's mediation of the Russo-Japanese War.

Russia and Japan had been on a collision course over their rival political and commercial ambitions in the Far East for nearly a decade. On February 8, 1904—in a frighteningly accurate preview of Pearl Harbor—the Japanese launched a surprise naval attack on the Russians at Port Arthur even as negotiations to settle differences between the two countries were being held. From New York Elihu Root, who shared T.R.'s admiration for Japanese military prowess, wrote the President in great excitement: "Was not the way the Japs began the fight bully? Some people in the United States might well learn the lesson that mere bigness does not take the place of perfect preparation and readiness for instant action." From the first the tide swept with Japan. Her armies landed in Korea and Manchuria, handily defeated the Russians in several encounters, and advanced toward Siberia. Finally Russia's Baltic Fleet, having come more than halfway around the world, was destroyed in the Tsushima Strait on May 27, 1905. The humiliating defeat led to an abortive revolution in Russia; the czar's throne was threatened as was the entire balance of power in the Far East. Yet, strangely enough, it was Japan, as drained by her victories as was Russia by her defeats, who wanted peace and asked Roosevelt to mediate. The President had begun his pressure on Russia in April, 1905, and was outraged at Russia's reluctance to negotiate. "The Czar is a preposterous little creature. . . ." he wrote Hay. "He has been unable to make war, and he is now unable to make peace." Japan insisted on direct negotiation between the two parties, not mediation by a third party, but Russia was even slow to accept Roosevelt's offer to bring about the meeting. ". . . the more I see of the Czar, the Kaiser, and the Mikado the better I am content with democracy," T.R. wrote to Lodge in reporting on his maneuverings. The Russians he found "treacherous and shifty"; the Japanese "entirely selfish, though with a veneer of courtesy. . . ." Not until June 10, when reports from his diplomatic network assured favorable replies, did Roosevelt issue a formal call for the conference. There were a few additional confused and comic exchanges before the two parties accepted and agreed upon Washington as the meeting place. "Oh Lord! I have been growing nearly mad in the effort to get Russia and Japan together," he wrote to Whitelaw Reid, his ambassador to England.

By the time all the conferees had gathered it was August, Roosevelt had moved to Sagamore Hill for the summer, and—to avoid Washington's brutal heat—the conference had been shifted to Portsmouth, New Hampshire. On August 5, T.R. entertained the two delegations on board the presidential yacht *Mayflower* anchored in Oyster Bay. The chief Russian negotiator, Count Serge Witte, stood a full foot taller than his Japanese counterpart, Baron Jutaro Komura. Neither the imperious Russians nor the sensitive Japanese were willing to surrender precedence in this initial meeting, and the air was tense as Roosevelt welcomed the two parties aboard and introduced one to the other.

Chatting loudly and somewhat recklessly in his imperfect French, the President got Witte on one side and Komura on the other and somehow steered the two together through the door into the dining salon. There would be no protocol troubles in seating either: luncheon was a buffet served from a round table. But first, Roosevelt picked up his glass, bid his guests do likewise, and proposed a toast—to which, he said, there would be no reply and which would be drunk in silence standing. "To the welfare and prosperity of the sovereigns and peoples of the two great nations, whose representatives have met one another on this ship,"

he began. It was the President's "earnest hope and prayer," he concluded, ". . . that a just and lasting peace may speedily be concluded
among them." The count and the baron were satisfied, the honor of czar
and mikado was upheld, and the luncheon continued on a pleasant social level. Witte and Komura even shook hands on parting.

Once the conference got underway, there were a number of crises
—principally over Japan's demands that Russia pay a war indemnity.
Roosevelt again intervened. "I am having my hair turned gray by dealing with the Russian and Japanese negotiators," he wrote his son Kermit
on August 25. "The Japanese ask too much, but the Russians are ten
times worse than the Japs because they are so stupid and won't tell the
truth." That day T.R. escaped from the pressures of trying to save the
peace conference by taking a dive in Long Island Sound aboard a United
States submarine—an exploit considered by the press as recklessly jeopardizing the Presidency. Four days later Japan broke the final deadlock
in the Portsmouth negotiations by agreeing to forego the indemnity and
divide the large island of Sakhalin with Russia. An armistice between
the two powers went into effect on September 1 and the negotiators
signed the Portsmouth Treaty on September 5. Four days after that, T.R.
celebrated the successful conclusion of his efforts in a busy day of entertaining at Sagamore Hill: he had the Japanese delegates to lunch, and
the Russians to dinner.

The world applauded Roosevelt's impressive accomplishment as
peacemaker and the following year he was awarded the Nobel Prize for
Peace. He turned over the cash award of $36,734.49 to a foundation for
the promotion of industrial peace in the United States, but the trustees
could never agree on how to spend the money. Twelve years later, in
1918, the money—with interest it then totaled $45,482.83—
reverted to Roosevelt, who donated it to war relief.

Following his triumph in the summer of 1905, Roosevelt went on
to play a leading role in assembling the Algeciras Conference in early
1906, which headed off a German-French confrontation over Morocco.
And although Czar Nicholas was given credit for it, it was Roosevelt's
initial suggestion that led to the convening of the Second Hague Peace
Conference in 1907, a gathering that attempted unsuccessfully to establish a world court.

To many people, in America as well as abroad, Roosevelt's emergence as a peacemaker was surprisingly uncharacteristic. It was well
known, of course, that Roosevelt was a jingo, one of those chauvinistic

expansionists who had not only welcomed but had, in a sense, helped precipitate the Spanish-American War of 1898. The very real but unacknowledged empire acquired in that war made a large navy—one of T.R.'s vigorously advocated causes—a necessity. It also made the Panama Canal he so energetically promoted a certainty.

Roosevelt was equally outspoken in his staunch defense of the Monroe Doctrine. Echoing Voltaire's acknowledgment of the Deity, he had once stated that "if the Monroe Doctrine did not already exist, it would be necessary forthwith to create it. . . ." In his annual message to Congress of December, 1904, the President proclaimed what came to be known as the Roosevelt Corollary to the Monroe Doctrine: the dictum against European intervention in Latin American republics transformed into an affirmation of an American right to do just that. Venezuela and the Dominican Republic had both so mismanaged their affairs as to threaten the intervention of European powers to collect overdue debts. Roosevelt stood squarely against such intervention; if anyone was to intervene it would be the United States. Without the approval of the Senate, Roosevelt stepped in to take over the administration of Dominican customs and the management of its debt payments. Roosevelt also took credit for having prevented Germany from interfering in Venezuelan affairs on an earlier occasion.

The President had already proved that a strong executive was needed to assert the enlarged national power; now he was demonstrating that a more authoritative nation could play a leading role on the world stage. The United States was growing up and reaching outward—and no one contributed quite so much to this dramatic development as did Roosevelt. It was he who had the conviction, the energy, and—not unimportantly—the flair for showmanship to do so.

4

A month after his electoral victory of November, 1904, Theodore Roosevelt sent up his annual message to Congress. In it he announced a major legislative goal of his second term: regulation of the railroads engaged in interstate commerce. As long ago as 1887 the Interstate Commerce Commission had been set up to supervise the railways and eliminate such abuses as discriminatory rates and secret rebates to favorite customers. But subsequent court decisions had rendered the commission virtually impotent by the end of the century—a newspaper cartoon depicted the I.C.C. as a scrawny figure emerging from the courts in undershirt and tattered pants held up by a single suspender. During his first term, T.R. had seen the enactment of an antirebate law, but it had failed to eliminate this particular evil. And so the President planned a more ambitious reform.

What Roosevelt advocated in his annual message was giving the Interstate Commerce Commission power to revise railroad rates, with the new rates to go into effect immediately and stay in effect until and if a court of review overturned them. The very next day, December 7, 1904, the President held a White House conference on railroad regulation; indeed no single other item of public business was so to preoccupy him for the next eighteen months. At first he had set himself another goal, tariff revision, but he soon abandoned this cause to concentrate on the railroads. "On the interstate commerce business, which I regard as a matter of principle, I shall fight," he wrote a New York magazine editor early in the new year. "On the tariff, which I regard as a matter of expediency, I shall endeavor to get the best results I can, but I shall not break with my party." But Roosevelt was soon to discover that pressure on railroad regulation was also to bring him dangerously close to a break with his party.

The conservative Republican leadership in the Senate was nearly unanimous in its opposition to any such innovation as the President was now proposing; indeed, some among them were publicly known as "railroad senators." Thus, Roosevelt got nowhere that year and in his message to the new Congress, convening in December, 1905, he was forced to reiterate his plea. He was asking for no radical reforms, the President insisted. The previous legislation against rebates would be strengthened; the inspection of company records, already provided for, would be insured; the courts would be empowered to expedite suits for infractions of the law. His one innovation had been announced a year earlier: the authority to fix maximum rates—but only where the existing rate had been challenged and found to be unfair. On January 4, 1906, William Peters Hepburn, a Republican from Iowa, introduced the President's bill in the House of Representatives; a month later it passed with only seven dissenting votes. The real contest was to come in the Senate, and there the battle lines were sharply drawn.

The Republican Old Guard was adamantly opposed to any regulation and drew up in ranks behind Senator Nelson W. Aldrich of Rhode

Island. Aldrich's small state, virtually a pocket borough, kept him in the Senate for thirty years. As Senate majority leader and chairman of both the Rules and Finance committees, he dominated the Senate as few other men have—but in 1906 his power was beginning to wane. New, intense Republican progressives from the Midwest and Far West —Albert J. Beveridge of Indiana, Robert M. La Follette of Wisconsin, William E. Borah of Idaho—were already challenging Aldrich and his coterie of archconservatives. In this and coming struggles they would pose the threat of a separate bloc that could swing over to the Democratic side to carry measures opposed by the G.O.P. standpatters.

An adroit parliamentarian, Aldrich saw that the Hepburn Bill lay in committee through March and maneuvered to have it reported out unamended—but with each committee member empowered to offer amendments on the floor of the Senate. His final stroke was to withdraw Republican endorsement of the measure by designating as floor leader not the ranking Republican on the committee but the ranking Democrat, "Pitchfork Ben" Tillman of South Carolina. Roosevelt had not been on speaking terms with the roughhewn Southerner since he withdrew a White House dinner invitation after Tillman had brawled with a fellow solon on the Senate floor. "The crossing of the big stick and the pitchfork should make a hot and spectacular finish," commented one newspaper. Roosevelt refused to be thwarted; through an intermediary he started communicating with Tillman in an effort to defeat Aldrich's next move: amending the bill to death. Although the President felt that judicial review was implicit in the original draft, Aldrich sought to broaden the scope of this review to allow the courts to pass not only on procedural matters but also on the facts in each case. Worse yet, he proposed that the revised rates not go into effect until after the judicial review—and this, of course, would bring endless delaying action in the courts.

A year earlier T.R. had written to a friend abroad that there were "several eminent statesmen at the other end of Pennsylvania Avenue" that he would gladly lend to the Russian government to serve as royal bodyguards whenever there was a likelihood of bomb explosions. And now he was writing to an English friend about his "rough-and-tumble time with Congress. . . ." He asked Nannie Lodge to invite him to dinner so they could discuss "the Hittite empire, the Pithecanthropus, and Magyar love songs, and the exact relations of the Atli of the *Volsunga Saga* to the Etzel of the *Nibelungenlied,* and of both to Attila"—to get his mind off the rate bill. It was a subject, he was writing to Senator Lodge in early April, that was dwarfing everything else. In the middle of that month the Democratic–progressive Republican coalition fell apart, but early in May Roosevelt worked out a compromise with the Old Guard, a compromise acceptable to all but a few radicals of the left and right. On May 18 the Hepburn Act passed the Senate with only three dissenting votes, a conference committee resolved differences with the House version, and T.R. signed the bill into law on the day Congress adjourned, June 30. A landmark piece of legislation, the act authorized the federal government to examine a railroad's books in order to determine reasonable rates to be charged. The matter of court review, T.R. ultimately acknowledged, was "academic" once the rate-making power had been conceded to the government.

At the closing of Congress Roosevelt also gave his approval to two additional reform measures, the Pure Food and Drug Act and the Meat Inspection Act. Although he was not really a leader of this particular crusade, T.R. had called for legislation to regulate interstate commerce in misbranded and adulterated food, drinks, and drugs in his annual message the previous December. Publication early in 1906 of Upton Sinclair's sensational novel about Chicago's meat-packing industry, *The Jungle*, focused the nation's attention on its meat supply. Humorist Finley Peter Dunne imagined the President reading Sinclair's book at breakfast. Mr. Dooley related what happened next: "Suddenly he rose fr'm th' table, an' cryin': 'I'm pizened,' began throwin' sausages out iv th' window. Th' ninth wan sthruck Sinitor Biv'ridge on th' head an' made him a blond. It bounced off, exploded, an' blew a leg off a secret-service agent, an' the scatthred fragmints desthroyed a handsome row iv ol' oak trees. . . . Since thin th' Presidint, like th' rest iv us, has become a viggytaryan. . . ."

Roosevelt betrayed a certain impatience with Sinclair and other writers then publishing lurid exposés in magazines and newspapers and on March 17, 1906, he gave them a name. That evening the President was a guest at a dinner of the Gridiron Club, the group of Washington correspondents famous for roasting government officials in hilarious skits to which the guests could reply in off-the-record speeches. Rising to speak that evening, Roosevelt took as his theme, the passage from Bunyan's *Pilgrim's Progress* describing the Man with a Muckrake, so preoccupied with turning over filth that he could not even look up to accept a crown being offered to him. Muckrakers the crusading journalists became, accepting Roosevelt's comparison not as the derogatory label it was meant to be but rather as a badge of honor.

Shortly thereafter Roosevelt appointed a government commission to investigate the conditions exposed in Sinclair's novel, and its report later that spring further roused the public to demand legislation. The New York *Evening Post* put its review of the government report on the meat industry in verse:

> Mary had a little lamb,
> And when she saw it sicken,
> She shipped it off to Packingtown,
> And now it's labelled chicken.

Such reactionaries as Senator Aldrich complained that government inspection of meat-packing plants and regulation of food and drug labeling interfered with the people's liberty to eat what they wanted to eat, but the tide was irresistible. Both acts moved slowly but surely through Congress and reached the President's desk for signature by the end of June. On July 1 T.R. arrived at Oyster Bay to begin another three-month vacation, well satisfied with the "astounding progress" made during the congressional session.

5

An obscure event of that summer of 1906—taking place far from the warm sun and cooling breezes of Sagamore Hill—was to cause Theodore Roosevelt himself deep distress in the months to come and to embarrass even his most ardent supporters.

Like many of his contemporaries, even so enlightened and so basically unprejudiced an individual as Roosevelt regarded black Americans with a kindly condescension. "Now as to the Negroes!" he wrote his friend Owen Wister on April 27, 1906. "I entirely agree with you that as a race and in the mass they are altogether inferior to the whites." Yet T.R.'s greatest hero in American history was Abraham Lincoln, and he believed passionately in emancipation and the gradual improvement of the black man's lot. In that same letter to Wister he went on to score Southern Democrats who denied the vote to blacks while insisting that their numbers be counted in determining representation in Congress.

And, he added, ". . . I do not know a white man of the South who is as good a man as Booker Washington today."

Roosevelt had long been an admirer of Booker T. Washington and heartily endorsed—again as did many of his well-meaning contemporaries—the Negro educator's goal of training blacks for industrial jobs. On October 16, 1901, a little more than a month after he had succeeded McKinley, T.R. had invited Washington to dine at the White House. He was surprised and dismayed by the violence of the South's response. "The action of President Roosevelt in entertaining that nigger," the rabid "Pitchfork Ben" Tillman was reported to have said, "will necessitate our killing a thousand niggers in the South before they will learn their place again." To a New England editor, Roosevelt complained—in a confidential letter—of the "idiot or vicious Bourbon element of the South" that was howling over the dinner invitation extended to Washington. "I shall have him to dine just as often as I please. . . ." As a matter of fact, T.R. never again did invite Washington—or any other Negro—to break bread with him at the White House, though he did continue to consult Washington on the appointment of blacks to federal offices in the South. Thus, it was not surprising that the Negro educator reluctantly stood by the President even after the furor that arose over an ugly incident of the summer of 1906.

Late in the spring three companies of the United States Army's Twenty-Fifth Infantry (Colored) had been posted to Fort Brown, Texas. The regiment's white officers had protested the move to Brownsville, a sleepy town on the Rio Grande River. "Texas, I fear, means a quasi battle ground for the Twenty-Fifth Infantry," one of them wrote. At their arrival toward the end of July, the black soldiers received anything but a warm welcome. There were actually few blacks in that part of Texas, and the Negro troopers found themselves on a social plane somewhat below that of the town's Mexican-Americans. With the white saloons closed to them, they had but two places to slake their thirst at the end of the parched days: a Jim Crow bar in a back room of one white establishment and an all-black saloon opened by an enterprising soldier in a shack on the edge of town. There was to be no mixing of the races in Brownsville; indeed the air in the town seemed heavy with barely repressed hostility.

Two weeks after the regiment's arrival, a white woman charged that one of the Negro soldiers had tried to rape her. The next day, Monday, August 13, Brownsville's mayor asked the post commander to keep all the soldiers in barracks that night; he feared a clash between the races because of white indignation at the reported rape attempt. An eight o'clock curfew was announced and by nine-thirty, the white officers later alleged, stragglers had been rounded up and all troops were present or accounted for on post. At eleven taps was sounded and the troopers retired for the night.

Shortly before midnight a wild flurry of shooting broke out in the town, leaving one man dead and another seriously injured. In the minds of Brownsville's terrified residents there was no doubt: the Negro soldiers were shooting up the town. Any number of witnesses was found to testify that they had seen the black troopers moving through the town's unlighted streets on that moonless night. Roused by the noise of firing, Fort Brown's officers called out the troops and took the roll; again, all were present or accounted for. Yet when the mayor arrived soon thereafter to accuse the soldiers, the post commander was inclined to agree with him. "I am afraid our men have done this shooting," he confided to a fellow officer.

Across the continent the calm of Oyster Bay was shattered by a telegram from a group of Brownsville citizens to the President. Twenty or thirty soldiers had participated in the raid, T.R. was informed, their officers could not restrain them, and at any moment the blacks again might attack the defenseless town. "We look to you for relief," the wire concluded, "we ask you to have the troops at once removed from Fort Brown and replaced by white soldiers." The first Army investigator arrived in Brownsville on Saturday, August 18, and a week later the Twenty-Fifth Infantry boarded trains for a transfer to Fort Reno, Oklahoma. Meanwhile twelve soldiers and one ex-soldier—discharged since the raid—had been named as the guilty parties and placed under arrest. No convincing evidence against these thirteen men, or any men of the Twenty-Fifth, was produced, however, and the attempt to determine guilt took a bizarre turn. On October 4, through the Army Inspector General, the President delivered an ultimatum: unless the members of the regiment stepped forward to name the guilty men, all 167 troopers would be summarily discharged.

Roosevelt was convinced not only of the soldiers' guilt but also that the entire regiment, including its veteran noncommissioned officers, was conspiring to conceal the crime. In a private letter the next month he wrote of "the grave and evil fact that the negroes too often band together to shelter their own criminals. . . ." No soldier volunteered to in-

82

form on his fellow troopers and on Monday, November 5, the President approved the dismissal order against the 167 men. His decision was not made public until the following evening, Election Day, after the polls had closed. Two days later, as the angry controversy over his draconian measure welled up across the country, T.R. stepped aboard the U.S.S. *Louisiana* for his trip to Panama.

During the President's absence, Secretary of War Taft was subjected to enormous pressure from those who opposed the dismissal; and on November 18—in an unprecedented action—he suspended the discharge order. From Puerto Rico, where he was stopping en route back from Panama, Roosevelt cabled his reply to Taft's message about the suspension. The discharge was not to be suspended unless there were new facts in the case. "I care nothing whatever for the yelling of either the politicians or the sentimentalists," T.R. wrote. "The offense was most heinous and the punishment I inflicted was imposed after due deliberation." The men were dismissed.

At this point, the Negro troopers gained an unlikely champion, Ohio's Senator Joseph B. Foraker. An early supporter of Roosevelt's nomination and election of 1904, Foraker had broken with the President over the railroad rate bill; he was one of three senators—and the only Republican—who voted against final passage. In 1906, however, Foraker was still a power in the party and at the opening of Congress on December 3, he rose to introduce a resolution directing the Secretary of War to furnish the Senate with all documents on the Brownsville affair. The case was to be reopened.

On December 19 T.R. replied with a message to the Senate which convinced Foraker that "he was irritated and full of the spirit of indignant resentment that the rightfulness of his action had been questioned." Early in January, 1907, the President submitted a new report which merely reaffirmed the previous conclusion that the black soldiers were guilty. Senator Foraker was unconvinced and succeeded in getting the Senate to approve hearings on the raid. The Senate Military Affairs Committee, however, was directed to conduct the hearings "without questioning the legality or justice of any act of the President in relation thereto." To a friend the nonplussed T.R. wrote that he was having "a perfectly comic time" with the Senate. The senators insisted that they could not desert Foraker without splitting the party. T.R.'s reply was that "if they split off Foraker they split off a splinter; but that if they split off me they would split the party neatly in two. . . ."

A few days later, Roosevelt and Foraker found themselves both guests at a dinner of the Gridiron Club. A cartoon in the souvenir program—in the crude humor of the day—showed T.R. simultaneously writing at his desk, shooting a bear, and kicking a Negro. The verse accompanying the drawing read:

> I'm busy with things night and day,
> A Rough Rider was once heard to say,
> Writing views, singing tunes,
> Killing bears, firing coons,
> Or composing an old Irish lay.

Another cartoon showed Foraker wooing the Negro vote with a jingle beginning "All coons look alike to me." The tasteless hijinks continued with a skit satirizing Roosevelt as an emperor, but this evening T.R. was not entering into the spirit of things—as uncomplaining Gridiron guests were expected to do. Asked to address the diners, Roosevelt gave an hour-long, impromptu defense of his administration. Justifying his actions in the Brownsville affair, he looked directly at Foraker.

Following the President's speech, the toastmaster called on the Ohio senator for an unscheduled rebuttal—"to bridge the bloody chasm." Forgetting himself, Foraker rose to make a direct, bitter attack on the President. Several times T.R. was heard to mutter "That is not so" or "I will not stand for it"; and a Supreme Court justice seated next to the President barely restrained him from jumping up to answer Foraker immediately. In the hubbub of cheering and shouts that broke out as Foraker finished, Roosevelt stood up and cried that the Negro soldiers were "bloody butchers" who ought to have been hung. "The only reason that I didn't have them hung was because I couldn't find out which ones of them did the shooting." Instead of sitting down, he stalked out of the hall. The story of the sensational clash between President and senator was all over Washington the next day and soon even in the papers.

Roosevelt refused to change his mind on this matter; and so did Foraker. Both men retired from public life early in 1909 stoutly maintaining their respective positions. The Senate hearings failed to uncover fresh evidence against the black soldiers. Courts-martial against two of their white officers—charged with failing to prevent the "riot"— ended in acquittals. No trooper was ever brought to trial for a specific crime, and fourteen of the soldiers were ultimately found eligible for re-enlistment. In 1972 the Army at last exonerated the black troopers and for the records changed their discharges to honorable. Roosevelt, however, never retreated from the position he had taken, as expressed in a letter of April, 1908, that there was no more question about the black troopers' guilt "than there is that Czolgosz shot McKinley, or that Guiteau shot Garfield and the move on behalf of these murderers is as essentially vicious as a move on behalf of Guiteau or Czolgosz would have been."

6

Later in 1907—and long before the final disgraceful scenes in the Brownsville tragedy had been enacted—Roosevelt found himself confronted with a crisis of a very different nature. A worldwide overexpansion of credit had led to "flurries" on the New York stock market in March and August. Several large firms declared bankruptcy and on October 23 the Knickerbocker Trust Company—unable to meet demands for withdrawal of funds on deposit—closed its doors. George B. Cortelyou, now Secretary of the Treasury, teamed with J. P. Morgan to bolster other trust companies with the deposit of public and private funds. But the crisis continued. A few days later, two officials of U.S. Steel paid a call on the President. Another firm in New York, they reported, was about to fail and such a collapse would undoubtedly precipitate a full-fledged panic—prelude perhaps to a long-term depression. Among the assets of this threatened institution was a controlling interest in the Tennessee Coal and Iron Company. U.S. Steel, Roosevelt's visitors said, was prepared to acquire the Tennessee securities but only on condition that the President would not challenge its acquisition as a violation of the antitrust law.

Roosevelt accepted at face value the steel men's claim that the take-over was of no great benefit to U.S. Steel and was only proposed in a spirit of public interest. The government would not dispute the purchase. The panic was averted, but Roosevelt's acquiescence in the steel corporation's maneuver was later to be a cause of acute embarrassment to him.

A happier event, as the year 1907 closed, was the departure of sixteen battleships of the United States Navy on an around-the-world cruise that was to last more than a year. T.R. conceived the epic voyage as a demonstration of America's emerging might. The vessels would sail down the east coast of South America, pass through the Straits of Magellan, visit several west coast ports, then cross the Pacific to Hawaii and the Philippines before returning through the Suez Canal and the Mediterranean Sea. Visits to Australia and Japan were later added, and the fleet made an emergency stop to help earthquake victims in Italy. Roosevelt came to consider the voyage of this Great White Fleet one of the grand accomplishments of his administration, and he would listen to no opposition to his scheme. Upon announcement of the voyage, there was an outcry from the East about removing the fleet from its traditional defensive base on the Atlantic. But when Congress at first refused to appropriate funds for the cruise, Roosevelt retorted that there was enough money to get the fleet out into the Pacific—and this he proposed to do. Congress could then think about money for getting the ships back.

It was a triumphant Roosevelt who boarded the yacht *Mayflower* on December 15, 1907, for the overnight trip to review the departing fleet at Hampton Roads, Virginia. The next day he made a speech and then signaled to Admiral Robley D. Evans: "Proceed to duty assigned." One by one the warships steamed past the presidential yacht before heading out to sea. As Roosevelt watched the long line of vessels pass in review and then disappear into the mists, he must have known that his "imperial years" were drawing to a close. When the big ships came up again over the rim of the horizon—their modern repetition of Magellan's voyage completed—T.R. would be a lame-duck President. But by that date, February 22, 1909, Roosevelt would have at least one major consolation to whatever sadness he felt at leaving office: his elected successor would be a man of his own choice.

⇜§ Chapter 6 §⇝

Choosing a Successor

Two weeks after his stunning electoral triumph of November, 1904, Roosevelt wrote to the British historian Sir George Otto Trevelyan a letter that soon became a "rambling digression" on why he had renounced a third term. Even if there were no anti-third-term tradition in the United States, T.R. explained, "it would be better to have some man like Taft or Root succeed me in the Presidency, at the head of the Republican party, than to have me succeed myself." Fully sharing his principles, either of those men would have the advantage of "freshness" and moreover would be "free from the animosities and suspicions which I had accumulated. . . ." Roosevelt, as was his custom, was starting the next campaign the minute the previous one was concluded—but this time the crusade would be in behalf of another.

The President was careful not to put in writing any regret he might have harbored over his premature renunciation; indeed, again and again during the next three years he was to repeat the declaration in one form or another. To Benjamin Ide Wheeler, president of the University of California, he wrote in the summer of 1906 that "under no circumstances" would he take the nomination in 1908. At the Gridiron dinner the following November he said he would not run again—and was amused to see the relief on Senator Aldrich's face. Early in 1907 Roosevelt confided to an old friend that he had "never for a moment altered my views as to the wisdom of my declaration. . . . It is time for someone else to stand his trick at the wheel." To his cousin Emlen Roosevelt T.R. wrote in exasperation at the end of 1907: "Most emphatically, I do not wish to run again for President." Since he had made this remark in private letters "several hundred times" and as often in private conversation, he did not see why it was necessary to make another public statement. But to stop speculation, Roosevelt released to the press on December 12, 1907, a statement that repeated the 1904 declaration and added that his decision was "final and would not be changed."

Consummate politician that he was, Roosevelt knew full well that you cannot fight something with nothing. To block any movement for his own renomination he needed an alternative candidate, and in 1905 T.R. launched a long and successful campaign to handpick his successor. Writing as an historian in 1887, Roosevelt had condemned Andrew Jackson, at the end of *his* second term, for designating Martin Van Buren as his successor. Two decades later, as President of the United States, T.R. repeated Jackson's maneuver—thus becoming the only other man in history to do so.

In Roosevelt's mind there were only two possible heirs apparent: Elihu Root and William Howard Taft. Early in 1903 Root, after a most successful tenure as Secretary of War, had announced his intention of resigning from the Cabinet by year's end in order to return to his lucrative New York law practice. The secretary agreed wholeheartedly with the President that his successor should be Taft, then serving under Root as civil governor of the Philippines.

A Cincinnati lawyer and former judge of the Ohio superior court, Taft had first come to Washington in 1890 to serve as United States Solicitor General under President Benjamin Harrison. There he met Theodore Roosevelt, a year his junior, then serving as a Civil Service Commissioner. Two years later Taft returned to Ohio to become a United States circuit judge for the Sixth Judicial Circuit—a pleasant and secure berth for the next eight years. Early in 1900 he was plucked from the bench by McKinley and made president of the commission sent out to the Philippines to study what should be done with America's distant new possession. He stayed on as civil governor, winning praise all around for his successful handling of many ticklish problems arising from America's trusteeship of the former Spanish colony.

Taft, a massive figure, weighing well over three hundred pounds, had the infectious amiability traditionally assigned the fat man. His perpetual smile, his deep-throated chuckle erupting into nearly uncontrollable laughter won for him instant love and trust. Joining the Roosevelt Cabinet at the beginning of 1904, Taft immediately took a commanding position in the administration—especially with Secretary of State John Hay sinking into his final illness. When T.R. left Washington in the spring of 1905 for a Rough Rider reunion and hunting trip out West, he cheerily told reporters that things would be all right, "I have left Taft sitting on the lid"—a remark that, considering the Secretary of War's girth, caused considerable amusement across the country.

At the death of Hay that summer, T.R. hesitated between elevating Taft to the State Department or asking Root to rejoin the Cabinet to fill the vacancy. As soon as he began thinking about the problem seriously, he wrote Senator Lodge, he saw that there was no reason for doubt. It was not a choice between Root and Taft, "but a choice of having both instead of one." Root became Secretary of State and Taft remained at the head of the War Department. Root's appointment brought immediate speculation in the press that the New York lawyer was T.R.'s choice as successor, and the President hastened to reassure Taft that such was not the case. In talking about Root rather than Taft as the next President, Roosevelt wrote, the public—like a child in the nursery—had merely "dropped its woolly horse and turned with frantic delight to the new cloth doll."

Roosevelt considered Root the better man, but he realized the impossibility of nominating or electing him to the Presidency. A brilliant attorney, Root faithfully served whatever client he had at the moment; as President, T.R. maintained, Root would be equally faithful in the service of his larger client, the American people. But the new Secretary of State was too closely identified with Wall Street and at the next election he would be sixty-three. Thus, by the summer of 1905, Roosevelt had more or less decided upon Taft as the heir apparent.

Taft himself would have preferred a seat on the Supreme Court, but twice he turned down Roosevelt's offer to name him to the high tribunal. Whatever ambition the easy-going Taft may have lacked was more than made up for by that of his wife, Nellie. Early in 1906 the Tafts were guests at a small White House dinner. Afterward, the party withdrew to the second-floor library, where the President sank into a chair, closed his eyes, and pretended to be in a trance. "I am the seventh son of a seventh daughter and I have clairvoyant powers," he intoned. "I see a man weighing three hundred and fifty pounds. There is something hanging over his head. I cannot make out what it is. . . . At one time it looks like the presidency, then again it looks like the chief justiceship."

"Make it the chief justiceship," the secretary said.

"Make it the presidency," interposed Nellie Taft.

At the end of a Cabinet meeting in March, Roosevelt asked Root and Taft to stay on to discuss the 1908 nomination and the current Supreme Court vacancy, which had been offered to Taft. The Secretary of War again expressed his preference for the bench but confessed that Nellie was "bitterly opposed" to his accepting the appointment, claiming that it would be the biggest mistake of his life. The troubled Taft informed the President that he was going to New York to discuss the matter with his elder half brother—and financial patron—Charles P. Taft. In the meantime, Mrs. Taft was requesting an audience with the President at which she could give her reasons against a Supreme Court appointment for her husband.

On March 15, 1906, Roosevelt wrote a long letter to Taft, following his "half-hour's talk with your dear wife." At the moment Taft was the man "most likely" to receive the G.O.P. nomination two years hence, an opportunity he would have to forego if he joined the high tribunal. On the other hand, if he accepted appointment to the Supreme Court, it would mean a quarter century of great work for the nation— with the possibility of stepping up to the Chief Justiceship, if that position became vacant before Roosevelt left the White House on March 4, 1909. It was a hard choice to make, the President observed, but "you yourself have to make it." Taft, strongly backed by Nellie and his brother Charles, made the choice. He declined the Supreme Court appointment and thereby became the leading candidate to succeed Roosevelt. The following December the Washington correspondents who made up the Gridiron Club picked Taft as the next President with a song about the Secretary of War that had as its chorus: "Waiting for Teddy's shoes."

As the presidential year of 1908 opened, a rival for the G.O.P. nomination suddenly appeared on the political horizon. Charles Evans Hughes overnight had won a national reputation as counsel to a committee of the New York state legislature that exposed abuses in the life insurance industry. Elected Governor of New York in 1906, Hughes was known as a stern defender of public morality, but his unsmiling countenance and formidable beard had earned him a reputation as an iceberg with chin whiskers. Nevertheless, the New York County Republican Committee endorsed Hughes for the Presidency on January 29, 1908. The governor agreed to "make plain his views on all important national issues" in a speech two nights later. But readers hoping to learn where Hughes stood found other, more important news on page 1 when they opened their papers on the morning of February 1. The previous day, timed perfectly to upstage the Hughes speech, T.R. had released the text of a special message to Congress—and it was this story that took all the headlines.

Roosevelt felt that Congress was already ignoring him, even as he entered his last full year in office. The lawmakers had failed to follow the recommendations of his regular annual message the preceding December and so now he issued a long, bellicose statement of his maturing progressive thought, calling for a general employers' liability act and compensation for injured government employees, increased government control over giant corporations, and federal regulation of securities issues—all ideas well in advance of the times.

The message caused "a great flutter in the dovecote," Roosevelt confessed with some pride in a letter on February 2 to his son Kermit. But as the nominating conventions approached, politicians were paying more attention to the prospective candidates and less to what he, the President, had to say. This special address, he added, was "well-nigh the last occasion I shall have to speak when all men, however unwilling, must listen, and I wanted to put my deep and earnest conviction into the message."

The call to a battle for progressivism contained in the special message of January, 1908, led to some truly impressive acrobatics by prominent political figures. Oscar Straus, a Cleveland Democrat who had entered the Roosevelt Cabinet a year earlier as Secretary of Commerce and Labor, admitted that he had been on both sides of the fence; "but that was not my fault," he claimed, "the fence had been moved." And Theodore Roosevelt found himself replying to a note of congratulation from William Jennings Bryan, then emerging as the front runner for the 1908 Democratic nomination—which would be the Great Commoner's third try for the Presidency. At a Gridiron dinner, Bryan once accused T.R. of larceny in appropriating so many of his own reforms. Good-naturedly, Roosevelt conceded the theft—adding only that the proposals were of very little use to the Nebraskan since he would never be in a position to see them enacted into law. And the special message brought Roosevelt at last to a parting of the ways with his old confidant Nicholas Murray Butler, the archconservative president of Columbia University. Butler wrote to say that the message had made "a very painful impression," that Roosevelt's friends spoke of it with grief and sorrow, while his critics and enemies were delighted. To Butler, T.R. replied that for the first time he regretted that this was not his first term and that he could not have "a showdown with my foes both without and within the party."

To a correspondent at this time Roosevelt indignantly wrote that charges he was using his office to bring about anyone's nomination were "false and malicious." As for the charge that he had timed the special message to deflate the Hughes boom: "If Hughes is going to play the game," the President told reporters, "he must learn the tricks." Nevertheless, with the failure of the Hughes candidacy to become airborne and with T.R.'s endorsement of Taft so widely known, there was little suspense about the forthcoming G.O.P. nomination. By mid-May, with only 491 convention votes needed for the nomination, Taft could already claim 563. The convention, scheduled to open in Chicago on June 16, promised to be a dull repetition of the 1904 gathering that had rubber-stamped T.R.'s nomination.

On June 1 Roosevelt wrote to Henry Cabot Lodge, who was scheduled to deliver the keynote speech at the convention, enclosing yet another statement of his noncandidacy "to be shown quietly to any of the Taft delegates who show the slightest symptoms of going for me. . . ." Not even the Secretary of War himself, T.R. confided to another friend, could be more anxious that Taft be nominated.

On the second day of the Republican convention, Senator Lodge rose to make his speech—and got only as far as his statement that "the President is the most abused and the most *popular* man in the country" when he was interrupted with a thunderclap of applause that quickly turned into a forty-nine-minute demonstration. Delegates clapping, shouting, cheering rose to their feet and started to sing "The Star Spangled Banner." Some, bearing aloft stuffed teddy bears, marched around the hall; others took off their coats and waved them overhead. From the galleries came a chant: "Four-four-four years more!" Several times Lodge banged his gavel, trying unsuccessfully to resume his speech. Finally the storm subsided, and the Massachusetts senator warned that any attempt to renominate the President would impugn Roosevelt's sincerity and good faith. He finished his address and the convention adjourned for the day.

Back in Washington the Tafts were following the convention by telegraph at the War Department. As the Roosevelt demonstration lengthened on June 17, Nellie Taft expressed her deep and bitter distrust of the President. The following day when her husband's name was put in nomination she proclaimed but a single wish: that the Taft demonstration would last longer than the Roosevelt one of the previous day. "Oh, my dear! my dear!" Taft clucked in nervous disapproval.

To Nellie Taft's intense disappointment, the Taft demonstration on June 18 lasted only twenty-five minutes. The President's daughter Alice Roosevelt Longworth was at the convention and described the other nomination speeches as "gusts of perfunctory oratory." The man who placed Hughes in nomination even forgot to mention the New York governor's name. On the first ballot Taft received 702 votes; Hughes, 67; with scattered votes for various favorite sons. A motion to make the nomination unanimous was quickly adopted. The following day Representative James Schoolcraft ("Sunny Jim") Sherman of New York was nominated as Taft's running mate.

To his new military aide Captain Archibald Butt—a Southern gentleman of impeccable social bearing and of unerring instinct for revelatory though never malicious gossip—T.R. confessed that the demonstration for him had merely allowed the delegates to let off steam; there was nothing more to it. Taft appeared at a Cabinet meeting the day after his nomination "radiantly happy," but Oscar Straus stayed after the meeting to confess to the President his sadness that the plan to name a successor had worked so well.

2

Two days after Taft's nomination, Roosevelt departed for his annual three-month vacation at Oyster Bay. One of the first letters he wrote from his summer home was to Henry Cabot Lodge, thanking the senator for his service at the convention and noting that most of what he could do for Taft had already been done. He did not wish "to become officious or a busybody"; Taft and his friends must run their own campaign.

It was simply not in keeping with Roosevelt's character, however, for the President to sit quietly on the sidelines—especially with even the remote danger that William Jennings Bryan, again, as predicted, the Democratic nominee, might at last gain the White House. The day before Taft's nomination, he had said that the Secretary of War would be elected "with a swoop; but we must all work on the assumption that it is a very hard contest!" As early as mid-July, T.R. was writing to Lodge to say that he did not see how Taft could be beaten, but this did not prevent him from sending a fairly steady stream of directives to the G.O.P. nominee.

"Poor old boy! Of course, you are not enjoying the campaign," he wrote to Taft on July 15. "I wish you had some of my bad temper! It is at times a real aid to enjoyment." Commenting on the draft of Taft's official acceptance speech, T.R. advised that the number of laudatory references to himself be cut down. "You are now the leader, and there must be nothing that looks like self-depreciation or undue subordination of yourself."

In late August he warned against overconfidence, reminding Taft that in 1904 he had never regarded his own contest with Parker "as anything but doubtful." On the other hand, Taft should not be "one particle discouraged"; the candidate's electoral vote was likely to be as high as McKinley's in 1900 or even his own in 1904. "Do not *answer* Bryan; attack him!" Roosevelt wrote a week later. In September he dispatched a "strictly private" letter to Taft concerning the candidate's golf playing. He would like the campaign staff to do everything possible to keep all mention of the nominee's fishing and golfing out of the press. The American people regarded politics "as a very serious business, and we want to be careful that your opponents do not get the chance to misrepresent you as not taking it with sufficient seriousness." He had received hundreds of letters complaining about Taft's golf, T.R. wrote in another letter. "It is just like my tennis; I never let any friends advertise my tennis, and never let a photo of me in tennis costume appear."

"Let the audience see you smile *always*," Roosevelt wrote to Taft on September 11, "because I feel that your nature shines out so transparently when you do smile—you big, generous, high-minded fellow." The President had just confided to Root that, for reasons he was "absolutely unable to fathom," Taft was not arousing the enthusiasm that his record and personality warranted. All he wanted to be sure of, T.R. wrote the candidate early in October, is that "the people of this country should get really to see and know you." That done, he had no fear of the outcome.

Although he declined to make any speeches in Taft's behalf—custom still prevented the President from actively campaigning, either for himself or for another—Roosevelt did write several long open letters of endorsement for publication in the late summer. For the past ten years, he wrote on September 9, as Governor of New York and President, he had been "thrown into the closest intimacy" with Taft, and on

94

every essential point the two "stood in heartiest agreement, shoulder to shoulder." The man to trust in an election campaign was the one like Taft, who "does not promise too much, but who could not be swayed from the path of duty by any argument, by any consideration. . . ."

The endorsement of Taft eventually became, in T.R.'s mind, a defense of his own stewardship—even a celebration of it. In some private letters he first wrote of "us" carrying the election but crossed the word out and substituted "Taft." At the end of September several Cabinet members were unexpectedly summoned to the White House. Bryan had attacked the administration, and T.R. wished to prepare a rebuttal. When Oscar Straus suggested that the President tone down his stiffly worded reply, Roosevelt remarked that the secretary must remember the letter was "not an etching but a poster." Roosevelt's aide Captain Butt almost hoped that Bryan would win. The Peerless Leader had pledged to serve only one term, which meant that T.R. could easily come back in four years, whereas he would have to stand aside for two terms should Taft be elected, and then it would be too late for a comeback. "If he would leave things alone and disappear for four years," Archie Butt wrote on September 25, "I believe, and so does every one here, I think, that the nation would call him to the Executive chair again. . . ."

An issue of the 1908 campaign, as it had been of the 1904 contest, was contributions from big business. First Roosevelt got Taft to dump Thomas C. du Pont as chairman of the G.O.P. campaign speakers committee—the du Pont Company was currently engaged in an antitrust suit brought by the government. Then T.R. moved to attack Bryan's campaign treasurer, Governor Charles N. Haskell of Oklahoma. Revelations about Haskell's connections with Standard Oil had just been made, and the President urged Taft to use the subject of Standard Oil contributions "to smash and cut Bryan. . . ." Roosevelt's offensive forced Bryan to ask for Haskell's resignation, and T.R. could gloat to Taft that, when the Democratic standard bearer had given him "a bully chance to hit him," he had done so "to some purpose."

In mid-October the President extended an invitation to Taft to stay at the White House, unless his managers thought such a close association would hurt him. To his son Kermit, after Taft's visit to the capital, T.R. wrote that the candidate was a "big generous fellow"; it seemed impossible that the people might prefer "a cheap faker like Bryan to such a fine man." But one could not predict "what twist the folly of mankind will take," he warned Kermit. Nevertheless, by month's end, he was writing the candidate that "the result of the election is now absolutely assured"; the Republicans had it "hands down."

On Election Eve, T.R. boarded the midnight train for New York —just as he had done four years earlier—en route to Oyster Bay to cast his ballot. "We've got them beaten to a frazzle," the President remarked as he left Washington. After voting on November 3, Roosevelt started back for the capital. As his train pulled out of Jersey City, a young man raced alongside and called to the President on the rear platform: "Four years more." T.R. was last seen shaking his head no.

The President's activities, however, were recorded on the inside pages of newspapers; it was Taft who got the front-page headlines. The candidate had opened his final day of campaigning with a speech at Dunkirk, New York. "I don't know whether you are as glad that Election Day is tomorrow as I am," he told his audience. "If you are, you are very happy." Thousands lined the streets of Cleveland, Taft's next stop, as he drove from the station to the armory for the second address of the day. Afterward, he stood up in his automobile to speak to an overflow crowd in the street. A parade greeted his arrival later on Monday at Youngstown where, after dinner, he gave the final speech of the campaign. A night train took him home to Cincinnati, where he would vote and then await returns at the home of Charles P. Taft. "Had he been a conquering hero, returning from a long and successful military campaign," reported the New York *Tribune*, "the people of his state could have given him no warmer or more enthusiastic welcome. . . ."

Alice Longworth was also in Cincinnati, where her husband was running for re-election to the House of Representatives, and the Longworths joined the circle of Taft family and friends to await the outcome. With voting machines in use at Buffalo and Indianapolis, early returns from those cities were expected to indicate how New York and Indiana —trend-setting states for the nation at large—would go. By early evening, it was apparent that Taft would roll up an impressive majority.

In Washington, members of a local Taft-Sherman marching club paraded up to the White House, gave three cheers for the victors, and asked to see the President. Roosevelt declined to come outside, or to make any election statement. Instead he telegraphed his congratulations to Taft in Cincinnati: "I need hardly say how heartily I congratulate you, and the country even more." Taft replied in a graciously worded message: "Thank you for your telegram. Without any expression from you I would know how deeply interested you have been in my success and how much you rejoice in it. It is your administration that this victory affirms." At midnight a throng of merrymakers from downtown Cincinnati, accompanied by several brass bands, reached the Charles Taft home and set off displays of "red fire." Stepping out on the front porch, the President-elect found the entire street filled with people—and to them he pledged to make his administration a worthy successor to that of Theodore Roosevelt, "and beyond that I claim nothing higher."

The final count was Taft, 7,677,788; Bryan, 6,407,982. The electoral count was 321 to 162. Taft had actually surpassed Roosevelt's popular vote of 1904, while Bryan increased the Democratic count by nearly one and a half million votes. Taft's plurality over Bryan was thus only half of T.R.'s over Parker. The Republican party remained in control of both houses of Congress, with an impressive two-to-one majority in the Senate.

Immediately after the election, Taft went to Hot Springs, Virginia, for a short rest. The first letter he wrote from the resort was to the President—to review the results of the election and to express his gratitude. "You and my brother Charley made that possible which in all probability would not have occurred otherwise. I don't wish to be falsely modest in this." T.R.'s reaction—on finding his efforts in behalf of Taft linked to the financial aid given by the candidate's brother—are not recorded. But, long after the glow of victory had faded, much was to be made of this letter.

3

In mid-November Taft returned to the capital, and among the matters he discussed with the President was the composition of his Cabinet. Upon his nomination the preceding June, Taft had resigned as Secretary of War. In his place T.R. had put General Luke Wright, a Tennessee Democrat whose appointment was a solid nonpartisan gesture in an election year. Roosevelt had explained to Taft that it would be hard to get a good man for the post with less than a year to go in his administration; could he promise Wright that Taft, if elected, would retain him in the office? Taft apparently assented. Indeed, according to Taft's own story, the nominee also told Roosevelt about this time that he "did not see how I could do anything else but retain all the old members of the

Cabinet who had been associated with me." Taft thought nothing more about the conversation and later was dismayed to hear that the President had practically told every member of the Cabinet that he would be retained. "I wish you would tell the boys I have been working with that I want to continue all of them," T.R. recalled Taft as saying. "They are all fine fellows, and they have been mighty good to me. I want them all to stay just as they are." T.R. had asked Taft to tell them himself, but he had demurred—not wanting to be bound by any pledges made during the campaign.

Following the election, it was learned that two members of the Cabinet would not stay on. Secretary of State Root would resign to become a United States Senator from New York, and Navy Secretary Truman H. Newberry wished to return to private life. A third member of the Cabinet, Secretary of the Treasury George B. Cortelyou, had had presidential ambitions of his own and even T.R. felt that he would not work well with Taft. Wright and the five others, however, might wish to remain.

On December 15, 1908, T.R. heartily endorsed Taft's nominee for Secretary of State: Philander C. Knox, his own former Attorney General, then a senator from Pennsylvania. Two weeks later he wrote in high humor to his successor: "Ha ha! *you* are making up your Cabinet. *I* in a lighthearted way have spent the morning testing the rifles for my African trip. Life has compensations!" A few days later, on January 4, 1909, he wrote in more sober vein; he had learned that Taft would not reappoint Attorney General Charles J. Bonaparte, Secretary of Commerce and Labor Oscar Straus, and Secretary of the Interior James R. Garfield, son of the former President. "Now I think it would be well for you to write them all at once that you do not intend to reappoint them," he advised, reverting to the avuncular tone he had used with Taft during the campaign. "They will be making their plans, and less than two months remain, and I do not think they ought to be left in doubt."

Taft decided to retain only James Wilson, Secretary of Agriculture since McKinley's first term, and George von Lengerke Meyer, whom he shifted from Postmaster General to the Navy Department. The others received letters on January 22 that their services would not be needed after March 4. Some in Washington tried to depict the Cabinet changes as the beginning of a rift between the outgoing President and his hand-picked successor. "Taft is going about this thing just as I would do,"

Roosevelt insisted to Archie Butt, "and while I retained McKinley's Cabinet the conditions were quite different. I cannot find any fault in Taft's attitude toward me."

Roosevelt seemed determined not to let any disagreement, or mis-understanding, with Taft on the Cabinet alter his assessment of his suc-cessor. "You blessed old trump," Roosevelt had written the nominee in mid-campaign, "I have always said you would be the greatest President, bar only Washington and Lincoln, and I feel mighty inclined to strike out the exceptions." "Taft is as fine a fellow as ever sat in the President's chair," Roosevelt wrote a few weeks after the election, "and I cannot ex-press the measureless content that comes over me as I think that the work in which I have so much believed will be carried on by him." This comforting thought, he concluded, prevented him from being "melan-choly at leaving the Presidency and taking my hands off the levers of the great machine." Having made up his mind to relinquish the Presi-dency gracefully and having convinced himself that Taft was a worthy successor, T.R. could not acknowledge any second thoughts about his own wisdom in these critical decisions. Self-doubt was never a charac-teristic of Roosevelt's personality.

Roosevelt was also determined to enjoy his Presidency to the fullest extent, to the last possible moment. "I am ending my career as President with just the same stiff fighting that has marked it ever since I took the office," he wrote an English friend. "But I am having a thoroly good time." Included in the good time was a libel suit against Joseph Pulitz-er's New York *World* for having said during the campaign that Charles P. Taft and Douglas Robinson, T.R.'s brother-in-law, had profited from the government's purchase of the New Panama Canal Company. Noth-ing ever came of the suit but Roosevelt expended a good deal of self-righteous wrath over the matter in these final months. He next became embroiled in a controversy with Congress over charges that he was using the Secret Service to spy on its members.

When overage army officers protested a presidential order that they demonstrate their fitness by a horseback ride of ninety miles in three days, Roosevelt showed that the President could do even better. Trailing Archie Butt and two others, T.R. rode to Warrenton, Virginia, and back—a round-trip of ninety miles—all in one January day. The party weathered a blizzard to return to Washington after dark, but the President disdained a carriage sent to meet him at the Aqueduct Bridge over the Potomac River. "By George we will make the White House

99

with our horses if we have to lead them," T.R. snapped, thinking of the tired mounts rather than of his exhausted companions. Edith Roosevelt met the party at the door of the White House, and to Archie Butt not even "Dolly Madison, even in her loveliest moments," could ever have been more attractive.

On February 12, 1909, Roosevelt went to Hodgenville, Kentucky, to dedicate a log cabin memorial at Lincoln's birthplace. And on Washington's birthday, he spent a glorious day at Hampton Roads, Virginia, welcoming the return of the Great White Fleet from its fourteen-month-long round-the-world cruise. The President, dressed in a frock coat and wearing a tall silk hat, was standing on the deck of the presidential yacht *Mayflower* at 10 A.M. as a tiny speck appeared over the horizon of the bay. Within a half hour the first ship was in sight. The flagship, as it drew up to the *Mayflower,* fired a twenty-one-gun salute; it took thirty minutes for the twenty-five vessels to pass in review—bands on their decks blaring "The Star-Spangled Banner." Later, offering a champagne toast to the fleet officers, T.R. said, "We stay-at-homes drink to the men who have made us so proud of our country."

At the January dinner of the Gridiron Club, T.R. had told the correspondents that this was the last time he would be their guest—and victim. Washington was no place for ex-presidents. Corinne Robinson, visiting her brother in the White House for the last time, found him "as gay as a boy let out of school." Sitting one morning in the executive office, she heard Roosevelt say again and again that there would be a new man in the saddle soon, "and there can't be two Presidents after March 4th." The acerbic Henry Adams sent the President a sadly humorous note: "After this spring, Andrew Jackson and I will be the solitary monuments of the Square. . . . I don't find the prospect amusing. Andrew may be as handsome as you, but he is not as good company at dinner."

One by one the Cabinet members gave their final dinners for the President and First Lady. And on March 1 Roosevelt invited thirty-one members of his Tennis Cabinet to a gala luncheon party at the White House. The guests ranged from French Ambassador Jules Jusserand and Supreme Court Justice William H. Moody down to two of T.R.'s friends from his ranching days in the Dakota Badlands. The President rose to address the group and there was scarcely a dry eye at the table when he had finished. Seth Bullock of South Dakota, the man designated to present the group's parting gift—a bronze statuette of a cougar—was too choked up to say anything and so, lunging across the table, started to claw away at the floral centerpiece that concealed the gift. T.R., thinking his old ranching friend drunk on the sherry, began to laugh, but he grew serious and fell silent when he saw the statuette. United States District Attorney Henry L. Stimson took over for Bullock, saying that he was unable to express what all of the guests were feeling—the love of a son for a father. At the conclusion of the lachrymose luncheon, all adjourned to the south lawn of the White House to pose for a stiffly formal group photograph: the grim-faced President seated at the center, flanked by his proud but saddened guests.

And then the sands of the Roosevelt administration had at last run out. The hostile New York *Sun* published a one-word editorial: "Thru!"

4

At 9:30 A.M. on Wednesday morning, March 3, Roosevelt was in the executive office to begin receiving an unending stream of well-wishers— shaking hands, signing autographs, and calling out the words that became a litany during the next twenty-four hours: "Good-bye and good luck!" After a lunch, he returned to the unscheduled farewell levee, breaking off only to go to the East Room to greet a group of governors in town for the Taft inauguration. His callers that day ranged from Cabinet officers and congressmen down to clerks and stenographers of the White House office staff; someone estimated he shook 2,500 hands. At 7 P.M. he ended the day's formal activities with a reception, again in the East Room, for Vice-President-elect Sherman and a delegation of citizens from Sherman's hometown of Utica, New York.

In a warm and unprecedented gesture, the Roosevelts had invited Mr. and Mrs. Taft to move into the White House a day early, have a quiet family dinner on the eve of the inaugural, and sleep that night in the Executive Mansion. "People have attempted to represent that you and I were in some way at odds during the last three months," Taft said in his letter accepting the invitation, "whereas you and I know that there has not been the slightest difference between us. . . ." He welcomed the opportunity presented by the invitation of dispelling rumors of a rift. The President-elect signed his letter "With love and affection, my dear Theodore." T.R. wrote back to say that Taft's letter was "so very nice—nice isn't anything like a strong enough word, but at the moment to use words as strong as I feel would look sloppy. . . ." And the President concluded with an endorsement of Taft's new form of address to his longtime chief.

The guests of honor arrived at the White House on Wednesday evening, shortly before the time set for dinner, with rain "coming down in bucketfuls." At the Gridiron dinner the previous January, a mock weather forecast had read: "March 3: Blizzard, T.R. preparing to leave the White House. March 4: Taft day—Rain, sleet, snow, high winds, thunder and lightning." As the actual day approached, however, the government forecaster was optimistic, predicting that Wednesday night would be fair and cooler after the passage of rain clouds. March 4 would be clear "with plenty of sunshine and invigorating air."

For the Roosevelts' final dinner in the White House the table had been laid for fourteen. At the last minute, however, Senator Knox and his wife sent their regrets; he would be detained on Capitol Hill in a treaty debate. In addition to the Tafts, the other guests were the Elihu Roots, the Nicholas Longworths, Admiral and Mrs. William Sheffield Cowles (she was Bamie, T.R.'s older sister), Miss Mabel Boardman, an old Taft family friend, and the perennially available bachelor military aide, Captain Archie Butt. (Butt, incidentally, had agreed to stay on in the White House under the new President, insuring the historian an uninterrupted flow of information in the frank private letters he sent almost daily to his sister-in-law, Clara.) Nellie Taft wore a white satin gown, with filmy tulle about the sleeves and bodice; Edith Roosevelt was somberly garbed in black.

The dinner proceeded without incident—though Elihu Root, known to the White House staff as the Crybaby, was seen to shed a few tears into his soup. After dinner all went upstairs, the men to smoke cigars in the President's study, the ladies to gather for coffee in the library. By this time the rain had turned to snow—a howling, driving blizzard. "I looked out the window," the trenchantly witty Alice Longworth later recalled, "and turning to the room said, 'It's snowing,' in a voice that, I fear, did not indicate regret at the prospect of a wretched day for the inauguration."

At 10 P.M. Taft excused himself for a short trip to the New Willard Hotel to address a group of Yale men, gathered to see the first alumnus of their college in history inaugurated President. And shortly thereafter the party at the White House broke up. Taft's speech at the Willard was curiously downbeat. To one of the Yale alumni, Gifford Pinchot, the President-elect sounded like a man "whose job had got him down even before he tackled it."

"Even the elements do protest," Taft remarked the following morning at breakfast as the storm raged on. "I knew there would be a blizzard when I went out," replied Roosevelt.

At 9:30 on Thursday, March 4, members of a joint delegation from the Senate and House arrived to escort Roosevelt and Taft to the Capitol. Before leaving, the pair posed for a photograph on the White House porch—Taft beaming his customary smile; T.R. presenting to the camera and history a totally impassive, entirely inscrutable gaze. The two mounted a carriage drawn by four horses and proceeded through the storm up Pennsylvania Avenue.

Taft was still hoping to hold the inaugural ceremony outdoors, in the wooden stand erected at the east front of the Capitol. But one look at Chief Justice Fuller—"white bearded and venerable"—convinced him that this would be impractical and unwise on such a day. It was the only time, men were saying, since the first inaugural of James Madison a full century earlier that the ceremony had to be held indoors, in the Senate Chamber.

William Howard Taft took the oath of office as successor to Theodore Roosevelt at 12:53 P.M. Forty minutes later, at the conclusion of Taft's inaugural address, T.R. bounded forward and grasped the new President by the shoulders. For a moment the two swayed in a clumsy bearhug, then broke to shake hands. "God bless you, old man," Roosevelt said. "It is a great state document."

Roosevelt had announced that he would not follow tradition and return to the White House with his predecessor—there to watch the inaugural parade. Instead, he had insisted, he would leave the city immediately following the inauguration ceremony. Learning of T.R.'s intent, Nellie Taft decided—despite all protests—that *she* would occupy the vacant seat in the presidential carriage. Vice President Sherman and other dignitaries would just have to follow in whatever order they pleased.

As the Tafts moved from the Senate Chamber to head up the inaugural procession back down Pennsylvania Avenue, Roosevelt slipped out a side door—but he was not unnoticed. A delegation of eight hundred members of the New York County Republican Committee formed a hollow square to escort the ex-President the few blocks to Washington's Union Station. As the group moved away from the Capitol, an accompanying band struck up the familiar "There'll Be a Hot Time in the Old Town Tonight"—and as they reached the depot, "Auld Lang Syne." "What's the matter with Teddy?" shouted Representative Herbert Parsons of New York, acting as a cheerleader. "He's all right," chanted the club members in response. At the station, T.R. bade farewell to his escort, calling out "Good-bye and good luck" as he disappeared into the private, presidential waiting room.

Edith Roosevelt and Alice Longworth had come directly from the White House. Members of the Cabinet and the French and Japanese ambassadors and their wives were also waiting at the station. Baron Takahira had roses for the ex-President; his baroness, unable to conceal her tears, presented the former First Lady with an additional bouquet. The train, delayed several hours by the continuing storm, did not leave Washington until 3:30.

The Roosevelts, "in most democratic manner," according to a newspaper account, traveled in the drawing room of an ordinary Pullman car, with no attendants, no Secret Service. After a porter brought messages of goodwill from his fellow travelers, T.R. went through the train shaking hands. At Jersey City, the Roosevelts transferred to the Manhattan ferry and were met in New York by their second son, Kermit, and the Douglas Robinsons, who urged them to break their journey at this point. But the couple was determined to sleep that night at Sagamore Hill.

The townsfolk of Oyster Bay had planned an elaborate welcome home for T.R. But as continued reports of the storm in Washington came in, most of the assembled crowd drifted away from the station. At last only a small gathering of about two hundred young people remained; some went sleighing to pass the time, but the hard core vowed to stay all night and into the next day if necessary to greet the town's most famous citizen. At 1:30 A.M., when news came that the train with the Roosevelts aboard was actually approaching, a huge bonfire was lit. Cheers went up as the familiar face appeared in a doorway. "I'm certainly glad to be here. By George, it's good to be back here," Roosevelt called. Then he put aside the drooping bouquet of roses he had carried all the way from Washington to shake every hand in sight.

At last the Roosevelts were able to get in a carriage for the short drive to Sagamore Hill. As they pulled away in the darkness, a reporter called out with a question about Roosevelt's future plans. "Not a word, boys," came the distinctive voice of the ex-President.

Colonel Roosevelt

ᴇᴄ§ Chapter 7 ᵇᴇᵛ

Through Darkest Africa

"When I stop being President I will stop completely," Roosevelt wrote to Henry Cabot Lodge in July, 1908, a month after he had seen Taft nominated by the G.O.P. to be his successor. There had been moments of doubt about his decision not to seek a third term, he confessed, moments in which he wondered if he "deserved a place beside your Dante's Pope, who was guilty of the great renunciation. . . ." But all those doubts proved "evanescent." T.R. was sure he had been right. He had a definite philosophy about the Presidency: "I think it should be a very powerful office, and I think the President should be a very strong man who uses without hesitation every power that the position yields; but because of this fact I believe that he should be sharply watched by the people, held to a strict accountability by them, and that he should not keep the office too long." Moreover, he declared to his old friend, when he was through with something, he was through with it; he was "under no temptation to snatch at the fringes of departing glory."

The following October 27, only a week before the election, and with only four months remaining of his second term, Roosevelt celebrated his fiftieth birthday. To the artist Frederic Remington he wrote the next day that he was still looking forward, not back. "I do not know any man who has had as happy a fifty years as I have had. I have had about as good a run for my money as any human being possibly could have; and whatever happens now I am ahead of the game."

Ever since the dramatic renunciation of November, 1904, there had been a lively interest, around the country as well as in Washington, in the post-presidential plans of Theodore Roosevelt. It was suggested that T.R. might succeed Charles W. Eliot as president of Harvard; by 1909,

Eliot would be seventy-five years old and, after forty years in the post, more than ripe for retirement. Nicholas Murray Butler thought that Roosevelt should succeed Thomas Collier Platt as United States Senator from New York; the declining Easy Boss's term would expire in 1909. In the summer of 1907 Roosevelt wrote to Taft that, should his plans for making the Secretary of War either President or Chief Justice fail, then Taft should become a senator from Ohio; perhaps after March, 1909, the two might meet as colleagues in the Senate chamber.

Henry Adams suggested that T.R. read the diaries of his grandfather, John Quincy Adams, who had started a second, and even more notable, career as a congressman after leaving the White House at the age of sixty-one. "Oh Lord!" T.R. replied, "I wish I did not sympathize with him . . . about being bored! The capacity to be bored whether treated as a sin or as a misfortune is an awful handicap." The question of what was to become of Roosevelt when his second term ended was easily answered, Philander C. Knox proclaimed at a Washington party: "He should be made a Bishop."

A more practical proposal came from Dr. Lyman Abbott, editor of *The Outlook,* a small but influential journal of opinion. Early in 1906 Abbott and his son Lawrence first suggested that T.R. join the magazine's staff as a contributing editor upon his retirement. It was too soon to make a decision, Roosevelt told the Abbotts, but they persisted and in the summer of 1908, after a conference at Sagamore Hill, the President agreed. In the first issue of the magazine following the election it was announced that Roosevelt, starting March 5, 1909, would be associated with *The Outlook*'s editorial staff as a special contributing editor. He would have an office in the magazine's New York headquarters, and all his contributions would be signed—to distinguish them from the weekly's regular editorial statements. *The Outlook* was to be "the exclusive channel for the expressions of [Roosevelt's] views on political, industrial, and social topics." He expected to write perhaps a dozen articles a year, from one to five thousand words in length each, for which he would be paid an annual salary of $12,000. The arrangement left him free to make public addresses on these topics, however, and to write for other publications on other subjects.

Among the other subjects T.R. no doubt contemplated writing about was the outdoor life and hunting—a passion since his ranching days in the Dakota Badlands three decades earlier. On a few occasions during his Presidency—down South and out West—he had been able to slip away from reporters and politicians to indulge his favorite pastime. Now, as he looked beyond his public career, Roosevelt began to plan for something much bigger and more ambitious, a hunting trip to Africa.

By March, 1908, as Roosevelt's plan for a safari through the Dark Continent took shape, he began soliciting advice from well-known big game hunters. "A year hence I shall leave the Presidency. . . ." he wrote one man. "I shall be fifty years old, and for ten years I have led a busy, sedentary life, and so it is unnecessary to say that I shall be in no trim for the hardest kind of explorers' work. But I am fairly healthy, and willing to work in order to get into a game country where I could do some shooting." He next asked about an itinerary, the expense, and the need for advance planning. He would like to be gone a year, "to see the great African fauna, and to kill one or two rhino or buffalo and some of the big antelopes, with the chance of a shot at a lion."

With expert advice from these hunters, the President confirmed plans for his trip and by June had worked out an itinerary. On or about April 1, 1909, he would sail from New York across the Atlantic and into the Mediterranean to Italy. There he would transfer to a vessel bound for East Africa via the Suez Canal. Landing at Mombasa about May 1, he would spend the next few months hunting in British and German East Africa, perhaps going as far as Uganda. About the first of the following year, 1910, he would strike the Nile and travel down it through the Sudan to Egypt, reaching civilization again about March 1.

Eighteen-year-old Kermit was asked if he would like to take a leave of absence from his freshman year at Harvard to accompany his father. His own holiday, the President explained, was coming at the age of fifty, after a busy life; if he went, Kermit had to understand that he was getting *his* holiday at the beginning of life and make up his mind to work doubly hard thereafter to justify having taken it. The question of whether he wanted to go was purely rhetorical, Kermit later wrote; whenever assigned to write a composition in school, he invariably described "some imaginary journey across the 'Dark Continent.' " Father and son had one serious discussion and the matter was settled. Kermit went; turned twenty on the trip; and when he returned, finished the four-year course at Harvard in two and a half years.

Roosevelt was anxious that this not be "a game-butchering trip" but rather a scientific expedition. Accepting his offer of wildlife specimens, the Smithsonian Institution agreed to send along three field naturalists and taxidermists. No government money need be spent, however, as the funds for the Smithsonian contingent would come from a private donation. The arrangement with the national museum was a great relief to Edith Roosevelt, T.R. noted; his wife had begun to fear she might be forced out of Sagamore Hill if he insisted on filling it with "queer antelopes, stuffed elephants, and the like."

As for Roosevelt's own expenses, those would be paid for by his earnings from writing about the journey. *Scribner's* magazine had originally offered Roosevelt $25,000 for a series of articles, later to be published as a book, on the safari. The President was about to accept when he received bids from *Collier's* and *McClure's* of $50,000 and $60,000 respectively. But Roosevelt preferred to write for *Scribner's,* publisher of several of his earlier works, and he asked the firm to meet *Collier's* offer of $50,000 for all serial rights and a 20 per cent royalty on book sales. He did not want to write for *McClure's,* he explained, and would overlook the difference between $50,000 and $60,000, though he could not ignore that between $25,000 and $50,000. *Scribner's* agreed to Roosevelt's demands, and the contract was signed—though *Collier's* upped its offer to $100,000 at the last minute. To his editor at *Scribner's,* Roosevelt wrote in appreciation that he knew the man to have the same standards of propriety as he did and would not advertise the articles or book until he left the Presidency, or at least until within two or three weeks of his leaving. To the disappointed chief of *Collier's* he wrote that he would have felt "thoroly uncomfortable as to my capacity for giving you the money's worth."

The safari, the President said to Archie Butt in June, 1908, "will let me down to private life without that dull thud of which we hear so much." By the time he returned from Africa, T.R. continued in a vein revealing either undue modesty or a complete lack of prescience, "it may be that I will have been sufficiently forgotten to be able to travel without being photographed." His chief, Captain Butt thought, was going to Africa as much for Taft as for himself. "If he were anywhere near telegraph lines it would be hard for the public not to suspect that Taft was being managed by him, and I think he wants to leave his secretary absolutely free with his own fate."

As with everything Roosevelt did, the country was soon taking an avid interest in the forthcoming big-game hunt. The Philadelphia *Ledger* made the astonishingly tasteless statement that, since T.R. had already enjoyed such a picturesque career, it would be fitting for him to meet death in some striking manner in Africa. The President was "immensely amused" by the article, but Edith Roosevelt did not find it quite as humorous. The British diplomat Cecil Spring Rice, an old friend, thoughtfully sent the President a pamphlet on sleeping sickness but predicted that the traveler would no doubt escape that dread disease by previously having been eaten by a lion or crocodile or killed by an enraged elephant or buffalo. Then too, Spring Rice pointed out cheerfully, malaria or a tribe of bellicose natives might do the job. The letter, T.R. reported, gave Edith a "keen tho melancholy enjoyment. . . ." She now felt entirely justified in adopting "a Roman-matron-like attitude of heroically bidding me to my death when I sail. . . ." Actually, friends claimed, Edith Roosevelt was nearly heartbroken at her husband's decision to go off on such a long and potentially dangerous journey; her only consolation, she confided to Archie Butt, was that worrying about the dangers of Africa would be no worse than "her anxiety when he is appearing in public, a target for every crank who comes to these shores." T.R. himself confessed that he would be homesick during such a long absence from Edith and the children. But he would not change his mind. The trip to Africa, he wrote an English friend, was his "last chance for something in the nature of a 'great adventure.' "

In December, 1908, the President learned to his intense annoyance that certain reporters were booking passage on his ship so as to accompany him to Africa and send back dispatches on the safari. He wrote immediately to the head of the Associated Press. An ex-President, he explained, is like any other citizen; he is entitled to no extra privileges. But, on the other hand, he should be treated no worse than anyone else. It would be "an indefensible wrong, a gross impropriety" to interfere with his privacy, "a wanton outrage" for a newspaper to try sending a reporter along. Any such attempt to cover his wanderings in the press would interfere with his "individual pleasure and profit" in the trip. Roosevelt would not speak to any newspaperman on the trip and would give out in advance that any statements attributed to him in the press during his absence were to be treated as false. He refused to relax this stringent regulation even for his friends the Abbotts of *The Outlook*—thus hoping to ensure that the only accounts of the safari would be his own in *Scribner's*.

The steamer for Italy on which Roosevelt and his son Kermit booked passage was the *Hamburg* of the Hamburg-American Line, scheduled to leave from Hoboken, New Jersey, on March 23, three weeks after the inauguration of Taft. On the previous day, T.R. spent seven hours in New York and Hoboken, saying good-bye to old friends and supervising the delivery and loading of his baggage at the pier. Father and son were to occupy four rooms on the starboard side of the promenade deck—previously the "Emperor William Suite." To accommodate its famous passenger, the German steamship line had redecorated the rooms, painting the walls predominantly red but livening them with pieces of armor and jute tapestry in blue and green.

After inspecting the rooms, T.R. went to the ship's gymnasium and tested the bars and other athletic apparatus. Finally he watched the loading of some two hundred cases, each approximately six feet by four feet, and all prominently stamped, "Theodore Roosevelt—Mombasa British East Africa."

Among the more interesting items of equipage Roosevelt would have on the safari was a light aluminum and oilcloth case, weighing a little less than sixty pounds, a load for one porter. The case contained T.R.'s Pigskin Library, the gift of his sister Corinne. Roosevelt had told his sister that he could not go anywhere, "not even into the jungles of Africa," without books to read. He had drawn up a list of some sixty volumes he wished to take, and Mrs. Robinson had had the books, trimmed to pocket size, specially bound in pigskin to withstand the rigors of the safari and the vagaries of the African climate.

Roosevelt's list ranged from the Bible and Shakespeare, Homer in Greek and Dante in Italian to the novels of Cooper, Scott, Dickens, Thackeray, and Mark Twain. The poems of Keats, Shelley, Browning, and Longfellow were included, as were the essays of Bacon, Lowell, and Holmes. *The Federalist* was tucked in alongside Gregorovius's history of Rome. And T.R. would be able to turn from the plays of Euripides to Bunyan's *Pilgrim's Progress* or Milton's *Paradise Lost.* En route he kept thinking of additions to be made to the Pigskin Library and later asked that *Alice in Wonderland,* Goethe's *Faust, Don Quixote,* and works of Montaigne, Molière, Pascal, and Voltaire, all in French, be sent out to Africa.

Wherever he went on the safari, Roosevelt was to carry a volume or two, tucked in a saddle bag or pocket, so that no opportunity for reading might be missed. "In consequence," he later wrote, "the books were stained with blood, sweat, gun-oil, dust, and ashes. . . ." Ordinary binding, he noted would have "vanished or become loathsome," whereas the pigskin "merely grew to look as a well-used saddle looks." To most of these books, T.R. was returning as an old friend; but he made one notable discovery about his literary tastes during the trip: "You will both be amused to hear," he wrote the Lodges from East Africa, "that at last, when fifty years old, I have come into my inheritance in Shakespeare. I never before really cared for more than one or two of his plays; but for some inexplicable reason the sealed book was suddenly opened to me on this trip."

The ex-President was already seen to be reading during idle moments of his final day in New York; the book was Charles Darwin's *Voyage of H.M.S. Beagle.* Monday evening Roosevelt returned to Oyster Bay for a quiet evening with the family—and for his private farewell to Edith. Neither the former First Lady nor any of the younger children would come to the pier for the sailing the following day; they would wave their good-byes from the piazza of Sagamore Hill. And for most of that day, Edith Roosevelt later told Archie Butt, she and the children wandered in the woods and tried to imagine what Theodore and Kermit were doing in New York. "But it was a dreadful day," she told the captain; the only one worse for her had been when her son Archie had lingered at death's door with diphtheria two years previously.

At 8:30 A.M. on sailing day, Roosevelt—accompanied only by Kermit—arrived back in New York. He was wearing an olive drab military uniform with the insignia of a colonel's rank on the collar and sleeves, a military overcoat, and the famous black slouch hat. "Mr. President" had become "Colonel Roosevelt"—the title he would prefer over all others for the rest of his life. The pair took an automobile to the Hudson tubes and then a train to Hoboken—after which T.R. stopped to thank the engineer for a safe ride under the river. In anticipation of a crush at the pier, most passengers had boarded the *Hamburg* the night before, and as the Colonel and his son appeared, a cheer went up from those lining the decks.

In Washington the new President had agonized over a gift for his departing predecessor. The ever-resourceful Archie Butt came up with the suggestion of a small gold ruler that concealed a pencil in one end —handsome enough to serve as a presidential gift and small enough to carry easily, Butt explained to his new chief. The aide even suggested an inscription: "Theodore Roosevelt from William Howard Taft, Goodbye—Good Luck." Taft approved, adding only the words, "and a Safe Return." The President dispatched Captain Butt, with a personal note, to deliver the gift in New York to Roosevelt.

Archie Butt found New York, on Tuesday, March 23, as excited over the sailing as if it had been another inauguration. People seemed "frenzied in their anxiety to get a glimpse" of T.R., Butt wrote his sister-in-law; they fought their way to the steamer's side even when there was no chance to see the ex-President. It took Butt himself some time to get near enough Roosevelt to be recognized, but when the Colonel saw his former aide, he reached out to grasp his hand and pull him over. "By George, it's good to see you again, Archie," he boomed. Roosevelt took the gift and letter, which he promised to read once the bedlam was over, and inquired about members of the White House staff. Someone called out in the crowd, and T.R.'s attention was directed to other well-wishers. "Let all Rough Riders hold up their hands so I can find them," the captain heard T.R. call, and the last he saw was the ex-President pushing his way through the crowd to his former comrades-in-arms.

An Italian-American band paraded up to the pier and serenaded Roosevelt—in thanks for the recent help given earthquake victims in their native land by the Great White Fleet. T.R. called reporters into his suite to say that he had received five to six thousand letters since leaving the White House. Because he had not been able to answer or even open four-fifths of them, he asked the newspapermen to publish his appreciation. "Someone told me, Colonel, that you are going to be our next President," one newspaperman broke in. T.R. raised both hands to cut off further questions and closed the news conference with a terse, "Goodbye, gentlemen."

The frenzied farewells continued for a good two hours until a fifth and final "All ashore" was sounded at 10:50 A.M. At that moment an Army cutter pulled up and out jumped Leonard Wood. The general, T.R.'s commander at San Juan Hill, bounded up the gangplank to find Roosevelt and give him a hasty greeting. He was the last visitor.

As the *Hamburg* pulled away from the Hoboken pier, a band struck up "The Star-Spangled Banner," and there was a deafening shriek of whistles and horns from the small flotilla of gaily decorated vessels that accompanied the big ship across New York harbor. The Douglas Robinsons rode in a tug alongside, where they could continue to wave at Theodore and Kermit—permitted, against all regulations, to stand on the bridge. High up on the port side shelter of the bridge the Colonel stood smiling and saluting with his soft black felt hat. Office windows in Lower Manhattan skyscrapers were lined with faces and from atop the

Singer Building—then the world's tallest—fluttered three signal flags spelling out the word "Farewell."

In the privacy of his cabin, Roosevelt later opened the letter from President Taft. It began with the warm, simple salutation, "My dear Theodore." If he had followed his impulse, Taft confessed, he would say "My dear Mr. President." The new Chief Executive could not overcome the habit of thinking of T.R. as President. "When I am addressed as 'Mr. President,' I turn to see whether you are not at my elbow. When I read in the newspaper of a conference between the speaker and the President, or between Senator Aldrich and the President, I wonder what the subject of the conference was, and can hardly identify the report with the fact that I had a talk with the two gentlemen."

After urging him to "undertake no foolhardy enterprise" and "observe those ordinary precautions" on his trip, the President turned frankly political in his letter. There had been a number of questions, arising since the inaguration, that he would like to have discussed with his predecessor. Some of the former President's friends in the West were probably already alienated from the new administration—or would be by the time of Roosevelt's return from Africa. Uncle Joe Cannon, the Speaker of the House, and Aldrich, still leader of the Senate, had promised to stand by the party platform and follow his lead, Taft claimed. But it was going to be difficult to push his program through: "I have not the prestige which you had or the popular support. . . ." Finally, the President pledged, he would do nothing in the White House without considering what T.R. would do under the same circumstances and without "having in a sense a mental talk with you over the pros and cons of the situation."

The Colonel called in a steward and dashed off a message, to be taken ashore by the pilot and telegraphed to Washington: "Am deeply touched by your gift and even more by your letter," Roosevelt wrote to Taft. "Greatly appreciate it. Everything will turn out all right, old man. Give my love to Mrs. Taft." The President apparently never received this wire, nor a subsequent greeting dispatched a half hour later—or chose to regard the messages as inadequate. The two men exchanged no letters for the next fifteen months and, Captain Butt later discovered, the President harbored a deep resentment that his gift had gone unacknowledged.

Passing through the Narrows, the *Hamburg* received a twenty-one-gun salute from Fort Hamilton. Another tug, carrying a party of sixty, followed the vessel all the way to Sandy Hook and, as the big ship pulled out into the open sea, a final signal was broken out: "Good Game." A remark widely attributed to J. P. Morgan reflected Wall Street's relief at Roosevelt's departure from the Presidency and its heartfelt wish that the last had been seen of the trustbuster. "America hopes," Morgan is supposed to have said, "that every lion will do its duty."

2

"An ocean voyage is to me always irksome," the restless T.R. wrote his elder sister, Bamie, after having crossed the Atlantic. The only thing to do, he said with resignation, was to enjoy it as much as possible. And this he found easy to do aboard the *Hamburg;* the Colonel was easily the most popular man on the ship. To Corinne Robinson he wrote that there were plenty of people aboard with whom he found it pleasant to talk "in English or in those variants of volapuk which with me pass for French or German."

On March 30 the *Hamburg* called at the Azores and three days later at Gibraltar, where Roosevelt was entertained by the British governor, a man "who looked as if he had walked out of Kipling. . . ." On April 5 T.R. left the *Hamburg* at Naples, where he was met by Edith's maiden sister, Emily Carow, and by the wife of his cousin James West Roosevelt and the American ambassador to Italy.

Failing to get a newsworthy quotation from the former President during his brief stopover in Naples, one enterprising if unscrupulous American reporter made up a story. In the alleged interview, T.R. was supposed to have declared that he had had Taft elected to carry out his policies—and if the new President did not do so, he would return from Africa and thrust aside his successor. The story was widely reprinted in the American press, and Archie Butt felt called upon to defend his former chief in front of the Tafts, telling them that the "interview" must be a fake. "Oh, I don't know," replied the skeptical and suspicious Nellie Taft. "It sounded just like him." When reports of the sensational story got back to the Colonel, he put out an immediate denial: "The interview is not a distortion; it is a deliberate, wilful invention without the slightest foundation." Once more, he reiterated his pledge not to give out any interviews for the next year. Responsible editors were immediately to dismiss any subsequent reports of conversations with him as pure fabrications.

Whatever his wishes, Roosevelt was not going to be successful in keeping away reporters. "The newspapers have been filled daily with minute accounts of your progress. . . ." Lodge wrote him. "The American people . . . follow it all with the absorbed interest of a boy who reads 'Robinson Crusoe' for the first time." Moreover, the Associated Press had decided to ignore his ban on newsmen; T.R. was always news and in Africa there was ever the chance of an accident, "the result of which might have been fatal to the hunter instead of the hunted." The wire service employed a certain Captain W. Robert Foran of British East Africa and saw that he was on the *Hamburg* when it left New York. The United Press was not to be outdone. Francis Warrington Dawson, Paris manager for the rival service and author of two novels Roosevelt had admired, arranged to be in Naples when the *Hamburg* docked. He, Foran, and a number of other correspondents who suddenly discovered the need for a long sea voyage to East Africa that month were aboard the *Admiral,* another German ship to which the Colonel and his son transferred at Naples.

In his new stateroom Roosevelt found flowers from the Kaiser and a telegram with the greeting *"Weidmannsheil!"*—the traditional German expression of good luck for a departing hunter. The following day, April 6, the ship put in at Messina, where T.R. could inspect the recent earthquake damage and where he met Victor Emmanuel III, "a nice, rather self-conscious little King." From Italy the *Admiral* steamed across the Mediterranean to Port Said, then through the Suez Canal and down the Red Sea to Aden. Turning south into the Indian Ocean, the vessel followed the coast of Africa to Mombasa, four degrees south of the equator. On April 21 the boat docked in a tropical downpour that reminded the ex-President of Panama. Captain Foran recorded the moment for posterity. "By gosh!" the Colonel is supposed to have said upon this occasion of his first close-up look at the tropical regions of the Dark Continent, "that's a wonderful sight." "Roosevelt's eyes were shining with intense excitement," Foran wrote; "his hands gripped the rail until the knuckles were bloodless, and his entire sturdy body seemed to be poised, expectant, like a well-trained pointer at work in the field."

The Colonel was welcomed at Mombasa by the Lieutenant-Governor of British East Africa. England had declared a protectorate over that vast land—the present independent republic of Kenya—only fourteen years earlier, in 1895. A railroad from Mombasa to the capital of Nairobi, 250 miles northwest, and on to the huge inland sea, Lake Victoria, had been built in 1903. But the country was still a frontier, one that delighted Roosevelt and reminded him of the western plains of America he knew so well from his ranching and hunting days.

T.R. did not linger on the coast. The day following his arrival at Mombasa, he left for the interior on the railroad whose route provided what he was later to call a journey "through the Pleistocene." The British had made a game reserve stretching one mile north of the track and several miles south, and the right-of-way teemed with African fauna who seemed to sense that the only danger was from the click of a camera shutter. So fascinated was the Colonel with the wildlife that he spent all the daylight hours, with the exception of meal times, perched on a special seat built across the cowcatcher of the locomotive. Birds hovered so near that he could almost catch them with his hands. At dusk the engine very nearly ran over a hyena; a lion and a rhino had been bagged by a previous train, T.R. was told; and giraffes had been known to cut telegraph lines with their necks as they loped across the tracks.

At the station of Kapiti Plains the Roosevelts first met their complete safari, one of the largest ever outfitted in East Africa. To the Colonel the array of natives and tents at the station looked as if "some small military expedition was about to start." In the front line, with an American flag proudly waving over it, was the ex-President's tent, flanked by the tents of other white members of the party, a dining tent, and a skinning tent. The natives were drawn up in ranks—first, the fifteen *askaris,* or rifle-bearers, smartly uniformed in white knickerbockers, blue blouses, and red fezzes. Behind them were the porters, recruited from several tribes to "minimize the danger of combination in the event of mutiny."

Since the aim of the expedition was to send back to the United States a large representation of African fauna, it was necessary to carry equipment that amounted to a traveling naturalist's laboratory and taxidermy shop combined, including four tons of salt to cure skins. Indeed, 200 of the 260 porters were needed to carry this scientific equipment. Immediately following a kill, the men would skin the animal—a job requiring brawn as well as skill when it came to such prey as elephants and rhinoceroses. Next, bones would be removed, cleaned, and packed for later reassembly, and the meat would be taken to feed the party or left as an unexpected feast for lurking predators.

In addition to normal provender for a safari, T.R. had specified that a few cans of Boston baked beans, California peaches, and tomatoes be put in each food box. Warm bedding was required because, even under the equator, nights would be cold at the higher elevations. And regardless of the climate, cleanliness would be observed. The Colonel's tent, in addition to a front flap to protect the entrance from the great heat, had a rear extension for a bath—always a hot bath, never a cold one in the tropics.

When hunting, Roosevelt would wear heavy shoes, with hobnails or rubber soles; a khaki-colored army shirt, and khaki trousers, the knees faced with leather and, to avoid extra wrap-around leggings, tight buttoning down to the ankles. As a concession to local custom, T.R. put aside his beloved black slouch hat and donned the traditional white sun helmet. Although he declined absolutely any publicity or pity about it, and refused to acknowledge even to himself that it was a severe handicap, Roosevelt's eyesight by this time was extremely poor. As a result of a sparring bout, his left eye was now virtually sightless; the astigmatism he had from birth made him helpless without the trademark pince-nez glasses. He never embarked on excursions such as the Cuban campaign in the Spanish-American War or the African safari, Kermit revealed, "without eight or ten pairs so distributed throughout his kit as to minimize the possibility of being crippled through any ordinary accident." In the tropics, of course, he would be subjected to the additional hazard of fogged over and wet lenses in the steamy heat and frequent rains. "It was a continual source of amazement" his son noted with pride, "to see how skilfully father had discounted this handicap in advance and appeared to be unhampered by it."

The Colonel would have three rifles: an Army Springfield, 30-caliber, stocked and sighted to his own deficient vision; a Winchester 405; and—the gift of a number of admirers, chiefly British—a double-barrelled 500-450 Holland and Holland elephant gun. "It is a perfect beauty and it shoots very accurately," T.R. wrote Kermit after he had practice fired the elephant gun, "but of course the recoil is tremendous." In time, Kermit had a chance to use the big gun, too, and later recalled that it was a standing joke with the party whether he feared the recoil more than a charging elephant. Less lethal equipment was the 4 x 5

Graphlex camera Kermit took along. Before leaving he had studied picture taking so that he could be the expedition's official photographer. To his father's additional delight, Kermit proved as good a photographer as he was a hunter and many of his pictures would later illustrate Roosevelt's book about the safari.

For personal attendants on the hunt the Colonel would have two gun-bearers, two *saises,* or horse-boys, and two tent-boys—one of whom made it his personal duty to see that Edith Roosevelt's framed photograph was always so arranged that the ex-President could see it the first thing upon entering his tent. One of his two horses was a sorrel he named Tranquility; the other, a brown he called Zebra-shape. To the natives the Colonel became known as Bwana Makuba, Great Master; to T.R.'s utter delight, Kermit was christened Bwana Merodadi, Dandy Master. A more candid native name for the ex-President was "the man with the big paunch"—tactfully translated for Roosevelt as "the man with unerring aim."

The Colonel took a sympathetic interest in the natives, but at least one effort of his to improve their lot went unappreciated. Hearing that the porters slept six to a tent, he ordered more tents from the coast so that they could sleep more comfortably only two to a tent. The natives protested this largesse. Six men to a tent insured warmth; with only two, they would be cold. The order for new tents was rescinded.

In addition to T.R. and Kermit, there would be the three naturalists representing the Smithsonian and two white guides. And for part of the trip at least there were to be representatives of the press after all.

It had been impossible for T.R. to avoid the reporters aboard the *Admiral,* en route from Italy to Mombasa, though he still refused to say anything for publication. Dawson of the United Press, however, had quickly won the Colonel's confidence by helping him put out his denial of the Naples "interview," and soon both he and Foran of the Associated Press were being treated as friends by the ever genial Roosevelt. Originally the Colonel had decreed that all reporters aboard must turn back at Mombasa, but at the port he relented further and told "the boys" that they could accompany him as far as Nairobi.

When Roosevelt reached the inland capital, he realized that the ban on reporters was actually working to his disadvantage. It did not stop the requests for interviews, nor did it halt the flow of false and often sensational reports back to Europe and America. In desperation he allowed the two wire service reporters to follow along in his wake, though he did not permit them to become permanent members of his expedition. During the first part of the hunt Nairobi was the base to which the safari kept looping back, and from the capital Dawson and Foran could easily keep in touch with the ex-President's party. But when the Colonel left East Africa for the interior and the long trip down the Nile to Khartoum, Dawson returned to America whereas Foran equipped his own safari and preceded the Colonel all the way to Egypt.

While he was still in Africa, Dawson became a particularly trusted helper of Roosevelt's—as a part-time secretary, to help with the undiminished flood of mail; as an editor of his articles for *Scribner's;* and finally, with Foran, as a press spokesman, who was allowed to release official bulletins of the safari's progress. The Colonel stipulated that he did not want to receive mail or send out any bulletins more often than every ten days or two weeks. To Dawson in Nairobi he would dispatch a native runner bearing a scrawled message reporting the kill and such sidelights as news of a dawn-to-dusk march or the fact that they had made a waterless camp because an oasis had dried up. Dawson would rewrite these reports and release them to an anxious world—via his own United Press and the rival Associated Press. With these releases stamped as official bulletins of the safari, the other reporters had nothing to send home and soon departed from East Africa.

3

The safari finally got underway at the Kapiti Plains station on April 24. Leaving the tracks, the expedition moved eastward, visiting various farms or ranches whose owners could direct them to the best game fields. The colonial government had offered to open the game preserves to the famous hunter from America, but Roosevelt refused this concession. He found in abundance zebra, wildebeest, hartbeest, gazelles of several kind, impala, mountain reedbuck, duiker, steinbuck, and the dikdik, an antelope the size of a hare. As Roosevelt's party traveled and hunted, it was seldom out of sight of game, and T.R. got a chance to shoot most of the plains animals. But at the outset the Colonel established the rule that they would shoot only what was needed for museum specimens or food.

Roosevelt readily confessed that it usually took him a number of bullets to kill his prey, but seldom, he claimed, did he only wound an animal and let it get away. As a naturalist, he dispassionately observed how each animal died and was careful to record, when the animal was being dissected, just what its stomach contained as a way of establishing the dietary habits of various species. He seemed particularly impressed with a crocodile later shot by Kermit along a river in the equatorial desert; the inventory of its stomach listed "sticks, stones, the claws of a cheetah, the hoofs of an impala, and the big bones of an eland, together with the shell plates of one of the large river-turtles. . . ." "I constantly felt while with him," one of the Smithsonian scientists later wrote, "that I was in the presence of the foremost field naturalist of our time, as indeed I was. . . ."

The Colonel was determined not to leave Africa without bagging the five most dangerous game: elephant, rhinoceros, buffalo, leopard, and lion. "If only I can get *my* lion," he told Dawson on the ship, "I shall be happy—even if he is small—but I hope he will have a mane!" Before the end of April he had shot the first four of the nine lions he would ultimately claim on the safari. It was late afternoon, and a ride since early morning had failed to raise any of the beasts they sought. En route back to the ranch where they were currently staying, however, the hunters took a detour into a shallow watercourse. First the spoor of two lions was detected, then shouts and rocks tossed into the underbrush brought loud grunts and great rustlings. The men dismounted, Roosevelt vowing that he would trust his aim rather than his ability to get away from a charging lion—"an elderly man with a varied past which included rheumatism does not vault lightly into the saddle," he wrote.

Suddenly, not thirty yards away from the Colonel, the first lion appeared. Roosevelt's initial bullet "ploughed forward through his flank," making the lion swerve so that the second bullet missed completely. A third bullet went through the spine and forward into the lion's chest. "Down he came," wrote T.R., "sixty yards off, his hind quarters dragging, his head up, his ears back, his jaws open and lips drawn up in a prodigious snarl, as he endeavored to turn to face us." The hunters could not be sure he was mortally wounded; if only grazed, he might have recovered, "and then, even though dying, his charge might have done mischief." T.R., Kermit, and their host for the day all fired and the beast fell dead. A short time later, Roosevelt caught up with the second lion and—resting his elbow on his gun-bearer's shoulder—took aim and killed the beast with two bullets. Both of the victims, alas, were maneless, but T.R. was nonetheless pleased with his accomplishment. Three days after this first successful outing, the Colonel shot two more lions —and watched with inexpressible pride that night as the natives brought in the huge victims on poles, deposited them before him as he stood in the moonlight near the campfire, and celebrated his triumph with a short, vigorous dance and wild, unintelligible chanting.

Nearly each day, even after the most strenuous outing, the Colonel forced himself to sit at his portable writing table to record incidents in his pocket diary—while they were still fresh in his mind—for the *Scribner's* articles. The other members of the party would long remember him laboring so, his absorbed face illuminated by a flickering light on the table, as they relaxed around the campfires. Most of the articles were later written out in longhand—though back in Nairobi he dictated some to Dawson, who banged them out on his typewriter, said to be the only machine in British East Africa and a very noisy one, prone to jamming. The reporter recalled a writing session from 9 A.M. one morning until 2:20 A.M. the following day. Transcribed in triplicate, the articles were sent to New York in batches as they were finished—sometimes two copies being sent out by separate runners as a precaution.

The arrival of the battered and stained blue canvas envelopes invariably caused excited pleasure at the *Scribner's* offices in New York. Because the articles were so spontaneous and perhaps because there was little or no time for polishing and revising, Roosevelt's writings about Africa—later published in book form as *African Game Trails*— have an immediacy, even a poetry that is found only in his writings three decades earlier about his ranching and hunting days out West.

By May 23 Roosevelt had finished the first two articles for *Scribner's,* and by June 1 four more: an incredible output of some 45,000 words in six weeks. In addition to accounts of his railway journey through the Pleistocene and his first lion hunt, he described plains hunting on East African ranches, and various encounters with rhinoceroses, giraffes, hippopotamuses, leopards, and buffalo. The eventual fourteen articles, varying in length from 5,000 to 15,000 words, were published in monthly installments in *Scribner's* between October, 1909, and September, 1910.

Edith Roosevelt, reading the pieces at home, could not have been relieved of her nervousness over her husband's absence by T.R.'s lengthy reports of East African table-talk—which seemed principally to center on "can-you-top-this" tales of lion-maulings. Henry Cabot Lodge, in high humor, wrote of his inexhaustible pleasure in reading that Kermit had shot "a noteworthy sow." And when a spirited account of the ex-President's lion hunting was published in America, Elihu Root commented, "Of course, Theodore shot three lions with one bullet and Kermit shot one lion with three bullets." Lodge reported the remark to T.R., who replied that if his former Cabinet officer persisted in such "hardened skepticism," he would return and personally "head an insurrection to put Tom Platt back in Root's [Senate] seat. . . ."

At the beginning of June, the Roosevelt safari marched into Nairobi, the protectorate's capital, then an attractive town with a native quarter, shops and bazaars mainly operated by Indians, and the comfortable homes of the European populace. The first specimens were dispatched to the United States, and the Roosevelts—father and son— were entertained at a number of dinner parties. There was more than a little bit of England in Nairobi. People dressed for dinner, and the menus were decidedly English and Continental—though departing guests were warned not to wander about in the night; there was always the possibility of a leopard lurking in the rose garden. From June through November the Roosevelt safari more or less made its headquarters at Nairobi, but with weeks-long treks in all four directions in search of various game.

Before the safari was six weeks old, the Colonel started worrying about money and sent a plea to Andrew Carnegie. The industrialist-turned-philanthropist was one of some thirty men who had contributed the funds needed to finance the Smithsonian's share of the safari; at that time Roosevelt knew the name of only three. For himself and Kermit, T.R. was paying about $20,000. But expenses had been much higher than anticipated, Roosevelt now wrote Carnegie; unless additional donations were forthcoming, the naturalists would have to return about August 1. Another $30,000 would be needed to finance the scientific expedition out of East Africa to the Congo and down the White Nile to the Sudan. At the end of July the Colonel learned that the Smithsonian, again through anonymous donors, had deposited another $10,000 on which the safari could draw—and this would somehow carry the party through to October. In that month Carnegie came up with the additional $20,000; but Roosevelt was forced to ask him for $7,000 more in December.

4

In Nairobi, Roosevelt was only a day away from the coast and from the ocean steamers that brought mail from Europe and America. In addition to Edith Roosevelt and his two sisters, Roosevelt found time to correspond, however irregularly, with Elihu Root and Henry Cabot Lodge; indeed, the Massachusetts senator reminded him that it was the first time in a quarter century that the two had not seen or written to one another every few days. "I am not sure when you will get this;" T.R. concluded one letter to Lodge, "the postman is a wild savage, who runs stark naked with the mail."

To Cecil Spring Rice the Colonel wrote that he was "dreadfully homesick" for his wife. "Catch me ever leaving her for a year again, if I can help it!" His consolation for being away from home was having his second son with him. To Theodore, Jr., he wrote in high praise of Kermit; it was hard for a father to realize that "the rather timid boy of four years ago has turned out a perfectly cool and daring fellow." Kermit, in fact, was proving a little too reckless, T.R. complained, "and keeps my heart in my throat, for I worry about him all the time. . . ." His son was not a good shot at the outset of the safari, "not even as good as I am, and Heaven knows I am poor enough; but he is a bold rider, always cool and fearless, and eager to work all day along." Kermit had just stopped a charging leopard at six yards after it had mauled a porter, he reported with pride.

Newspapers from the United States were available in Nairobi only one month after date of publication, but the ex-President claimed not to have read a paper since leaving home and consequently knew nothing of domestic politics or world events. His isolation was not to last. "I am horribly puzzled by the letters I am now receiving from home about political affairs," he wrote Ethel later in the year, "and the scrape I shall be in as soon as I land in connection with the congressional elections; but this I shant worry you about, for I do'n't see that any one can help me in the matter." The most important current political issue was the tariff, and during the summer of 1909 Lodge kept the Colonel posted on the fight in Congress for tariff revision.

The 1908 Republican campaign platform had called for a revision of the protective tariff, to be enacted by a special session of Congress immediately following the inauguration of the next President. It was not specifically stated in the tariff plank that the revision was to be downward, but it was generally assumed that a reduction of the high duties on imports would be sought—and Taft made it clear in his acceptance speech and in other campaign utterances that he expected lower duties to be established. The Dingley tariff of 1897, still in force, had raised duties to an all-time high. "No matter how great an improvement the new tariff may be," Uncle Joe Cannon had once said, "it almost always results in the party in power losing the election." T.R. had wisely sidestepped the issue during his seven and a half years in office, but Taft made tariff revision the first goal of his new administration.

Although he possessed a keen judicial mind, William Howard Taft was essentially a lazy man—a failing that can perhaps be attributed to the lethargy brought on by his tremendous girth. And as President, he developed a disarming if thoroughly annoying way of dozing off even during an important conversation—perhaps a manifestation of the classic form of escapism. His predilection for impromptu naps was the despair of his military aide, Archie Butt. The new President, apparently, could drift off to sleep anytime, anywhere. If it was after dinner, his guests would merely have to wait until the big man's own snores awakened him or until Butt loudly and purposefully slammed shut or dropped a book—it was not possible to leave the presidential presence, however somnolent, without permission. Following an intimate White House dinner for Cabinet members once, the President called for some music to be played on the Victrola but fell asleep during the first selection. He then awoke only to request the Prize Song from "Die Meistersinger" but drifted off again before the record could be put on. Attorney General George W. Wickersham then wickedly suggested the sextette from "Lucia de Lamermoor," since "it would wake anyone but a dead man." The party waited patiently through the selection but it failed to rouse their slumbering host. "He must be dead," the Attorney General remarked with awe. At the opera one evening, Butt agonized through an entire act, hoping that the President would awake when the lights came on at intermission, before the audience was treated to the spectacle of the placid Chief Executive happily dozing through a command performance. And again, to Captain Butt's utter horror, Taft fell asleep during a funeral at which he was a front-row mourner, while on still another occasion he was the embarrassed companion of a fast-asleep President making a campaign tour of New York City in an open car.

"Archie," Taft confided to his aide soon after the inaugural, "it seems to me I will never catch up with my work. . . . there is so much to be done and so little time to do it in that I feel discouraged." Butt secretly agreed, estimating that the new President would "be about three years behind when the fourth of March, 1913, rolls around."

No doubt Taft intended to call the special session of Congress in March, 1909, with a strong demand for downward revision. But he somehow never got around to writing a tariff message and merely stated, in a brief note to the two houses, that Congress was being convened to revise the tariff—in which direction, he did not reveal. The new Congress was, of course, controlled by the G.O.P., with Nelson Aldrich continuing as leader of the Senate and crude, crafty Uncle Joe Cannon still Speaker of the House of Representatives. But many of the Old Guard had retired, been defeated, or died. An incipient new wing of the party was coalescing around a small but distinguished coterie of progressive Midwestern senators: Robert M. La Follette of Wisconsin, Jonathan P. Dolliver and Albert B. Cummins of Iowa, Albert J. Beveridge of Indiana, Joseph L. Bristow of Kansas, Moses E. Clapp of Minnesota. In fact, Aldrich had few able supporters other than that aloof, inscrutable Brahmin Henry Cabot Lodge. In the House, the preceding December, thirty progressive Republican representatives had joined the Democratic minority in an attempt—only narrowly defeated—to oust Uncle Joe from the Speaker's chair. As one historian has noted, "a party within a party was being born. . . ."

Taft was later brilliantly characterized by Senator Dolliver as "a large amiable island surrounded entirely by persons who knew exactly what they wanted." That such was indeed the case was clearly demonstrated at the very outset of his administration. On March 9, a few days before the opening of the special session, Aldrich, Cannon, and Representative Sereno E. Payne of New York called at the White House to tell the President of the new alliance between the G.O.P. insurgents and the Democratic opposition—an alliance that again threatened to topple the Speaker. Unless Taft supported the Old Guard leaders, they could not promise success for tariff revision. Taken in by these practiced old-time politicians, or perhaps at last revealing his basically conservative leanings, Taft cast his lot—in the first month of his Presidency —with the men regarded by many as the most reactionary and outdated members of his party. Taft used his patronage lever to ensure that Cannon was retained as Speaker, but in the protracted and acrimonious tariff fight that followed, the Old Guard succeeded in defeating the heroic efforts of the insurgents to win a general and genuine downward revision of duties.

"I am dealing with very acute and expert politicians," Taft told his wife during the tariff debate, "and I am trusting a great many of them and I may be deceived." Taft foolishly agreed to stay out of the fight until bills had passed both houses and the differences were being resolved in a conference committee. While the measure was still being debated, he was told, it would be too early for presidential intervention. Later, in the conference committee, he was informed that it was too late to exert pressure for any other than minor changes. Progressive Republicans in both houses joined many Democrats in the negative vote, but the Payne-Aldrich tariff was nonetheless passed at the end of July and went to Taft for signature. Speaking for the Republican Old Guard, Lodge claimed that there were to be four hundred reductions in the schedule of tariffs, with only thirty increases. But it was the size of the reductions and the importance of the products on which duties were lowered—or raised—that really mattered. And thus, the act must be considered as a continuation of the protection extended to Eastern industry at the expense of Western and Southern producers of raw materials.

"I could make a lot of cheap publicity for the time being by vetoing the bill," the President wrote privately, "but it would leave the party in a bad shape. . . ." In defense of party loyalty then, and somehow convincing himself that the bill was not a betrayal of his campaign pledges, the President signed it into law on August 5, just as a terrifying thunderstorm—grim preview of the political storm to follow—broke outside the White House.

"Apparently you have come out as well as we could hope on the tariff question," Roosevelt wrote to Lodge from Mount Kenya early the next month. Having heard only Lodge's version of the tariff battle, the Colonel did not then perceive the potential for political division in the measure. The ex-President was certainly not yet aware of the swelling protest, especially in the West, against the Payne-Aldrich tariff and the growing resentment against the man who had signed it into law. "Shades of Theodore Roosevelt!" shrieked the Des Moines, Iowa, *News*. "May ghosts of animals he has killed in Africa ever haunt him for having foisted on the country this man Taft." Another Iowa newspaper was already predicting that only Roosevelt, upon his return, could give the country progressive leadership.

5

By mid-October the Colonel had finished four more articles for *Scribner's,* for a total of ten, and this took him through a series of adventures deep within the British protectorate. A sixty-mile trek across the desert south of Nairobi had brought the safari by the first week of June to the Sotik, a huge limestone plain on the border with German East Africa —and there for the next five weeks the party enjoyed the most successful and varied shooting of the entire safari. The bag included all the by-then familiar plains animals, plus lion, rhinoceros, hyena, and giraffe. The nights were cool and in the evenings, after dinner, members of the party gathered around a blazing fire and listened to Kermit strumming his mandolin.

When Warrington Dawson returned to the United States, he sought an interview with Corinne Robinson, to give T.R.'s younger sister a first-hand account of life in Africa. Mrs. Robinson seemed incredulous when told that the Colonel spent his evenings resting. "I have never known my brother Theodore to rest," she said, apparently concerned that such unaccustomed inactivity might mean ill health or declining powers. Dawson explained what he meant by resting. At night they would sit around the campfire and talk first about the day's hunting. Shortly the conversation would branch out to cover medieval history and literature, astronomy, perhaps the question of whether or not Louis XVII escaped from the Temple, then European politics and socialism. Mrs. Robinson, with relief, interrupted Dawson's recital. "If that's what you call resting," she said. "—Yes, I can accept, now, your original statement that my brother Theodore rested!"

From the Sotik the safari traveled north to Lake Naivasha, and there the prey was hippopotamus. As the party was skirting the shores of the lake in a steam launch one day—the Colonel in the bow with his Springfield, Kermit next with his camera, a guide steering—it met one of the "self-confident, truculent" beasts. The three men transferred to a smaller rowboat and drew near the animal. Roosevelt's first bullet only ticked the hippo, which spun around, plunged into the water, "and with his huge jaws open came straight for the boat, floundering and splashing through the thick-growing water-lilies." Its object, T.R. coolly noted, may only have been to escape into deep water, but the open jaws seemed to indicate that it might be "bent on mischief." Again and again, Roosevelt fired, once directly into the cavernous opening of the hugh jaws, which thereupon were closed "with the clash of a sprung bear trap." As the Colonel fired, his son clicked the camera; Kermit said that, until the hippo was dead, he saw it only through the "finder." For a half hour afterward, the accompanying natives chanted an improvised song praising Bwana Makuba and expressing the hope that he would award them the delicious hippo meat.

What made this latest feat remarkable, Roosevelt later revealed, was the fact that the instant he had spied the hippo along the shore T.R. felt the first wave of an attack of fever sweeping over him—not any African fever, he was convinced, but rather a recurrence of the fever he had picked up eleven years earlier during the Cuban campaign. He had to fire though shaking with the chill, and the moment the hippo was dead, he curled up in the boat and "had my chill in peace and comfort." It was one of only five days the ex-President was ill the entire trip. Kermit suffered two days from tick fever and one of sunstroke but was otherwise well throughout.

The next major excursion, taking most of the month of August, was an elephant hunt on the slopes of 17,000-foot-high Mount Kenya, eighty miles north of Nairobi. Camping at chill elevations as high as 10,000 feet and tramping for days in fine rain through "tangled forest and matted jungle," the Colonel's party tracked the elusive animals. At last they caught up with a herd but in the thick growth they could tell their prey was at hand only by the sound of cracking boughs and "curious internal rumblings of the great beasts." Stepping in the giant footprints, where there were no twigs to crack and thus give him away, T.R. stalked the elephant herd until a turn in the path brought him into sight of one only thirty yards away. He felled his first elephant with two bullets, but at that instant the bushes to his left parted and another bull elephant charged. The Colonel jumped aside, but the beast passed so close that it could have touched him with his trunk. That night they camped under a clear sky with a young moon hanging at tree-top level. Standing before a roaring fire, T.R. toasted slices of elephant's heart on a pronged stick—a delicacy he pronounced delicious. In the next few days, he shot four more of the eight elephants he would finally take.

Each victim was carefully chosen to fill the grouping needed for the Smithsonian.

The previous year Roosevelt had entertained Carl Akeley, the noted American naturalist and big game hunter, at the White House. Akeley told the President of his own plans for a safari to East Africa, where he hoped to get a group of elephants for the American Museum of Natural History in New York. The two made a tentative date to meet, so that Roosevelt would have a chance to shoot one or two of the animals for the American Museum.

The Chicago *Tribune* seized upon this projected rendezvous as a splendid opportunity to circumvent the Roosevelt ban on correspondents: the newspaper dispatched its cartoonist John T. McCutcheon as a member of the Akeley expedition. McCutcheon's qualifications for joining a safari were slim indeed; by his own admission, he "had not shot at anything for three years, nor hit anything for ten." Yet, like everyone who goes to Africa with a gun and a return ticket, he later wrote, he had two overweening ambitions: "One was to kill a lion and the other to live to tell about it."

The Akeley party reached Mombasa on September 16 and went immediately to Nairobi. There Akeley found a letter from the Colonel suggesting that they meet in mid-November in the vicinity of Mount Elgon, 220 miles northwest of the capital. After some weeks of hunting near Nairobi, the Akeley safari set out for Mount Elgon, taking the railroad part way and then organizing an overland march from the last station. McCutcheon was impressed by the efficiency of the East African mailmen, runners who bore messages over incredible distances in short times and always seemed, like Stanley, to find their Livingstones. Messages from Roosevelt kept arriving but for the eleven days of their overland march from the railroad, Akeley and McCutcheon had no guarantee that they would actually encounter the Colonel. On the morning of November 14, moving in a direction suggested by the latest runner, they heard shots off to their left and soon saw, about a mile away a large safari that could only be Roosevelt's.

The two safaris immediately went into camp, and Roosevelt rode over to greet Akeley. Straight-faced, the American hunter handed the Colonel a message that had just arrived from Nairobi. Dated November 6 and from America, it read: "Reported here you have been killed. Mrs. Roosevelt worried. Cable denial American Embassy, Rome." The party erupted in laughter as T.R. recited aloud the bizarre request. McCutcheon described Roosevelt as a man who "certainly didn't look dead." He was rugged and healthy; his "cheeks were burned to a ruddy tan and his eyes were as clear as a plainsman's." The ex-President easily laughed and joked with the new arrivals and appeared to be a man with no cares or worries in the world. The Akeley party brought news from America, particularly political news, and the Colonel commented on this "with a frankness," McCutcheon noted, "that compels even a newspaper man to regard as confidential." The protectorate officials, it seems, had interpreted T.R.'s expressed wish for privacy even more strictly than he had perhaps intended, with the result that almost no one had been permitted into the regions through which his safari was traveling; and it was thus an absolute treat to receive visitors from home.

It was quickly arranged that Roosevelt and Akeley would start on their elephant hunt the next morning, and the parties separated for the night. Elephant hunting, as the Colonel had learned on Mount Kenya, can be a tedious and wearing experience, but he was unusually lucky this time. Just at noon the following day, the hunters spied some elephants, including the two cows and a calf Akeley needed for the group he was assembling for the New York museum, and they were quickly shot.

Returning to the carcasses the next morning, they saw something that had to be sketched by McCutcheon and photographed by Kermit to be believed. During the night a hyena had crept up to one of the dead elephants and begun feasting. The hyena had actually eaten his way inside the rib cage of the elephant and then, bloated by his gorging, found he could not turn around to get out. In a frenzy he had bitten his way through the dead elephant's stomach lining and stuck out his head. The drying membranes, however, had apparently contracted and trapped the hapless beast, who managed only to kick one leg clear. And there, for the hunters to see, was the blissfully satiated but effectively imprisoned hyena, gazing out from the dead elephant's stomach much as he might be looking out a window. The hyena was promptly shot, and the extraordinary scene recorded for posterity.

At lunch the following day, the Colonel laughed over stories that he had been drunk or crazy during his final months in office. "I may be crazy," he said, "but I most certainly haven't been drinking hard." After regaling the party with various stories about his White House years, he told them of a recent episode during a buffalo hunt. A rhino had appeared, which threatened to charge the party and scare away the buffalo.

Absorbed in the stalk and forgetting rank, one of the other hunters had told T.R. to hurry away and shoo off the rhino while they closed in on their prey. "So you see," the Colonel concluded, "there's an occupation. That settles the question as to what shall we do with our ex-Presidents. They can be used to scare rhinos away."

6

After parting ways with the Akeley safari, the Roosevelt expedition returned for a last time to Nairobi. The original safari had now broken up and the porters had been dismissed, because the Colonel could take only a few personal attendants with him into Uganda and to the Nile. Additional provisions were gathered for the march through the interior, all previously collected specimens were prepared for shipment to the United States, and T.R. packed the final contributions from America to his Pigskin Library. On December 18 the greatly reduced party boarded the train for the railroad's inland terminal on Lake Victoria. En route to the lake they passed the African watershed; up to that point the lands through which they had been traveling were drained by rivers flowing eastward into the Indian Ocean. Now the streams and rivers spilled westward, into the great inland lakes that harbored the headwaters of the Nile. And those waters eventually would carry Roosevelt north, to Egypt, the Mediterranean, and Europe.

It took the steamer twenty-four hours to cross the unruffled waters of Lake Victoria, from Kisumu to Entebbe, the seat of the British governor in the Uganda protectorate. Dark clouds settled over the land they were leaving, T.R. reported, but a rainbow welcomed them to the new region. "At nightfall, as the red sunset faded," he wrote in a poetic vein, "the lonely waters of the vast inland sea stretched ocean-like, west and south into a shoreless gloom. Then the darkness deepened, the tropic stars blazed overhead, and the light of the half moon drowned in silver the embers of the sunset."

The following morning, cruising along the equator, Roosevelt the poet became Roosevelt the scientific observer. He reported—again in greater detail than at least Edith Roosevelt, should she be reading the article in Oyster Bay, would like to have heard—the ravages of sleeping sickness, which had virtually depopulated Uganda only a decade earlier. Carried by the biting fly related to the tsetse, the "dreadful scourge" had killed 200,000 "in slow torment." Islands in the lake that had previously thronged with members of fishing tribes were now totally desolate. But, upon landing in Uganda, Roosevelt commented that "there was nothing in the hot, laughing tropical beauty of the land to suggest the grisly horror that brooded so near."

The Colonel's party was greeted in Uganda with the usual efficient courtesy of the British officials. Among the events scheduled for the former President was a visit to a Church of England mission, where the native children had been patiently drilled to sing a phonetic greeting:

> *O se ka nyu si bai di mo nseli laiti*
> *Wati so pulauli wi eli adi twayi laiti silasi giremi.* . . .

Luckily the Colonel was quick to detect the melody of "The Star-Spangled Banner" in the curious words and politely he beamed his approval.

From the great lake the party moved north, spending Christmas on the march—there being no reason to celebrate the day, T.R. noted with unmistakable regret, unless there were small folks to hang up stockings the night before and gleefully rush to open presents in the morning. On January 5, 1910, they reached Lake Albert Nyanza, after an overland trek from Victoria of 160 miles. There were two more months of travel ahead of them—principally in pursuit of the mysterious white rhinoceros of the Lado region and the giant eland in the Belgian Congo, but the memorable hunt was now drawing to its inevitable conclusion. From Lake Albert they could take boats that would carry them to the Bahr el Jebel, or White Nile. Soon Roosevelt would be traveling through lands he had visited four decades earlier on a trip up the Nile with his family as a boy of fourteen.

A "crazy little steam-launch," two sailboats, and two large rowboats carried the party north into the Lado. Two days after leaving Lake Albert, they pitched camp in a grove of thorn trees, where the "nights were hot, and the days burning." The river was "alive with monstrous crocodiles," the smoke of prairie fires drifted across the horizon, and mosquitoes, bats, and large carnivorous ants came with twilight to the wild, desolate country of papyrus marshes and rolling plains that rose into distant hills and low mountains. Only Theodore Roosevelt could have found it "a very pleasant camp" and write with no intention of humor that he "thoroughly enjoyed it."

The next morning the hunters set out in pursuit of the rare white rhino, following dung deposits through tangled grass higher than their heads. And with the usual Roosevelt luck, they located their prey the first day and got the specimens for the National Museum. The taxidermists had to fend off marauding lions come to enjoy a rhino feast and a prairie fire momentarily threatened to wipe out the entire camp—but the outing was judged an unqualified success.

"Kermit and I continue in the best of health; but this is not a mere health resort!" T.R. admitted in a letter to Lodge at the end of their month-long stay in the Lado. "All the other members of the party have been down with fever or dysentery; one gun bearer has died of fever, four porters of dysentery and two have been mauled by beasts; and in a village on our line of march, near which we camped and hunted, eight natives died of sleeping sickness during our stay." Balancing out the health hazards perhaps was the opportunity afforded in the Lado for culinary surprises. The Colonel noted with approval a breakfast of scrambled crocodile eggs and a stew of buffalo kidney.

A curious cloud rose about this time on T.R.'s horizon. A runner one day brought the Colonel news that on January 7 Taft had dismissed Gifford Pinchot as chief of the United States Forest Service in a dispute with Taft's Secretary of the Interior, Richard Achilles Ballinger. Pinchot had been T.R.'s leading adviser on conservation matters and an intimate member of the Tennis Cabinet. To Pinchot Roosevelt wrote that he could scarcely credit the news, although it did make him uneasy. He had been able to follow political developments "very imperfectly," he noted; perhaps Pinchot could write with details, care of the American Embassy in Paris.

Early in February the party left the White Nile for a loop into the Belgian Congo to hunt the giant eland, and on the last day of that month the hunters boarded a steamer for the two-week trip that would take them nearly one thousand miles north to Khartoum in the Sudan.

Roosevelt's safari was over. The last article for *Scribner's* was written, and a preface was composed for the volume to be published later that year. *African Game Trails, An Account of the African Wanderings of an American Hunter-Naturalist* he would call the book, and it was dedicated to Kermit Roosevelt, "My Side-Partner in our 'Great Adventure.'" All of Roosevelt's love and enthusiasm for the Dark Continent went into the Foreword:

" 'I speak of Africa and golden joys'; the joy of wandering through lonely lands; the joy of hunting the mighty and terrible lords of the wilderness, the cunning, the wary, and the grim.

"In these greatest of the world's great hunting-grounds there are mountain peaks whose snows are dazzling under the equatorial sun; swamps where the slime oozes and bubbles and festers in the steaming heat; lakes like seas; skies that burn above deserts where the iron desolation is shrouded from view by the wavering mockery of the mirage; vast grassy plains where palms and thorn-trees fringe the dwindling streams; mighty rivers rushing out of the heart of the continent through the sadness of endless marshes; forests of gorgeous beauty, where death broods in the dark and silent depths."

There were sights forever fixed in his mind, he continued, ". . . memories of the lion's charge, of the gray bulk of the elephant, close at hand in the sombre woodland; of the buffalo, his sullen eyes lowering from under his helmet of horn; of the rhinoceros, truculent and stupid, standing in the bright sunlight of the empty plain." Some things could be told but for others there were no words, "no words that can tell the hidden spirit of the wilderness, that can reveal its mystery, its melancholy, and its charm."

Later, with the naturalist Edmund Heller, he would publish a two-volume scientific work based on the expedition, *Life Histories of African Game Animals.* But for this first, popular work he was content merely to list the score for game he and Kermit had shot. For T.R.: nine lions; eight elephants; thirteen rhinoceroses; six buffaloes; and fifty-three other species—for a grand total of 296. For Kermit: eight lions; three elephants; seven rhinos; four buffaloes; and sixty-five other species, including three of the leopards that had eluded his father and two rare bongo —for a total of 216. The two Roosevelts kept about a dozen trophies for themselves. Of the rest, what was not shot merely for meat was preserved for the Smithsonian. Sixty-one large mammals were collected and one hundred and three small mammals, including the newly classified *Pelomys roosevelti,* or iridescent creek rat. Also among the small mammals observed en route was a nocturnal tree hyrax, found in the high forests near Mount Elgon. These "squat, wooly, funny things," Roosevelt discovered to his great amusement, were known among the local white settlers as "Teddy bears."

Again the dispassionate scientific observer, the Colonel could not conclude his book without a discourse on the use of "spiritous liquors" for medicinal purposes in the tropics. At the outset of the safari, a friend had presented him with a bottle of rare brandy "for emergencies." Early on, T.R. decided that hot tea was just as good a stimulant when he was feeling "feverish or exhausted from a hard day's tramp," and so he handed the bottle over to one of the guides—who also apparently had little use for it. Making a final reckoning at Khartoum, the guide asked T.R. what he should do with the bottle of brandy. The Colonel suggested that it be donated to the store of the steamer that had brought them north. But before parting with the bottle, he measured the remaining contents. In eleven months on safari, Roosevelt noted carefully, he had taken just six ounces of alcohol.

~§ Chapter 8 §~

In the Presence of Kings

In mid-March, 1910, the eyes of the world seemed fixed on Khartoum. The capital of what was then the Anglo-Egyptian Sudan is near the point where the Blue Nile coursing down from the mountains of Ethiopia joins the White Nile to form the Nile proper—and it was the place where Roosevelt, descending the White Nile from the large interior lakes of Africa, would re-enter civilization.

Lawrence Abbott, son of the editor of *The Outlook,* had been greatly disappointed the previous year when the Colonel had declined to make an exception to his ban against newspapermen and had withdrawn permission for the younger Abbott to accompany him to Mombasa. But in a postscript to a letter written to Abbott in December, 1909, T.R. asked him to come to Khartoum. Abbott excitedly took passage on a ship bound for Naples, where he could transship for Alexandria, Cairo, and the upper reaches of the Nile. Happily, he found himself on the same boat with Edith Roosevelt and eighteen-year-old Ethel, also bound for Khartoum, and offered to act as their escort.

Not only would the Colonel be emerging from the heart of the Dark Continent—perhaps with more recent adventures to tell than those currently appearing in *Scribner's*——it would also be the first time in nearly a year that he could be interviewed by the press. Hoping to find headlines, a number of editors sent reporters to Egypt. What did the former President think of the job his successor was doing? What were his views on the controversial Payne-Aldrich tariff of 1909? What were his reactions to the dismissal of Gifford Pinchot? Rival correspondents chartered steamboats to race upriver and stand at the jungle's edge, pencil and pad in hand, to record the every word of Bwana Makuba.

John Callan O'Laughlin of the Chicago *Tribune* found the Colonel in the "high spirits of perfect health"; he seemed to have lost the careworn look of his last months in office. "His face was brown, and his moustache, lightened by the sun, showed a few more gray hairs," the reporter wrote. "His jaws were clean of fat, and his well-worn khaki hung loosely on his muscular frame."

T.R. told "the boys" he was glad to see them and asked them for news from home. One by one he sat with them in the stateroom of his steamer and exchanged confidential views, purely "off the record." For publication he would only authorize the statement that he had nothing to say on politics, that he would give no interviews, and that any report of an interview was to be regarded as false. "Here was a tremendous reward for the long and expensive journey we had undertaken!" lamented O'Laughlin. Roosevelt was more than eager to show the reporters the skins and bones of his specimens and to introduce them to the loyal natives accompanying this remnant of the safari; but as for politics, "no, not a word." Later, in Khartoum, he would confide to Lawrence Abbott his belief that his political career was ended. "No man in American public life has ever reached the crest of the wave as I appear to have done without the wave's breaking and engulfing him."

The British officials came out to welcome the steamer to Khartoum on March 14, and flags flew from housetops and from boats lining the bank. Various sights—including the governor's palace where he would be staying—were pointed out to Roosevelt. "Where is the railroad station?" he asked impatiently.

"Surely I never, never wrote mother that I was not homesick!" Roosevelt had written his daughter "Ethely-bye" several months earlier. "If I did, I put in a 'not' by mistake. . . . I have been homesick all the time, and grow steadily more so." T.R. and Kermit were standing on the platform as the train from the north pulled into the Khartoum station and Edith and Ethel Roosevelt stepped down. Husband and wife had been separated just nine days short of an entire year.

An essential part of Theodore Roosevelt's plan for his African safari was to have Edith waiting for him at Khartoum when he emerged from the jungles. Then, as a reward for his wife's sacrifice in letting him be gone for an entire year, he would take her on a trip through Europe —to see the hill towns of Italy, the French cathedrals, the English country lanes in spring, perhaps spend a day at the Louvre. He would no longer be President and the two of them were to travel strictly as private citizens. The tour, he had written Lodge on August 8, 1908, must be made on his own terms. "If it means that I have to make a kind of mock triumphal progress and spend my time at dismal and expensive entertainments which I shall loathe even more than the wretched creatures who feel obliged to give them, why I won't go, and shall simply come straight home." Within ten days he had received, and accepted, an invitation that ultimately altered the nature of his European trip and turned it into the triumphal—though certainly not "mock triumphal"—progress he had hoped to avoid.

While T.R. was still President the chancellor of Oxford, Lord Curzon, had invited him to deliver the Romanes Lecture for 1910 and receive an honorary degree from the university. Roosevelt was more than delighted to accept. In October, 1908, Jules Jusserand had come to the White House with an invitation from the French government for Roosevelt to deliver an address at the Sorbonne, and again the President accepted. It was only a matter of time, he predicted to Archie Butt, before the German ambassador arrived with an invitation—the Kaiser would surely not let the English and French get ahead of him.

Although he had corresponded with the Kaiser and, in a sense, collaborated with him on such matters as the Algeciras Conference—and although some people had described the two as similar characters— Roosevelt did not particularly want to meet the German emperor. The problem, he confided to a friend, was how to keep from hurting Wilhelm's feelings by seeing his uncle the King of England and not him, and yet avoid giving the impression that the Kaiser would be doing him a favor by inviting him to Berlin. But the invitation came, as expected, and before the end of the year the University of Berlin was added to the European itinerary. While working at getting Taft elected as his successor, Roosevelt had composed the Oxford and Sorbonne addresses and written a draft of the Berlin speech.

With the floodgates thus opened, the invitations came pouring in, and T.R. accepted a surprising number of them—from Victor Emmanuel III, to return to Rome; from ancient Franz Josef of Austria-Hungary; from Norway, to deliver an acceptance speech for the Nobel Peace Prize he had been awarded in 1906.

With so many official functions now being scheduled, Roosevelt foresaw one problem: what was he to wear when presented at court? He wrote to his friend Whitelaw Reid, American Ambassador to the Court of St. James's, with a suggestion. "My idea . . . is that I should take with me the dress uniform of a colonel of United States cavalry (which I am entitled to wear as an ex-Colonel of the Spanish War—not a paper colonel, either, but one who saw service)." Captain Butt thought it was a splendid idea—a cavalry colonel's uniform was brilliant with plumes and gold lace and could be worn with high patent leather boots. Edith Roosevelt got wind of the plan and quashed it with devastating wit. "Theodore," she said, ". . . if you insist upon this I will have a vivandière's costume made and follow you throughout Europe." Yet apparently it still did not occur to Roosevelt that his trip was going to be a royal progress.

When he arrived in Khartoum, Lawrence Abbott was astonished to discover that the Colonel had made no special arrangements for the forthcoming tour of Europe. He planned to buy the tickets for his family, check their baggage, write his own letters, and keep track of all their engagements. In short, he expected to travel from Khartoum through Europe "like any American tourist." Abbott quickly convinced the Colonel that this was totally impractical and volunteered his own services as a secretary-tour manager.

Abbott's first assignment at Khartoum was to translate the nearly indecipherable manuscript of an article on the Pigskin Library that T.R. had drafted for *The Outlook,* which was edited by Abbott's father. One night of wrestling with this problem convinced him that he was going to need help, and Abbott cabled New York for a stenographic secretary. This man, Frank Harper, joined the party in Rome. Meanwhile, Cal O'Laughlin of the Chicago *Tribune* was also made a permanent member of the party, which would then consist of the four Roosevelts, the three men acting as secretaries, a maid, and a valet. Abbott took charge of finances, buying a ledger in which to keep the accounts, and at the end of the trip could report to Roosevelt that he had a credit of about three thousand dollars. So uninterested was T.R. in money for the trip, reported Abbott, that if he had told the Colonel he was three thousand short he probably would have been surprised it was not more.

The Roosevelt party spent three days at Khartoum, days filled with official receptions, tours, and speeches. On March 17 they left by train for the north and the following day, at Wady Halfa, transferred to the steamer *Ibis* for a two-day cruise on the Nile. At Abu Simbel they went ashore to inspect the temple of Ramesses II, where Ethel Roosevelt— Baedeker in hand—acted as guide. The Colonel was outraged to discover that previous visitors had cut their initials in the rock. Such vandals should be treated just as those who defaced the natural wonders of Yellowstone Park were; they should be apprehended and compelled to return and undo "their despicable work." At Shillal, they boarded another train and, after additional sightseeing at Karnak and Luxor, arrived at Cairo on the twenty-fourth.

Among the welcomers at the Cairo station was Oscar Straus, whom Taft had appointed ambassador to the Ottoman Empire as a consolation for not keeping him in the Cabinet. Straus showed T.R. a recent magazine article about his successor's first year in office "which plainly showed that much ground had been lost." Once more the former President expressed regret that Straus and James Garfield had not been retained by Taft.

In Cairo the Roosevelts stopped at the famed Shepheards Hotel. Visits were exchanged with the khedive; the pyramids and Sphinx were seen by moonlight; and on March 28 the Colonel spoke at the National University. Although technically a part of the Ottoman Empire, Egypt was in effect a British protectorate—but one with aspirations of self-government. The Egyptian premier Butros Ghali, a Coptic Christian, had recently been assassinated by a member of the Nationalist party, a group composed largely of young Moslem students who believed in Egypt for the Egyptians—and Roosevelt had been warned not to refer to the incident. T.R. took as the subject of his university address "Law and Order in Egypt," and in the speech he not only condemned the assassination but also preached on the virtue of self-restraint in the matter of sovereignty. "God is with the patient, if they know how to wait," he said, quoting an Arab proverb he had picked up in the Sudan. Students paraded in protest the next day, but officialdom lauded the Colonel's sentiments and his courage in expressing them in public.

At Cairo, as at Khartoum, Roosevelt found bundles of mail awaiting answers. Among the invitations he had to consider was one from the Kaiser asking him to stay at the palace. Mrs. Roosevelt, however, was not included in the invitation, and T.R. wrote the American ambassador in Berlin to decline the Kaiser's offer and say that he would stay with his wife at the embassy instead. Wilhelm got the hint and broke tradition to include Mrs. Roosevelt. A more serious problem loomed over the proposal that the former President visit the Vatican.

By the age of fifty, Theodore Roosevelt—one of his biographers notes—had fulfilled the dream of every American boy: he had led a cavalry charge, shot a lion, and been President of the United States. To make his life perfect he needed only a fight with the pope.

From Gondokoro on the White Nile, Roosevelt had written to the American ambassador at Rome, John G. A. Leishman, that he would be pleased by the honor of a presentation to Pope Pius X. At Cairo he found waiting for him a reply from the ambassador. Leishman had made an inquiry through the Reverend Thomas Kennedy, rector of the American College in Rome, and from him received a message for the ex-President: "The Holy Father will be delighted to grant audience to Mr. Roosevelt on April 5th and hopes that nothing will arise to prevent it such as the much regretted incident which made the reception of Mr. Fairbanks impossible."

On his recent visit to Rome former Vice President Charles W. Fairbanks had been scheduled to see the pope, when it was revealed that he would the same day lecture before the American Methodist mission in the Eternal City. One of the more zealous missionaries, a man with the delicious name of Ezra Tipple, had not made easier the efforts of his group to convert the papal diocese to Protestantism by referring to Pius as "the whore of Babylon." The pope refused to see Fairbanks on the same day he was to favor the Methodists with a visit.

To Ambassador Leishman, Roosevelt promptly replied that— although he recognized the pope's right to receive or not receive anyone he chose—he could not "submit to any conditions which in any way limit my freedom of conduct." He still hoped that the pope would find it "convenient" to receive him. The answer from the Vatican was that the audience "could not occur except on the understanding expressed in the former message." If Roosevelt recognized the Methodist presence in Rome, then the doors of the Vatican were closed to him. The Colonel's response was terse: "Proposed presentation is of course now impossible."

O'Laughlin was a Catholic and anxious not to have a headline row between Roosevelt and the pope develop out of the incident. When the Roosevelt party reached Naples, he hurried on to Rome and sought a meeting with Cardinal Rafael Merry del Val, the Papal Secretary of State. The cardinal's amazing attempt at a compromise was an offer for the pope to receive the Colonel based on a secret pledge not to visit the Methodists—though it could be given out to the press that there was no such agreement! It was an offer, T.R. later wrote, that "a

Tammany Boodle alderman would have been ashamed to make," and he refused to be a party to any such deal. The ex-President published a defense of his action in *The Outlook,* and most of his fellow citizens— including a number of American Catholic clerics—praised his resolution. "I have just been administering private discipline to the Pope and the Kaiser, on questions of ethics and etiquette respectively," Roosevelt wrote Senator Lodge; "in consequence I may see neither. . . ."

The final ludicrous scene in this comedy of errors was enacted when the Roosevelt party—via steamer from Alexandria to Naples —reached Rome on April 3. The Reverend Tipple, gloating over Methodism's apparent victory, issued a new attack on the Holy Father. This, T.R. sadly concluded, seemed to make the pope right in refusing to share the former President with the Protestant upstarts. The Colonel promptly canceled a public reception at which the Methodist delegation was to be presented to him; any churchmen he would see, including Tipple's associates and some American Catholic clerics in Rome, would be seen in private.

Apart from having to remove the Vatican from his itinerary, Roosevelt greatly enjoyed his visit to the Italian capital. He renewed his acquaintance with Victor Emmanuel and found the king's family equally pleasant. But he was given an awkward lesson in Italian court etiquette when he arrived at the Quirinal Palace for a state dinner. Stopping at the cloakroom, he endeavored to leave his silk top hat with attendants, but it was returned to him "with every symptom of surprise and horror," and he walked into the reception room still with his hat in hand. He was presented to the queen and asked to take her in to dinner. Again, to T.R. at least, this seemed like an appropriate time to dispose of the unwanted headgear but he found no takers. He was expected to walk into the dining room with the queen on one arm and his hat on the other. It reminded him, he later wrote, of nothing so much as the Jewish weddings on the Lower East Side of New York—which he had attended as police commissioner—where participants wore their hats through the ceremony. He was vastly relieved when a servant materialized as the dinner guests were seating themselves and bore away all the hats.

The Italian king caused "frightful agitation" when he called at the hotel for Roosevelt and embarrassed T.R. by insisting that the former President take the right-hand seat in the carriage. As the Colonel went to place wreaths on the tombs of the king's father and grandfather, a fearful thunderstorm broke out. "Whenever Caesar began an expedition which was crowned with success," one of the dignitaries portentously remarked to O'Laughlin, "Jove blackened the sky, sounded his war drums and sent bolts toward the earth."

From Rome the party headed north. Kermit and Ethel, Abbott, O'Laughlin, Harper, and the servants went directly to Genoa, but Theodore and Edith Roosevelt hoped to repeat the wedding trip over the Cornechi they had taken twenty-three years earlier. The couple started out from Spezia in an old-fashioned three-horse carriage and got as far as the village of Sestri Levante before being discovered. The municipal authorities called upon them at the hotel and a band came to serenade them. The next day natives and tourists seemed to line the route wherever they went and by noon they realized that their private enjoyment was at an end. Reluctantly they abandoned the sentimental journey and rejoined the rest of the party at Genoa. It would be two months—and not until just as he was leaving England for America—before Roosevelt again experienced any privacy.

On April 10 the Roosevelts reached Porto Maurizio, where Edith Roosevelt's maiden sister made her home. The picturesque seaside town, sixty miles southwest of Genoa and only twenty miles from the French border, had approximately six thousand residents at the time; O'Laughlin estimated the crowd meeting them at the railroad to number six thousand. Emily Carow's hillside villa stood in a flowering garden overlooking the sea and was named Villa Magna Quies—Villa of Great Quiet. The three days the Roosevelts were at Porto Maurizio were anything but ones of great quiet. There were ceremonies to open Boulevard Roosevelt and to present Miss Carow's distinguished visitor with the freedom of the city, an evening festival, numerous visitors, and a procession of messengers bearing letters and telegrams—usually requests of one type or another. "These good people have expectation as to what I can do," T.R. said in exasperation to Abbott, "that would not be justified if I were George Washington, Abraham Lincoln, and the Angel Gabriel all rolled into one." The writers wanted autographs, stamps, picture postcards, his views on subjects ranging from the Shakespeare-Bacon controversy to the referendum, articles or lectures on antelopes, politics as a career for a young man, or Hungarian immigration to the United States. But one petitioner's request for an interview was readily granted.

2

A tall, lean, angular man whose enormous walrus moustache gave his head an outsize appearance, Gifford Pinchot had become chief of the Division of Forestry in the Department of Agriculture in 1898. The division then had a staff of eleven and an annual appropriation of $28,520. But its biggest handicap was the fact that the government forests—43,000,000 acres of forest reserves plus several times that sum of unreserved public timberlands—fell under the jurisdiction of the Public Land Office in the Department of the Interior. Pinchot was a tireless crusader, with a messianic vision of himself as the champion of public over private rights to the nation's resources. At the end of three years, in July, 1901, he saw his division upgraded to a bureau, with a staff of 179 and an appropriation of $185,440. Two months later Theodore Roosevelt became President.

Whether or not Pinchot actually converted Roosevelt to the cause of conservation of natural resources remains in doubt. The two met during Roosevelt's term as New York governor, found they shared a love of the outdoors, and promptly became fellow partisans of conservation and warm personal friends. Pinchot helped Roosevelt on that part of the new President's first annual message to Congress, in December, 1901, dealing with forestry and irrigation. With his typical disregard for tradition and precedence, T.R. worked directly with the chief forester, bypassing his Secretary of Agriculture.

On February 1, 1905, Pinchot achieved his principal goal as forester, when Roosevelt signed an act transferring the forest reserves—renamed national forests—to his bureau, the Forest Service. Pinchot, an inner member of the Tennis Cabinet, next worked closely with T.R. on the formation in 1907 of the Inland Waterways Commission, to study ways of relieving overland transportation congestion. The commission's report revealed that water transportation was but part of the larger problem of conserving and utilizing natural resources. And thus, on May 13, 1908, Roosevelt had convened the White House Conservation Conference, with the governors of all the states in attendance. At the conference T.R. paid special tribute to Pinchot as the man "to whom we owe so much of the progress we have already made in handling this matter of the co-ordination and conservation of natural resources." The governors' conference, Pinchot later declared, made conservation "the characteristic and outstanding policy" of T.R.'s administration, "almost in the twinkling of an eye." Roosevelt the conservationist now stood next to Roosevelt the trustbuster and Roosevelt the canal builder.

Along with most other Roosevelt disciples, Pinchot accepted T.R.'s designation of Taft as his successor—but with little enthusiasm. At a conservation conference in Washington a month after the election, Pinchot's tepid support for Taft became mingled with a vague unease. "There is one difficulty about the conservation of natural resources," the President-elect said in his opening remarks. "It is that the imagination of those who are pressing it may outrun the practical facts." This was blasphemy to Pinchot, to whom there was no such thing as too much virtue. Next came the news that Taft would not retain James Garfield, another dedicated conservationist and fellow member of the Tennis Cabinet, as Secretary of the Interior, and Pinchot's sense of foreboding deepened.

Garfield's successor was Richard Achilles Ballinger, a Seattle lawyer and former reform mayor of that city, who had served for a year under Garfield as Commissioner of the Public Land Office but had returned to private life in March, 1908. The Land Office, of course, was the Forest Service's bureaucratic rival and only the friendship and essential agreement between Garfield and Pinchot had kept the historic feud between the Interior and Agriculture departments quiescent during the later Roosevelt years. "Jim and I think alike concerning the matters in which the Forest Service and the Department of the Interior are closely related. Ballinger and I might clash," Pinchot said when he learned of the appointment.

And clash they did—spectacularly. In the summer of 1909 an Interior Department investigator charged Ballinger with irregularities in awarding coal mining claims in Alaska to a syndicate said to be backed by J. P. Morgan and Daniel Guggenheim. A presidential review—it would later be called a whitewash—cleared Ballinger, and the man who had made the charges was dismissed. Apparently willing to believe the worst about Taft's Secretary of the Interior, Pinchot took up the discharged employee's cause, which soon was getting wide publicity.

"Gifford Pinchot is out again defying the lightning. . . ." Taft wrote his brother Horace at the end of 1909. It was an accurate prediction of the forester's next move. In defiance of a direct order from the President that government officials correspond with members of Congress only through the heads of their departments, Pinchot wrote early in January, 1910, to Senator Jonathan Dolliver of Iowa, chairman of the Committee on Agriculture and Forestry, criticizing the removal of the Interior Department employee. After Senator Dolliver read the letter on the floor of the Senate, Taft conferred with his Cabinet for four hours and even sought the advice of Elihu Root, then a New York senator. "There is only one thing for you to do now," Root told the President, "and that you must do at once." In a letter dated January 7, Taft removed Pinchot from office. "Well, Archie," the President told his military aide, ". . . I have done all the harm I could. Come for me at three, and let's get some pure air in our lungs and the cobwebs off my brain." And the two went for a long ride and then a walk in the country.

The news of Pinchot's removal, first rumored and then confirmed, reached T.R. in Africa. Roosevelt wrote to Henry Cabot Lodge that he would of course say nothing for publication. "It is a very ungracious thing for an ex-President to criticize his successor," he wrote Pinchot on March 1. Perhaps the ex-forester could meet him in Europe, before his return to the political battlefields of the United States. "I wish to see you before I in even the smallest degree commit myself."

Pinchot left for Europe almost immediately upon receipt of the letter and on April 11 appeared at the Villa Magna Quies at Porto Maurizio. He brought with him a number of letters from such progressives as senators Dolliver and Beveridge and Kansas newspaperman William Allen White, letters that, as one historian has stated, "fairly bristled with acrid comment" on the Taft administration. "One of the best and most satisfactory talks with T.R. I ever had. Lasted nearly all day, and till about 10:30 at night," Pinchot noted in his diary for the day. There can be little doubt as to which side of the controversy the Colonel saw as he continued his triumphal journey through Europe.

3

Fearing that the ladies might become overtired, Roosevelt left his wife and daughter at Porto Maurizio and went with Kermit to Venice, Vienna, and Budapest. Waiting at his hotel in Vienna on the morning of April 15 was Henry White.

Often described as America's first professional diplomat, White had served in various European capitals and had been named ambassador to

France by his old friend Theodore Roosevelt. To nearly everyone's astonishment Taft, soon after taking office, asked for White's resignation; it was said that twenty-five years earlier White had somehow slighted the Tafts when they stopped in London during their wedding journey. When the news reached the Colonel, deep in Africa, he wrote White immediately to express his dismay. He had told Taft that he regarded White as "without exception the very best man in our diplomatic service." Taft had assured both Roosevelt and Lodge that White would be retained in Paris, T.R. now recalled. Of course, Roosevelt added somewhat cryptically, it was "not a promise any more than my statement that I would not run again for President was a promise." Henry White was in Vienna at T.R.'s request, and the two freely discussed domestic politics, no doubt again with some emphasis on the failings of the Colonel's successor. Roosevelt, Lawrence Abbott told White at this time, "particularly resented" the President's action in dismissing the ambassador and seemed "quite unable to get over it."

The Colonel found his popular reception in Vienna even greater than that of Rome—just as if he were President again and visiting San Francisco, Seattle, St. Louis, or New Orleans, he wrote. The streets and squares around his hotel were completely blocked and when he drove to Schloss Schönbrunn to dine with Emperor Franz Josef, he found the entire route lined with well-wishers. The emperor, then in the sixtieth year of his reign, did not strike T.R. as a very able man, "but he was a gentleman, he had good instincts." Franz Josef offered to open the royal hunting preserves to Roosevelt, and the court was shocked when he declined—in Austria, such an invitation was a command. At a state dinner the Colonel was horrified by Austrian court custom with regard to finger bowls. Following each course, the emperor and his guests rinsed their mouths with water from the finger bowls and then expectorated into the bowls. Roosevelt, while presumably declining to follow custom in this instance, had learned by then how to get along with kings.

With one notable exception—Queen Wilhelmina of Holland —he liked all the royalty he met. Each sovereign he encountered, T.R. claimed, "was obviously conscious that he was looking a possible republic in the face, which was naturally an incentive to good conduct." Most members of the royalty spoke English, so T.R. could converse freely with them; otherwise he spoke French "with daring fluency."

Why any king would want to see him, the Colonel could not at

first imagine. But soon he sensed that his visits were "a relief to the te-
dium, the dull, narrow routine of their lives." And then there was the
sense of rivalry. Once the Kaiser had invited Roosevelt to the palace,
every other crowned head wanted him as a guest, almost as if to bask in
the reflected glory of the renowned American. Each king would write to
the next "and tell the one ahead what sort of barbarian I was and what
I might say," T.R. later recalled. "In fact, I think each ruler screwed his
throne down a little tighter as I approached."

When he arrived at a new palace, the Colonel found the king or
prince eager to hear the tales that had so pleased his brother monarch
on the previous stop. Especially popular, in addition to accounts of the
safari, were tales about the Rough Riders and ranching days in the Dakota Badlands. The royal auditors hung on every word, although occasionally they would have to interrupt with requests for clarification of
such terms as "a two-gun man." Ever afterward, T.R. noted, he would
bear testimony to the courtesy, good manners, and sense of responsibility
and duty of the various sovereigns he had come to know. But, as an average, they were not very high in intellect and force of personality;
"there was no use trying to talk of books" with them, he said. A constitutional monarch, Roosevelt concluded, is no more than a "sublimated
American vice-president," with an exalted social position.

"I have never demanded of knowledge anything except that it shall
be useless," Roosevelt wrote with facetious hyperbole. Yet, as a voracious
reader with a photographic memory, he was able to digest and retain
vast stores of unrelated and apparently irrelevant information. Until he
went abroad on this trip, he confessed, he had never "derived the slightest benefit, however small, from such things as a knowledge of Moslem
travels in the thirteenth century, or Magyar history, or the Mongol con-
quests, or the growth of the races of Middle Europe and the deeds of
their great men." It was this ability to talk knowledgably and at length
on so many subjects that made the ex-President such an entertaining
guest.

To avoid wounding political sensibilities, it was necessary that Roosevelt visit Budapest, capital of the other half of the Dual Monarchy—
and again he found his great knowledge useful in scoring points with
his hosts. Received in the legislative hall at Budapest, the Colonel found
his audience immensely pleased by his "allusions to Arpád, St. Stephen,
Matthew Corvinus and other Hungarian heroes, to the battle of Mohács,
to the provisions of the Golden Bull of one King Béla, and to the cu-

rious indirect results of the Bogomil heresy, and the double part played by racial and religious considerations in causing the Protestants of Hungary and Transylvania to side with the Turk rather than with the Austrian. . . ." Among politicians, T.R. concluded in describing his popularity with the Hungarians, "the one-eyed is apt to be king—so far as concerns foreign history, or indeed so far as concerns any branch of abstract knowledge not dealing with applied politics, applied economics, or money-making."

Before leaving Budapest Roosevelt called upon Francis Kossuth, son of the Hungarian patriot of the revolution of 1848. "I am ill," Kossuth told Roosevelt, "but if you had not been kind enough to call on me, I would have been conveyed to your hotel on a litter." He had been raised in an atmosphere of liberty as typified by America, Kossuth said, and had "peculiar feelings of pleasure and sympathy" toward the United States. Returning from a visit to a state farm on his last day in the Hungarian capital, Roosevelt found his carriage blocked by a crowd of tens of thousands outside the hotel. He rose to make a few remarks and when his words were translated into Magyar, wrote O'Laughlin, "there was a shout of appreciation which rolled over to the berg across the river and came back in a thundering echo."

From Budapest the two Roosevelt men took a train to Paris, where they were reunited with Mrs. Roosevelt and Ethel on April 21. In the French capital they were guests at the American embassy of Robert Bacon, T.R.'s Harvard classmate and briefly his Secretary of State in 1909, the man Taft had picked to put in Henry White's place—perhaps as a conciliatory gesture. At Paris Roosevelt was also greeted by his old friend Jules Jusserand.

Jusserand was waiting nervously at the platform when the train pulled into the station. He peered into each coach, O'Laughlin noted, until "he caught sight of his quarry"; for the ambassador had crossed the Atlantic especially to be with Roosevelt and apparently felt he would not be doing his duty if he left T.R. with one hour of freedom during his week in the French capital. There were calls on the officials of the Third Republic, the usual sightseeing, an evening at the Comédie-Française, a visit with Edith Wharton, and a tour of Auguste Rodin's studio.

It was already known that the Kaiser planned a military review for the Colonel, and the French—anxious that they be taken seriously as a military power and not merely appreciated for their charm and refinement—insisted on a martial display too. Roosevelt showed up at

Vincennes in "the usual dreadful dress of the 'visiting statesman,' with frock coat and top hat"; but a colonel of the cavalry regiment asked him if he would not rather watch the sham battle on horseback. T.R. readily agreed, a pair of leggings was found to put over the striped pants, and a few days later Roosevelt learned that his mount had practically been canonized by the overwhelmed men of the regiment.

Roosevelt's speech at the Sorbonne was scheduled for April 23, and long before the appointed hour the streets surrounding the hall were filled with such an enormous crowd that even ticketholders had difficulty in reaching the doors. An audience of three thousand packed an amphitheater decorated with statues of France's great—Pascal, Descartes, Lavoisier, and others. A solemn group of university officials and academicians sat ranged on the speaker's dais, and when the Colonel rose to speak, he stood before a simple backdrop of the American and French flags. "Citizenship in a Republic" was the topic of the sermon for the day—and preach Roosevelt did.

Speaking in English, but with an occasional extemporaneous sentence in French for special emphasis, the ex-President reminded his audience that in a monarchy or dictatorship the quality of the ruler is all-important. In a republic, such as his and theirs, the quality of the individual citizen is the supreme issue. The virtues he wished to stress included "the will and the power to work, to fight at need, and to have plenty of healthy children." The greatest curse is the curse of sterility, he maintained; "and the severest of all condemnations should be that visited upon wilful sterility." In a less didactic vein, he paid tribute to the French tradition "that a high artistic and literary development is compatible with notable leadership in arms and statecraft." The length of this tradition in France was illustrated, he said, by the fact that the earliest epic in a modern tongue, *The Song of Roland,* celebrated the military achievements of Charlemagne. The conclusion of the address, noted Lawrence Abbott, was greeted with "a long-continued storm of applause."

"I find that Paris is still everywhere talking of Mr. Roosevelt," a friend wrote Abbott a fortnight later. It was amazing, he continued, that the *blasé* city had not only "kept up its interest in him without abatement for eight days; but that a week after his departure should still find him the main topic of conversation. . . ." The newspaper *Temps* printed 57,000 copies of the Sorbonne address and distributed them free to every schoolteacher in France.

4

The members of the Roosevelt party spent only twenty-four hours in Belgium, but they were cordially welcomed to Laeken Palace by King Albert and Queen Elizabeth. T.R. slipped off to see some things on his own in Brussels, but the king came upon him and insisted on driving him about in the royal carriage. Every evening, the queen told the Colonel, she read aloud to the king; it seemed that they led "a thoroughly wholesome life."

Because of his Dutch ancestry, Roosevelt had been especially looking forward to his visit to the Netherlands, and a large, friendly crowd greeted him when he changed cars at the frontier. That day, April 29, he was invited to lunch at Hetloo Palace by Queen Wilhelmina and her consort, Duke Henry. T.R. later described the queen as "excessively unattractive and commonplace, and obviously both conceited and bad-tempered." She reminded him of "a puffed-up wife of some leading grocer" in an American small town, the type of lady who was proud of her social position and insistent on taking precedence over other leading ladies of the ville. The duke, Wilhelmina's "fat, heavy, dull husband," led a dreadful life, Roosevelt discovered. As the party rose from the luncheon table, Wilhelmina commanded Henry to take Roosevelt into his own room. Not hearing her request, Henry turned questioningly toward the queen. To everyone's intense embarrassment, Wilhelmina lost her temper, grew réd in the face, and snapped out, "I said *take Mr. Roosevelt into your own room.*" T.R. tried to ignore the incident and asked Henry about his daughter, Juliana. "I hope she has a brother," Henry said frankly, "otherwise I pity the man that marries her!"

There were stops at Amsterdam, with a pilgrimage to see the Rembrandts at the Rijksmuseum, and at The Hague and Haarlem—all made more pleasant because the visit to Holland had been nicely timed to coincide with the national tulip festival. The Colonel charmed one group he met by reciting the words of a Dutch nursery rhyme that had been handed down in his family.

In Copenhagen, the next stop on the itinerary, the Roosevelts were asked to stay at the royal palace—to the consternation of the diplomatic corps, especially the Russian ambassador. "I understand Mr. Roosevelt is now nothing in his own country," the Russian complained to his American counterpart. "He is not even an Excellency; and yet he and his family are staying in the rooms the Czar occupied last Summer." Actually, Roosevelt was not sure he liked staying in palaces, agreeing with Lawrence Abbott that the royal residences were often deficient in modern plumbing—though ". . . you can't ring your bell and complain of your room!"

Since the Danish king was on holiday in southern Europe, the Roosevelts were to be entertained by Crown Prince Christian and his wife, Crown Princess Alexandra. The prince, "accompanied by a brilliant suite," drove to the station to meet the Roosevelt party. Said to be the tallest man in Europe, Christian stood at the center of a circle of attendants, court officials, and diplomats as the train pulled into the station. The dramatic effect, the American ambassador noted with satisfaction, was going to be worthy of the event. But somehow Roosevelt missed his cue and—wearing "an army coat and an ancient sombrero"— descended two cars away from the royal party. Christian stretched his long legs to run down the platform, and his attendants, unable to keep up, went helter skelter in confusion. Barely listening to the formal words of presentation, the Colonel said "Now I have lost my baggage. Let's go look for it." Due to some error, the trunks had not come on the same train and would not arrive until 7:30 P.M.

Later, at the palace, the prince came in person to tell Mrs. Roosevelt that "they had asked some people to dinner" at seven—it was really a formal court dinner—with a reception immediately afterwards. Rather than delay everyone, the guests of honor could come in their traveling clothes—if Edith Roosevelt did not mind. She did not, and went in to dinner on the arm of the prince "looking perfectly gracious and at ease" in her traveling suit. An admiring court lady told the American ambassador that "nobody but royalty could have made a situation of that kind go off so well."

The object of the swing north through the Low Countries to Scandinavia was to allow Roosevelt to deliver his formal address of acceptance for the 1906 Nobel Peace Prize at Christiania (Oslo). It was rumored that the Norwegians had been offended by his stated inability to come earlier and that, until he fulfilled the customary obligation, no other American would be considered for the honor. The obligation proved to be a disguised delight, for the Roosevelts fell in love with the Norwegian royal family—King Haakon, Queen Maud, and seven-year-old Crown Prince Olaf—who were their hosts, again at the royal palace.

Following the reception at the Christiania station, a parade through the city, and luncheon at the American legation, T.R. retired to a private suite at the palace to catch up on his correspondence. Suddenly the king wandered in with some questions about the schedule—and then asked if the Colonel would not like some tea. "By George, your Majesty, the very thing I should like!" he replied and over tea the two got acquainted. Kermit and Ethel were enlisted in Olaf's boyish games, and before long T.R. succumbed and romped with the prince, "as I used to romp with my own children when they were small." If Norway ever became a republic, he wrote to a friend, he and Edith hoped that the Norwegian royal family would come to live near them at Sagamore Hill; he would be delighted to have the exiles as neighbors.

Haakon and Maud commiserated with the Roosevelts over their approaching stop at Berlin, for they recalled their own recent visit to the Kaiser with "lively horror." They had felt "drilled" by Wilhelm and were almost afraid of the servants. The Colonel reassured them that— since he had already taught the Kaiser etiquette in the matter of Mrs. Roosevelt's invitation to stay at the palace—he was not concerned about being intimidated.

The Nobel address, prepared while he was still in Africa and delivered on May 5, was curiously—but not surprisingly considering Roosevelt's views—bellicose at the outset. Peace he described as only generally good in itself; "it is never the highest good unless it comes as the handmaid of righteousness; and it becomes a very evil thing if it serves merely as a mask for cowardice and sloth, or as an instrument to further the ends of despotism or anarchy." The bully, the brawler, the oppressor is to be despised and abhorred, he stated, but no more than the coward or the voluptuary. "No man is worth calling a man who will not fight rather than submit to infamy. . . . No nation deserves to exist if it permits itself to lose the stern and virile virtues. . . ."

Having defined peace as something far more positive than the absence of war, he went on to give prescriptions for achieving it: arbitration treaties, until further advance had been made in the matter of an international police force; development of The Hague Tribunal, or a world court; limitation of armaments, especially naval armaments, by international agreement. And finally he called for a League of Peace, a combination of the Great Powers not only to keep peace among themselves but also to prevent—by force, if necessary—peace being broken by others.

Roosevelt delivered his Nobel speech despite the onset of an attack of bronchitis. The Colonel always taxed his high, thin voice to the utmost and was frequently troubled with throat ailments that occasionally caused him to lose his voice altogether. On the rest of the trip he would require "a good deal of doctoring"; but he managed to keep every engagement, though there were some bad times for him ahead.

It was not the Colonel's voice that curtailed his activities in Sweden and Germany, however, but news that greeted him upon his arrival in Stockholm on May 7 of the death of King Edward VII of England. The eldest son of the prolific Victoria, Edward was related by blood or marriage to virtually every royal house in Europe—both Kaiser Wilhelm and Czar Nicholas were his nephews. All Europe was plunged into mourning, some of the events scheduled for the Colonel's two days in Sweden had to be cancelled, and T.R. saw a way out of the invitation to stay at the palace in Berlin. In view of Edward's death, he wired Wilhelm, it might be better for the Roosevelt party to stay at the American embassy during the stop in Germany—and the Kaiser agreed.

Because he was in mourning, the Kaiser could not come to the station in Berlin on the morning of May 10 and his official representative arrived too late to greet the Roosevelt party. The Colonel, of course, did not mind the lack of another lavish reception ceremony and went in a private automobile to the embassy. But all morning, O'Laughlin wrote, "German officialdom seemed to tumble all over itself" in an effort to make up for the mistake. At noon the Roosevelts, accompanied by the chancellor and the foreign secretary, took a special train out to the New Palace at Potsdam. Resplendent in the white uniform of a general and wearing a glittering brass helmet surmounted by a silver eagle, the Kaiser met Roosevelt on the steps of the palace.

After lunch, the party withdrew to a reception room known as the *Muschelsaal* for the iridescent mussel shells stuck in the plaster by an artist at the time of Frederick the Great—a "typically Prussian notion of aesthetics," noted Lawrence Abbott with scorn. T.R. and Wilhelm withdrew to one corner of the gaudy room for a lively chat, while the rest of the party tried to look busy at the other end. After some time, Lawrence noticed the official in charge of the affair nervously consulting his watch; he then went to the chancellor, and the two went to the minister of the interior. All three officials approached the empress. The agitation now seemed so heightened and generalized that Abbott asked a military aide what was wrong. It seemed that the special train back to Berlin was scheduled to leave at four; if it did not leave on time, all the trains on that line would be thrown off schedule. Yet no one dared to interrupt the Kaiser's private conversation with Roosevelt. Finally Wilhelm himself noted the time, good-byes were quickly spoken, and the party was rushed to the station "piling into the vehicles with very little attention to the precedence which had been scrupulously observed" en route to Potsdam that morning.

Theodore Roosevelt and Kaiser Wilhelm had often been compared with one another. A *Punch* cartoon of 1905—banned in Germany —had depicted T.R. with his moustache greased and twirled upwards in imitation of Wilhelm's, glaring at his Prussian look-alike. Although the Colonel spoke German, they probably conversed in English which was the Kaiser's second language. In several long talks during Roosevelt's five days in Berlin, the two discussed any number of topics. The former President had an answer even when Wilhelm asked frankly how he was regarded in America. "Well! your Majesty, I don't know whether you will understand our political terminology," T.R. quickly responded, "but in America we think that if you lived on our side of the water you would carry your ward and turn up at the convention with your delegation behind you—and I cannot say as much for most of your fellow sovereigns!" The Kaiser seemed immensely pleased at the analogy and soon the two learned that they had at least one thing really in common: "a cordial dislike of shams and of pretense." In this category they both put Andrew Carnegie's crusade in behalf of international peace.

Cashing in on the goodwill engendered by his financing of the scientific part of the African safari, Carnegie had been after the Colonel to speak to the Kaiser about arbitration and disarmament. Stories that the former President would be lecturing Wilhelm on these subjects appeared in the press, and the German Foreign Office, through an Austrian intermediary, got in touch with T.R. while he was still in Vienna. What was Roosevelt going to talk to Wilhelm about? The Colonel replied that he had no special intention to bring up the subjects of arbitration or disarmament but would not steer clear of them if they came up in normal conversation. Through an official leak, the Berlin papers then carried an announcement that Roosevelt would be speaking to the Kaiser about universal peace and commented that this would be a breach of etiquette.

The Colonel was almost grateful; whether or not he spoke to the Kaiser on such incendiary topics, he could always tell Carnegie that it had not been possible. And no one could blame him, if nothing came of any efforts to convert Wilhelm from his devotion to militarism.

Rather than argue the merits of arbitration and disarmament with his new friend, the Colonel of the Rough Riders, the Kaiser invited him to attend a sham battle on May 11, the first civilian to be invited along on field maneuvers of the German army. Kermit and Henry White, who had showed up from Vienna, were included in the invitation. Wilhelm was in another gaudy uniform; T.R. wore a riding suit and the famous black slouch hat. The Kaiser kept Roosevelt at his side the entire afternoon and the next day sent him a number of photographs taken of the two on horseback. The candid shots were quite unexceptional but the penciled remarks of the Kaiser on the back were not. "When we shake hands, we shake the world," read one inscription. On another the sham battle was described as something to take care of that old "peace bore" Andrew Carnegie. Hearing of the Kaiser's indiscretion, the foreign office tried to get the photographs back, saying they would be suitably framed. Roosevelt declined to return them, explaining that he would have them mounted himself—which he did, with double glass so that the inscriptions could also be read.

The address at the University of Berlin, on the day following the sham battle, was more of a medical than a forensic triumph for Roosevelt, for the doctors had warned him against speaking for any length of time and a reader stood by in case his voice failed. The Kaiser was in the audience, German academics lined the speaker's platform, and a chorus of students sang a medley of songs including "Hail, Columbia" and "The Star-Spangled Banner." But even the devoted Lawrence Abbott found the speech, entitled "The World Movement," uninteresting.

The Colonel opened with a tribute to German culture, including a reference to Charlemagne who now, as Karl der Grose, was a part of the Teutonic tradition. Finally, after a nearly interminable review of world history, the Colonel in his peroration called attention to the movement toward world civilization "throbbing in every corner of the globe," a movement that would "bind the nations of the world together while yet leaving unimpaired that love of country in the individual citizen which in the present stage of the world's progress is essential to the world's well-being." None of his auditors could have taken exception to such a platitude, and the speech was officially announced as another success for the touring statesman.

Roosevelt did not really enjoy his visit to Germany. In Sweden tens of thousands had gathered at every place he passed through; in Germany he found only a few hundred at each stop, and those were "courteous, decorously enthusiastic, and that was all." Everywhere in the Kaiser's realm, he was treated "with proper civility, all the civility which I had a right to demand and expect; and no more." Passing back into Holland again, he found another "wildly enthusiastic mob" of perhaps ten thousand at the first stop. The Roosevelt magic had not evaporated; it was merely Prussian discipline and self-control—or perhaps, T.R. wrote, the "Germans did not like me, and did not like my country."

5

In Berlin the Colonel had received a cable from President Taft asking him to serve as the special ambassador of the United States at the funeral of Edward VII, and thus when T.R. arrived in London on May 16 he was greeted for the first time on the tour as an official representative of his country. "The President has named Mr. Roosevelt to represent us at the King's funeral," Archie Butt wrote his sister-in-law. "With him and the Kaiser present, it will be a wonder if the poor corpse gets a passing thought."

The Roosevelts had planned to stay at the home of Arthur Lee, a friend of many years who was then a member of Parliament. Instead they were taken to Dorchester House, the official residence of American Ambassador Whitelaw Reid. The family circle was soon enlarged by the arrival of Alice Longworth, who brought all the latest political gossip from Washington and sat up half the first night talking to her father. To her, Roosevelt confessed his disappointment at the course taken by the Taft administration and said it would be impossible for him to speak in its behalf in the forthcoming congressional elections.

Another arrival from the United States was Elihu Root. Writing to the Colonel in February, 1910, Root had compared the two administrations as a change from an automobile to a cab. "Taft is big and good natured and easy going and lets things drift considerably. That is sometimes a good thing but not always. He is making a good President . . .

but he has not yet altogether arrived." The administration, Root continued, had not had a smooth path. "A good many of the so-called insurgents are talking Roosevelt against Taft and you will have to be pretty careful when you get here . . . not to say things that have meanings ascribed to them that you have never thought of. . . ."

"I really think you ought to try to see me for a moment while abroad," T.R. had said in replying to the New York senator on April 27. "People complain that I see Pinchot. . . . They also complain that I don't see men representing the other side." Root was bound for The Hague to argue a case before the international tribunal and stopped off in London at the end of May for a long talk with Roosevelt at Dorchester House. Visiting London a decade later, Root found himself passing the ambassadorial residence. "It is there I had an interesting interview with Roosevelt," he told a companion. "And if he had done as he promised me—kept out of things political—we would have been spared much of our past trouble." But at the time he knew better. Before leaving the United States, Root had been told by Lodge of T.R.'s promise to maintain silence on political affairs—and was asked if the pledge did not seem to indicate failing powers. "It seems almost to mark the approach of senility," Root observed.

A third—and happily nonpolitical—visitor to the English metropolis was Seth Bullock, the marshal of North Dakota and T.R.'s beloved friend from his ranching days. The ex-President had asked Bullock and his wife to meet him in London because, after all the encounters with royalty, he needed to see some of his own kind of people again. The marshal was so happy to see Roosevelt, he told Kermit, that he felt like hanging his hat on the dome of St. Paul's and shooting it off. The feigned fear of just such Rough Rider hijinks had been behind a recent *Punch* cartoon in which the lions at the base of the Nelson column in Trafalgar Square were shown guarded by policemen; a sign warned the returning big game hunter "These lions are not to be shot."

The funeral of Edward VII was the last tribal gathering of Europe's royalty before the thrones of so many of them were consumed in the holocaust of World War I. Among the seventy special ambassadors, only Roosevelt and the French foreign minister, Stephen Pichon, were not reigning sovereigns or princes of royal blood. But Dorchester House, nonetheless, became one of the most popular gathering spots in London and the Colonel one of the most sought-after celebrities in the city. Roosevelt was given a special state carriage and a guard of six grenadiers in towering bearskins, who formed up and saluted every time he left Dorchester House—entrances and exits that, to his amusement if not discomfort, were also marked by bugle blasts. In addition to the two aides assigned him by the British, he enlisted Henry White as an adviser on the intricate protocol involved in a royal funeral.

Roosevelt was received the very first day by the new king, George V, and Queen Mary. That same day the crown prince and crown princess of Denmark and King Haakon of Norway broke tradition by calling on their recent guest at Dorchester House. "Confound these kings," T.R. said to Lawrence Abbott, "will they never leave me alone." Next Roosevelt and White drove to Buckingham Palace, where the Kaiser was staying, and were relieved to find Wilhelm out. As they were about to leave, however, the German emperor drove up, jumped out of his carriage, and said "It is a great piece of luck. I have an hour to spare, and we can have a good talk together." Roosevelt demurred, saying he had nothing like that much time on this busy morning. "How much time can you give me?" asked the Kaiser. Glancing at his watch, the Colonel replied, "I'll give you twenty minutes." And Wilhelm seemed grateful.

The evening preceding the funeral, all the ambassadors were invited to a formal dinner at Buckingham Palace, an event that emerges in T.R.'s later description as very much like an old-fashioned Irish wake. Each guest upon arrival said some word of "perfunctory condolence" to King George—"and then on with the revel!" There was not even a pretense of grief as the group sat down to dinner—the new king in the middle of the table on one side, the Kaiser opposite him, and all the rest seated with no apparent attention to rank. The Colonel found himself seated between Prince Henry of Prussia and a Hanoverian prince whose name he never caught.

Upon entering the room, Roosevelt had been greeted by Ferdinand I, self-proclaimed Czar of Bulgaria. But the imperious Wilhelm came over, stopped in front of Czar Ferdinand, and said pointedly: "Roosevelt, my friend, I want to introduce you to the King of Spain; *he* is worth talking to!" Roosevelt was surprised and delighted when Alphonso XIII remarked that he admired not only his public career but his military career, "though I am sorry that your honors should have been won at the expense of my countrymen." The former Colonel of the Rough Riders replied with a tribute to the valor of Spanish troops in the late war, adding only that they had been poorly led.

T.R. next encountered Duke Henry, the hapless prince consort of

Holland but again the Kaiser interrupted. Apparently no one regarded Henry as being of the slightest consequence and he "drifted off with fat meekness." The King of Denmark, "a nice old boy," greeted T.R. and then introduced his brother the King of Greece, "also a nice old boy, but a preposterous character as a king." At one point in the evening, Roosevelt was observed surrounded by a cordon of kings, talking loudly and striking a clenched fist against the palm of his other hand in a characteristically emphatic gesture. "Oh, I would never have taken that step at all if I had been in your place, your Majesty," he told one monarch, and to another he said: "That is just what I would have done; quite right."

As the only man in ordinary evening dress, Roosevelt stood among the magnificently costumed royalty as a penguin amidst an array of peacocks. Even Pichon was wearing clothes "stiff with gold lace" and all sorts of sashes and orders. As the representative of the other great republic, the Frenchman seized upon T.R. as a natural ally. Irritated by the consideration being shown in London to members of France's former royal family, Pichon took Roosevelt aside now and asked what color coat the coachman assigned him had worn en route to the dinner. His coachman, Pichon complained, had worn black; those of the royalty, red! Roosevelt said he thought his had worn black, too, but that it did not really matter to him. He would be perfectly content if the coachman wore a green coat with yellow splashes—"un paletot vert avec des taches jaunes," in his reckless French. Pichon took him seriously and T.R. spent the next quarter hour trying to convince the astonished Frenchman that it was a joke.

Promptly at eight the next morning, May 20, Roosevelt, again in evening dress, arrived back at Buckingham Palace for the funeral procession to Windsor. He and Pichon had been assigned to the same carriage, and now the Frenchman was complaining that theirs was an ordinary carriage whereas the royalty would have glass coaches. Never having heard of a glass coach, "excepting in connection with Cinderella," T.R. felt perfectly satisfied with their quite handsome vehicle and persuaded Pichon that they should get in nonetheless. Next the French foreign minister hissed that "ces Chinois" were to precede them in the procession. T.R. responded that anyone as gorgeously attired as "ces Chinois" *should* go first, but Pichon was not amused. The final straw, as far as the volatile Frenchman was concerned, was the fact that a third party was to be put in the republican carriage—"ce Perse," a Persian prince Roosevelt described as "a deprecatory, inoffensive-looking Levantine."

Pichon fairly vaulted into the carriage now, slammed himself into the left rear seat, and flung his arm protectively over the right rear seat, indicating that Roosevelt and not "ce Perse" would have the place of honor. The unfortunate Persian prince meekly climbed in and sat opposite the two republican representatives, "looking about as unaggressive as a rabbit in a cage with two boa constrictors." Pichon continued to rail that "toutes ces petites royautes" even "le roi du Portugal" were preceding them, but Roosevelt—turning serious—admonished him not "to make a row at a funeral." The advice apparently had a "sedative effect" on the Frenchman. The funeral was held without a public explosion, and at the luncheon at Windsor Castle following the ceremonies, Roosevelt was seated at the king's table; Pichon, at the queen's.

A final bizarre episode of the funerary festivities occurred four days later when the Roosevelts paid a courtesy call on Queen Mother Alexandra, Edward's widow. Mixed with Alexandra's grief was her reluctance to vacate Buckingham Palace for the new king, her son, and her almost morbid delight in how well preserved Edward's body had been right up to the time of burial. Alexandra's sister the Dowager Empress of Russia was on hand, and the two old ladies asked Edith Roosevelt if they could kiss her at parting. Being half of New England blood, T.R. noted, Edith was "not of an expansive temperament, and endured rather than enjoyed the ceremony." As he was breaking off the interview with the royal ladies, the Colonel heard the unmistakable sound of a child's voice out in the corridor. It proved to be Norway's Crown Prince Olaf, who had heard that his great friend Roosevelt was in the palace and was waiting for the sort of romp he had so enjoyed in Christiania. T.R. obliged the boy by tossing him in the air and rolling him on the floor. Olaf's laughter penetrated the walls, and the dowager empress opened the door again to see what might be going on, and Roosevelt momentarily paused. "But aren't you going on with the play?" pleaded Olaf.

The funeral over, the Roosevelts tried to get in a little sightseeing and one day visited the National Gallery. Within an hour reporters had caught up with them and one described T.R. gazing at Frith's "Derby Day" and sighing "Ah! Tempora mutantur!" *Punch* tried to make something of the event, and its editor wired Roosevelt if the quotation was correct. Not imagining the man to be serious, the ex-President replied: "Statement incorrect. In commenting on pictures I never use any language as modern as Latin. On the occasion in question my quotations were from cuneiform script, and the particular sentence referred to was the pre-Ninevite phrase 'hully gee.' " Puzzled, the editor acknowledged receipt of the disclaimer and let the matter drop.

The Colonel had a more satisfactory encounter with British humor when he appeared at Cambridge on May 26. Not to be outdone by Oxford, the younger university had awarded T.R. an honorary LL.D. and invited him to speak at Cambridge Union, the famous student debating society. The students had formed up in two long ranks for the arrival of the distinguished American, leaving a pathway down which the Colonel was to pass. At a turn in the path, Roosevelt found a stuffed teddy bear seated on the pavement, a paw stretched out in greeting. And at the moment the degree was actually bestowed in the chapel, another teddy bear was lowered on a pulley arrangement. Roosevelt was delighted; on a similar occasion, he was told, Charles Darwin had had a monkey dropped on him.

The student newspaper had greeted Roosevelt's arrival at Cambridge with a verse:

> Oh, we're ready for you, Teddy, our sins are all re-
> viewed;
> We've put away our novels and our statues in the
> nude;
> We've read your precious homilies and hope to hear
> some more
> At the coming visitation of the moral Theodore.
> No, seriously, Teddy (we're proud to have you here);
> Your speeches may be out of date, your methods may
> be queer,
> But you've done some pretty decent things without
> delay or fuss,
> And you're full of grit inside you—and that's what
> appeals to us.
> So we're ready for you, Teddy, but take my good ad-
> vice:
> Though sin is really naughty we find it rather nice;
> So when you come to speak to us, in Providence's
> name,
> Give the go-by to the Sunday chapel missionary
> game.

Holding up the paper as he rose to address the Cambridge Union, Roosevelt said—to general student laughter—that he would try to preach as little as possible, "but you must take your chance, for it is impossible to break the bad habit of a lifetime at the bidding of a comparative stranger." T.R.'s sermon was entitled "The Conditions of Success," its message was that the degree of success did not matter but rather how a person carried himself in any position; and at the conclusion the Colonel told the students he was glad he had violated the poet's plea not to preach.

Roosevelt was slated to give the second major address of his nearly month-long stay in England five days later, on May 31. The setting was London's historic Guildhall, which boasted one of Europe's finest Gothic interiors, and the occasion was the bestowal upon the former President of the freedom of the City of London. The Lord Mayor of London presided over a brilliant gathering of England's political and social leaders. Ushers in medieval costume and bearing maces conducted the distinguished visitors one by one through the hall and to the dais to be presented. The diverse assembly included the Bishop of London, the painter John Singer Sargent, and Roosevelt's newfound friend, Foreign Secretary Sir Edward Grey. An elaborate scroll, granting Roosevelt the freedom of the city, was presented in "a suitable gold box" that turned out to be a baroque creation decorated with American and British flags and flanked by a miniature lion and bison.

Roosevelt had been thinking about this speech while he was still in Africa, and he had discussed it with Grey and other members of the British government. The subject was British rule in Africa, which he had closely observed in East Africa, Uganda, the Sudan, and Egypt. In the first three protectorates he had found nothing to criticize and much to praise, but he had a stern message concerning Egypt. "Now, either you have the right to be in Egypt or you have not; either it is or is not your duty to establish and keep order," he told the Guildhall audience. If the British had any feeling that they should not be there, "why, then, by all means get out of Egypt." If, as he sincerely believed, England should be in Egypt, then it had an obligation to maintain order and prevent such regrettable incidents as the assassination of Butros Ghali. Little Englanders, who were then already questioning Britain's self-appointed role as colonial governor and civilizing agent of so much of the world were offended by Roosevelt's frankness. But staunch colonialists were delighted. One old man of eighty-four sent a message of congratulation addressed simply to "His Excellency 'Govern-or-go' Roosevelt." The London *Spectator* described the Colonel's speech as the chief event of the week, claimed that only "timid, fussy, and pedantic people" objected to it, and thanked him for reminding England of her duty.

In those late May and early June days, the Roosevelts were in and

out of London, staying mostly with Arthur Lee at his house in London
or at his country home, Chequers Court. They met many old friends and
were introduced to any number of notables, mostly at small, relatively
informal gatherings. There was even time for such sightseeing as a visit
to Stratford-on-Avon. And finally, on June 7, came the day of the Romanes Lecture at Oxford, the appearance that was the original reason
for stopping in Europe en route back home from Africa and that was
now to be the culminating event of the entire triumphal progress.

The Oxford ceremony awarding Roosevelt a D.C.L. was conducted
in Latin—though happily programs giving an English translation
were provided for all the guests. Lord Curzon, Chancellor of Oxford,
opened the conclave with a request that the "Reverend Doctors" and the
"Masters of the University" signal their assent to the granting of the degree. Ascertaining their approval, he called out "Ite, Bedelli! Petite
Virum Honorabilem!" ("Go, Beadles, and bring in the honorable gentlemen!"). As Roosevelt was ushered in, Curzon attempted to mix solem-
nity with levity in a Latin exclamation that has been translated as:

> Behold, Vice-Chancellor, the promised wight,
> Before whose coming comets turned to flight,
> And all the startled mouths of sevenfold Nile took
>   fright.

In his presentation speech, the vice-chancellor recounted that Roosevelt
twice had been elevated to the Presidency. "May we not presage that
still a third time—most auspicious of numbers—he may be called
upon to take the reins of government?" Referring to the safari, the
speaker noted that the Colonel's "onslaughts on the wild beasts of the
desert have been not less fierce nor less successful than over the many-
headed hydra of corruption in his own land." Now, like another Ulysses,
he was returning home, "after visiting many cities and discoursing on
many themes." And it was Oxford's pleasure to listen to the final such
discourse.

Curzon responded to the vice-chancellor's introduction with another reference to a third term, calling Roosevelt the "most strenuous of
men, most distinguished of citizens to-day playing a part on the stage of
the world . . . peer of the most august Kings, queller of men, destroyer
of monsters wherever found, yet the most human of mankind. . . ." "Ite,
Bedelli! Ducite Doctorem Honorabilem ad Pulpitum!" ("Go, Beadles,
conduct the Honorable Doctor to the Lectern,") he concluded.

Roosevelt's Romanes Lecture was the longest and the most ambitious of his European addresses. He took as his subject "Biological Analogies in History" and attempted to demonstrate that there was a parallelism—however inexact—between the birth, growth, and death of species in the animal world, and the birth, growth, and death of societies in the history of mankind. He showed that just as some species became extinct, leaving no true descendants, so certain civilizations of the past, like those of Mesopotamia, vanished with no one to inherit or pass on their greatness. On the other hand, other civilizations, most notably that of Rome, lived on in the various nations that had sprung from their crumbling empires. The lesson for the present was clear: which was the civilization of Great Britain and the United States to be?

Rome fell to attack from without, Roosevelt pointed out, only because of the incurable ills within; "while we should be vigilant against foes from without, yet we need never really fear them so long as we safeguard ourselves against the enemies within our own households; and these enemies are our own passions and follies." Once more T.R. had an opportunity to preach the "homely commonplace virtues"; "it needs but little of the vision of a seer to foretell what must happen in any community if the average woman ceases to become the mother of a family of healthy children, if the average man loses the will and the power to work up to old age and to fight whenever the need arises." It was his fervent hope, that "our children and children's children to endless generations" should continue to play a dominant part in the world. "But whether this be denied or granted by the years we shall not see, let at least the satisfaction be ours that we have carried onward the lighted torch in our own day and generation," he concluded. "If we do this, then, as our eyes close, and we go out into the darkness, and others' hands grasp the torch, at least we can say that our part has been borne well and valiantly."

The address, although politely received, was not judged to be an important scientific or historical statement. For scholars, it was too obviously the generalization of a widely cultivated if not deeply reflective or innovative mind. "In the way of grading which we have at Oxford," said the Archbishop of York, "we agreed to mark the lecture 'Beta Minus,' but the lecturer 'Alpha Plus.' While we felt that the lecture was not a very great contribution to science, we were sure that the lecturer was a very great man." Another Oxonian observed that the biological analogies in history, as propounded by Roosevelt, were three in number: "Longitude, Latitude, and Platitude."

Two days after delivering the lecture, Roosevelt was enjoying what was only the second interlude of privacy and pure enjoyment on the European tour—the first having been the aborted carriage ride with Edith in Italy. The last twenty-four hours T.R. spent in England were in the company of Sir Edward Grey, tramping in the valley of the Itchen and through the New Forest, the English bird lover instructing and comparing information with the American one. On June 10 the Roosevelts boarded a German liner at Southampton for the eight-day voyage to New York. Bidding good-bye to Europe, to one of the most exciting and varied periods of his life, and to an entire phase of his career, the hunter and wildly acclaimed world statesman turned his face toward home and an uncertain but challenging and possibly provocative future.

Theodore Roosevelt
with the man he chose
as his successor,
William Howard Taft
(Theodore Roosevelt Birthplace)

The family at the White House
(from left): Ethel, Kermit, Quentin, Edith, Ted, Theodore, Archie,
Alice and Nicholas Longworth
(Theodore Roosevelt Birthplace)

On safari in Africa: T.R. with a fallen rhino

The big-game hunters: Kermit (second from left) and T.R. (center), with a guide and Smithsonian scientists

The Colonel of the Rough Riders on maneuvers with the Kaiser, May, 1910

Roosevelt in Paris, April, 1910

The glorious welcome home in June, 1910: T.R. doffing his top hat at rear of upper deck; against the smoke stack at far right: F.D.R. in boater and Eleanor

Sagamore Hill from the west lawn; part of the railing has been removed to convert the piazza into a platform from which to address visiting delegations.

(Theodore Roosevelt Birthplace)

The large, comfortable, eclectic North Room at Sagamore Hill

Henry Cabot Lodge
(Brown Brothers)

T.R. with Edith
during the 1912 campaign

Robert M. La Follette
(Brown Brothers)

Friends and Enemies:

Elihu Root
(Culver Picture)

The ex-President about to go up with Arch Hoxsey outside St. Louis in October, 1910

(Theodore Roosevelt Birthplace)

Hiram Johnson

(Brown Brothers)

The Bull Moose campaigning in New Jersey, 1912

Another inauguration: Taft with his successor,
Woodrow Wilson, in March, 1913

≈§ Chapter 9 §≈

Return of the Hunter

Shortly after seven on the morning of June 18, 1910, the huge hull of the *Kaiserin Auguste Victoria* emerged from the mist at the lower end of Ambrose Channel leading into New York harbor. The German passenger liner moved smoothly along at eighteen knots an hour, followed by an escort consisting of the battleship *South Carolina* and five torpedo destroyers. Passengers lined the rails of the four upper decks, waving and shouting as the Hamburg line tug came alongside, carrying that day an unusual complement of anxious newspaper reporters. Quickly the newsmen found the object of their morning excursion: in a large port of the upper promenade, flashing his famous smile and waving his tall silk hat, stood Theodore Roosevelt. The hunter was home, and sailing into the most glorious and ecstatic welcome New York had ever extended to a native son.

The reporters' shouts of recognition were cut short by three long blasts of the tug's whistle, and these touched off a cacophony of horns and whistles from the scores of river and harbor craft thronging the channel from shore to shore. The liner and her escort steamed majestically on to the quarantine station off Fort Wadsworth, where the flotilla was greeted with a twenty-one-gun presidential salute. Proudly standing by on board as the Colonel took the salute were his wife, Edith, his two daughters, Alice Longworth and Ethel, and his son and hunting companion, Kermit. At 7:55 the *Kaiserin* dropped anchor and was promptly boarded by the port's health officer. Behind him came Senator Lodge, Nicholas Longworth, and—representing President Taft as he had at T.R.'s departure fifteen months earlier—Captain Archie Butt. Roosevelt, now stationed on the upper bridge, watched the escorting vessels pass in review to the starboard side of the liner. As eight bells struck, bugles were sounded on the warships, bands on two of them launched into "The Star-Spangled Banner," and flags were broken out from stem to stern.

A few minutes later the revenue cutter *Manhattan* pulled up to the *Kaiserin,* a port on the liner's main deck opened, and out was pushed a resplendent new gangplank with crimson carpet and white manropes. First up the gangplank from the cutter was William Loeb, T.R.'s former secretary and now Collector of the Port of New York. Roosevelt greeted the new set of welcomers and then, preceded by his wife, left the *Kaiserin* for the *Manhattan.* On board the cutter the couple found their three sons who had been left at home, Ted, Archie, and Quentin. "Think; for the first time in nearly two years I have them all within reach," exclaimed Edith Roosevelt. They also found waiting for them T.R.'s two sisters and their husbands, Admiral and Mrs. William S. Cowles and Mr. and Mrs. Douglas Robinson; and sundry other friends and relatives including the ex-President's niece Eleanor and her young husband, Franklin D. Roosevelt.

A breakfast had been planned aboard the cutter, but there were too many hands to be shaken and too many pictures to pose for—and luckily the Roosevelts had already eaten aboard the *Kaiserin.* The *Manhattan* cast off from the liner and moved into the harbor where it was met by the *Androscoggin,* a steamer bearing the official reception committee. The *South Carolina* fired a final salute of twenty-one guns, and the Colonel transferred once more, this time to the reception vessel.

As chairman of the welcoming committee, Cornelius Vanderbilt pinned a medal on T.R.'s chest and took him to the line of two hundred official greeters waiting to shake hands. "I'm *so* glad to see you!" he told each man in turn, the "so's" sounding to a reporter like a string of exploding firecrackers. "All Jersey's for you," volunteered the Governor of New Jersey. "Oh, who could talk politics on a day like this?" retorted the Colonel with good-natured exasperation. Spying his old friend from police commission days Jacob Riis, Roosevelt called down the line: "Oh, Jake! A am glad to see you. I've got *more* things to tell you." Lyman Abbott suggested that the reception was bound to increase circulation of *The Outlook,* which now boasted the former President as its contributing editor. "Oh, who could bother with circulation on such a day as this?" T.R. laughed. "First thing I know he'll want me to edit a special pink sporting supplement."

Finally Vanderbilt broke off the handshaking and took the Colonel to the bridge for the start of a naval parade, but T.R. slipped away to return to the deck and shake hands with members of the Seventh Regiment Band, which responded by launching into a chorus of "Home, Sweet Home." Trailed by smaller craft, the *Androscoggin* steamed up the Hudson River, hugging close to the New Jersey shore, then turned at a point near Fifty-ninth Street, and followed the Manhattan shore back to the Battery. Promptly at eleven, Roosevelt crossed a gangplank to set foot once more, after his long absence, on American soil. The "return from Elba," noted *The New York Times,* was taking place on the ninety-fifth anniversary of the battle of Waterloo.

Mrs. Roosevelt and the children had been taken directly from the *Manhattan* to the Battery and were now waiting for the Colonel on a specially erected speakers' stand. Since early morning people had been flocking to Battery Park to await the formal reception ceremony, and a crowd of 100,000 completely filled the space. Seventy-five known pickpockets had previously been rounded up by the New York police, for it was feared that this would also be a grand day for thieves.

The welcoming ceremonies had been scheduled to last an hour, but they were over in just ten minutes. New York's Mayor William Gaynor gave a welcoming speech of only a few sentences, and T.R.'s reply was equally brief. Reporters found particular significance, however, in a sentence in which he said that he was "ready and eager to do my part" in solving the problems of the country.

Shortly after eleven Roosevelt got in the first of fourteen carriages that were to carry the reception committee up Broadway and Fifth Avenue to Fifty-ninth Street. The Rough Riders were forming up for the parade and T.R. greeted them with a shout, "I certainly love my boys." The police commissioner cruised ahead in an automobile to clear a path and check on his patrolmen, stationed at ten-foot intervals the entire length of the march. Next came the mounted police, a police band, the Rough Riders, and then the Colonel's carriage. For most of the route, T.R. stood up in the seat smiling and waving his silk hat. In an age when the six-day work week was still standard, the sidewalks and windows of the skyscrapers on Lower Broadway that Saturday morning were filled with office workers. At Fourth Street the parade turned west to Washington Square and passing under the arch there entered Fifth Avenue. Vanderbilt, sitting opposite the Colonel, read from a list of delegations posted en route up the avenue—and Roosevelt could thus greet in turn the members of Republican clubs from as far away as Pittsburgh and Chicago, veterans' organizations, and societies representing various ethnic groups.

There were further dense crowds at Madison Square, and at Thirty-eighth Street the carriage passed the house where Edith Roosevelt and the children were waiting for the private luncheon party that would follow the parade. Several people en route broke through the police cordon to shake hands with T.R., a woman tossed him a flower from a tall building, and at one point a man stood chanting into a megaphone, "Our next President." The crowds lining the route were later estimated at one million. The Colonel, claimed the *Times,* "should have been surfeited with adulation if ever man was."

The parade broke up at the Fifty-ninth Street plaza with a final brief ceremony at 1 P.M. Perspiration beaded the Colonel's face after the long ride in the sun, but he went over to say good-bye to the Rough Riders and other veterans of the Spanish-American War. Five thousand of the marchers went off to the Twelfth Regiment Armory for a typical army meal of pork and beans, hardtack, stewed beef, pickles and coffee, served on tin plates and cups, as T.R. joined his family for the private luncheon at the Fifth Avenue home belonging to the grandfather of Eleanor Alexander, Theodore Roosevelt, Jr.'s fiancée. "Oh, Pop, look at your hat!" called out Alice from a window as he pulled up to the house. From being held and waved the entire morning, across the harbor and up Fifth Avenue, the hat had become limp and twisted. The Colonel laughed and entered the house.

Shortly after three the sunny skies over New York grew so dark that office lights had to be turned on, the temperature dropped twenty degrees, from 82 to 62, a breeze of 10 miles an hour turned into a gale of 60, and in a violent rain storm lasting only five minutes thirteen people in the metropolitan area lost their lives. By four the storm was all over.

Meanwhile the Roosevelt party, in several closed automobiles, drove through the rain to the Thirty-fourth Street ferry, crossed the East River to Long Island City, and boarded a special train for Oyster Bay. En route additional crowds, having braved the rain, stood watching the train pass, and at one point it had to jerk to a sudden stop to avoid hitting on-lookers who had pushed on to the tracks. The twenty-five-mile journey took an hour and a half. Triumphal arches had been erected along the main street of Oyster Bay and all the public buildings and stores were gaily festooned. Cheers, firecrackers, and a children's choir of five hundred voices greeted T.R.'s emergence from the train. Showing no fatigue from the long day, Roosevelt responded graciously to a welcoming speech and then got in a carriage for the short drive to Sagamore Hill.

"I have nothing to say," he said to reporters pressing him for his views on politics. "There is nothing I can say. There is one thing I want, and that is absolute privacy. I want to close up like a native oyster."

Sunday morning the family drove back in to Oyster Bay to attend church services—an occasion marked by two innovations: the Roosevelts traveled by automobile instead of carriage, and twelve-year-old Quentin wore his first pair of long trousers. Senator Lodge and the Longworths had spent the night, and Secretary of the Navy George von Lengerke Meyer appeared at midday. The Colonel took his exercise after breakfast by marching up and down the veranda telling hunting tales to Lodge and Nicholas Longworth, who seemed hard-pressed to keep up with him and avoid running into chairs. Reporters showed up in the afternoon and, though he allowed them to sit and chat on the porch, the Colonel refused to grant an interview for publication.

The Roosevelts returned to Manhattan on Monday, to attend the wedding of Theodore, Jr., to Miss Alexander. Curious crowds had gathered outside the Fifth Avenue Presbyterian Church at Fifty-fifth Street to await the arrival of social and political figures, and a cheer broke out as the Colonel himself appeared. At the last moment he had impulsively invited the Rough Riders, in town for the welcoming ceremonies of the previous day, and as many as possible were squeezed into the church for the ceremony.

Earlier in the day T.R. had turned up at the offices of *The Outlook* to catch up on his correspondence. Later he walked unnoticed across Twenty-second Street to *Scribner's,* to discuss publication of *African Game Trails.* Emerging from *Scribner's,* however, he was recognized by people on the street. From then until he reached the safety of *The Outlook* again, reported the *Times,* "it was a go-as-you-please foot race with a surging, perspiring crowd in which the strenuous ex-President won and left his admirers panting outside the doors."

To his sister Mrs. Robinson, Roosevelt later confessed that he found the incident most unpleasant. Unlike the friendly enthusiasm of Saturday's reception, he said, this gathering "represented a certain hysterical quality. . . . *That type* of crowd, feeling *that* kind of way," he concluded, "means that within a very short time they will be throwing eggs at me." Peary's feat of reaching the North Pole the preceding year was still being widely discussed, and to another friend T.R. now said that he—like the celebrated explorer—had no place to travel but south.

2

At its dinner in February, 1910, Washington's Gridiron Club had staged a "Back from Elba" skit. Wearing long military cloaks and Napoleon hats decorated with the monogram T.R., members came trouping in to the song:

> *When Teddy comes marching home again,*
> *Hurrah! Hurrah!*
> *We'll give him a hearty welcome then,*
> *Hurrah! Hurrah!*
> *The club will cheer, the boys will shout,*
> *The malefactors will all go out,*
> *And we'll get jobs when Teddy comes marching home.*

Talk of a third term for the Colonel—constant in some quarters since the designation of Taft as his successor in 1908—had tended to rise as the reputation of the new President fell. When she left for Africa to meet her husband, Edith Roosevelt bore messages from well-meaning friends that T.R. should avoid the brewing dispute between Republican regulars and insurgents by staying out of the country for another year or so. "Why not for life?" Henry Adams wrote a friend abroad. "The ostrich business won't work forever even among the Hottentots."

Arriving at Gondokoro on the White Nile in mid-February, T.R. was handed a letter from Lodge. "I think it is of the first importance that you should say absolutely nothing about American politics before you get home," the Massachusetts senator advised his friend. "You cannot form any accurate judgment until you do get home, for the simple reason that you have been away so long that there is a mass of facts which you cannot master until you are on the ground and can review the whole situation here." There was "a constantly growing thought" of Roosevelt's return to the Presidency, Lodge added, but it was mainly by men who were making use of the famous name against the Taft administration for their own purposes. The Colonel readily agreed to maintain silence on domestic politics; as for a return to the Presidency, it did not seem wise—"from any side"—to be a candidate again. "I have had the crown, I have had everything possible, and there is nothing left for me to grasp at. . . ." Yet, he concluded, "I shall neither seek nor shirk any responsibility."

The exchanges between Roosevelt and Lodge continued as T.R. proceeded through Europe. From Porto Maurizio, Italy, on April 11— the day he conferred with Gifford Pinchot—the Colonel wrote of his growing disenchantment with Taft. "The qualities shown by a thoroughly able and trustworthy lieutenant are totally different, or at least may be totally different from those needed by the leader, the commander." He could not help feeling that the administration, while adhering to the objects of his own policies, had pursued its goals in a spirit and with methods that "rendered the effort almost nugatory." Roosevelt still hoped that Taft would "retrieve" himself; yet, even if the condition of the Republican party proved hopeless, "I most emphatically desire that I shall not be put in the position of having to run for the Presidency, staggering under a load which I cannot carry, and which has been put on my shoulders through no fault of my own." When he returned, T.R. promised his friend, he would speak as little as possible— and even then he would have to exercise extreme care "to avoid saying things which, no matter how impersonal and general I keep them, shall seem to stand in contrast with what has been done in the past year."

By this time even Lodge could see that the G.O.P. was about to founder on the issue of the tariff and the other apparent failures of the Taft administration. He was now most anxious that T.R. "should so steer your course that no human being could say that you allowed Taft and the Party to go to defeat in 1910 in order to clear the way for you in 1912." The Colonel, replying from Christiania, Norway, on May 5, agreed that the outlook was black. For a year after Taft had taken office, T.R. now confessed, he would not let himself think ill of his successor. Finally, he had to admit not only that Taft had gone wrong on certain points but that "deep down underneath I had all along known he was wrong, on points as to which I had tried to deceive myself, by loudly proclaiming to myself that he was right." Once again he promised public silence on politics, this time specifically for two months after reaching the United States. "Ugh! I do dread getting back to America, and having to plunge into this cauldron of politics."

President Taft was looking very poorly, Archie Butt told his sister-in-law in the spring of 1910. He was tying himself to his desk and had a difficult summer ahead of him. "It is hard on any man to see the eyes of everyone turn to another person as the eyes of the entire country are turning to Roosevelt." Yet the President never said anything except in praise of his predecessor. "I never once heard him murmur against the fate which keeps him almost in a secondary place in the public eye." For a time the President had considered going to New York himself, to extend his greetings to the returning hunter in person. But William Loeb argued against it, saying that "it will be a T.R. day and there will be no other note sounded."

Late in May Taft wrote out in longhand what his biographer Henry F. Pringle has called "the most poignant letter, perhaps, among all the untold millions that presidents of the United States—so often bothered and troubled men—have written." He had not written to Roosevelt since his departure in March, 1909, Taft explained, because he had not wished "to invite your judgment on matters at long range or to commit you in respect to issues that you ought perhaps only to reach a decision upon, after your return to the United States." But at last he felt that he could unburden himself. "It is now a year and three months since I assumed office and I have had a hard time. I do not know that I have had harder luck than other presidents but I do know that thus far I have succeeded far less than have others." He had conscientiously tried to carry out T.R.'s policies, the President claimed, but his method of doing so had not worked smoothly.

The Payne-Aldrich tariff, Taft argued, was "a good bill and a real downward revision." As for other matters, Congress was then debating railroad regulation, and Taft predicted that the administration bill would pass, as would a postal savings bank measure. He tried to find comfort in a new conservation measure, statehood for New Mexico and Arizona, and a bill offering protection to railroad workers. But he could not long suppress his pessimism. The insurgents—La Follette, Cummins, Dolliver, Bristow, Clapp, Beveridge, Borah—had done their best to defeat his administration. "They have probably furnished ammunition enough to the press and the public to make a Democratic House. Whether they will bring on a Democratic administration in three years remains to be seen."

Finally the President included a note of personal despair. In mid-May, 1909—less than three months after her husband's inauguration —Nellie Taft had suffered a nervous collapse, with brief symptoms of paralysis, that had prevented her from fulfilling her duties as First Lady for an entire year. "Mrs. Taft is not an easy patient," the President confided, "and an attempt to control her only increased the nervous strain." Now, a year later, she could take part in receptions where she was required to speak only formula greetings. But dinners and other occasions where she might be called upon to converse more extensively were still ruled out. He did not admit it, but over the White House those months must have hovered the tragic shade of Ida McKinley.

Roosevelt received the President's letter in London, only two days before he was to sail for home, and his reply was brief but reassuring and courteous. His talk with Root, the Colonel reported, had been very satisfactory. "I am of course much concerned about some of the things I see and am told; but what I have felt it best to do was to say absolutely nothing—and indeed to keep my mind as open as I kept my mouth shut!" He realized that the sickness of the one Taft loved had added to his burden, but he and Edith felt genuine pleasure at learning how much better Mrs. Taft now was.

Two days before the arrival of the *Kaiserin Auguste Victoria* in New York, the President handed to Archie Butt the letter his aide was to deliver in person to the returning hunter. The letter beginning "My dear Theodore" had gone through several drafts, for Taft wanted it written in a manner that offered not the slightest suggestion of any rift in their former friendship—and yet he did not want to appear to be fawning or seeking favors from his predecessor. Most importantly, it included a cordial invitation to the Colonel and Mrs. Roosevelt to come to Washington and stay at the White House. Captain Butt thought that it should be accompanied by a personal note from the First Lady to *her* predecessor, and the President told him to return that evening for Mrs. Taft's letter. When he appeared at the White House after dinner, Butt found the Tafts chatting with their guests. "Nellie," the President said quietly, "will you go and do that for me, dear?" Mrs. Taft left the room without a word, went upstairs, and shortly returned with the note to Edith Roosevelt.

On June 20—two days after his arrival in New York and the very day of his son's wedding—Roosevelt acknowledged the President's invitation. It had touched him greatly, he wrote, and also what Mrs. Taft wrote to Mrs. Roosevelt. "But I don't think it well for an ex-President to go to the White House, or indeed to go to Washington, except when he cannot help it." Later he would have to go to the capital to look over the trophies of the safari but he thought it best to wait until "all of political Washington had left." He had been conferring with Nicholas Longworth and George Meyer and was pleased at their reports of progress with current legislation. He was especially glad to learn that Taft had insisted on adding two battleships to the fleet and had got them from Congress.

After his triumphal reception in New York, T.R. was indeed maintaining silence on political issues. But this did not mean he was isolating himself from politics. In addition to Longworth, Meyer, and Lodge—all of whom could be relied upon to give favorable reports of the administration—T.R.'s steady stream of visitors at Oyster Bay his first week back included Gifford Pinchot, James Garfield, and Robert M. La Follette—none of whom could be expected to say anything kind about his successor. Answering reporters' questions as he left Sagamore Hill, the Wisconsin senator expressed pleasure with his conference. The Colonel was "in fighting trim"; without doubt, he was the "greatest living American."

In addition to holding court at Sagamore Hill during these summer months of 1910, Roosevelt was making frequent trips into New York City, where he had taken up his duties as a contributing editor to *The Outlook*. Nominally he came to the *Outlook* offices on Fourth Avenue at Twenty-second Street to hold conferences with the other editors and to submit his signed editorials to the weekly publication. But the offices always seemed teeming with people anxious to see the ex-President and his diary recorded a steady stream of visitors there, too. In fact, he often found it difficult to extricate himself from unscheduled interviews and impromptu conferences at his New York office.

One visitor later recalled T.R. bursting out of his office, his arm linked to that of another man and engaged in an animated monologue. The Colonel steered the man to the exit and then returned to say that he had had to keep talking to prevent the other man from starting a discourse that it would be impossible to terminate. In such cases, men of quite disparate views often left Roosevelt's presence with the distinct impression that he agreed wholeheartedly with them. His continuing prominence caused a good deal of criticism, but the Colonel explained his dilemma to Lawrence Abbott. There were two elevators at the *Outlook*. "If I go down in the front elevator," T.R. said, "my critics call it ostentation; if I go down in the side elevator, they call it secretiveness!"

In Washington the President wrote a confidential memorandum for members of his Cabinet. "You may have noted that there are a good many interviews being held at Oyster Bay with the insurgents and others and that sometimes authentic statements are made and sometimes statements that are not authentic—or at least statements made one day are denied the next. I think it is very important that nothing should be said on the subject one way or the other by either myself or any member of the Cabinet for the present." In private Taft could give vent to his true forebodings. "I do not see how I am going to get out of having a fight with President Roosevelt. . . ." he remarked to Archie Butt. "He seems to have thrown down the gauntlet. . . . I have doubted up to the present time whether he really intended to fight my administration or not, but he sees no one but my enemies, and if by chance he sees any supporters of the Administration, he does not talk intimately with any of them. . . . I confess it wounds me very deeply. I hardly think the prophet of the square deal is playing it exactly square with me now."

Nellie Taft was equally pessimistic—and made an uncannily accurate prediction at this time. "Well, I suppose you will have to fight Mr. Roosevelt for the nomination," she told her husband, "and if you get it he will defeat you. But it can't be helped. If possible you must not allow him to defeat you for the renomination. It does not make much difference about the reelection."

Actually Roosevelt himself was far from thinking of such a direct challenge to the President—if one can believe what he was writing to such an intimate political friend as Gifford Pinchot at the end of June. He keenly shared the ex-forester's disappointment with Taft; indeed, he felt it even more deeply "because it was I who made him President. . . ." Yet both he and Pinchot must realize that in two years circumstances would probably make it not only necessary to renominate Taft "but eminently desirable to re-elect him over anyone whom there is the least likelihood of the Democrats naming."

On June 25 Congress adjourned and, as was customary, the President went to the Capitol the final evening to sign last-minute bills. He was accompanied by Solicitor General Lloyd Bowers, his new private secretary Charles D. Norton, and Archie Butt, who recorded the dramatic ceremony: the President conferring with Bowers on the legislation to be signed; the stream of representatives and senators, come to shake the President's hand or request the pen with which he had signed some favorite bill. Afterward, close to midnight, the presidential party went gaily riding and singing through the moonlight before returning to the

White House. Butt had noticed that none of the insurgents had stopped to greet the President, that Senator Borah had even come into the room, talked to someone else, and left without speaking to Taft. Suddenly, the President broke the carefree mood of the night ride: "Bowers, did you notice the utter absence of the insurgent Senators in my room to-night? I don't give a damn. If they can get along without me, I presume I can do the same without them."

Two days later, reading the newspapers at breakfast, the President learned that Colonel Roosevelt was planning to visit him at the summer White House at Beverly, Massachusetts, to which the Tafts were about to repair. "I hope he will not come," Taft said to Archie Butt. "He can scarcely do so without my inviting him, and I don't propose to do that. I invited him to the White House, and he declined to come, giving some good reasons from his point of view possibly, but not from mine, so I am not in a position to ask him again." Indeed, concluded the President, he did not want to see Roosevelt until the Colonel had had time to think over the political situation thoroughly and make up his mind as to what course he would pursue. "He says he will keep silent for at least two months. I don't care if he keeps silent forever." Taft apparently relented, however, and three days later the two men met—for the first time in sixteen months.

In the afternoon of June 30 Archie Butt stood on the porch of the President's summer house at Beverly with Jimmy Sloan of the Secret Service. The two had been posted as lookouts for the arrival of their former chief. In his proper, rather old-maidish way, the captain had just remarked that the meeting would put to rest all the false reports of enmity between the two. "It does not mean anything," replied the cynical Sloan. "I know this man better than you do. He will come to see the President to-day and bite his leg off to-morrow." Shocked, Captain Butt did not immediately reply and was happily diverted by the sight of a large motor car turning in at the driveway. As soon as he recognized Roosevelt, and his companion of the day Senator Lodge, he went inside to notify the President. Taft emerged from the house just in time to greet the Colonel as he stepped from the automobile.

"Ah, Theodore, it is good to see you," exclaimed Taft.

"How are you, Mr. President? This is simply bully," replied Roosevelt.

"See here now, drop the 'Mr. President,' " said Taft, playfully hitting his former patron on the shoulder.

"Not at all," remarked the Colonel. "You must be Mr. President and I am Theodore. It must be that way."

Taft did not press the issue; yet, Archie Butt could not help notice, thereafter he addressed Roosevelt as Mr. President—which eventually drew a protest from T.R. "The force of habit is very strong in me," Taft explained. "I can never think of you save as Mr. President."

Roosevelt was introduced to Charles Norton and was warmly greeted by Butt. Taft linked arms with the Colonel and guided him around the corner of the veranda where they could all sit down. A butler appeared and the President asked what everyone would have to drink. The Colonel joked that he needed rather than wanted a Scotch and soda, but no one took anything. Lodge and Butt asked for cigars but found they had to step around the corner, out of the ocean breeze, to light them. The captain took this opportunity to ask the senator if the two men should be left alone. Lodge revealed that he had raised this point on the way over and that T.R. had definitely asked not to be left alone with the President.

Taft brought up the subject of New York state politics, the ostensible reason for T.R.'s call, but the discussion proved to be only desultory. When Mrs. Taft and the Tafts' daughter, Helen, appeared, the political conversation ceased altogether. "Now, Mr. President," Taft boomed, "tell me about cabbages and kings." And for an hour the Colonel regaled the party with a spirited account of his recent trip through Europe.

Finally the time came to leave and as the Colonel rose, Senator Lodge said that the two might just as well decide then what should be given out as to the meeting; there were some two hundred reporters at the gates. Roosevelt suggested that, if the President had no objections, he would say simply that he had paid a personal call and had spent a most delightful afternoon. "Which is true as far as I am concerned."

"And more than true as far as I am concerned," the President chimed in. "This has taken me back to some of those dear old afternoons when I was Will and you were Mr. President." And on this amicable note, they parted.

"Well, Archie," the President said to his military aide after the Colonel had disappeared, "that is another corner turned." Captain Butt reported Lodge's remark that Roosevelt had not wanted to be left alone with him. "I think he felt just as I did," reflected Taft, "that it was best to have simply a social personal visit and not give any opportunity for confidences which might be embarrassing."

3

Roosevelt had come to Beverly from Cambridge, where the previous day he had attended the Harvard commencement—and the thirtieth reunion of his class of 1880—and where he had held a conversation of much greater significance for his political future than the exchange of pleasantries with Taft.

Charles Evans Hughes, elected to a second two-year term as Governor of New York in 1908, was currently locked in mortal combat with Republican Old Guard bosses in the state—especially William Barnes, Jr., described by one historian as "the new and not so easy" successor to Thomas Collier Platt. The governor had just accepted appointment by Taft to the Supreme Court, to take effect with the opening of the fall term. But before resigning his gubernatorial office, Hughes was determined to make a fight for a bill instituting the direct primary in elections for state offices. Barnes had hinted that Roosevelt's silence on this controversial issue meant that he sided with the bosses in opposition to the measure. Despite T.R.'s emphatic statement on June 22 that such rumors were "entirely without justification"—and anyone who continued to claim he opposed the primary was thus eligible for membership in the Ananias Club—Hughes still felt isolated.

At the Harvard commencement, the New York governor—present to receive an honorary degree—found himself walking next to the former President in the academic procession. The two were seen to be talking together so earnestly that the march pace was actually slowed. Later, they sat next to one another on the platform and continued their discussion.

In the audience that day was T.R.'s old acquaintance Winthrop Chanler, who observed Hughes and Roosevelt conversing quietly but intensely. "Look at the two of them!" he whispered to a friend seated nearby. "Do you know what Hughes is saying? He's telling Roosevelt that the Republican party is in a bad way in New York, and that Roosevelt's duty is to jump in and back the direct primary. And Theodore is going to do it." The observation was an accurate one: Hughes convinced Roosevelt to come out for the primary bill. In an open telegram that evening the Colonel called upon the state legislature to pass the measure.

"Hughes had dragged him to the edge of a definite pond," the novelist Owen Wister later wrote in sadness, "and into the pond he plumped. What a small pond after all—one bill in one State—for an ex-President to notice! And then, the pond flowed speedily into a brook, and the brook speedily into a river, and down the river he went toward a sea that neither he nor friend nor enemy dreamed of."

On July 1, two days after Roosevelt had sent his telegram, the G.O.P. Old Guard again called up the primary bill in the New York state legislature and, in concert with the Democratic minority, defeated the measure. The very next day Lloyd C. Griscom, chairman of the New York County Republican Committee and an increasingly disenchanted Taft supporter, called on T.R. at Oyster Bay and apparently persuaded the ex-President to lead the opposition to Barnes. "One thing I don't want to become, or rather seem to become, is a factional leader in New York State politics," the Colonel shortly thereafter wrote the Kansas newspaper editor William Allen White; but in effect this is the role he now assumed. Roosevelt declared his candidacy for the temporary chairmanship of the New York Republican convention to be held at the end of September in Saratoga. Barnes promptly nominated his own candidate: Vice President James S. "Sunny Jim" Sherman of Utica—and implied that Sherman had the endorsement of President Taft.

The President was careful not to commit himself publicly to the Sherman candidacy but, goaded on by his private secretary, Charles Norton, he conferred almost daily by telephone with the Vice President on strategy to defeat Roosevelt. On August 16 the New York Republican State Committee voted, twenty to fifteen, to recommend that the state convention select Sherman as temporary chairman. That afternoon, as he was stepping into his automobile for a ride with Norton and Archie Butt, the President said: "Have you seen the newspapers this afternoon? They have defeated Theodore." Norton started to laugh and was soon joined by Taft, who could seldom prevent his deep-throated chuckle from erupting into a hearty guffaw. "We've got him—we've got him," cried the secretary, "as sure as peas we've got him."

"Like hell you've got him," thought Butt, seething in silence. "He is laughing in his sleeve at the whole kit and caboodle of you, and he'll eat you up when the time comes." The good captain was beginning to feel the strain of a divided loyalty—between the Roosevelt he so admired, respected, and even idolized and the Taft he was genuinely if somewhat patronizingly fond of.

Roosevelt at first felt almost relieved to be out of the fight, but Taft kept the issue alive by his next move, a typically inept blunder on the President's part. He released a statement to the press saying that he had advised Sherman to confer with Roosevelt and thought that this should have indicated support of the former President for the temporary chairmanship. "It is not the kind of fight into which an ex-President should be required to go. . . ." T.R. had written Lodge. "Twenty years ago I should not have minded it. It would have been entirely suitable for my age and standing. This whole political business now is bitterly distasteful to me." Nevertheless, Roosevelt re-entered the contest, and on September 19 he met Taft at New Haven, Connecticut.

Not even Archie Butt knew who had requested the conference, but Taft led him to believe that the initiative came from the Colonel. "I am in the dark as to the object he seeks," the President told his aide, "but he has kept me in this state of mind ever since he has been back. Archie, no one knows how deeply he has wounded me. I shall always be grateful for what he did for me, but since he has come back he has seared me to the very soul."

Groping for an explanation of the widening rift between him and his former chief, Taft on another occasion told Butt that the letter the captain had carried to the ex-President on the day he left for Africa had precipitated the quarrel. In the letter Taft had said that he would never forget what Roosevelt and his brother Charley had done to make him President. It was this—linking T.R.'s political support with the financial aid of his wealthy brother—that had so angered the Colonel that he did not even reply to the letter; Taft had the story from someone on the steamer with Roosevelt that day. Actually, Taft had made this statement in an earlier letter, written immediately after the election of 1908, and T.R. *had* responded to the farewell message. Taft's anxiety was obviously clouding his memory.

With the developing estrangement hanging so heavily in the air, the second meeting between the two men that summer of 1910 proved to be a dramatic encounter. Captain Butt, ominously concluding a letter to his sister-in-law the morning of September 19, asked: "Comes he in peace or comes he in war?" T.R. left Oyster Bay in a speedboat but out in Long Island Sound ran into bad weather and had to put in to shore at Stamford. He then completed the journey to New Haven—where the President had just attended a meeting of the Yale Corporation—by automobile. The two met at the home of Henry White, had lunch with Norton, Griscom, and a few other guests, and then—at T.R.'s suggestion—were left alone in the dining room, with Jimmy Sloan standing guard at the closed door. "The Colonel is too foxy a guy to let any of these chumps hear what he says," Sloan said to Archie Butt.

Seeing the faces of the President and the ex-President as they emerged from the dining room, Captain Butt concluded that nothing had been accomplished—indeed, that "if they are not farther apart than ever, at least they are no nearer." The two men left the house in the same car, and Colonel Roosevelt tried to amuse the party by telling funny stories. The President, noted Butt, "wreathed his face with a purely physical smile and laughed aloud, but it was all strained."

When reporters at New Haven made light of the meeting and implied that Roosevelt had sought it, the Colonel angrily charged that Norton—acting for the President—had called the conference. Norton urged a counterstatement but the President let the matter rest. Sadly, he remarked to Archie Butt that "if you were to remove Roosevelt's skull now, you would find written on his brain '1912.' But he is so purely an opportunist that should he find conditions changed materially in another year and you were to open his brain, you would not find there 1912, and Roosevelt would deny it was ever there." The President, Captain Butt was now convinced, felt an open fight with his predecessor was inevitable—and was even anxious to have it come. "Such is politics as seen from the inside, dear Clara," Butt concluded one of his almost daily letters to his sister-in-law. "Aren't you glad that Lewis is in the wholesale cotton business?"

Despite his reservations and forebodings, Taft decided that he must support Roosevelt even against his own Vice President; it was impossible, he told Elihu Root, to support Barnes and the "dead lot" now arrayed against the Colonel.

"We're going . . . to beat them to a frazzle," T.R. said as he stepped from the train at Saratoga on the eve of the Republican state convention; "remember the word frazzle." The clergyman opening the conclave on September 27 with the traditional prayer caused unintentional merriment with his invocation: "Bless this assembly, which is gathered to take sweet counsel together."

By a vote of 568 to 443, Roosevelt was elected temporary chairman and in his keynote address he mentioned "our able, upright and distinguished President" and even spoke favorably of the Payne-Aldrich tariff. He stated that Governor Hughes's direct primary legislation was the central issue of the forthcoming campaign. Later, when challenged on this point by a member of the Old Guard, T.R. rose again to say "We have now come to the vital moment of this Convention. By your votes you are to determine whether the Republican party in the State of New York is to be the party of progress or the party of the Bourbon and the reactionary." Again Roosevelt carried the day; the convention endorsed Hughes's program and went on to nominate as his successor Henry L. Stimson, a former law associate of Elihu Root's, the man T.R. had appointed as United States Attorney for the Southern District of New York, and a member of the Tennis Cabinet.

Stimson had not sought the nomination; indeed, in mid-summer he had ridden over from his own Long Island estate to Sagamore Hill to discuss with the Colonel what he considered the unpleasant prospect of running for governor. T.R. said he understood his friend's position perfectly; Stimson did not want to run for governor "unless such circumstances should arise as would, for instance, make it necessary for me [Roosevelt] to run against my will again for President." Stimson protested to the last. "If I run and am defeated, as looks almost certain, it will be a defeat for you," he told his former chief three days before the convention.

4

Despite the intensity of the drama and the prominence of the cast of characters, the fight in New York was not the sole nor even the principal arena for Roosevelt's political activities in the summer and autumn of 1910. Indeed, even before he had returned to the United States in mid-June, the Colonel had begun to accept speaking engagements about the country; and these speeches would put him square in the middle of that year's congressional elections—the first in which regular Republicans would be contending not only against Democrats but against the insurgents within their own ranks.

On August 23—the day after he re-entered the fight for the temporary chairmanship—T.R. left Oyster Bay on a 5,500-mile tour that took him through upstate New York, Ohio, Illinois, Iowa, and Nebraska, out to Wyoming and Colorado, and back through Kansas, Missouri, North and South Dakota, Minnesota, and Wisconsin to Pennsylvania: fourteen states in nineteen days. It was a trip, he wrote his son Ted before leaving, "which I perfectly dread." But happily *The Outlook* had furnished him with a private railroad car; it was the only way he could agree to make such an extensive journey. Roosevelt hated to tell people that he would not make speeches unless his expenses were paid, but "to go from place to place frowsy and unkempt, with a handbag, and surrounded by a mob of people who are governed by a mixture of admiration and hilarity, is exceedingly unpleasant, and so very tiring that there is always a good chance of my breaking down."

Traveling in style and with the usual entourage of reporters, Roosevelt continued to steal the headlines from the President. Even before he left on his western trip, Archie Butt noted, the former President was getting two columns of newspaper space to every one devoted to the Taft administration. "Really, Mr. Roosevelt seems to fill more of our lives in Washington when away from it than he did when he was here," the captain concluded as the campaign lengthened.

During this first long trip following his return from Africa and Europe, the Colonel spoke on a good many subjects: conservation, regulation of industry, public morality (he declined to attend a banquet in Chicago until his hosts had agreed to bar Senator William Lorimer, whose election was then being challenged as fraudulent and who would eventually be expelled from the Senate). He usually spoke in the generalities that he defended as necessary to put across his principles but which his critics attacked as mere platitudes. And his reception everywhere was remarkable. The audiences he addressed ranged from a businessmen's breakfast and a Granger gathering to a Chicago political club and the Colorado legislature. He spoke in public squares, at picnics, under a tent, in a ball park; the crowds he drew varied in size from three hundred to several thousand. And even where he did not pause to speak, groups of fervent supporters stood in the rain for hours just to cheer his passing train. But of all the speeches on his tour, the one delivered on August 31 at the dedication of the John Brown battlefield at Osawatomie, Kansas, created the greatest immediate stir and remained as the most indelible memory of the 1910 campaign.

While still traveling in Europe, Roosevelt had received from Lodge a recommendation that he read *The Promise of American Life,* a book published the preceding November by a middle-aged architectural critic and emerging political philosopher named Herbert Croly. T.R. picked up a copy of Croly's book in London, promptly read it, and soon was recommending it to others and even quoting from it.

Roosevelt was later to call *The Promise of American Life* "the most powerful and illuminating study of our national conditions which has appeared for many years." He generously overlooked the fact that Croly was not an uncritical admirer of his. Indeed, the author claimed that T.R. had done little to promote "candid and consistent thinking." Instead, Croly observed, Roosevelt "has preached the doctrine that the paramount and almost the exclusive duty of the American citizen consists in being a sixty-horse-power moral motor car." Roosevelt could afford to overlook this sarcasm, for Croly made the chapter on his own Presidency a climax in American political development, speaking in it of a "new Federalism or rather new Nationalism." And it was this last phrase that T.R. took for the theme of his sermon of the day at Osawatomie.

Roosevelt had conferred with Gifford Pinchot, who was usually accompanied by James Garfield, a number of times earlier in the summer; in fact, the two men were on the train with the Colonel, en route from Colorado to Kansas, the day before the Osawatomie speech. Pinchot's brother Amos later claimed that the ex-forester had written the controversial speech for T.R.; and before leaving on his western trip, the Colonel had notified Pinchot that he had taken the Osawatomie speech "substantially as you left it, with one or two additions, and two or three changes." To Henry Cabot Lodge he later explained that most of the statements in the speech had previously been made during his years as President. "I may have here and there strengthened them, or made them a little clearer, but substantially what I said at Osawatomie consisted of assembling those points made in my messages to Congress which I regarded as of the most importance for the moment." Root agreed, adding that his only objection to the New Nationalism was calling it new.

In his opening remarks on the John Brown battlefield Roosevelt echoed Herbert Croly: "Our country—this great Republic—means nothing unless it means the triumph of a real democracy, the triumph of popular government, and, in the long run, of an economic system under which each man shall be guaranteed the opportunity to show the best that there is in him." Then, in a somewhat dubious comparison, he attempted to link Abraham Lincoln's efforts to preserve the Union with those of present-day reformers attempting to solve twentieth-century problems—he was speaking to an audience containing a large number of Grand Army veterans and was, after all, dedicating what has been called the opening battlefield of the Civil War. (Roosevelt's hero had always been Abraham Lincoln; a photograph of Lincoln's funeral procession in New York purports to show the six-year-old Theodore at the window of his father's house watching the line of march.) And now, to prove that the time was ripe for another Lincoln to heal the division between the citizenry and the special interests, he cited his great predecessor on labor and capital.

" 'Labor is prior to, and independent of, capital,' " Roosevelt recited. " 'Capital is only the fruit of labor, and could never have existed if labor had not first existed. Labor is the superior of capital, and deserves much the higher consideration.' "

Pausing, perhaps to let the words sink in, Roosevelt continued: "If that remark was original with me, I should be even more strongly denounced as a Communist agitator than I shall be anyhow. It is Lincoln's. I am only quoting it; and this is one side; that is the side the capitalist should hear. Now, let the working man hear his side.

" 'Capital has its rights, which are as worthy of protection as any other rights. . . . Nor should this lead to a war upon the owners of property. Property is the fruit of labor; . . . property is desirable; is a positive good in the world.' "

The history of mankind, the Colonel said as he launched into his main theme, is one of "conflict between the men who possess more than they have earned and the men who have earned more than they possess. . . ." At the present moment in history, he told his audience, this conflict appeared as "the struggle of freemen to gain and hold the right of self-government as against the special interests, who twist the methods of free government into machinery for defeating the popular will."

Government, federal and state, must be freed from the "sinister influence or control of special interests." As the special interests of cotton and slavery had threatened the nation's political integrity before the Civil War, "so now the great special business interests too often control and corrupt the men and methods of government for their own profit." The special interests must be driven out of politics, he exclaimed.

The Osawatomie address, however, was not to be one only of dubious historical parallels and platitudinous and repetitive generalities. The ex-President soon became specific in his references to property and large corporations and advanced certain proposals that were to form the core of his New Nationalism over the course of the next two years and to bring down upon his head a storm of abuse. "The citizens of the United States must effectively control the mighty commercial forces which they themselves have called into being."

Before the corporations could be controlled properly, he continued, there must be an end to their political activity. To accomplish this goal, there must be effective publicity of corporate affairs and a prohibition agaihst the use of corporate funds for political purposes. There must be government supervision of all corporations doing interstate business— not just of such public-service corporations as the railways. Franchises, such as those for public transportation, should be granted for a limited time only, and perhaps such control and supervision as implied in the granting of franchises should be extended to combinations that controlled the other necessities of life, such as meat, oil, and coal. Corporate officials should be held personally responsible for company wrongdoings.

Yet this was not the famous trustbuster speaking. Combinations were the result of "an imperative economic law which cannot be repealed by political legislation," he stated. As a matter of fact, the effort to prohibit combination had failed. "The way out lies, not in attempting to prevent such combinations, but in completely controlling them in the interests of the public welfare." He therefore suggested an increase in the powers both of the Federal Bureau of Corporations and the Interstate Commerce Commission.

Moving on to another topic, he suggested the establishment of a tariff commission, to revise schedules one at a time and thus avoid the political logrolling of a general revision by Congress—implying but not actually charging that this is what had happened with Payne-Aldrich. Elsewhere, T.R. called for a graduated income tax and an inheritance tax, a revision of the monetary system, full accounting for campaign expenditures, and even the recall of public servants.

His program, Roosevelt conceded, called for a more active governmental interference in social and economic conditions than the nation was accustomed to, but "we have got to face the fact that such an increase in governmental control is now necessary." He was not asking for overcentralization, only that the people "work in a spirit of broad and far-reaching nationalism when we work for what concerns our people as a whole."

The Osawatomie speech has been characterized by one historian as perhaps the most radical ever given by an ex-President, and it gained for the Colonel intensified and even fanatical support throughout the Midwest and Far West. On his train the next day, he was joined by Kansas Governor William R. Stubbs, Senator Joseph L. Bristow, and newspapermen William Allen White and William Rockhill Nelson, who were all progressives and now "hysterically jubilant" over their hero's utterances. "Roosevelt for 1912" was the catchword up and down the aisles of the train, and at a subsequent gathering in Kansas City T.R. listened to a song calling for his return to the Presidency. The Colonel remained impassive in the face of such talk, however, and continued not only to commend insurgents but also to say a kind word now and again for the President.

Reading reports of the Osawatomie speech in the newspapers, Henry Cabot Lodge grew alarmed and wrote immediately to say that people in the East were "startled" by what his old friend had said and were now "holding you up as little short of a revolutionist. . . ." Lodge himself was not startled, for he had discussed all these topics with "my dear Theodore" often; it was merely "the Kansas crowd and the insurgents generally who have given the impression of extreme utterances when the utterances were not extreme and only a presentation of the policies you have been advocating for some time."

What did concern Lodge was what Roosevelt had said, elsewhere on his trip, about the courts. Court procedures certainly needed to be reformed, Lodge conceded, but it was not "helpful to criticize specific decisions. . . ." He was "very conservative" on the matter of court decisions; "I think that to encourage resistance to the decisions of the courts tends to lead to a disregard of the law." In his reply the Colonel said, disarmingly if inaccurately, that he found it curious "that what people think is most revolutionary in my speech should be merely a quotation from Lincoln." And he quickly proceeded to defend his criticism of court decisions that had created a neutral ground in which neither state nor federal government had any power to intervene. At any rate, he believed that—as he had been told by regulars and insurgents alike en route —his tour of the West had helped secure "a fairly united party support for the Republicans at this election."

5

Roosevelt in his subsequent forays along the campaign trail that autumn of 1910—to the South, to New England, back to the Midwest, and extensively through New York State—certainly acted as if he believed he could heal the party's wounds. He campaigned specifically for Cummins in Iowa, Beveridge in Indiana, a young progressive named Robert P. Bass successfully seeking the New Hampshire governorship, and of course Henry Stimson in New York.

In the New York fight, T.R. was now more or less on his own. Having drawn Roosevelt into the factional fight in the Empire State, Governor Hughes—as the Colonel sarcastically wrote Lodge—now assumed "the lofty position that as a prospective Justice of the Supreme Court he cannot take any sides in the contest. . . ." He was not very pleased with Taft, Roosevelt confessed to his friend, "but, thank heavens! I made Taft President and not Hughes, who was the only possible alternative."

The ex-President journeyed to Boston to speak eloquently for Lodge, who erroneously believed his Senate seat threatened. And he was amused by an invitation to come to Ohio, where the regular G.O.P. candidate for governor, Warren G. Harding, having defeated Garfield for the nomination, now promised to adopt the Osawatomie speech as his platform if only T.R. would intervene in his uphill and ultimately unsuccessful contest against Democrat Judson Harmon. One place where he would not campaign was New York's Dutchess County, where the young husband of his niece Eleanor, Franklin D. Roosevelt, was making his first bid for office, a seat in the New York State Senate—as a Democrat. "Franklin ought to go in politics without the least regard as to where I speak or don't speak. . . ." he wrote his sister Bamie. "He is a fine fellow. . . ."

Oblivious to charges of inconsistency, he attacked parts of the Payne-Aldrich tariff where, as in the South and West, it was particularly unpopular and supported it in New York where it was part of Stimson's campaign platform. And in *The Outlook* of September 17 he wrote that he thought the present tariff "is better than the last, and considerably better than the one before the last." Such an endorsement caused the insurgents, especially La Follette, to cry out in dismay. The Wisconsin senator was really too much of a radical for Roosevelt, and the ex-President managed to speak at Milwaukee without mentioning his name.

The irrepressible Colonel knew how to get headlines even when he was not actively politicking. In 1905 he had become the first President to descend in a submarine when he boarded the U.S. Navy submarine torpedo boat *Plunger*. Now he became the first Chief Executive to go up in an airplane. On October 11, he took time out from campaigning for the progressive ticket headed by Missouri's Governor Herbert S. Hadley to visit an aviation meet at Lambert Field, eighteen miles outside of St. Louis.

As his car pulled up, Roosevelt was greeted by a flyer named Arch Hoxsey, who informed him that they shared the same birthday, October 27, and that this fact gave Hoxsey a special claim on the former President. "I want you to take a short spin with me in the air," Hoxsey said. "You can, with perfect safety, trust yourself in my hands." "Now?" T.R. asked. "Yes," answered Hoxsey, "this is good a time as we can ever get. It is calm, and ideal flying machine weather. Will you go?"

Roosevelt hesitated a moment and then agreed, asking only that the flight not be publicly announced. Walking the hundred feet to his flying machine, Hoxsey felt himself already in the clouds. "Now, Hoxsey," he told himself, "no funny business when you get this fellow up, because if you spill him you can never square yourself with anybody."

The Colonel had charged ahead and was already scrambling among the wires when Hoxsey reached the airplane. The aviator asked his passenger to exchange the famous slouch hat for the regulation cap and goggles and when the two were secured in their seats, he opened up the engine and took off. Making the first pass of the grandstand, at a height of about 150 feet, Hoxsey sensed an unaccustomed wiggle in the flying machine. Turning, he saw T.R. waving vigorously at the crowd below. "Be careful, Colonel; don't pull any of those strings." T.R. smiled broadly and said, "Nothing doing." Informed that the ex-President was aloft, the assembly below lapsed into an awed and frightened silence. Hoxsey made two laps of the field—in three minutes and twenty seconds—and landed his famous passenger to wild cheers. The guards had difficulty in restraining the crowd, which wished to break through and congratulate the two.

"It was great! First class!" Roosevelt said, pumping the aviator's hand. "It was the finest experience I have ever had. I wish I could stay up for an hour, but I haven't the time this afternoon."

Whether circling an aviation field at St. Louis or dedicating a battlefield in Kansas, Roosevelt was acting like a candidate himself in the 1910 Congressional campaign. The hostile New York *Sun* kept repeating a month before the election: "The time to beat Roosevelt in 1912 is on November 8, 1910." To most observers this is precisely what seemed to happen.

The election was a debacle for the Republican party, with both regulars and insurgents toppling everywhere to their Democratic opponents. The G.O.P. retained control of the Senate, but the House of Representatives—for the first time in sixteen years—would be controlled by the Democrats, and by a sizable margin, 228 to 162. The Democrats would also have twenty-six of the forty-eight governorships, with Judson Harmon defeating Harding in the President's home state of Ohio and—a particularly bitter blow to T.R.—John A. Dix swamping Stimson in the New York contest. Massachusetts picked a Democratic governor, Eugene N. Foss, as did New Jersey, which elected the former president of Princeton, Woodrow Wilson, a candidate of the state's Democratic machine running as a reformer. Republican losses in the progressive West were less, however, and there would be some new insurgent faces in the Senate: Miles Poindexter of Washington, Asle J. Gronna of North Dakota, and John D. Works of California. California also picked a progressive Republican governor, Hiram Johnson. But Iowa's Dolliver had unexpectedly died in October and, with Indiana going Democratic, Beveridge would be retired from the Senate.

Joseph Pulitzer's New York *World,* which had warned throughout the campaign that a vote for Stimson in 1910 was a vote for Roosevelt in 1912, now happily proclaimed that the former President was extinguished from political life—by 1912 he would be a half-forgotten myth. In December the Gridiron Club, which at the beginning of the year had applauded a "Back from Elba" skit, now featured T.R. in a "Retreat from Moscow" act. "Cabot Lodge tries to keep his head above water," wrote Henry Adams. "Roosevelt for the moment has gone under. A gang of unknown men float on the surface."

Roosevelt himself was curiously ambivalent about the returns. "Well! we got thoroughly thrashed yesterday," he wrote one friend, "but I am enlisted 'for three years or the war,' and we will see this thing through." And the next week in an *Outlook* editorial, he said, "The fight for progressive popular government has merely begun and will certainly go on to a triumphant conclusion in spite of initial checks and in spite of the personal success or failure of individual leaders." "Well, 'Every dog has his day; but the nights belong to the cat,' " T.R. wrote his son Ted on November 11. And to Senator Lodge that same day he wrote that "the bright spot in the business is that I think it will put a stop to the talk about my being nominated in 1912, which was beginning to make me very uneasy."

A few days after the election, Taft left Washington for a cruise down the Atlantic coast and through the Caribbean to Panama, where he would inspect current progress on the canal. During the President's absence Roosevelt visited the capital for the first time since he had left office and was enthusiastically received wherever he went. There was a reception for the Colonel at the National Press Club and three thousand people were turned away from Convention Hall when he appeared to lecture on "Wild Man and Wild Beast in Africa." Mrs. Taft and her daughter, Helen, had gone to New York, but T.R. called at the White House anyway and left his card. Even though there was no one official to greet him, the ex-President was warmly welcomed by the servants and clerks, each of whom received a pleasant greeting or joking question from his beloved former chief. It was the only happy day the White House staff had had in two years, head usher Ike Hoover told Captain Butt, "and not one of us would exchange it for a hundred-dollar bill."

Yet, as the autumn lengthened into winter, visitors to Oyster Bay found Roosevelt increasingly downcast. "I think that the American people feel a little bit tired of me, a feeling with which I cordially sympathize," he told one friend. Lloyd Griscom came away from one Sunday at Sagamore Hill alarmed by the Colonel's depression; "all his old buoyancy seemed to be gone," Griscom told Archie Butt, "and he really seemed to be a changed man." Butt reported the remark to Taft and thought he saw tears forming in the President's eyes. It distressed him deeply, Taft said, to think of his former friend "sitting there at Oyster Bay alone and feeling himself deserted." The American people were strange in their attitude toward their heroes, he continued, waxing philosophical. "They have even led their idols on and on to cut their legs from under them later and apparently to make their fall all the greater." Captain Butt agreed. Roosevelt had had "all the adulation which has never been the President's," he wrote a few days later, "and is now more abused and condemned than ever the President was or will be."

The hunter had returned in triumph, and the king who had voluntarily abdicated was come to view and judge the actions of his hand-picked successor. But if Roosevelt, in 1910, was also a general returning to the field of action, the first clear blast of his trumpet summoning the old legions to renewed endeavor had gone unanswered. Roosevelt returned to the political arena was, for the moment, Roosevelt rejected.

æ§ *Chapter 10* ê»

A Fissure in the G.O.P.

American election campaigns traditionally begin the morning after the preceding contest is decided. After the balloting of 1910, however, more than two months passed before the first significant event of the 1912 campaign took place. Then, on January 21, 1911, a small group of men gathered at the Washington home of Senator Robert M. La Follette to make a portentous move.

For nearly a year the Wisconsin senator had been discussing with like-minded senators and representatives the need for an organization to promote progressive legislation in the various states they represented. And during the holiday recess of Congress in December he had drafted a declaration of principles for such an organization and submitted it to several of his colleagues. After some modifications, the declaration was mailed to leading progressives in a number of states. With it went an invitation to attend the meeting at La Follette's home. At this gathering announcement was made of the formation of the National Progressive Republican League. In addition to the coterie of insurgent senators, the League's charter membership boasted six governors, including Hiram Johnson of California and Francis E. McGovern of Wisconsin. Gifford and Amos Pinchot subscribed to the organization, as did James Garfield, Louis D. Brandeis, Ray Stannard Baker, and William Allen White. Senator Jonathan Bourne of Oregon was elected president.

The declaration of principles was brief and forceful. Popular government in America, it was claimed, had been "thwarted" and progressive legislation "strangled" by the special interests, which controlled "caucuses, delegates, conventions, and party organizations." Through this control of the political machinery, it was charged, "legislation in the public interest has been baffled and defeated." Cited as examples of this frustration of the public will was the long struggle, "but partially effective," for the control of railway rates and services, for tariff revision, for regulation of trusts, for reconstruction of banking and monetary laws, and for conservation of coal, oil, gas, timber, water, and other natural resources.

Not until popular government had truly been established in the states and in the nation would government become responsive to the popular will. To this end, the League advocated five reforms: (1) direct election of United States senators, then still chosen by state legislatures; (2) direct primaries for the nomination of elective officials; (3) direct election of delegates to the national party conventions, with an opportunity for voters to indicate their choices for President and Vice President; (4) amendment of state constitutions to provide for the initiative, referendum, and recall; and (5) a thoroughgoing corrupt practices act.

Among the people from whom La Follette had solicited support in December was Theodore Roosevelt. "Now, Colonel," he had written, "can't you consistently give this movement the benefit of your great name and influence?" But the Wisconsin senator absent-mindedly forgot to include a copy of the draft declaration—indeed, even forgot to sign his name to the letter. Later, when Roosevelt had received more specific information from Bourne, he replied to La Follette. "I wish I could see you personally, for I am rather doubtful whether it is advisable for me to be one of the signers of such a call. I should like to have gone over it with you." To Bourne, T.R. was even more negative, saying that he felt it unwise to go into a movement in which "a small knot of men" were attempting to dictate popular policies "instead of rallying the people to their support."

To William Allen White, who joined La Follette and Bourne in urging him to endorse the League, the Colonel wrote that he could do more for the movement from the outside than he could as a founding father. "Now, my dear Senator," he asked in a subsequent letter to La Follette, "don't you think that the way I can best help the league is by cordial endorsement of it over my signature in *The Outlook?*" And on January 14 he published a forceful editorial statement in favor of what he called Progressive Nationalism, citing Wisconsin—under La Follette's leadership—as the state that had advanced farther than any other in securing "both genuine popular rule and the wise use of the collective power of the people to do what cannot be done by merely individual effort. . . ." But T.R. reserved his stronger and more detailed endorsement for the issue dated January 21, the very day of the Washington conclave he declined to attend.

"Most Western Progressives, and many Eastern Progressives (including the present writer)," T.R. said of the declaration, "will assent to the five propositions, at least in principle." Yet he hedged on endorsing recall, saying that "it is sometimes very useful, but contains undoubted possibilities of mischief" and was unnecessary for short-term elective officials. The only argument he could see for its use was in the case of officials elected or appointed for life—and in the United States this was true only of the judiciary. On this subject he promised to speak later.

Roosevelt then narrowed the discussion—and the point at which he began to part company with the League's founders—to the proposal for the initiative and referendum. As regards these two measures, the Colonel charged that "the anticipations of their adherents and the fears of their opponents are equally exaggerated." Ordinary citizens "neither can nor ought to spend their time in following all the minutiae of legislation"; this work must be delegated to their legislators. The advocates of the initiative and referendum, Roosevelt said, must remember that those measures were "in themselves merely means and not ends." The New England town meeting, he explained, was in fact an even more radical form of popular government; the genuinely progressive leader would no more ostracize a New England state for failure to adopt the initiative and referendum than he would a Western or Southern state for not adopting the town meeting.

Roosevelt knew, as did everyone else, that the principal reason for the formation of the National Progressive Republican League was to block Taft's renomination in 1912—and indirectly to promote the candidacy of La Follette. In five years as governor of Wisconsin, La Follette had succeeded in making that state one of the most progressive in the nation, securing regulation of railroad rates, instituting the direct primary, and reorganizing and equalizing the tax structure. In December, 1905, he had resigned the governorship to take up his duties as a United States senator.

A compelling figure with his shock of bristling hair and deep-set, penetrating eyes, La Follette brought to Washington the self-righteous conviction of a temperance reformer and the fervor of an Old Testament prophet. Indeed, he titled the chapter in his autobiography dealing with those first years of his twenty-year-long career in the upper house "Alone in the Senate." No one else, he sincerely believed, perceived the progressive movement with quite his unclouded vision; no one else was ready to fight for it with quite his uncompromising and incorruptible stance.

Roosevelt was quickly dismissed by the new Wisconsin senator. The then President, La Follette later charged, "acted upon the maxim that half a loaf is better than no bread." As for himself, La Follette declared, half a loaf was fatal; it "dulls the appetite, and destroys the keenness of interest in attaining the full loaf." He absolutely scorned what he called T.R.'s "rhetorical radicalism" and claimed that Roosevelt invariably offset his attacks on special interests with equally drastic assaults on those seeking to reform abuses. "This cannonading, first in one direction and then in another," La Follette wrote, "filled the air with noise and smoke, which confused and obscured the line of action, but, when the battle cloud drifted by and quiet was restored, it was always a matter of surprise that so little had really been accomplished."

Roosevelt never really came to know La Follette during the three years his Presidency overlapped the latter's senatorial career and they remained strangers to one another in 1911. He was diffident about explaining to La Follette his reasons for not endorsing the League, T.R. wrote White, "partly because I do not know him well enough to be sure that he would not misunderstand me. . . . ." Later, the Colonel's doubt and uncertainty about La Follette ripened into a hearty ill will, as he came to think of the Wisconsin senator as "half zealot and half self-seeking demagogue" and a "vindictive and unscrupulous faker."

That the newly formed National Progressive Republican League would boom La Follette for the Presidency was shortly confirmed by Senator Bourne, in a speech delivered at the end of March in Boston. The 1912 race, the Oregonian predicted, would be between La Follette and New Jersey's new Democratic governor, Woodrow Wilson. Roosevelt, as far as the progressives in the Republican party were concerned, was on trial; only if he endorsed concrete reforms did the ex-President have a chance for the G.O.P. nomination. La Follette, however, was determined not to give Roosevelt such an opportunity. After securing pledges of financial support from, among others, the Pinchot brothers, he accounced his candidacy on June 17, 1911.

Roosevelt, meanwhile, was far from writing off Taft as La Follette and Bourne were so blithely doing. The Colonel had even effected a reconciliation of sorts with his successor following the congressional elections—though he had once more declined an invitation to stay at the White House. "I think you are a trump to ask me to come to the White House," he wrote the President, "and I should accept at once if I were going to the Gridiron dinner. But I am not going; I have repeatedly refused. I don't think it would be wise for me to go there." Despite the rebuff, Taft had sent T.R. a draft of his annual message to Congress in December, 1910, and the Colonel had replied that there was nothing for him to say about it "save in the way of agreement and commendation." Later in the month, the President had sought Roosevelt's advice on the nation's currently strained relations with Japan, and in January, 1911, the Colonel wrote that Taft's proposed reciprocity treaty with Canada was "admirable from every standpoint."

As for 1912, Roosevelt was writing to a variety of correspondents that whereas before the fall elections there had been perhaps one chance in ten that he would be forced into making the race for a third term, now there was but one chance in a hundred—or perhaps a thousand. The best thing for the party to do, he concluded, was to "do what we can with Taft, face probable defeat in 1912, and then endeavor to reorganize under really capable and sanely progressive leadership." The Colonel demurely refrained from mentioning the name of the man he thought could provide such leadership after 1912, a man who would be leader of the opposition during a transitional Democratic administration and ultimately the G.O.P. standard bearer in 1916.

2

Roosevelt did not long remain despondent over the defeat of 1910. It was not in his nature to brood sullenly over the past—nor to regret for an instant any action taken or left undone. In the New York contest, he now wrote Lodge, he had acted "just as an ex-President ought to act . . . to put the party on a higher and cleaner plane as regards both honesty and popular responsibility. . . ." As for charges that he had been inconsistent or had spoken unwisely, he backed every word uttered during the summer and fall of 1910, he told another correspondent. Early in 1911 Roosevelt's eye was on the future—and the prospects once more seemed bright.

And now there was a special reason for happiness. Theodore, Jr., who had moved to California to pursue a business career following his marriage to Eleanor Alexander, wrote in January to say that his wife was expecting their first child. Edith Roosevelt was no more delighted than was he, the Colonel wrote his son. "I do'n't care a rap whether it is a boy or a girl." Home, wife, children were the things that really counted in life, he continued. "I have heartily enjoyed many things; the Presidency, my success as a soldier, a writer, a big game hunter and explorer; but all of them put together are not for one moment to be weighed in the balance when compared with the joy I have known with your mother and all of you. . . . Really, the prospect of grandchildren was all that was lacking to make perfect mother's happiness and mine."

The family circle at Sagamore Hill had shrunk to three, with only the Roosevelts' younger daughter, nineteen-year-old Ethel, still living at home. Alice, of course, was in Washington, where her husband, Nicholas Longworth, was becoming an increasingly powerful member of the House of Representatives, a solidly conservative Republican, regular and still loyal to the Taft administration. Kermit was back at Harvard. The third son, Archibald, was at a preparatory school in Arizona, while thirteen-year-old Quentin, T.R. wrote a friend, had "electrified Groton by standing high in his class, something which neither he nor any of his brothers ever did before."

For once Roosevelt was not feeling pinched in regard to finances. Despite the popular conception, he was not really a wealthy man; his inheritance from his father provided but a modest income. Through his long public career, he had constantly worried about supporting a large family on small official salaries. But now he had the $12,000 per year from *The Outlook*, plus royalties from *African Game Trails*, which he expected to run as high as $40,000 in 1911.

The Roosevelts were soon to have a chance to see their eldest son and his wife, for the Colonel was planning another extensive speaking tour. The previous year he had accepted an invitation to deliver the annual Earl Lectures at the University of California at Berkeley—a series in which an eminent Christian scholar or thinker was "to speak upon themes calculated to illustrate and disseminate Christian thought and minister to Christian life." Although he claimed to dread another triumphal procession, Roosevelt said it would be impossible to pass through so many states en route to California without stopping in nearly each to make a speech or two. "I have felt very strongly that I wanted to appear in every section of the country," he wrote Ted in San Francisco, "and as nearly as possible in every State, once, to thank the American people for having made me President. . . ."

His five-week-long journey—from March 8 to April 15—would take him through Georgia, Alabama, Mississippi, and Louisiana to Texas, then on to California via New Mexico and Arizona, and back through Nevada, Oregon, Washington, Idaho, and Montana to Wisconsin. This time there would be no private car, and the Colonel would travel alone to New Mexico, where he would be joined by his wife and Ethel. In Arizona the couple would stop to see Archie and in San Francisco they would be joined by Quentin, so that they could have a family reunion of ten days to two weeks with the western branch of the family.

At the outset of Roosevelt's 1911 trip there was a flurry of excitement that, for once, had nothing to do with domestic politics and his increasingly controversial involvement in them. South of the border in Mexico, Francisco Madero had raised the flag of insurrection against the corrupt regime of Porfirio Diaz, the first act in the long, bitter, and confusing Mexican revolution. To protect American citizens and property in Mexico, the War Department massed twenty thousand troops on the border; at Guantanamo in Cuba two thousand marines were put on alert, with a fast cruiser squadron ready to take them across the Caribbean should the need arise.

The fifty-two-year-old ex-Colonel of the Rough Riders caught the whiff of battle smoke and en route to El Paso, Texas, on March 14 wrote hurriedly and passionately to President Taft. He did not want to participate in any mere war with Mexico—"it would not be my business to do peculiarly irksome and disagreeable and profitless police duty of the kind any occupation of Mexico would entail." But if there was a chance of a big war erupting, one in which Mexico would perhaps be backed by Japan or some other great power, "then I should wish immediately to apply for permission to raise a division of cavalry, such as the regiment I commanded in Cuba."

"I have noted carefully your wish," the President promptly replied, "and if the occasion offers—which Heaven forfend—I shall be glad to conform to your desires." But Japan did not intervene, the war with Mexico failed to materialize, and Roosevelt missed his opportunity for renewed military glory. When next he wrote the President, it was from San Francisco on April 1: "Well, thank Heaven! I am coming to the end of the last speaking tour I shall ever make."

There had been diversions en route, especially a descent into the Grand Canyon with Archie and the dedication of the Roosevelt Dam near Phoenix. The Earl Lectures at Berkeley—the original reason for making this trip—proved to be of the type of vague but emphatic moral uplift that caused even so devoted an admirer as William Allen White to entitle his introduction to a volume of Roosevelt speeches "Saith the Preacher."

The Roosevelts were back at Oyster Bay in time to watch the incomparable Long Island spring unfold from their veranda at Sagamore Hill. There were still visitors to the comfortable frame house but perhaps fewer were political callers—and certainly these were less insistent than those who had come during the preceding election year. Tuesdays and Fridays the Colonel generally took the train in to Manhattan to spend the day at his *Outlook* office, polishing his editorials, holding conferences, dictating a steady stream of correspondence. And there were always public gatherings to which an ex-President would be invited and which he would find it impossible to avoid attending.

On June 6 the Colonel went to Baltimore to attend the silver jubilee of Cardinal Gibbons, where he encountered the President. A newspaper account of the meeting described the two as shaking hands vigorously, whispering together, and even breaking into unrestrained laughter. But when another reporter wrote that T.R. had promised Taft support for the 1912 nomination, Roosevelt promptly denied the story. Two weeks after their meeting in Baltimore Taft wrote the ex-President a short note thanking him for a silver wedding anniversary present. The letter, dated June 18, 1911, was to be the last exchange between the two men for several years.

The Colonel was not publicly endorsing anyone for the nomination that summer and autumn of 1911, not Taft—though he was still resigned to the President's candidacy—and certainly not La Follette. Nor was he ready to re-enter the political arena himself. A number of people, interpreting the Western trip as a bid for political support, had written to suggest formation of an organization to promote a Roosevelt candidacy the next year; to all of them, the Colonel wrote a prompt and firm "No, thank you." And to Iowa farm editor Henry Wallace he wrote, at the outset of summer, that he planned to follow the advice given by a New Bedford whaling captain to his mate; the captain had told the mate "that all he wanted from him was silence and damned little of that."

"Our life is very happy here," the Colonel wrote to his old friend Cecil Spring Rice in late August. "I almost feel as if it was a confession of weakness on my part to be as thoroughly contented as I am." There were moments when he would like to be back in public life, he continued, but these were fleeting. "Twenty years ago, or ten years ago, I should not have been at all happy living as I now am living, because I should have felt that I had no business to have quit the arena, that it was ignoble to be merely an onlooker instead of doing my part in the strife." Now, however, he only wanted to continue working—presumably a continuation of his literary pursuits—for the eight years remaining before Quentin's graduation from college. "Then all the children will have been launched in life, and I shall be sixty years old, and I shall feel that I have a right to draw out of work entirely."

It was not to be. Indeed, only two months after he wrote this prediction of a serene future, Roosevelt's seclusion and solitude at Sagamore Hill were shattered forever.

3

October 27, 1911, was Theodore Roosevelt's fifty-third birthday. But the celebration of this particular milestone was not to be an occasion for untroubled gaiety at Sagamore Hill. That morning's newspapers announced that the Taft administration had filed suit the preceding day against the United States Steel Corporation for violation of the Sherman Antitrust Act. Taft had taken up T.R.'s mantle as trustbuster and, indeed, would end his term in office with a better record of prosecutions than his predecessor had left. The government's most important case of the year had been prepared in secrecy, to prevent speculation in U.S. Steel shares, by a special assistant to Attorney General George W. Wickersham; and the President—in his characteristically indolent manner—had not bothered to read the particular charges against the steel corporation, though he had been briefed on the impending action. Had he done so, it is possible that the final rupture with Roosevelt might have been avoided, that the Republican party might have been spared its conclusive and fatal division in the following year's presidential election, and that the course of American politics might not have been so fundamentally altered in the years following 1912.

Among the allegations in the government's suit was one in which it was charged that U.S. Steel had engaged in monopolistic practices when it acquired the Tennessee Coal and Iron Company during the panic of 1907—and that the steel company's executives had deceived

President Theodore Roosevelt in order to make the acquisition. On that occasion Elbert H. Gary and Henry Clay Frick of the steel corporation had come to Roosevelt with a proposal. A large block of Tennessee Coal and Iron shares, they explained, was held by a "certain business firm" that was about to go under. The collapse of this firm—it was the brokerage house of Moore & Schley, though the President was not so informed—might pull down other Wall Street institutions, turning the panic into a severe depression that would undermine the closing years of Roosevelt's administration. The steel executives, acting in the public interest, they assured T.R., proposed to buy Tennessee Coal and Iron for $45,000,000—more than the property, which they said they did not really want, was worth. But they would go ahead only if the President could promise them that no antitrust action would be taken against U.S. Steel because of the acquisition. Believing that he had to reach a quick decision, Roosevelt told the two men that—though he could not advise them to make the purchase of the coal and iron company—he would not object to it.

Now, four years later in 1911, the Taft administration's suit was charging that the acquisition had indeed been a violation of the Sherman Act. This left the public with but two conclusions to reach: Roosevelt had either been duped by the steel executives, as the government's petition claimed, or he had connived with them to break the law; he was either a fool or a villain. The charge struck Roosevelt, Taft's biographer writes, "deep in his Achilles heel, his ego."

The Colonel could not have been entirely unprepared for this accusation. The preceding April Taft had called into special session the Sixty-second Congress, elected in November, 1910. For the first time since 1895 the Democrats controlled the House of Representatives; Uncle Joe Cannon had been replaced as Speaker by Missouri's Champ Clark. The G.O.P. still retained nominal control of the Senate, but thirteen insurgent senators formed a separate caucus, demanded special recognition as a minority within the Republican party, and asked that one-fifth of Republican committee assignments be made from their ranks. At the same time forty-six progressive congressmen declared that they would no longer be bound by the decisions of the Republican caucus. Thus, as one historian has concluded, by the spring of 1911 "there were really three distinct parties in the national legislature."

Taft had summoned Congress into the extraordinary session solely to deal with his proposed reciprocity treaty with Canada. The President got his treaty—with more opposition from his own party than from the Democrats—only to have Canada later fail to ratify it. But once in session, the legislators went charging off in all directions on their own. Among their activities was an investigation of U.S. Steel, and Roosevelt had been invited to testify before a House committee on August 5.

It had been his duty in 1907, the Colonel told the congressmen, to stop the panic and not "to form any judgment as to whether the representatives of the Steel Corporation were anxious to get possession of that company . . . or whether they were only anxious to save the situation caused by the panic." Actually, he conceded, he thought then—as he still did in 1911—that both motives were in the minds of the steel executives. "What was the predominant motive was of no consequence. . . . The question was of saving the plain people, the common people, in all parts of the United States from dreadful misery and suffering; and this was what my action did." He had never had any doubt of the wisdom of his action, the Colonel concluded, "not for a moment."

He had testified only unwillingly, Roosevelt wrote a few days later to his eldest son, because "it does not seem to me proper for a Congressional Committee to get an ex-President before them on a matter where all they can possibly say is that they think his judgement was wrong —and where, incidentally, his judgement was absolutely right." For T.R. there could be no confession of error. It would be unfair to accuse him of any conscious villainy in reaching the gentlemen's agreement with the steel executives; yet, he was certainly remiss—if not actually foolish—in his failure to probe further before so readily assenting to their proposition.

However impervious to charges of wrongdoing in the steel matter, Roosevelt was far from unmoved by the government suit of October 26. Taft had been a member of his Cabinet in 1907, had known of the action regarding Tennessee Coal and Iron, indeed "had been emphatic in his commendation," the Colonel wrote a friend two days later. Perhaps the President did not know of Wickersham's move but this was no excuse; it was his own concept of the office that the President was responsible for every action of importance taken by his subordinates. "I am sorry to say," he wrote to James Garfield on October 31, "that I think . . . that both he [Taft] and Wickersham are playing small, mean and foolish politics in this matter."

Roosevelt did not confine his rage over the government suit to private letters but set out at once to prepare a rebuttal, which appeared in the November 18 issue of *The Outlook*. The Taft administration's law-suits to break up large corporations, T.R. charged, were futile and counterproductive. "The effort to restore competition as it was sixty years ago . . . is just as foolish as if we should go back to the flintlocks of Washington's Continentals as a substitute for modern weapons of precision." It was absurd to treat the size of a corporation as a crime in itself. Nothing was to be gained by breaking up huge interstate or international industrial organizations that had not offended other than by size. Such efforts could be compared to attempts "to dam the Mississippi, to stop its flow outright." That would be an effort certain to result in failure and disaster, whereas building levees along the river could control its waters and avoid floods. The nation likewise should adopt a policy "of attacking, not the mere fact of combination, but the evils and wrong-doing which so frequently accompany combination."

The *Outlook* article, one close historian of this period has observed, regained for T.R. the support of solid and conservative business leaders who had been frightened off by the Osawatomie speech in 1910. One friend wrote to call the article an "impregnable and powerful" campaign platform. The Colonel himself, a month later, acknowledged that his newly enunciated position on trusts "was generally accepted" as having brought his name forward once more for the 1912 nomination; the strong undercurrent of feeling for him had merely "come to the surface."

Early in the new year of 1912 Henry Stimson, who had entered the Taft administration as Secretary of War, journeyed to Oyster Bay to sound out the Colonel on his present feelings about the President. Roosevelt, Stimson reported in Washington, was "as hard as nails and utterly implacable"; his personal animosity toward the President dated precisely to the filing of the steel suit. On January 14 Archie Butt—now a major—was invited to a luncheon at the Longworth home and was asked to take in Corinne Robinson. The breach between her brother and Taft, Mrs. Robinson told Major Butt, was now irrevocable; Roosevelt would never forgive his successor for allowing him to be maligned in the U.S. Steel prosecution.

"When I think of the old days at the White House and how these two men seemed to love one another," Mrs. Robinson lamented, "it makes me very unhappy to think of the great chasm which lies between them now. How they would get together and talk and discuss matters! And I remember the way their laughs would mingle and reverberate through the corridors and rooms. . . ." If only the two men could get together again, the Colonel could be made to understand the President's position, Mrs. Robinson's companion suggested. "Oh, Major Butt," she replied sadly, "it is too late now."

4

Roosevelt, even after the announcement of the government's suit against U.S. Steel, continued to tell people that Taft's renomination was probably inevitable and that he would have to support the President, who was better than anyone the Democrats were likely to bring forth. On October 27, in a long letter to Governor Hiram Johnson of California, he said that he himself would make a weak candidate, especially in the East where it would be thought he had betrayed his old friend Taft and had intrigued to have himself nominated. Moreover, he did not want to be sacrificed to lead "the forlorn hope" the campaign of 1912 was likely to prove for the G.O.P. ". . . I ought not to be asked to have my throat cut when the throat-cutting would damage me and in addition, what is infinitely more important, would damage the progressive cause we have at heart."

La Follette's candidacy, meanwhile, seemed to be gathering steam. Three hundred progressives from thirty states gathered in Chicago on October 16 to endorse the Wisconsin senator as "the logical candidate" for the Republican nomination the following year. At the Chicago conclave, La Follette later wrote, there was "but one discordant note." It was sounded by James Garfield. The Ohioan had come to the meeting directly from New York, where he had conferred with Roosevelt, and expended most of his energies at Chicago in trying to prevent the conference from making a specific endorsement of La Follette. Two weeks later the Wisconsin senator was shocked to read an *Outlook* editorial that described what he considered the unqualified progressive endorsement at Chicago as "a recommendation rather than a committal of the movement to any one man." Garfield's action, and the *Outlook* editorial, La Follette said, "revived my distrust regarding Roosevelt."

In an attempt to relieve his anxiety that the Colonel might suddenly enter the race, La Follette dispatched two emissaries from his camp to New York, Chicago newspaperman Gilson Gardner and the muckraking journalist Ray Stannard Baker. Gardner returned to tell his chief that Roosevelt was surprised at the strength of the La Follette candidacy and disappointed by it. He had come away from the interview with the distinct impression that the Colonel wanted to be President again, that up until then he had stood aside only because he thought Taft could not be beaten for the nomination.

Gardner and Baker has asked Roosevelt to announce that he would not accept the nomination under any circumstances; many progressives were withholding their support from the Wisconsin senator until they saw which way the ex-President would move. Roosevelt refused, just as he had refused similar requests from the Taft camp. He explained that no man had the right to ask him whether or not he would cross such a bridge until he came to it. "At present I am not convinced that I will be brought anywhere near the bridge in question," he told Baker.

La Follette next considered writing a public letter to Roosevelt, forcing him to answer the question of whether or not he would be a candidate. A conference was held at Gifford Pinchot's home in Washington and several drafts of a letter to the Colonel were prepared. But the Wisconsin senator suddenly abandoned the effort in disgust. He realized that any such letter would have to carry a give-and-take proposal that would pledge him to support Roosevelt if the sage of Sagamore Hill decided to enter the contest after all. La Follette had no intention of withdrawing in favor of Roosevelt; as he had told his supporters from the very outset of his campaign, he was in the race until nominated or defeated in the convention. Nothing infuriated him more than the swelling chorus of charges that all along he had been but a stalking horse for the former President.

Square in the middle, of course, was the large man in the White House. The special session of Congress had ended on August 22 with more minuses for the President than pluses, with the insurgents within the G.O.P. giving Taft as much if not more trouble than the opposition Democrats. It was all so very discouraging to the amiable Chief Executive. And now there was apparently to be a fight, against either La Follette or Roosevelt, or both, for the 1912 nomination. "The truth is that I am not very happy in this renomination and re-election business," he wrote his brother Charles in September. "I have to set my teeth and go through with it as best I can. I am not going to squeal or run away. . . ."

Archie Butt found the President seemingly obsessed by his predecessor. "Just now the trouble with the Colonel hangs over him like a big, black cloud and seems to be his nemesis. He frets under it, I can see," Butt wrote. Careful to say nothing in public, Taft was now speaking slightingly of Roosevelt in private—and the words, of course, found their way to Oyster Bay. There was no longer even a fragment of respect for their once close friendship. The Colonel felt the same way. He did not want to be drawn into any attack on Taft, T.R. wrote to Henry Cabot Lodge at the end of December, "but Heavens and earth, what a floppy souled creature he is!"

By then Roosevelt had a new cause for displeasure with his successor, the arbitration treaties the administration had negotiated with England and France. The move, the Colonel argued, was "one of intolerable folly and hypocrisy." Such treaties would bargain away the national honor, and he besieged Lodge and Root to lead an effort in the Senate to modify them. T.R. brusquely declined to attend the New York Citizens' Peace Banquet, at which the President would speak on his arbitration treaties, because—as he told reporters—"I am not hungry."

Christmas came to Sagamore Hill. Edith Roosevelt had been thrown from a horse early in the autumn, had been unconscious for thirty-six hours, had experienced severe headaches, and had suffered a temporary impairment of her senses of taste and smell. But the former First Lady had recovered by year's end and was able to preside happily over the holiday family reunion. The Longworths arrived from Washington and in the morning of December 25 Roosevelt and his son-in-law "solemnly" chopped wood, "an occupation at which he is even worse than I am," T.R. wrote Theodore, Jr.; and in the afternoon the two took a three or four hours' walk, "a form of exercise in which I am even worse than he is." The only cloud over the holiday was the absence of Ted, his wife, Eleanor, and Roosevelt's first grandchild, their daughter Grace, born the preceding summer; "it was not really Christmas as long as Gracie was not present," the Colonel wrote his son. "Christmas loses some of its fine edge when the youngest child is a boy a half inch taller than his father!"

The new year of 1912 was but two days old when politics intruded once more. Representative George W. Norris of Nebraska, a La Follette supporter, had written the Colonel asking him to demand that the Secretary of State of Nebraska remove Roosevelt's name from the primary ballot. This would mean that he must now declare that he would not accept the presidential nomination if it were offered him, T.R. answered Norris; and this was still a bridge he could not cross.

Historians have scrutinized Roosevelt's voluminous correspondence through 1911 and into the early months of 1912, and have sifted the conflicting testimony of those who spoke to him at the time—all in an effort to find the precise moment at which he decided to become a candidate for the Republican nomination. Such exhaustive efforts are perhaps futile and really unimportant. The transition from a critical but reluctant supporter of Taft to a determined and implacable opponent was a gradual one. It can only be said that at the beginning of January, 1912, Roosevelt—indeed, as he wrote Norris—was not ready to cross that bridge; but at the end of the month he had decided he must become a candidate.

Through December Roosevelt had continued to protest that his nomination would be a personal "misfortune" and a "calamity." "In my opinion," T.R.'s old friend of the police commissioner days, newspaper-man Joseph Bucklin Bishop, wrote on the first of the month, "the matter has already passed out of your hands. Whether you wish to be the candidate or not does not weigh a particle. The party needs you and will take you willy-nilly." And on December 2, Roosevelt wrote to Dan Hanna, the son of Mark Hanna and publisher of the Cleveland *Leader,* approving an editorial stating that the progressives could count on Roosevelt's leadership if and when it was needed. But to William Allen White, who had written to say that the Colonel's campaign ark was afloat, T.R. replied that he was "feeling a warm sympathy for those friends of Noah who assured him that it would not be much of a shower." Whereas he had formerly asked individuals booming his candidacy to cease their efforts, one historian has noted, he now invited them to Oyster Bay to discuss the situation.

The Colonel was protesting, in a letter of January 9 to William L. Ward, Republican national committeeman from New York, that he did not want the nomination to come "as the result of artificial stimulus." He agreed completely with Ward's earlier assertion that the nomination, if it came at all, must come as the result of "an honest widespread desire of the people and not as the result of the slightest manipulation on the part of any individual, or set of individuals." In fact, T.R. sent Ward's statement to a number of his other correspondents.

Ward, however, did not heed his own advice. On January 13 he joined Cal O'Laughlin, T.R.'s traveling companion from Khartoum through Europe, William Franklin Knox, a former Rough Rider and now a Michigan newspaper publisher, and James Keeley, editor of the Chicago *Tribune,* in setting up a Roosevelt National Committee in Chicago. Ward soon recruited to the committee a number of Eastern and Midwestern professional politicians equally determined to promote a Roosevelt candidacy. The campaign ark was indeed afloat—though it was still uncertain if Noah would come aboard.

5

La Follette began to panic. It was clear to him at least that Roosevelt would soon declare his candidacy—and that this would precipitate a stampede of progressives from his own camp to that of the Colonel's. He sadly recognized that even among the intimate members of his own campaign organization there were men ready to bolt to Roosevelt. Nonetheless, in a statement issued to the press on January 29 he reaffirmed that he would be in the race "until the gavel falls in the convention announcing the nominee."

Four days later the Wisconsin senator attended the annual banquet of the Periodical Publishers' Association in Philadelphia. Tired from his previous speaking engagements, upset by the news that his small daughter must have an operation, discouraged by a conference in Washington that, he believed, had revealed "the studied undermining" of his candidacy by his own supporters, La Follette considered canceling his talk to the publishers. Once before, in his first term as Governor of Wisconsin, he had pushed himself too hard and had had a breakdown leading to reports that he was losing his mind. Nevertheless he went to Philadelphia on February 2, "knowing that to speak there would make demands upon me which, at that time, I could ill afford."

The publishers' dinner proved to be a complete disaster for the beleaguered La Follette. Woodrow Wilson of New Jersey spoke first, giving an address of "flawless art" that held the eight hundred guests spellbound. Rising at his turn, La Follette bowed to Wilson, observed that if any Democrat were to be elected President that year he hoped it would be the New Jersey governor, and began his speech. He was going to tell his audience the true story of money in the United States, he said, and how it was stolen from those to whom it rightfully belonged. But first he launched into a bitter, gratuitous, and—considering his audience—ill-considered attack on journalists.

People at the various tables began to squirm and look at one another in surprise and dismay. A few rose to leave. "There go some of the fellows I'm hitting," La Follette shouted at them. "They don't want to hear about themselves." The chairman called the senator to order for engaging in personal abuse, and he continued. Now his listeners realized with horror that entire passages of the speech were being repeated, that instead of turning over pages of his manuscript as he finished them the senator was hopelessly shuffling them together. Soon shouts of "Sit down!" were heard from the audience and more people rose to leave. But La Follette refused to stop and went on with the incoherent speech, mumbling, repeating, shouting. He spoke for two and a half hours and when he finished it was after midnight and there were few left in the room but the embarrassed guests at the head table.

Reports went out the next day that La Follette had suffered a nervous breakdown and had withdrawn from the presidential race. With what one historian has called "indecent haste," the Pinchots, Medill McCormick of Chicago, and others switched their allegiance from the Wisconsin senator to Roosevelt. It was announced from La Follette headquarters that the senator, ill from overwork, would cancel all engagements and take a two-week sick leave. When he returned to the campaign trail, however, he would find his presidential hopes all but vanished.

Roosevelt was now only awaiting the right opportunity to announce his candidacy—though he continued to protest that he was not seeking the nomination. On January 16 a long "Private & Confidential" letter had gone to New York publisher Frank Munsey. "I am not and shall not be a candidate," T.R. declared. He would neither seek the nomination nor accept it if it came as a result of "an intrigue." Yet he could not make a public statement that would take him out of the race, one that "would make it difficult or impossible for me to serve the public by undertaking a great task if the people as a whole seemed definitely to come to the conclusion that I ought to do that task." The best course, he still maintained, was to keep public silence on the nomination. Among those who received copies of the Munsey letter was Elihu Root. "No thirsty sinner ever took a pledge which was harder for him to keep than it will be for you to maintain this position," Root replied.

Roosevelt was thirstier than Root imagined—or at least his friends were convincing him of his thirst. A number of progressive Republican governors had joined the chorus of those demanding he take the lead of a crusade against Taft. T.R. decided, only two days after he wrote the Munsey letter, that he could no longer remain silent and that his declaration should come in the form of a response to a round-robin petition from what came to be called "the seven little governors"— the chief executives of West Virginia, Nebraska, New Hampshire, Wyoming, Michigan, Kansas, and Missouri.

The "somewhat 'cooked' letter," as Alice Longworth called it, was dated February 10 and certainly did not take her father entirely by surprise. In it the seven governors declared that it was their belief that a large majority of Republican voters favored his election. Roosevelt represented "as no other man represents those principles and policies . . . necessary for the happiness and prosperity of the country." In asking the Colonel to declare that he would accept the G.O.P. nomination if it came to him "unsolicited and unsought," the governors said that they were not considering Roosevelt's personal interests. If the ex-President declined to accept the nomination, he would be "unresponsive to a plain public duty."

Roosevelt's brief response, dated Saturday, February 24, was published in the Monday newspapers. The governors' letter, he noted, put a heavy responsibility on him, "expressing as it does the carefully considered convictions of the men elected by popular vote to stand at the heads of government in their several states." After agreeing that this was a matter not to be decided with reference to the personal preferences of any man, he came to the point. "I will accept the nomination for President if it is tendered to me, and I will adhere to this decision until the convention has expressed its preference."

The ebullient Colonel could not wait for the publication of his letter to the seven little governors, however. On February 21, arriving in Columbus, Ohio, to give a speech before the state's constitutional convention, Roosevelt was once more asked if he was in the race. To the inquiring reporter, T.R. replied—adding a colorful and enduring phrase to the vocabulary of American politics—"My hat is in the ring."

Chapter 11

When Friends Become Enemies

An unusual number of important people called upon Theodore Roosevelt at his *Outlook* office in New York on February 14, 1912, among them Oscar S. Straus. The Colonel gave his former Cabinet officer galley proofs of the speech he intended to deliver the following week before the Ohio Constitutional Convention at Columbus. After reading the speech, Straus confided to one of the magazine's editors that he was frankly shocked; T.R. had gone too far to the left, he felt. "I hear you don't like my speech," Roosevelt said to Straus later. It was fine, all but one part, Straus started to explain. But Roosevelt snapped that his mind was made up; uncharacteristically for him, he did not want to hear any counterarguments.

Actually the Colonel had solicited a number of opinions on the speech and had already revised it to accommodate the suggestions of other critics. After reading the first two drafts of the speech, Amos Pinchot had written to say he felt that Roosevelt was putting in too many qualifying statements. If the speech gave that impression, T.R. replied, and if it did not convince sincere progressives that he was taking a sufficiently well-defined radical position, then it would be a failure. It would mean that the country was not ready to "tolerate my leadership at all." Roosevelt had qualified his statements to make them precise; the tendency among public men—progressives as well as conservatives, he was sorry to say—was "to utter a string of easy, well-sounding, and rather cheap, half-truths." But he was determined to utter whole truths, "which are complex and difficult of statement."

The Columbus speech was to be the platform for T.R.'s campaign for the G.O.P. nomination; it was also, even his most devoted followers would come to feel, a fatal misstep. Rising before the Ohio convention, Roosevelt began by demonstrating his Republican orthodoxy; seven times in the first seventeen paragraphs he cited Lincoln. With Lincoln, he held that "this country, with its institutions, belongs to the people who inhabit it. Whenever they shall grow weary of the existing government, they can exercise their constitutional right of amending it"—as these men had gathered at Columbus to revise their state constitution.

But Roosevelt had not traveled to the Midwest merely to lecture on Ohio's new constitution. He had come to announce his position on the controversial issues of the day, to draw together and restate most of the doctrines about which he had been speaking and writing since the campaign of 1910. Quickly the Colonel endorsed such reforms as the short ballot, direct preferential primaries for the election of delegates to the national nominating conventions, direct election of United States senators, and the initiative and referendum. He still did not see the necessity for the recall of short-term elective officers and believed in the recall of judges only "as a last resort, when it has become clearly evident that no other course will achieve the desired result." Then Roosevelt stepped to the brink and—in the opinion of his detractors—plunged into a murky abyss.

"But when a judge decides a constitutional question, when he decides what the people as a whole can or cannot do," the Colonel declaimed, "the people should have the right to recall that decision if they think it is wrong." Lincoln in his campaign for the Presidency had denounced the Dred Scott decision, Roosevelt noted. The people took his side and—though the word recall was not used—the decision was effectively nullified. Yet T.R. was not advocating recall of United States Supreme Court decisions, only those of a state's highest court. If a considerable number of people felt that a particular decision, declaring a statute unconstitutional, was "in defiance of justice," then the people by petition should be able to bring the issue before the full electorate. The voters would decide whether or not to sustain the decision. This popular verdict was to be accepted as final—"subject only to action by the Supreme Court of the United States."

The people were not infallible, Roosevelt conceded, but they "have shown themselves wiser than the courts in the way they have approached and dealt with such vital questions of our day as those concerning the proper control of big corporations and of securing their rights to industrial workers." He then proceeded to detail instances in which state courts had declared unconstitutional laws attempting to regulate hours of work for women and to hold corporations liable for injuries sustained by their employees on the job. "I wish I could make you visualize to yourselves what these decisions against which I so vehemently protest really represent of suffering and injustice. I wish I had the power to bring before you the man maimed or dead, the women and children left to struggle against bitter poverty because the bread-winner has gone."

The shockwaves set off by the speech at Columbus and by T.R.'s subsequent letter to the seven little governors announcing his candidacy traveled fast and reached far. Partisans felt compelled to state their positions—for or against Roosevelt's advocacy of the recall of judicial decisions; for or against his effort to wrest the Republican nomination from Taft and risk a fatal sundering of the G.O.P.; for or against his decision to break tradition and seek what would be, in effect, a third term. New political alliances were forged; old relationships were severed; and friends were friends no longer.

"You can hardly exaggerate the consternation into which the Roosevelt cohort has been thrown by his actual cavortings now going on," Henry Adams wrote a friend on February 25, "and there is not one of your intimates but is squirming like a skinned eel at the hole into which he has thrown them." The Colonel's friends were wondering, Adams said, what he expected of them. "Even so clearheaded a man as Root" thought that T.R. had in mind not the Presidency, "but that he aims at a leadership far in the future, as a sort of Moses and Messiah for a vast progressive tide of a rising humanity." All of the critics, Adams concluded, now accepted his old theory that Roosevelt was insane. "I see nothing for him but the asylum." Less apocalyptic was the comment of California Congressman William Kent on Roosevelt's declaration of candidacy. "Terrible Ted," he said, had gone "with the girl so long he had to marry her."

Four days after delivering the Columbus address, on Sunday, February 25, Roosevelt was a dinner and overnight guest at the Boston home of Judge Robert Grant. Among the other guests were the historian William Roscoe Thayer and William Allen White of Emporia, Kansas. In defending his speech, which Thayer had found too radical, the Colonel said that he wished to draw into "one dominant stream" all the na-

tion's intelligent and patriotic men, "in order to prepare against the social upheaval which will otherwise overwhelm us." Did the ex-President
mean to found a great centrist party, such as the one Cavour had
founded for the liberation of Italy, asked Thayer, who had just completed his two-volume study of the Italian statesman. "Exactly," replied
T.R. But, Judge Grant now asked, would the present leaders of the
G.O.P. support him in this endeavor. "No," answered the Colonel.
"None of them; not even Lodge, I think." The judge pressed him further. "But the situation is complex, I suppose? You would like to be
President." "You are right. It is complex," said Roosevelt. "I like power;
but I care nothing to be President as President. I am interested in these
ideas of mine and I want to carry them through, and feel that I am the
one to carry them through."

Years later White would remember Judge Grant's guests reading
the statement announcing T.R.'s candidacy—the letter replying to the
seven little governors—that was to be given out that evening for publication in Monday's newspapers. The Kansas editor suggested a few sty-
listic changes and then told the Colonel that if he was determined to
make such a mistake as running for the Presidency again, he would help
him "with all my heart to make it as terrible as possible." And White left
Boston on the midnight train for New York and Washington, "full of
bewildered zeal for a cause that I did not then entirely approve."

Monday afternoon in the capital White went to see Kansas Congressman Victor Murdock, whom he found to be "amazed and not altogether delighted with the Colonel's statement." But Murdock had also
broken with the President, thought La Follette was hopeless, and believed that Roosevelt could win. "Victor," White said, "the Colonel
thinks it's 1860, and it looks to me about like '56. He's not running
against Douglas. He's running against Buchanan." Murdock smiled and
replied: "Bill, he's running against Franklin Pierce. This rebellion has a
long, long way to go before it wins."

Henry Cabot Lodge had called in the gentlemen of the press to declare that he was opposed to the constitutional changes advocated by
Roosevelt at Columbus and that he must continue to oppose the policies
now advocated by his oldest and closest associate in politics. ". . . but I
cannot personally oppose him who has been my lifelong friend, and for
this reason I take no part whatever in the campaign for the presidential
nomination." "I have had my share of mishaps in politics," Lodge wrote
the Colonel on February 28, "but I never thought that any situation

could arise which would have made me so miserably unhappy as I have been during the past week." The Columbus speech had served to reveal their differences of opinion on constitutional issues. He had long known, Lodge continued, that the two did indeed differ but he had not fully realized how wide was the difference. It had been impossible to keep silent and risk misrepresentation of his own position, Lodge concluded, and so he had given the statement to the press. "It is at least honest although it gives no expression to the pain and unhappiness which lie behind it."

"I don't know whether to be most touched by your letter or most inclined to laugh over it," the Colonel replied on March 1. Nothing Lodge could do would make Roosevelt lose "my warm personal affection for you." He had known for a couple of years that the two of them were heading in opposite directions as regards domestic politics; but he would not now try to justify his own viewpoint for fear it would be attacking Lodge's. "Of course, you will stand by your convictions," the Colonel said. "Now, don't you ever think of this matter again." But the end was written to a political alliance that stretched back more than a quarter century.

President Taft had apparently been following his rival's pronouncements carefully and promptly denounced T.R.'s proposal for the recall of judicial decisions. "Such extremists," he stated, "would hurry us into a condition which would find no parallel except in the French Revolution or in that bubbling anarchy that once characterized the South American Republics. Such extremists"—naming no names but making it perfectly clear to whom he was referring—"are not progressive—they are political emotionalists or neurotics."

No lingering tatter of friendship between Taft and Roosevelt remained to be swept aside by the Columbus speech, but elsewhere there were to be sad and painful partings of the way. Henry Stimson made his choice and announced it in a speech delivered at Chicago on March 5. He had first entered politics under the aegis of Theodore Roosevelt, he still believed in Roosevelt's policies, and he still considered himself the Colonel's friend. But those who were now forcing T.R. to make the race against Taft were "jeopardizing instead of helping the real cause of progress in the nation." Stimson had sent a copy of the speech to Sagamore Hill, with a letter saying he thought that T.R. was making a mistake and that "the horizon of my little world was swimming a good deal and it is hard to look forward to a time when I am not working or thinking with you. . . ."

"Heaven's sake!" the Colonel replied. "You have so often been right that it is perfectly possible that I am wrong and I needn't tell you, my dear fellow, that I do not care a rap about your attitude in favor of Mr. Taft." He had always known that Stimson would have to be for the renomination of the President he now served as Secretary of War. As for the Chicago speech, T.R. continued, he did not have time to read it. "The newspapers waste their time if they try to tell me anything that you have said against me."

To some old friends Roosevelt would not be so charitable. Chicago publisher H. H. Kohlsaat had written to suggest that he withdraw from the race against Taft. "If you were my worst enemy," T.R. replied in the white heat of anger, "you could not advise me to do anything more utterly destructive of my good name, more utterly damaging to my character. . . . I am astounded—and I mean this—that you should write me such a letter."

Kohlsaat had earlier admonished Roosevelt to adhere to the statement made on election night of 1904, that he considered the full term to which he had then been elected his second and would not accept nomination to a third term in 1908. "I would cut that hand off right here," Kohlsaat later had Roosevelt saying, as he put his finger to his wrist, "if I could recall that statement to the Associated Press." Less dramatically, but more plausibly, Roosevelt early in 1912 was explaining away the 1904 statement. What he had renounced was only renomination, as the incumbent, in 1908; he had not meant the statement to apply to 1912 anymore than it should apply to 1916, 1928, or even 1948. The prohibition against third terms should stand only against three consecutive terms. When he turned down a third cup of coffee at breakfast, it did not mean he was denying himself coffee at lunch, dinner, or anytime later on in life. The third-term issue, as far as the Colonel was concerned, simply did not exist.

What T.R. could not acknowledge—perhaps even to himself— was that he wanted a third term rather desperately. He was very nearly obsessed with power, more so in the period after he left the White House than during the years in office when power—often as much power as he wished to exercise—was within his grasp. Yet Roosevelt was a highly moralistic man. Deep within, he must have sensed that there was something dark and almost unnatural about this craving for power, something not spoken about, something best ignored. No one can ever know the inner turmoil he endured as the two conflicting natures struggled for supremacy. When the desire for power overcame his very real reluctance to return to office, the Colonel would begin to make elaborate excuses for what many considered his erratic and contradictory behavior.

Elihu Root was another who would not follow his old chief in this new crusade. Roosevelt was essentially a fighter, "completely dominated by the desire to destroy his adversary," the New York senator told a friend. The Colonel instinctively grabbed any weapon that could be used to that end. Thus, he was now saying things and taking positions that, Root claimed, were inspired simply by his desire to win. "I have no doubt he thinks he believes what he says, but he doesn't. He has merely picked up certain popular ideas which were at hand as one might pick up a poker or a chair with which to strike." And the elegant, brilliant, and supercilious former Cabinet officer, who had long regarded the Colonel fondly if patronizingly, became—next to Taft—Roosevelt's most implacable adversary.

The unhappiest person of the year 1912, according to Alice Longworth, was her husband, Nick. He was the congressman from Taft's home district in Cincinnati and, moreover, firmly in sympathy with the President. Alice naturally was for her father "without reservation." "I have got to come out [for the nomination]," the Colonel had written his son-in-law on February 13. "You let me know how matters are in your district and I will try to smash up any Roosevelt creature who antagonizes you."

Equally unhappy, though few realized it at the time, was Archie Butt, unable to choose between Roosevelt and Taft as the gap between his former and present chiefs widened. "The clash which must follow between these two men is tragic," Butt wrote on February 14. "It is moving now from day to day with the irresistible force of the Greek drama. . . ." The President, noticing that his normally cheerful and vigorous military aide seemed depressed and unduly fatigued, kindly suggested that he take a leave and go abroad. Thus, on March 2, five days after Roosevelt's declaration of candidacy had been published, Major Butt sailed for Europe. The ship on which he booked his return passage, six weeks later, was the *Titanic*. Four years earlier Butt had written to his mother that although he had no favorite hymn he would like to have "Nearer, My God, to Thee" played at his funeral. And it was Archie Butt, remaining on board to help others abandon ship after the giant vessel had struck an iceberg, who asked the ship's band to play the famous hymn as the *Titantic* slipped beneath the icy waters of the North Atlantic. There would be no more intimate letters to "Dear Clara," no more inside glimpses of the disintegrating Taft administration.

William Rockhill Nelson, publisher of the Kansas City *Star,* was in Washington shortly after the Columbus speech and the announcement of T.R.'s candidacy. The *Star*'s office was next to that of *The New York Times,* and Nelson stopped by to discuss the speech with Oscar King Davis, Washington correspondent of the *Times.* "I'm for Roosevelt, first, last, and all the time. I'm for him right or wrong," Nelson exclaimed. Although he could not pretend to like everything the Colonel did or said, this was going to be a fight to the finish, "and every man in this country has got to get on one side or the other. My side is with Roosevelt. Where are you going to stand?" There was only one answer for O. K. Davis, who shortly thereafter resigned from the *Times* to serve in the Roosevelt campaign.

For others the choice would be more difficult. Novelist Owen Wister recalled that he had once visited T.R. in the White House during a demonstration of jujitsu. When he failed to understand the holds, Roosevelt tried to make it all clear by locking a strangle hold about the writer's neck. "It may have taken thirty seconds," Wister related. But "my Adam's apple was sore for three days. Swallowing hurt. Of course he never knew it, and of course I never told him. In 1912 he had no notion of how it hurt to swallow some of the things he was saying."

In Washington President Taft went walking with Archie Butt after reading dispatches of the Columbus address. Now that the Colonel's hat was in the ring, he confessed to a "strong presentiment" that he would be beaten in the convention. He promised to fight to the end but when his friends claimed victory for him—Taft told the major in one of their last chats—"remember that I feel I am losing a battle and that I am not blind myself, no matter what my friends may put out." Mrs. Taft expressed great discouragement when the news of T.R.'s candidacy was released. "I told you so four years ago and you would not believe me," she complained to her husband. "I know you did, my dear," the President said, chuckling, "and I think you are perfectly happy now. You would have preferred the Colonel to come out against me than to have been wrong yourself."

2

To most people who met him Roosevelt seemed larger than he actually was: a stocky, close to two hundred pound, five-foot-ten or eleven. In 1912, at the age of 53, he was at the peak of his mental and physical powers. He had long legs but a short trunk, with a barrel chest and sloping, boxer's shoulders. His head, wrote William Allen White in the best physical description we have from a contemporary, "often, perhaps generally, was thrust forward from the neck, a firm short pedestal for his face. . . ." White said that T.R.'s countenance was dominated by his large, pugnacious nose, while the drooping moustache covered a sensitive mouth. The heavy underlip T.R. used "as a shutter, purposely to uncover a double row of glittering teeth that were his pride." The Colonel used this display of dentures, the Kansas newspaperman claimed, as "a gesture of humor or rage." Teeth bared, his slightly cleft chin thrust forward, Roosevelt would work his jaw muscles with "an animal ferocity."

T.R. had a high, wide brow from which his hair line had not receded an inch. He kept his stiff hair, which inclined to curl, shortly cropped, giving him an aspect of virility, wrote White, "so real that, looking at Roosevelt's hair, one could understand how Delilah thought she could sap Samson's strength by shearing him." T.R.'s narrowly set eyes, only one of which by this time retained any vision, peered out from the flashing pince-nez glasses that were another trademark. With the glasses off—never in public, of course—Roosevelt's ferocity vanished. Waxing somewhat fanciful, White described the two men he saw in Roosevelt: "One was a primitive—impetuous, imperious, splashing in a reservoir of vigor; the other was sophisticated, not ever quite furtive, but often feline."

To White and many of the others who would blindly, unquestioningly follow him in the quixotic crusade of 1912, Roosevelt was "big, overwhelming, towering, monumental, a very Goliath of a personality inflated out of a common man by surplus energy." He was overcharged, hyperactive, superenergetic—a man, it should have been obvious, who could never have accepted the passive role of elder statesman at "the ripest time of his life." Yet, "with all his Cyclopean features," White found him well balanced in mind and body. "If he was a freak," the admiring Kansan concluded, "God and the times needed one."

It was this seemingly superhuman figure who commanded the attention of a vast audience at New York's Carnegie Hall on the evening of March 20—a crowd come to hear T.R. deliver his first major address since the already famous Columbus speech. It was to be the kickoff of the most vigorously contested fight for a nomination in the nation's history, one that held particular fascination because of the former personal and political friendship of the two major contestants. Five thousand were turned back at the doors of Carnegie Hall, but the capacity crowd inside respectfully fell silent as the Colonel rose to make his speech.

The fundamental issue of the campaign for the nomination, Roosevelt stated at the outset, was the question of whether or not the people were fit to govern themselves. He felt they were; his opponents—President Taft and his backers—felt they were not. He was supporting such reforms as the direct primary and the initiative and referendum because of his faith in the people. His opponents, because they feared the will of the people, were opposing such reforms. Not known for his ability to perceive shades of gray, Roosevelt once more was presenting a simple choice between black and white.

The President, Roosevelt claimed, upheld the position of that "large number of reputable and honorable men who, down at bottom, distrust popular government, and, when they must accept it, accept it with reluctance, and hedge it around with every species of restriction and check and balance, so as to make the power of the people as limited and as ineffective as possible." Taft, in short, favored a government for all the people, by a representative part of the people—what T.R. found to be "an excellent and moderate description of an oligarchy." The President's calm advocacy of such a position differed only in manner of presentation from the view "nakedly set forth" by one of his supporters who had said Roosevelt's proposal for the recall of judicial decisions was "equivalent to allowing an appeal from the umpire to the bleachers." He for one, said T.R. warming to the metaphor, did not see self-government in the United States as a game in which the populace —having paid the price of admission—should be content to sit in the bleachers and watch powerlessly as the professional politicians in the arena below waged their contest. The Constitution, said the Colonel slipping into another easy-to-understand metaphor, is not "a straightjacket to be used for the control of an unruly patient—the people."

Taft had described Roosevelt's controversial recall plan as giving in to "the fitful impulse of a temporary majority." But, the Colonel now reminded his audience, the method of review he proposed might take as long as two years from the time of the election of the legislature that passed an act later declared unconstitutional by a state court. On the other hand, a presidential campaign then lasted approximately four months from the time of the nominating conventions to the general election. How had Taft reached the Presidency, other than by "the fitful impulse of a temporary majority."

"I am not leading this fight as a matter of aesthetic pleasure," T.R. said as he approached his peroration. "I am leading because somebody must lead, or else the fight would not be made at all." The task facing Americans was to strive for social and industrial justice, goals to be achieved through the genuine rule of the people. In order to succeed, he concluded, "we need leaders of inspired idealism, leaders to whom are granted great visions, who dream greatly and strive to make their dreams come true; who can kindle the people with the fire from their own burning souls." Such leaders, however, were but instruments, "to be used until broken and then to be cast aside. . . ." Any leader worth his salt would care no more about being cast aside than a soldier going into battle should care that his life may be forfeit in order to win the victory. "In the long fight for righteousness the watchword for all of us is spend and be spent. It is of little matter whether any one man fails or succeeds; but the cause shall not fail, for it is the cause of mankind."

As he reached the stirring conclusion to his speech, the Carnegie Hall audience—virtually as one man—leaped to their feet, cheering and wildly applauding. In the crowd that night was William Barnes, leader of the Old Guard Republican faction in New York. Asked later why he rose with the rest and responded so enthusiastically to the man he was pledged to oppose, Barnes confessed, "Why, I was on my feet before I knew it. Roosevelt, confound him, has a kind of magnetism that you cannot resist when you are in his presence."

Barnes would remain loyal to the President—and indeed would become one of T.R.'s most bitter foes—but Roosevelt's campaign for the nomination was already creating some particularly curious political bedfellows. Even before publication of Roosevelt's letter to the seven little governors saying he would accept the nomination, a campaign organization had been put together under capable, genial Senator Joseph M. Dixon of Montana. With headquarters in New York, Dixon's executive committee would provide the professional know-how for the hordes of dedicated amateurs who would be carrying the Roosevelt banner across the country. Such well-known progressives as Governor Hiram Johnson of California, ex-Senator Albert J. Beveridge of Indiana, senators Moses Clapp, Jonathan Bourne, Joseph Bristow, Miles Poindexter, and William Borah, and Representative George Norris of Nebraska joined the Roosevelt ranks. But so too did the politicians William Flinn of Pennsylvania and William L. Ward of New York's Westchester County—"as reactionary a boss as ever stood beneath the G.O.P. banner," according to Amos Pinchot. The omnipresent Pinchot brothers and James Garfield stood with the Colonel, of course, as did George Walbridge Perkins.

A former insurance company executive and a partner in the House of Morgan, Perkins had helped form the International Harvester Company, the Northern Securities Company, and the United States Steel Corporation. Perkins had impressed Roosevelt as a public-spirited man when the two met during the latter's term as Governor of New York, and T.R. had appointed him to the Palisades Interstate Park Commission. In 1910 Perkins, then two years short of his fiftieth birthday, had resigned from Morgan to devote himself to public affairs—some would say king-making and preparation for becoming a power behind the throne. George Perkins thoroughly agreed with Roosevelt that large corporations, properly supervised by government, were more efficient than small, competing ones, and he took the somewhat radical view—for a man of his background—that workers should share in corporate profits and should be protected in retirement with pensions.

In 1912 Perkins was described by the pudgy and envious William Allen White as being "handsome . . . slim and trim, exquisitely undertailored." In the campaign—in which he soon came to play a leading role—Perkins made quick decisions, spoke softly, smiled easily, was "as careful of the punctilios as a preacher at the front door of the church." White watched him with grudging admiration but nonetheless felt him to be a sinister influence and grumbled about this to the Colonel. One of the nastier charges of the campaign involved T.R.'s failure as President to have prosecuted International Harvester for violation of the antitrust law—and the subsequent, presumably coincidental appearance in his campaign entourage of the man who had fashioned the corporation, George W. Perkins. Along with New York publisher Frank Munsey, Perkins would provide the principal financial backing for the Roosevelt candidacy—right through the general election. Indeed, one

Western progressive was soon complaining to the Colonel that the Roosevelt organization was "merely George Perkins and a pushbutton."

As for Munsey, whose newspaper acquisitions and consolidations caused him to be feared and hated in the journalistic profession, William Allen White would have the last, acid word. Writing Munsey's obituary thirteen years later, White claimed that Munsey "contributed to the journalism of his day the great talent of a meat packer, the morals of a money changer and the manners of an undertaker. He [had] . . . succeeded in transforming a once noble profession into an eight per-cent security." But in 1912 White stood shoulder to shoulder with Frank Munsey, placing his tiny Emporia *Gazette* in line with the Munsey chain. T.R.'s additional newspaper support would come from Medill McCormick's Chicago *Tribune,* William Rockhill Nelson's Kansas City *Star,* E. A. Van Valkenberg's Philadelphia *North American,* Henry L. Stoddard's New York *Evening Mail,* and the five newspapers—including the Indianapolis *Star* and Denver *Times*—owned by John C. Shaffer.

The Colonel would make much—especially in a speech delivered in Louisville, Kentucky, on April 3—of the fact that President Taft was being supported by the bosses of the G.O.P. Old Guard. "These men know him well," Roosevelt said of the President's conservative backers, naming names, "and have studied his actions for three years, and they regard him as being precisely the kind of Progressive whom they approve; that is, as not a Progressive at all." But he ignored the complaints of those progressives who objected to the presence of Ward and Flinn among his train of supporters. And although Roosevelt loved to swing out against the "malefactors of great wealth," he readily accepted large contributions from Perkins and Munsey—$15,000 from each in the contest for New York delegates to the convention. There were splendid openings for "practical malefactors of great wealth" in the Roosevelt camp, commented *Life* magazine—if only they promised to burn their letters and apply at the back door.

Curiously, Taft was finding it difficult to raise funds for his own renomination campaign. The Republican National Committee seemed to think that the President's brother Charley would again come through with the necessary financing. "I am not made of money," Charles Taft had protested. "The committee has got no money, and it can't raise any, and it will be the same thing after the convention. . . . My only complaint is that they expect me to do it all." A millionaire friend of his,

Charles Taft noted, was complaining about the expense of getting a European prince—through the marriage of his daughter—into the family. "He ought to have tried getting a president into one," Charley observed.

3

The presidential election of 1912 would be the first in which primaries played a significant role. At the beginning of the year only a handful of the forty-eight states—notably California, Nebraska, New Jersey, North Dakota, Oregon, and Wisconsin—had some sort of primary legislation on their books. In six additional states—Illinois, Maryland, Massachusetts, Ohio, Pennsylvania, and South Dakota—bills establishing primaries were quickly pushed through the state legislatures, Roosevelt supporters backing the measures, Taft men generally opposing them. With election procedures set by so many different state legislatures, the primaries varied widely from state to state, as they still do.

In some states there was to be a true presidential preference primary, allowing registered voters of each party to mark ballots for the man they wished their party to nominate at its coming national convention. On the Republican side, this narrowed to a choice of Roosevelt, Taft, or La Follette. In other states, voters would cast their ballots for a slate of delegates pledged to support a particular candidate at the convention. Some states allowed primaries at the district level only, to select delegates to a state convention where the delegation to the national convention would ultimately be chosen. But in an overwhelming number of states the delegates to the national nominating conventions would be selected by the state conventions, whose delegates were not selected by the people but rather by the party machinery. And in 1912 the Republican state conventions were largely controlled by Taft men.

By the time the Roosevelt campaign for the nomination was officially launched, it was already too late to do much about the South, where there were no primaries, only state conventions. The Florida gathering on February 6, first in the nation, had set the pattern. Taft men, firmly in control of the convention, settled most contests brought up from district meetings in favor of the President. At this point, the Roosevelt men marched from the hall in a body, held a rump convention, and nominated their own slate of delegates to the national convention, which was scheduled to open in Chicago on June 18. Ormsby McHarg, an opportunistic defector from the Taft administration and unofficial roving campaign manager for T.R., seized upon this as his principal strategy for the remainder of the campaign. Rather than allow Taft to reach the convention with a monolithic block of Southern votes, he would contest the results of all Southern conventions and see that rival delegations appeared at Chicago.

A newspaperman sympathetic to Roosevelt later explained McHarg's reasoning. Since there would be no opportunity to develop the Colonel's strength until the Northern and Western primaries were held, it was essential not to let an impression be formed that Taft—because of his showing in the South—was unbeatable. A chart showing Taft with 150 delegates and Roosevelt with 18 would not inspire any confidence in T.R.'s campaign. But one showing Taft 23, Roosevelt 18, contested 127 would give an altogether different picture. The friendly journalist even claimed that these early contests were never intended to be taken seriously. But eventually it was on this very issue—the seating of contested delegates—that the convention and the nomination were to hinge.

At the outset even the Colonel had reservations about McHarg's method of operating. Some of his opponents were charging that McHarg was securing Southern delegates by the promise of money or patronage, T.R. wrote on March 4. He was certain the stories were false, but he wanted from McHarg a denial that he was securing delegates by improper means.

Even with such a resourceful politician as McHarg at work, it was an uphill fight for the Roosevelt men. Taft supporters, they charged, had been using federal patronage to ensure that Southern delegations to the national convention in June would be solidly pro-Taft. Local postmasters were instructed to bring Taft delegations to state nominating conventions, or face removal. Against such tactics, Roosevelt could only rail, occasionally win a victory, and later at Chicago enter official protests.

To no one's surprise these district and state conventions—running from February through the spring—were acrimonious affairs, at which physical violence often broke out. Nearly every district gathering in Missouri ended in a fist fight and mob rule; so many members of one conclave came armed with baseball bats that it was dubbed the "ball bat convention." But Oklahoma—only five years a state and still frontier country—provided the most violent scenes. Just before the state convention was to open on March 14, the Old Guard state committee ruled that two hundred Roosevelt district delegates would not be seated—whereupon the Colonel's followers pushed aside the doorkeepers and seized control of the hall. The pro-Taft presiding officer was allowed to convene the meeting, but a Roosevelt man stood behind him, hand on his holster, "ready for an emergency." One delegate died of a heart attack and three others were carried out after fist fights. Somehow, amidst the pandemonium, T.R. won the state's ten delegates-at-large and six of the ten district delegates. Two of Taft's four Oklahoma delegates were later to be contested at Chicago.

At the very outset of the campaign, the Roosevelt team had decided to make its major effort in the primary states. Thus, on March 6, Senator Dixon sent a letter to Representative William B. McKinley of Illinois, manager of the Taft campaign, challenging his opponent to abide by the result of preferential primaries. Taft's manager replied with a haughty statement that gave the Roosevelt men all the publicity they wanted—and new evidence for the Colonel to use in his efforts to show that the G.O.P. nomination was being unfairly engineered by the President. "I do not favor changes in the rules of the game while the game is in progress," McKinley answered.

Roosevelt had originally intended to make relatively few speeches in his quest for the nomination, at one time toying with the idea of limiting himself to one major address in each state where a primary was to be held. But with the South seemingly so tied up for Taft and with the prospect of waging a real fight only in the primary states, the Colonel campaigned that spring of 1912 as no other man in history—with the possible exception of the indefatigable William Jennings Bryan—had ever before campaigned for the Presidency.

On March 26, six days after the Carnegie Hall address, he left on a whirlwind swing through the Midwest that took him, by month's end, to Indiana, Illinois, Missouri, Iowa, Minnesota, Wisconsin, and Michigan. In April he made four trips—to the South and Midwest, to New England, once more to the Midwest as far as Oklahoma and Arkansas and back through North Carolina, and finally to New England again—with only a day or two between each excursion for rest and strategy conferences at Oyster Bay. In May he concentrated on Ohio and New Jersey—nearly a week in each—and Maryland and Pennsylvania.

The pace very nearly proved too much even for the vigorous Colonel. "I got through Nebraska and Kansas all right," he wrote on April

20 to O. K. Davis, ". . . but my voice has gone and there must be no repetition of such a program. . . ." For his next effort, in New England, there were to be no speeches from the rear platform of his railroad car, no open-air speeches at all, and only major addresses in Boston and several other cities. "It is folly to try to make me continue a car-tail campaign," he concluded crossly. "After this all arrangements for speaking trips must be purely tentative until I have sanctioned them in detail."

At the beginning the Colonel had been discouraged by the monotonous regularity with which state conventions in the South had ended in Taft victories. In mid-March he was writing to Arthur Lee in England that there was only "the very smallest chance" of winning the fight, with the odds running about four to one against him. And there was little cause for joy in the Roosevelt camp when the results of the first three primaries were known. In North Dakota—which held the first presidential preference primary, on March 19—Roosevelt had allowed himself to be backed by the conservative faction of the state G.O.P. and he was roundly defeated, 23,669 votes to 34,123, by Senator La Follette, who was still clinging pathetically to his presidential aspirations. Taft finished a very poor third, with but 1,876 votes. T. R. asked Senator Dixon to issue a statement that La Follette's triumph was, after all, a victory for progressivism and that North Dakota's delegation—after a complimentary first-ballot vote at the convention for the Wisconsin senator—would come to him. But Taft supporters were gleeful over the Colonel's setback. "The impression prevails here," one wrote, "that when North Dakota kicked Teddy's hat out of the ring, Teddy was sitting in his hat."

Of the ninety district delegates to the national convention selected in New York's primary on March 26, eighty-three were for the President; only seven, for Roosevelt. "They are stealing the primary elections from us," Roosevelt howled in protest after the defeat in his home state. "Never has there been anything more scandalous than the conduct of the Republican New York County machine in this fight." The Colonel had become so violent, Taft confided in a private letter a few days later, "that some people fear he is losing his mind, others say he is drinking. . . ." His conduct was "certainly that of a desperate man who stops at nothing. . . ."

Roosevelt wisely stood aside in Wisconsin, allowing La Follette to sweep his own state on April 2, with a nearly three to one edge over the

President. But then the tide turned suddenly and dramatically for Roosevelt. Medill McCormick's Chicago *Tribune* had pushed so relentlessly for a primary that the Illinois governor was forced to call a special session of the legislature. A primary bill was hastily enacted on March 30 and the election was held only ten days later, on April 9. The Colonel won twice as many votes as Taft and was rewarded with all but two of the state's fifty-eight delegates. O. K. Davis clearly saw a bandwagon start to roll, and he and other smug insiders at Roosevelt headquarters formed a private club of "Before April 9th" men. The Illinois triumph was repeated four days later in Pennsylvania, where Roosevelt won fifty-five of the state's sixty-four district delegates and later, at the state convention, was given all twelve of Pennsylvania's delegates-at-large.

4

"One of the burdens that a man leading a cause has to carry," President Taft wrote his brother Horace the morning after the Pennsylvania primary, "is the disappointment that his friends and sympathizers feel at every recurring disaster." Reading the results of the vote in the Keystone State, Taft confessed that he had "felt more sorrow at Nellie's disappointment and yours, and that of all who have become absorbed in the fight, than I did myself." He had hoped to have the nomination clinched by May 1, but now it looked as if he would have to depend on the states that would be voting later.

The news that month of April was not all bad for the President, however. T. R. won all eight district delegates, as well as the four delegates-at-large, selected by the Maine state convention on April 10. But that same day Taft carried the Vermont convention after ceding only two district delegates to his rival. Although Roosevelt won a decisive victory in Nebraska on April 19, Taft garnered two-thirds of the Republican vote in the New Hampshire primary held four days later. And finally conventions in Michigan, Kentucky, and Indiana selected largely pro-Taft delegations.

The seesaw nature of the contest made for frayed nerves, inflamed passions, and overheated tempers. State troopers were unable to contain the violence that erupted at the Michigan gathering. There was a fist fight on the speaker's platform, ex-Senator Beveridge of Indiana was unable to give his keynote address because of the uproar, and the pro-Roosevelt forces—in the same hall and from the same platform—simultaneously selected a rival delegation to the official Taft slate. Roosevelt carried two district primaries in Washington State but the delegation ultimately selected by the state convention was unanimously for Taft. The two major protagonists split the last two primaries held in April: Oregon voting for T.R.; Massachusetts, for Taft. The results in the Bay State, on April 30, were particularly curious. Whereas Taft carried the preferential vote by 3,500 votes, the eight delegates-at-large pledged to T. R. won by 8,000 votes over the Taft slate. "Well, isn't the outcome in Massachusetts comic?" the Colonel wrote to Senator Lodge. "Apparently there were about eighty thousand people who preferred Taft, about eighty thousand who preferred me, and from three to five thousand who, in an involved way, thought they would vote both for Taft and for me."

When the results of the Illinois and Pennsylvania primaries indicated that he could not be certain of renomination, Taft had reluctantly decided to wage an open fight against Roosevelt—though he felt such campaigning to be beneath the dignity of his presidential office. "Whether I win or lose is not the important thing," he told a visitor. "But I am in this fight to perform a great public duty—the duty of keeping Theodore Roosevelt out of the White House."

En route to Boston, where he was to make a major address on April 26, Taft spoke a number of times from the rear platform of his special train. "This wrenches my soul," he would concede in opening his remarks. "I am here to reply to an old and true friend of mine, Theodore Roosevelt, who has made many charges against me. I deny those charges. I deny all of them. I do not want to fight Theodore Roosevelt, but sometimes a man in a corner fights. I am going to fight." Acknowledging that Roosevelt had been responsible for his elevation to the Presidency, Taft added—candidly, if injudiciously—"It is a bad trait to bite the hand that feeds you."

At Boston Taft raised the third-term issue. The job Roosevelt wanted to undertake "may take a long time, perhaps the rest of his natural life. There is not the slightest reason why, if he secures a third term, and the limitations of the Washington, Jefferson and Jackson tradition is broken down, he should not have as many terms as his natural life will permit," Taft charged. "If he is necessary now to the government, why not later?"

By the time he had finished his Boston speech that evening, Taft was physically and emotionally drained. Barely able to speak above a whisper, he returned to his private car. A newspaperman, seeking clarification of some point contained in the President's address, found Taft alone in his private compartment, slumped over, his head between his hands. He looked up at the reporter, said chokingly "Roosevelt was my closest friend," and then abandoned himself to uncontrollable weeping.

Roosevelt promptly answered Taft, calling the President's attempt to defend his administration as progressive "the grossest and most astounding hypocrisy." But he did not wish the campaign to become one of personalities, he loftily told reporters. "I am glad you liked the way I answered Taft," the Colonel wrote O. K. Davis on April 28. "I then practically dropped him partly because I think stamping on a man I have knocked down is both useless and discourteous."

But vituperation did not end there—and indeed it reached a new level of intensity as the struggle opened for the May primary states. In Massachusetts, the President had told one audience to condemn him if it wished but by witnesses other than Theodore Roosevelt. "I was a man of straw," he said in a remarkable confession for a man seeking re-election to the highest office in the land, "but I have been a man of straw long enough. Every man who has blood in his body, and who has been misrepresented as I have been is forced to fight." And then, speaking at Hyattsville, Maryland, on May 4, he made the most unfortunate statement of that, and possibly any other, presidential campaign. "I am a man of peace," the President told his audience, "and I don't want to fight. But when I do fight I want to hit hard. Even a rat in a corner will fight."

With Taft comparing himself to a man of straw, a dog biting the hand that fed him, and a cornered rat, it would have seemed there was little Roosevelt could add. But in Ohio, where the campaign to win control of the President's home state delegation got underway in mid-May, new and ever more bitter epithets were hurled. The President, according to Roosevelt, was a "fathead" and a "puzzlewit"; T.R. was labeled by Taft as a "dangerous egotist," "a demagogue," a "flatterer of the people." In the week before the vote on May 21 the Colonel traveled 1,800 miles, crisscrossing the state to give ninety scheduled talks. The President traveled even farther and gave more speeches; on one occasion the two private railroad cars were halted next to one another and a hopeful crowd gathered to see if the candidates—or at least their supporters —might not engage in a knock-down brawl on the spot. With such excitement being generated by the two principal contestants, it is no wonder that La Follette's campaign in Ohio—one in which the Wisconsin senator flailed mercilessly at both Taft and Roosevelt—was all but ignored by the press and people.

Before setting out for Ohio, the President had written in discouragement to his brother Horace. Even such supporters as Root and Stimson were holding back now, apparently afraid of Roosevelt's welling strength. Seats in the Roosevelt bandwagon were already being eagerly sought and he expected many more to clamber aboard when—as he thoroughly anticipated—the results in Ohio and California indicated that he could not win renomination. Taft's pessimism was justified. Roosevelt did carry California and Ohio and subsequently scored victories in Maryland, New Jersey, and South Dakota before the primary season ended on June 4.

The people—at least in the states where some sort of primary was held—had spoken. In those contests, La Follette had received thirty-six delegates, Taft forty-eight, and Roosevelt two hundred seventy-eight. In the popular balloting La Follette wound up with a total of 351,043 votes; Taft 761,716; and Roosevelt—a narrow but nonetheless impressive majority over the combined votes of his two opponents —1,157,397. As final preparations were made for opening the convention in Chicago on June 18, the President would seem to have every reason for being gloomy; and Colonel Roosevelt, every right to be optimistic.

Standing
at Armageddon

Roosevelt wound up his campaign for the Republican nomination with a speech on May 30 at Gettysburg, Pennsylvania. The next day he was back in New York, where he intended to divide his time between Sagamore Hill and the *Outlook* offices in Manhattan until the decision of the G.O.P. convention was known. Reporters came to him with a rumor then circulating that he would disregard the time-honored tradition that kept a candidate at arm's length from the deliberations of a convention and go to Chicago. "Fake, pure fake!" snapped the Colonel. Yet, he added, he could still change his plans; "if circumstances demand, of course I'll go."

There were to be 1,078 delegates to the Chicago conclave; a simple majority of 540 was needed to secure the nomination. At the close of the primary and state convention season, Taft and Roosevelt each claimed that such a majority was within his grasp. A poll of delegates, conducted by the New York *Tribune,* revealed 469½ for Roosevelt and 454½ for Taft. La Follette and Iowa's Senator Albert B. Cummins, a belated entrant, each had small followings. But the outcome of the final vote, it was now clear, rested with the 254 delegates whose right to sit was sharply contested by the two leading candidates. The disputes were to be settled, in the first instance, by the Republican National Committee, meeting in Chicago prior to the opening of the convention.

The fifty-three member National Committee had been selected by vote of the 1908 convention—a gathering so thoroughly dominated by Theodore Roosevelt that it had unquestioningly accepted his designation of Taft as successor. But these party stalwarts were now, more than two to one, for the President. The day before the National Committee was to hold its first session on the disputed seats, T.R. announced that he was sending the Pennsylvania politician William Flinn to Chicago to rally and lead his supporters. On June 8, receiving news of the first adverse decisions of the committee, the Colonel charged that "again and again we have sent to the penitentiary election officials for deeds not one whit worse than what was done by the National Committee at Chicago yesterday." In *The Outlook,* three days later, he denounced the continued seating of disputed Taft delegates as "a fraud as vulgar, as brazen, and as cynically open as any ever committed by the Tweed regime in New York forty years ago."

The President meanwhile had returned to the Olympian seclusion of the White House. He surprised many by the choice of an orator to put his name in nomination: the handsome, genial proprietor of the Marion, Ohio, *Star* and unsuccessful G.O.P. candidate for governor in 1910, Warren G. Harding. "I know you can do it well," Taft wrote, asking Harding to speak for him, "and I should be delighted to . . . have it done by a man who represents the state so worthily as you do." On June 14 Taft was quoted as saying, "All the information I get is that I will be nominated on the first ballot."

The National Committee made but a slight pretense of hearing all the evidence about the contested delegates before reaching a decision on each dispute. Both sides were allowed to submit affidavits—often quite massive documentation—and then to support the evidence with half hour oral presentations. A fair decision, without more thorough investigation, was probably impossible.

The committee meetings were often marked by nearly as much invective and actual physical violence as had marred the state conventions whose riotous deliberations it was now supposed to be calmly reviewing. Fist fights almost broke up several sessions, and the award of two California delegates to Taft brought forth from Roosevelt headquarters a blistering broadside, a minor masterpiece of political invective: The National Committee was engaged in a "saturnalia of fraud and larceny," one that had seemingly reached the "limit of folly and indecency." Not content with "the political emoluments of pocket-picking and porch-climbing," the "doomed and passion-drunk committee" was now assuming "the role of the apache and the garroteer."

"I do not want any contest decided in my favor merely for the purpose of giving me the majority," Taft had magnanimously declared on May 31 as he directed that the deliberations of the committee be open to the press. He was confident that the evidence to support the majority of his rival's contests was "flimsy" and representative of the "bluff and bluster of the general Roosevelt campaign." The President was happily proved very nearly correct with the early admission by some of the Colonel's own supporters that many of the contests in the South, instigated by Ormsby McHarg, were spurious. The public, learning that the Roosevelt camp had made false charges, began to doubt that any of the challenges were valid. Actually Roosevelt did have reason enough to challenge the results in a number of primaries and state conventions. But when the National Committee concluded its hearings, 235 of the disputed seats were awarded to Taft and only 19 to Roosevelt.

The fact that Roosevelt was watching the fight in the National Committee from afar did not mean he was playing a passive role. Alice Longworth arrived at Sagamore Hill the first week in June and found things "popping." A steady stream of visitors appeared at the front door, reporters came up the long hill from the village twice a day to chat with the candidate on the veranda, a delegation of four hundred Masons materialized on the front lawn one afternoon, two telegraph operators kept an open wire to Chicago in the third-floor gun room humming—until at last Alice and her stepmother fled to the privacy of a summer house. Rumors proliferated that T.R. would go to Chicago to take up a battlefield command.

Among the passionately committed followers of the Colonel was nineteen-year-old Nicholas Roosevelt, the son of his first cousin and Oyster Bay neighbor J. West Roosevelt. Preparing to leave Cambridge at the end of his second year at Harvard, Nicholas received news from Kermit on Thursday, June 13, that the family was packing for the possible trip to Chicago the next day. The young man caught the first train for New York, reached Oyster Bay at midnight, and Friday morning showed up at Sagamore Hill—where he joined Cousin Edith, Cousin Theodore, and other members of the family at the breakfast table. The meal was constantly interrupted with new dispatches from Chicago. Edith still hoped that they would not have to go but everything was in readiness for a departure that afternoon. "Nick," the Colonel said as he was about to go upstairs after breakfast, "I am taking Ferrero and Herodotus with me to amuse myself and get my mind off the business if I go to Chicago."

Roosevelt had decided to take Edith with him that morning to his office at *The Outlook* in New York and there reach a final decision about the trip to Chicago. Other members of the family would follow later. As the pair climbed into their automobile for the drive into the city, the Colonel remarked to his young cousin, "I guess we'll meet at a lot of Phillipics soon." And as the car turned in the drive, he called back, "But we may fly back here tonight—and by gracious! I hope we do!"

Reporters who met the Colonel upon his arrival in New York noticed that he was wearing his famous wide-brimmed slouch hat—the Rough Rider headgear, the Acceptance Hat of 1900. No one was surprised when it was announced early in the afternoon that the Roosevelt party would leave on the Lake Shore Limited for Chicago at 5:30.

Nicholas Roosevelt phoned for a ticket, left Oyster Bay immediately, and joined the group at Grand Central. Among the entourage would be Kermit; Theodore Douglas Robinson, Corinne's oldest son; George Roosevelt, son of T.R.'s cousin Emlen; Frank Harper, the Colonel's private secretary; and James Amos, his valet. To avoid a gathering crowd at the station, Edith and Theodore Roosevelt were brought down to the tracks in a freight elevator at the last moment and joined the party in a front compartment car. Another entire Pullman car had been booked by reporters.

At several stations en route to Chicago small crowds had gathered to cheer Roosevelt's passing and at Elkhart, Indiana, T.R. called from the rear platform, "We will fight to a finish! We will not stand for theft." At South Bend Cal O'Laughlin boarded the train with fresh news from Chicago. The revulsion against the National Committee's decisions was so great, he reported, that some newspapers were switching their support from Taft to Roosevelt. Nicholas described Cousin Theodore as "bubbling with cheerfulness."

The welcoming crowd at Chicago Saturday afternoon had broken through police lines and was yelling and surging about on the platform as the Lake Shore Limited pulled in. The young cousins had instructions "to keep tight with the old man," so Nicholas and George, Frank Harper and Teddy Robinson formed a phalanx around the Colonel to move him through the throng. Outside was "a sea of cheering people." The Roosevelt party got into several flag-decorated automobiles and moved into what Nicholas Roosevelt later described as the most thrilling and remarkable experience of his life.

"People packed the windows and lined the roofs and the elevated tracks and were so thick in the streets we could hardly move in the procession. . . ." Nicholas wrote in his diary. "Everyone was howling with delight, and cries of 'Teddy!' filled the air. At the cross streets, as far as we could see to either side, or back or forward, people were wedged in like pins. Everyone cheered. Everyone screamed. Everyone was hurled along in the irresistible force of the delighted mob." Newspapers later estimated the crowd at 50,000 people. "If ever an American was a hero of a hot and crowded hour," wrote William Allen White, "it was Theodore Roosevelt that day in Chicago." Someone with more detachment —and a sense of humor—had had ten thousand handbills printed and distributed, announcing that Colonel Roosevelt would walk on the waters of Lake Michigan at 7:30 Monday evening.

In the front car of the motorcade leaving the station stood the Colonel, smiling and bowing to right and left. Nicholas Roosevelt and several of the younger members of the party, riding in another open car, could not resist jumping up and down in their seats, cheering and shouting—"altho we were part of the show." Marching in the parade was California's delegation to the convention, hoisting aloft a banner inscribed "California's 26 for Roosevelt"—a defiant challenge to the National Committee's awarding of two delegates to Taft. And on all sides marching bands added to the noise and pandemonium; the most frequently played number, of course, was the Spanish-American War song and T.R.'s perennial campaign tune, "There'll Be a Hot Time in the Old Town Tonight."

Earlier in the week George Henry Payne, a New York newspaperman who had joined the Roosevelt campaign, had come to Perkins with the suggestion that the New York delegation—though nearly solid for Taft—be met upon arrival at the station and marched to its hotel by a Roosevelt band. Perkins thought it was an amusing idea and told Payne to go ahead. Barnes and his delegation were so "scandalized and angered," noted O. K. Davis, that Payne decided to use this device again. Soon Roosevelt bands were appearing everywhere, meeting delegations at the railroad stations, parading through the city, playing in hotel lobbies and at the convention hall. No one—except Payne— had time even to think of where the bands were coming from, but at the end of the convention a flabbergasted George Perkins was presented with bills amounting to more than ten thousand dollars.

Amos Pinchot reached for new literary heights in trying to describe Chicago during those two weeks in June. The city thronged with "a gay and noisy carnival crowd that was nevertheless grimly eager for the final drive. . . . Every lobby along the lake front boiled and bubbled with gossip and the whispering of intrigue, though the real intriguers whose scheming meant anything were far from the madding crowd, behind the locked and mysterious doors of well-guarded suites." The days were sweltering, Pinchot recalled, and the noise of bands and torchlit processions made "night hideous and sleep difficult." Chicago was bursting with labor leaders, foreign observers, farmers and cattlemen, small businessmen and industrialists, students and college professors, social workers and lobbyists, and of course politicians—"the really big men of the convention and their handy men and hirelings from the lowest infernos of politics, who wielded mysterious influence, and were followed by an underworld contingent of racketeers, gamblers, thieves, prostitutes, such as flock to convention towns, jubilant in the expectation of rich harvests."

Finley Peter Dunne's Mr. Dooley had a more earthy description. The G.O.P. convention, he said two days before it opened, was going to be "a combynation iv th' Chicago fire, Saint Bartholomew's massacree, the battle iv th' Boyne, th' life iv Jessie James, an' th' night iv th' big wind." Was he going? "Iv coarse I'm goin'! I haven't missed a riot in this neighborhood in forty years. . . ." But he wanted a seat, Dooley concluded, far enough away so that he would not be splattered with the blood.

The Roosevelt party was taken, that Saturday afternoon, to the Congress Hotel, where the Colonel was given a large second floor suite; he and Edith would also have private rooms elsewhere in the hotel. It was impossible even in the large conference room reserved for welcoming ceremonies for Roosevelt to greet all those who had gathered at the Congress to see him, so he stepped to a balcony overlooking Michigan Avenue and delivered an impromptu tirade against his enemies, concluding with a pledge to the crowd in the street below that he "would not take it lying down." "Soak 'em, Teddy! Give it to 'em!" someone cried out. As he returned to the suite, newspapermen pushed forward for a statement. How was the Colonel feeling, one asked. Ready for a fight? T.R. smiled grimly and replied with a favorite expression: "I'm feeling like a Bull Moose!"

2

What Roosevelt had decided not to take lying down, of course, were the decisions of the National Committee that had awarded most of the disputed delegates to Taft—decisions that appeared to have given his rival a majority of votes in the convention scheduled to open on Tuesday. Roosevelt would bring the fight to the floor of the convention and to do this he had to challenge the Old Guard's arrangements for organizing the assembly.

The National Committee had selected Elihu Root as the temporary chairman and keynote speaker of the convention, and William Barnes —in behalf of the New York delegation—had wired all Taft delegates to support the committee's choice. The designation of Root —T.R.'s former Secretary of War and Secretary of State, the man he had once called "the ablest man that has appeared in the public life of any country in any position in my time"—posed a true dilemma for the Colonel. Root, of course, had declined to join Roosevelt in the progressive camp, but he had also declined to campaign for Taft. In order to join the public discussion and contrast Roosevelt with Taft, Root had written the President in mid-May, he would have to betray certain confidences of his previous offices under T.R. and thus appear disloyal to his former chief. Yet Roosevelt, as far as he knew and certainly in public, had never said a word about him that was not "kindly and laudatory." If he were to take part in a public attack, "I should be subject to universal condemnation. . . ." At sixty-seven, Root concluded, his fighting days were over. But in agreeing to chair the convention, Root put himself at the very center of the decade's nastiest political fray.

Roosevelt quickly decided that he would not abide by the National Committee's designation of Root and instead proposed for temporary chairman Governor Francis E. McGovern of Wisconsin—hoping thereby to win over the small but determined bloc of La Follette delegates. It was essential that the Roosevelt forces have a friendly, or at least a neutral, man as presiding officer, for the Colonel had resolved to appeal the decisions of the National Committee concerning the contested delegates first to the Credentials Committee and, as a final resort, to the convention itself. As his floor manager in this effort, T.R. chose Herbert Spencer Hadley, the first Republican governor of Missouri since

Reconstruction and one of the seven little governors who had signed the February appeal. Hadley was a dignified, unfailingly courteous man yet a forceful and persuasive speaker, tall, thin, with a pallor that betrayed only slightly his record of ill-health. It was decided that Governor Hadley, at the first opportunity after the opening of the convention on Tuesday, would offer a motion to amend the temporary role of delegates submitted by the National Committee so as to substitute the names of seventy-two Roosevelt men whose claims had been rejected.

Why seventy-two? The following year Nicholas Murray Butler, by then a scornful critic of Roosevelt's, found himself on a train bound from New York to Boston with Hadley. Now that the fight was over, Butler asked, perhaps Hadley could tell him why the Roosevelt men had made the seating of those seventy-two delegates the crucial issue of the convention. Well, Hadley had admitted with a smile, it would do no harm to tell the story now. He, Senator Borah, and Frank Kellogg of Minnesota, had reviewed the decisions of the National Committee and decided that in twenty-four cases there was strong evidence to support the claims of the Roosevelt delegates. The three men went to the Colonel and said that they wished to contest the twenty-four seats on the floor of the convention. "Twenty-four seats!" Roosevelt is supposed to have exclaimed. "What is the use of contesting twenty-four seats? You must contest seventy-four if you expect to get anywhere." And thus, Hadley told Butler —who got the final total wrong—the number was raised to seventy-two.

As the testimony of a hostile witness, Butler's account— published a quarter century later—is certainly suspect. But even a sympathetic student of the progressive movement has conceded that perhaps no more than thirty T.R. delegates were stolen by the Taft forces. And thirty votes would not have been enough to give Roosevelt a majority of the convention; seventy-two might have.

The bargaining, trading, arm twisting, and log rolling that went on in and about the downtown Chicago hotels in the days preceding the opening of the convention were intensive and apparently almost uninterrupted, save for the absolute minimum number of hours needed for eating and sleeping—and many a courted delegate would complain of getting too much of the former and not enough of the latter. Excitement seemed to mount hourly. Word reached Roosevelt headquarters that Timothy Woodruff—once T.R.'s lieutenant governor—was wavering from support of Taft and might bring over a sizable bloc of New

York delegates. Indeed, Woodruff confided to Alice Longworth that his wife had threatened to go to Reno if he did not switch—and he feared she was serious. Barnes and his ally Senator Murray Crane of Massachusetts were said to be willing to sacrifice the Republican party to get the nomination for Taft; this more than defeat of the Democratic nominee in November was their goal. The sixty-six pro-Taft black delegates from several Southern states were rumored to be forming a caucus —to offer themselves to the highest bidder. It was also being said, on no real evidence, that Senator Cummins would release his ten Iowa delegates to vote for the Colonel on the first ballot. Taft's peak strength, it was estimated on Saturday night, was 536, four short of a majority.

After dinner Saturday evening, Nicholas Roosevelt decided to play spy and attend a Taft rally in the Louis XVI room of the Congress Hotel. Successive messengers had been sent to the lobby to announce the gathering; as each announcement was made, a chorus of Roosevelt supporters would shout: "All postmasters attend!" The room, Nicholas discovered, was only half full, although the chairman kept urging people to stand clear of the doors so others could be admitted. The principal speaker, William Barnes, was described by the blissfully biased Nicholas Roosevelt as "a big fat pig, with tiny eyes sunk in his puffy cheeks . . . [the] regular caricature of a boss." He could scarcely help laughing when Barnes spoke of saving the country, the Constitution, liberty itself from a Roosevelt monarchy. Behind Barnes stood a party hack, leading perfunctory applause at the end of very nearly each line of the speech. It was pathetic, the Colonel's young cousin concluded—and thereafter maliciously advised people wishing to escape the whirlwind centering on Roosevelt to seek peace and quiet at the deserted Taft headquarters.

The Roosevelts went to church on Sunday morning, but the afternoon and evening were completely given over to politics. A constant stream of humanity flowed in and out of the Roosevelt rooms, leaving behind a litter of torn paper and cigar butts. Eight or ten men sat in attendance at desks and answered phones until two in the morning. It sometimes took policemen an hour to clear the rooms for a private conference so strong was the pressure from outside of people wanting to get in. It took William Draper Lewis of the University of Pennsylvania Law School twenty minutes to get through the antechambers to keep an appointment with Roosevelt in a private room beyond. He found the Colonel alone, sitting in a rocking chair and reading, apparently oblivious to the pandemonium outside. As Lewis entered, T.R. looked up from his book; the volume, Dean Lewis discovered, was Herodotus.

Senator Dixon provided another circle of calm in the eye of the hurricane. Amos Pinchot later recalled the genial Montanan presiding quitely at a long mahogany conference table, smiling and telling everyone that the outcome would be favorable to the Roosevelt cause—apparently in possession of some secret information denied all others. But Alice Longworth, arriving in Chicago with her husband, said that none of the supposed insiders had "any more accurate idea of what was going to happen than had the crowds walking to and fro on Michigan Avenue. . . ."

Monday evening Roosevelt agreed to deliver the major address at a meeting in the Auditorium to rally his supporters. At his arrival, the crowd of five thousand went wild and could not even be stopped by the organist's playing of "The Star-Spangled Banner." Roosevelt had been working on his speech since leaving New York and had told his cousin Nicholas that it must be the greatest effort of his life.

His personal fate, or that of Mr. Taft, mattered little, the Colonel said. What did matter was the protest against "a crime which strikes straight at the heart of every principle of political decency and honesty, a crime which represents treason to the people and the usurpation of the sovereignty of the people by irresponsible bosses, inspired by the sinister influences of moneyed privilege." He was speaking, of course, of the conspiracy of the National Committee to steal delegates from him. He demanded now only that neither set of contestants—his own "sixty to eighty lawfully elected delegates" or the equal number of "fraudulent" Taft delegates seated by the committee—be allowed to vote in the convention until the remaining one thousand delegates pass on the contests. Roosevelt next commented on the campaign for the nomination. The primary states that he had carried so impressively represented two-thirds of the Republican electoral vote in the last general election. If he carried those states against the Democratic challenger in the fall, he would be within three votes of a majority in the electoral college.

Finally, after a brief review of the aims of the progressive movement and a lament that more men of privilege were not marching with him, the Colonel strode into his peroration. "We who stand for the cause of the uplift of humanity and the betterment of mankind are pledged to eternal war against wrong whether by the few or by the many, by a plutocracy or by a mob. We believe that this country will not be a permanently good place for any of us to live in unless we make it a reasonably good place for all of us to live in. . . ." Again he stated that his own fate was immaterial; he was to be used as any man committed to the battlefield was to be used. By putting far above personal interests the triumph of the high cause for which they battled, they would not lose. But it would be far better to fail honorably than to win by such foul methods as those of the adversary. "But the victory shall be ours and it shall be won as we have already won so many victories, by clean and honest fighting for the loftiest of causes. We fight in honorable fashion for the good of mankind; fearless of the future; unheeding of our individual fates; with unflinching hearts and undimmed eyes;"—and then in a ringing final phrase he summoned his troops to the biblical battlefield many of them had probably never heard of, thus blessing the endeavor as a new holy crusade—"we stand at Armageddon, and we battle for the Lord."

Curiously Nicholas Roosevelt did not think the speech—save for the stirring finale—was among Cousin Theodore's best efforts. Far better, he claimed, was a talk given later that evening to a private gathering of all the Roosevelt delegates by California Governor Hiram Johnson. In an unrecorded, impromptu speech Johnson summoned the delegates to join him in making history, to follow Roosevelt out of the Republican party if necessary. Were they with him? Johnson asked in conclusion. To a man, the delegates sprang to their feet with cheers and cries of "yes, yes." Governor Stubbs of Kansas jumped down from his perch on a rolltop desk and shouted, "Johnson will be our Vice-President. Yes sir, Roosevelt and Johnson—we'll nominate them, and we'll elect them, too."

3

Medill McCormick's Chicago *Tribune* carried a banner across every page of its issue of Tuesday, June 18, the day the convention was to open: "THE EIGHTH COMMANDMENT: THOU SHALT NOT STEAL." The Coliseum, where the proceedings were to be held, became in the portentous words of a *Tribune* editorial "the temple at Gaza and Samson is between the pillars."

The convention was opened by Victor Rosewater, an unassuming

Omaha newspaper editor who had just succeeded to the chairmanship of the Republican National Committee upon the death of the incumbent. His plea that the delegates sit still and look pleasant for the official photograph was answered by a rude shout that it would be the first and last time that the throng would act in harmony. Just about the only uncommitted and unangry attendant was William Jennings Bryan, in Chicago as a newspaper reporter. The other newsmen stopped their partisan wrangling to welcome Bryan with applause to the press table. If he proved so popular at the forthcoming Democratic convention in Baltimore, one reporter suggested, he might once more emerge as the party's nominee. The three-time loser scoffed at the idea. "My boy," he said, "do you think I'm going to run for President just to get the Republican party out of a hole?"

Rosewater, on the speaker's platform, could not conceal his nervousness in convening the assembly. Word had reached him the night before that—after the traditional invocation by a clergyman and after he had gaveled the meeting to order—Governor Hadley would rise to introduce a motion that the seventy-two disputed Taft delegates not be permitted to vote until the contests had been resolved by the Credentials Committee. Rosewater's instructions were to rule the Hadley motion out of order. "Victor," Senator Boies Penrose of Pennsylvania had advised him, "as soon as you make that ruling tomorrow you had better take a running jump off the platform before someone can take a shot at you."

T.R.'s valet, James Amos, later revealed that there may have been a chance the jocular prediction would come true. Quite late on Monday evening Amos had been roused by the sound of an argument outside the door leading to Roosevelt's private suite. A former Rough Rider, obviously drunk, was demanding that the detectives on duty admit him to see his old friend Teddy. To calm the man, Roosevelt agreed to receive him. "I'm goin' to take this thing in my own hands," the man said, pulling out two pistols from under a long coat. "As soon as Rosewater makes that ruling, I'm goin' to fill him full of lead. Then I'm goin' to plug that old guy Root." At last Roosevelt succeeded in steering the man back to the door, whispering to Amos to take care of the situation. The two detectives wanted to lock him up but Amos hit upon a better plan. Since the Rough Rider was already "half full of liquor," they plied him with more drinks "until the other half was full." When Rosewater made his expected ruling—that Hadley's motion was out of order —the Westerner was sleeping it off somewhere far from the Coliseum.

Before any motion could be entertained, Rosewater declared, the convention must be properly organized—with selection of the temporary chairman as the first order of business. The nomination of Governor Mc-Govern of Wisconsin for this post was enthusiastically seconded by such Roosevelt supporters as Hadley and Johnson. But then La Follette's campaign manager sought recognition and was allowed to make a statement from the platform. "This nomination is not with Senator La Follette's consent," he declared. "We make no deals with Roosevelt. We make no trades with Taft." The single-minded Wisconsin senator had meant what he said a year earlier in announcing his candidacy: he was in the race until the decision of the convention was announced. The hall fell silent for a moment; then a low humming swelled into a chorus of hisses.

The New York delegate who nominated Root oleaginously quoted T.R.'s description of Root as "the ablest man . . . in public life." Cheers broke out, however, at the mention of Roosevelt's name. "You need not hesitate to cheer Roosevelt in my presence," the speaker interjected. "I cheered him seven years. . . . [but] Elihu Root was good enough for Roosevelt and he is good enough for me."

When the roll call of states for votes on the temporary chairmanship was completed, Root was declared elected by a vote of 558 to 501 for McGovern, with 19 scattered or uncast votes. William Flinn stalked up to the rostrum, looked the haughty Root in the eye, and shouted: "Receiver of stolen goods!" If the seventy-two challenged votes had been denied Taft, of course, Root would not have been elected temporary chairman, a sympathetic McGovern would have taken the chair, and possibly—just possibly—the final outcome of the convention would have been changed. But it was not to be. The Roosevelt men lost the first major skirmish, Root took the gavel, and the result was virtually a foregone conclusion.

At the second session of the convention, on Wednesday, June 19, Governor Hadley again rose to introduce his motion that the seventy-two challenged Taft delegates not be permitted to vote on any question until the contests had been resolved. His height accentuated by a long frock coat, Hadley calmly presented his case in a speech that clearly demonstrated he had done his homework. The loud applause that rewarded his effort swelled to an ovation—and for a moment the thought crossed several minds in the hall that the convention was on the brink of a stampede to Hadley as a compromise candidate. At that instant, however, a woman in the gallery unfurled a huge portrait of T.R., and the Hadley ovation turned into a twenty-minute Roosevelt demonstration that was only quelled by repeated bangings of Root's gavel. Hadley's motion lost, 567 to 507, but the contests were nonetheless referred to the Credentials Committee.

Meeting through the next three days, the Credentials Committee ruled in favor of Taft on all seventy-two contests. And in the full convention the minority report filed by Roosevelt men on the committee was rejected each time by a comfortable majority of delegates including, of course, the votes of the disputed seventy-two. The closest the Roosevelt forces came to victory was in the case of two contested California delegates, which Taft won 542 to 529. As each new vote was announced and at each bang of Root's gavel, cheers and boos broke out anew. The convention, Taft's opponents charged, had become a steamroller. Soon Roosevelt supporters, on the floor and in the galleries, were periodically chanting slow "choo-choos" that culminated in loud cries of "toot-toot." To augment their voices thousands brought pieces of sandpaper to rub together. A Mississippi delegate rose on a point of order and was recognized by Senator Root. "The point of order is that the steamroller is exceeding the speed limit." After the laughter died out, Root conceded the point but gave as his justification for the speed the necessity of winding up the convention so the delegates could return home on Sunday.

To add to the hilarity and if nothing particular seemed to be transpiring, the New Jersey delegation would rise on signal and give a cheer:

> . . . . Who are we?
> We are the delegates from New Jersey.
> Are we in it? Just you wait.
> We'll give Teddy twenty-eight straight.

The New Jersey demonstration, Nicholas Roosevelt recalled, would generally be followed by a chant from the Massachusetts delegation, led by the historian Albert Bushnell Hart: "Massachusetts eighteen, Massachusetts eighteen, Massachusetts eighteen! Roosevelt, first, last, and all the time!" Similar calls would come from West Virginia and California, someone would start the chant "We want Teddy!" and the convention would dissolve into pandemonium.

At one session Nicholas Murray Butler was seated on the platform next to Senator Penrose. Haughtily looking down at the obstreperous Pennsylvania delegation led by Penrose's rival William Flinn, Butler asked the senator how such men got themselves elected delegates to a national convention; he for one had never hoped to see their like outside a street riot. "Oh," replied Penrose, "those are the corks, bottles, and banana peels washed up by the Roosevelt tide."

"If I could nominate . . . Hughes by a withdrawal it would give me great pleasure to bring it about," the President had written to a political confidant on the eve of the convention. "My chief purpose in staying in is to defeat Mr. Roosevelt, whose nomination . . . would be a great danger and menace to the country." Were he to withdraw, Taft wearily concluded, his support at the convention would go not to the former New York governor he had appointed to the Supreme Court two years earlier but to Roosevelt, "and that I cannot permit." The President was in the fight to the finish just as he knew Roosevelt was, for he had undoubtedly read T.R.'s recent reply to a reporter's question about compromise in Chicago. "I'll name the compromise candidate," the Colonel had exclaimed. "He'll be me. I'll name the compromise platform. It will be our platform."

4

As the steamroller moved noisily and almost merrily forward at the Coliseum, the conferences at Roosevelt headquarters grew lengthier, more frequent, and more intense. "We are frittering away our time," Hiram Johnson thundered at one meeting. "We are frittering away our opportunity. And, what is worse, we are frittering away Theodore Roosevelt." The time had come, Johnson said on Friday evening, to make a choice: whether to stay in the Republican party and accept Taft as the nominee, or bolt to form a new party with T.R. as standard bearer.

Years later Amos Pinchot described the actual birth of the new party. A group of perhaps twenty insiders had gathered in the Colonel's suite; some were seated at a conference table, others slumped in armchairs or stood leaning against the walls. Roosevelt was nervously pacing the room in silence. Off in a corner Perkins and Munsey were whispering intensely to one another. Gradually everyone else in the room fell silent, trying not to stare at the two financiers. Suddenly their whispering stopped, Munsey made a decisive gesture, and the two walked over to Roosevelt. Each placed a hand on one of his shoulders and one or the other said, "Colonel, we will see you through."

With the final reports of the Credentials Committee adopted and the organization of the convention thus completed, the actual nominating of a candidate was to get underway on Saturday, June 22. Henry J. Allen of Kansas rose to read a brief message from Theodore Roosevelt: "The Convention as now composed has no claim to represent the voters of the Republican Party. It represents nothing but successful fraud in overriding the will of the rank and file of the party. Any man nominated by the Convention as now constituted would be merely the beneficiary of this successful fraud. . . ." The Colonel did not release his delegates from their obligation to vote for him—if they voted at all. But he asked the Roosevelt delegates to decline to vote on any further business before the convention.

Nominating speeches for the several candidates were subsequently made, and a roll of the states called. The balloting proceeded along predictable lines—Taft building slowly to a narrow majority; the great number of Roosevelt delegates abstaining—until Massachusetts was reached. The chairman announced that the state cast eighteen votes for Taft with eighteen abstentions. When the tally was challenged, a poll of the individual delegates was called. The first name on the list was that of a Mr. Fosdick, a delegate-at-large pledged to Roosevelt. He answered "Present, but I refuse to vote." Cheering broke out, and Root banged for order. Striding to the front of the platform Root leaned out and shouted at Fosdick, "You have been sent here by your state to vote. If you refuse to do your duty, your alternate will be called upon." Fosdick's name was called again. "No man on God's earth can make me vote in this convention," he called out. Root then called the alternate, by a quirk of the confused Massachusetts primary a Taft man. The "howl of derision and hate" that greeted this vote, one observer claimed, was unequalled in the entire convention. But Root continued to call upon alternates to Roosevelt delegates from Massachusetts who refused to vote, with the result that two more votes were chalked up for Taft.

Root did not again halt the roll call, and the ballot was at last completed. Taft received 561; Roosevelt, 107; La Follette, 41; Cummins, 17; Hughes, 2; absent, 6. But 344 Roosevelt delegates remained silent and not voting through the roll call. Vice President "Sunny Jim" Sherman was renominated and the convention adjourned. Senator Reed Smoot of Utah, a leading standpatter, came smiling up to Nicholas Murray Butler: "Well, she's did! What next?"

Even as the convention was lurching toward its conclusion that

Saturday evening, another mass Roosevelt rally was being held in Chicago's Orchestra Hall. Governor Johnson presided, speakers were called upon to mark time until the Great Man himself appeared, an event that brought the usual tumultuous greeting. The Colonel told the crowd—in actuality a rump convention of the now fractured Republican party—that he would accept the nomination of a new party. He asked the bolting delegates to return home, find out the sentiment of the people, and return to a new convention to select candidates and adopt a progressive platform. Indeed, if the delegates in the meantime found another candidate, Roosevelt would be happy to support him—a "pretty politeness," Alice Longworth called the offer. There was no doubt in any mind that evening who the standard bearer of the new party of progressivism would be. The assembly, Mrs. Longworth said, was "chockablock with a sort of camp-meeting fervor. . . ." Everyone acted as if he had suddenly and unexpectedly been presented with the one gift in life he had most longed for—Theodore Roosevelt leading a new crusade.

Theodore and Edith Roosevelt stayed on in Chicago through Monday, but Alice left on the Sunday afternoon train for Washington with her husband. Seated in the dining car, surrounded by admiring members of the Old Guard, was Elihu Root. Mrs. Longworth swept up to his table, leaned over, and hissed "toot-toot" in his face. A final, pithy comment on the disastrous convention was given a few days later by Chauncey Depew, the genial ex-senator from New York. "The only question now," he said, "is which corpse gets the most flowers."

≈§ Chapter 13 §≈

A Bull Moose
at Large

"**N***othing new* is happening in politics," Woodrow Wilson wrote in the spring of 1912, "except Mr. Roosevelt, who is always new, being bound by nothing in the heavens above or in the earth below. He is now rampant and very diligently employed in splitting the party wide open—so that we may get in!" The New Jersey governor was only expressing the commonly held view of his fellow Democrats that the rift in the G.O.P. could have but one result: victory for their own party in the November elections. And, of course, he was also giving voice to his personal hope that he, as the Democratic standard bearer, would be leading the victorious hosts that fall.

Wilson had already made one of the most meteoric rises in American political history. Less than two years earlier he had been the generally popular but also controversial president of Princeton University, a serious scholar who had written a number of important books on American history and government. George Harvey, the conservative editor of *Harper's Weekly,* had mentioned Wilson for the Presidency but few took the suggestion seriously. Then in a surprise move, the old line political bosses of New Jersey's Democratic party picked the Princeton schoolman for the gubernatorial nomination in 1910; he was judged to be an attractive candidate yet a man, once elected, who would be responsive to their demands. When Wilson appeared at Trenton's opera house to accept the nomination, one of the politicians caught his first glimpse of the candidate. "God, look at that jaw!" he said to a companion. The sharp thrust of the prominent jaw, the firmly set mouth, the steely eyes behind rimless glasses—all indicated that Wilson, perhaps, was not going to be a man easily controlled by the bosses.

In office Wilson indeed turned on his sponsors and pushed through the legislature of 1911 an impressive program of reforms. From around the nation progressives of both parties began looking in wonder and admiration to the Garden State and its surprisingly dynamic new leader. By the beginning of 1912 Wilson was one of the four leading contenders for the Democratic nomination that year—the others being Governor Judson Harmon of Ohio, Representative Oscar W. Underwood of Alabama, and Speaker of the House James Beauchamp ("Champ") Clark of Missouri.

One cartoonist depicted Harmon as the candidate of the Midwest and the Northeast; Underwood, of the South; Clark, of the trans-Mississippi West—and only Wilson as the national candidate. But Wilson's energetic campaign for the nomination faltered badly, he lost key primaries to Clark, and the Missourian entered the convention—which opened in Baltimore on Tuesday, June 25, three days after the Republicans had nominated Taft—with a commanding lead in delegate strength. Yet, since a two-thirds majority of the 1,088 delegates was needed for victory at the Democratic convention, Wilson and the others stayed in the race. And in the background was the specter of a fourth nomination for William Jennings Bryan, who would be leading the Nebraska delegation to the convention.

Among Wilson's ardent supporters on the eve of the convention was Joseph Pulitzer's New York *World*. Wilson alone of the Democrats in the field seemed capable of defeating Theodore Roosevelt, the "most cunning and adroit demagogue that modern civilization has produced since Napoleon III." Arriving in Baltimore for the convention, Franklin D. Roosevelt said that his wife's cousin Kermit Roosevelt had told him, "Pop is praying for the nomination of Champ Clark."

Like the Republican gathering the week before, the Democratic convention erupted into bitter internecine warfare over the first item of business: the election of a temporary chairman. The candidate of the Democratic National Committee was Alton B. Parker, the colorless conservative who had been so decisively defeated for the Presidency by Theodore Roosevelt in 1904. Bryan had his own candidate: Senator John W. Kern of Indiana, his vice-presidential running mate in 1908.

Sixteen years had elapsed since the Boy Orator of the Platte— giving his famous Cross of Gold speech at Chicago—had stampeded the 1896 convention into giving him his first nomination at the age of thirty-six; and those years weighed heavily on Bryan as he rose to nominate Kern. Time, noted William Allen White, who was covering the convention as a reporter, "had broadened his girth, thinned his hair, taken youth out of him." Slightly stooped now, with "a little too much weight in jowl and belly," Bryan in his alpaca coat and wrinkled trousers "had a frowsy look." Pale and grim, his thick black eyebrows furrowed over his piercing eyes, a grizzled fringe of ruffled and moist hair at the back of his balding dome, his mouth "a thin dagger-slit across his broad face," Bryan began speaking—and for a moment the old magic radiated out over the hall. But the palmetto fan he clutched in his right hand began to tremble, he spoke at much too great a length, and soon cries of "Parker! Parker!" welled up. The unfortunate Bryan, concluded the *World* reporter, "had begun as a prophet, concluded as a bore and sat down amid a roar one-quarter of enthusiasm, three-quarters of relief."

Kern next dramatically withdrew from the contest in favor of Bryan himself, and a Texas delegate exclaimed that "the fight is on and Bryan is on one side and Wall Street is on the other." In the subsequent roll call, most Clark delegates voted for Parker; the Wilson men stood with Bryan; and Parker won 579 to 508. This initial vote, Wilson's biographer Arthur S. Link has concluded, convinced thousands of progressive Democrats that Clark had allied himself with Wall Street and Tammany Hall against Wilson and Bryan. Among the interested observers at Baltimore was Alice Longworth, who found it "comforting to see that there was no more sweet harmony in the Democratic ranks" than in those of the Republican party—though the Democrats had a "capacity for sustained volume of noise that no Republican lungs can ever equal."

A new height of drama was reached at the session held Thursday evening. Bryan had been told that New York's ninety votes would be switched from Harmon to Clark on an early ballot, and the news strengthened the Great Commoner's resolve to move against what he considered the Tammany-Wall Street alliance. From his seat in the Nebraska delegation, he rose to introduce a resolution that the convention go on record as being opposed to the nomination of any man supported by J. Pierpont Morgan, Thomas Fortune Ryan, August Belmont, "or any other member of the privilege-hunting and favor-seeking class." Moreover, Bryan moved that the convention "demand the withdrawal . . . of any delegate or delegates constituting or representing the above-named interests." As it happened, Belmont was a New York delegate, and Ryan, one from Virginia. "My God . . . what is the matter with Bryan?" the presiding officer hissed to a neighbor on the platform. "Does he want to destroy the Democratic party?"

Bryan started down the aisle toward the platform, to defend his resolution in a speech. He found his way blocked by an infuriated delegate who shouted, "Are you a Democrat?" The rumpled Nebraskan paused, drew himself up, and coldly answered: "My Democracy has been certified to by six million and a half Democratic voters. But I will ask the secretary to record one vote in the negative if the gentleman will give me his name." Even Bryan seemed disturbed by the storm he had summoned, however, and he ultimately withdrew his demand for the expulsion of Ryan and Belmont.

That night and into Friday morning, the nominations for President were finally made. The first ballot was taken at seven o'clock in the morning: Clark, 440½; Wilson, 324; Harmon, 148; Underwood, 117½; with fifty-six scattered votes, including one for Bryan. The weary and overwrought delegates then adjourned until Friday afternoon.

On the next eight ballots only minor shifts in the voting were recorded, but on the tenth ballot New York—as had been expected—cast its ninety votes for Clark. This brought Clark up to 556, a majority but not the two-thirds majority required. Following the convention from the Speaker's office at the Capitol, Champ Clark readied a telegram of acceptance and confidently told a visitor that he would have the nomination on the next ballot. From his summer home on the New Jersey shore, Wilson sent his floor manager a wire asking that his delegates be released to vote for Clark.

In the previous sixteen Democratic conventions, stretching back to 1848, the candidate winning a simple majority had never been denied a two-thirds vote. Wilson himself was on record as opposing the two-thirds requirement as undemocratic. But as the roll call continued on the tenth ballot, North Dakota held fast for Wilson and an Oklahoma delegate—shouting that he would not join Tammany in the nomination—started another demonstration for the New Jersey governor. Underwood's delegates likewise refused to be stampeded; allied with the Wilson men, they could continue to prevent Clark from attaining the two-thirds majority. And at 4:03 Saturday morning the convention again adjourned. Wilson's manager pocketed the withdrawal statement, and the convention went into a fifth session on Saturday afternoon.

The next break for Wilson came on the fourteenth ballot when Bryan arose to say that Nebraska could no longer support a candidate backed by Tammany Hall and was thus shifting its support from Clark to Wilson. Abandoning even a pretense of journalistic impartiality, William Allen White stood on the reporters' table and cheered along with the galleries. Only Tammany, "irreconcilable reactionaries" from the South, and a few scattered bosses, he wrote, "clung to the spars and lifeboats of the wrecked Clark liner, and all the country knew that Clark's day was done—that the progressives were about to win a victory in Baltimore to offset the defeat in Chicago." When the convention adjourned on Saturday, after the twenty-sixth ballot, the vote stood: Clark, 463½; Wilson, 407½; Underwood, 112½; Harmon, 29; miscellaneous, 79.

Sunday was officially a day of rest, but the bargaining and negotiating continued through the day-long adjournment. When balloting resumed on Monday, July 1, Wilson had picked up additional strength. Sizable blocs of votes from Indiana, Iowa, Vermont, Michigan, and Wyoming appeared in his column; and on the thirtieth ballot Wilson actually passed Clark in the count. But still the nomination eluded him, as it had the Speaker. Then, on Tuesday, Illinois cast fifty-eight votes for the New Jersey governor—and thus set the stage for Wilson's ultimate triumph. At the beginning of the forty-sixth ballot, Alabama announced that Underwood's name was being withdrawn. In quick succession the Harmon and Clark delegates were also released—though Missouri insisted on voting for her favorite son to the end—and Wilson was nominated with an avalanche of 990 votes.

Underwood refused the vice-presidential nomination, and the convention picked instead Governor Thomas R. Marshall of Indiana—a man whose sole subsequent contribution to political thought was the remark that what the country really needed was a good five-cent cigar.

The country was exhausted from two weeks of such intense political activity, first at Chicago, then at Baltimore. The victors, Taft and Wilson, were as weary and troubled as the losers. And Theodore Roosevelt pondered his next move, briefly regretting that he was committed to running as the candidate of a third party. "I should much have preferred to have kept out of this fight," he wrote a friend on July 10, a week

257

after the Democrats had straggled out of Baltimore. "Perhaps if Wilson had been nominated first, I should have done so." With another progressive in the race, he knew his own chances of election were greatly diminished. Even so ardent a partisan as Alice Longworth confessed that her "hopes were far from robust."

2

The summer of 1912 was a time of decision for America's men of politics. For the Democrats among them it was a relatively simple choice; despite the bitter and protracted wrangling at Baltimore, most of them would rally behind the victor of the convention. Even should the disappointed followers of Clark, Underwood, and Harmon find the vaunted progressivism of Wilson difficult to accept, it was unlikely they would move in any great numbers to the Republican nominee. If anyone was leading a forlorn hope in 1912, it was William Howard Taft. "Sometimes I think I might as well give up as far as being a candidate is concerned," the President wrote his wife in July. "There are so many people in the country who don't like me."

The choice for Republicans, of course, was an especially agonizing one. Some among them—notably Lodge, Root, and Stimson—had long since announced that they must part ways with Roosevelt, however deep their personal friendship, however close their former political alliance. At the Chicago convention, the lines between Taft and Roosevelt supporters had been clearly marked. But at the end of the riotous gathering, there were some surprising defections from the Colonel's camp. It had been one thing to challenge Taft for leadership of the G.O.P.; quite another to bolt the party and join T.R.'s quixotic crusade.

On the Sunday following Taft's nomination, Governor Hadley had come to the Congress Hotel to say good-bye to Roosevelt before leaving Chicago. The Missourian had already intimated that he would not follow T.R. out of the party, and there was a welling resentment at Roosevelt headquarters against the man who had signed the governors' plea to T.R. to enter the contest and who had been floor leader of the Colonel's forces at the just concluded convention. As Hadley entered the hotel suite, the people clustered about Roosevelt fell silent, standing "like graven images." But T.R. greeted Hadley warmly, took him aside for a whispered conversation, and then bade him farewell. "He will not be with us," Roosevelt said after Hadley had departed, "but we must not blame him."

At least one of the other seven little governors took an equally dim view of the Roosevelt revolt; on July 8 Michigan's Chase Osborn advised "all good Republicans . . . [to] refuse to join the malcontents in a new party." Senator Borah of Idaho tried to sit on the fence, staying in the party but remaining aloof from the Taft candidacy. Iowa's Senator Cummins announced that he would personally vote for Roosevelt but would not join a new party. La Follette, opposed to both Taft and Roosevelt, stayed within the Republican party but privately expressed his hopes for a Wilson victory. Roosevelt, the embittered Wisconsin senator wrote, "offered no reason for a third party, except his own overmastering craving for a third term."

In six states—California, Kansas, Maine, Nebraska, South Dakota, and West Virginia—progressives retained control of the Republican party machinery; there was no separate ticket below the presidential line; and such men as governors Stubbs, Vessey, and Glasscock, Senator Crawford, and Representative Norris could have Roosevelt and remain within their state's party organization. But with the single exception of Montana's Dixon, no incumbent Republican senator or governor seeking re-election in 1912 joined the new party. William Flinn of Pennsylvania remained true to Roosevelt, but William Ward and Ormsby McHarg, coldly practical politicians, quietly stole out of the Roosevelt tent.

The Colonel was not as philosophic and understanding about some of these defections as he had been about Hadley's. "What a miserable showing some of the so-called Progressive leaders have made," T.R. wrote in anger to Cal O'Laughlin on July 9. "They represent nothing but mere sound and fury. A year or two ago, when it was merely a question of loud words, they were claiming to be much further advanced than I was, but they have not the heart for a fight, and the minute they were up against deeds insteads of words, they quit forthwith."

The Colonel reserved his most exquisite venom for a public denunciation of Elihu Root in the New York senator's role as chairman of the adjourned Republican convention. In *The Outlook* for July 6 Roosevelt described Root—because of his recognition of the two Taft alternates from Massachusetts—as a "modern Autolycus, the 'snapper-up of unconsidered trifles.'" But T.R. could not seem to get those trifles off his mind, for in the very next issue of the magazine he referred to those two votes as being "publicly raped at the last moment from Massachusetts." Root felt the thrusts keenly and hesitated about entering the lists against Roosevelt in the fall campaign; in the end, he would make only one major address in support of the President.

In the summer of 1912, as in the primary campaign leading up to the G.O.P. convention, the unhappiest man in politics was Nicholas Longworth. At the end of July he and Alice journeyed to Sagamore Hill for a family conference. The Colonel, his daughter, and his son-in-law sat a long time on the piazza debating whether or not Alice should be allowed to go to the Progressive party convention, scheduled to open in Chicago the first week in August. Alice later recalled that she and her father had rocked in their chairs with characteristic violence as Nick and the Colonel "held a sort of court of justice" on her. At last it was decided that it would not be fair to Longworth—standing for re-election to the House of Representatives as a regular—if his wife went to the insurgent gathering. "They were both simply angelic," Alice later wrote, "really so sorry for me, and I may say that I was so sorry for myself that I was sniffling." But she had promised to abide by the decision of the menfolk and returned to Washington, where she tried not to be too unpleasant, with, she reported, "only intermittent success."

On July 8 Senator Dixon's call for a convention of what had been dubbed the Bull Moose party had been published. Despite major defections from the progressive movement, there were still some prominent names among the sixty-three signers of the call. And thus, on Monday, August 5, six weeks to the day after he had left, Colonel Roosevelt was back at the Congress Hotel in Chicago.

Every state except South Carolina was represented when the first convention of the Progressive party was called to order at the Coliseum, but some states had sent three or four times the authorized number of delegates so that there were more than two thousand persons seated on the floor of the hall. Amos Pinchot surveyed the scene from the gallery and found it far from reassuring. He conceded that there were a large number of "superior, intelligent, and deeply earnest people"; but the convention majority, he felt, was made up of persons "bent chiefly on riding to power or prestige on Roosevelt's broad back." This "nondescript army," Pinchot charged, had "aims as far apart as the poles from the equator." Yet it was "miraculously kept united by the magnetism of one electric personality, and the pervasive thought that somehow something worthwhile and exciting was about to eventuate through their chief's magic."

Less a political convention than it was an old-time camp meeting of religious revivalists, the Bull Moose gathering alternated between periods of frenzied, unrestrained welcome of its heroes and solemn, even tearful attention to what they had to say. On the opening day, Governor Hiram Johnson marched proudly in at the head of his California delegation, singing "I want to be a Bull Moose, and with the Bull Moose stand!" Roosevelt's former friend Chicago publisher H. H. Kohlsaat snidely reported that it was worth coming in from Lake Forest just to see Oscar Straus—as Secretary of Commerce and Labor, the highest ranking Jew in T.R.'s administration—leading the New York delegation in a lusty rendition of "Onward, Christian Soldiers." But the muses were perhaps most imaginatively served by a new verse for "The Battle Hymn of the Republic":

> *The moose has left the wooded hill;*
> *his call rings through the land.*
> *It's a summons to the young and strong*
> *to join with willing hand:*
> *To fight for right and country;*
> *to strike down a robber band,*
> *And we'll go marching on.*

Ex-Senator Beveridge of Indiana delivered a keynote address on Monday evening that brought the delegates roaring to their feet and breaking into a renewed chorus of song: "He is trampling out the vintage where the grapes of wrath are stored. . . ." But the greatest ovation, of course, was reserved for the hero of the hour, the knight in shining armor, Theodore Roosevelt, when he was introduced to the convention on Tuesday. His appearance was greeted with a fifty-five minute demonstration and his address "A Confession of Faith"—only half of its 20,000 word length actually delivered—was interrupted by applause and cheers no less than 145 times.

The platform of the Progressive party, he told the Coliseum audience, must be a "contract with the people." If the people accepted this contract by putting them in power, then they must feel themselves under obligation to fulfill the promises of that platform "as loyally as if it were actually enforceable under the penalties of the law." What T.R.

proceeded to outline in his speech would be incorporated wholesale into the Progressive platform the next day.

He had made his "Confession of Faith" so lengthy, the Colonel said in conclusion, because he wanted his audience to know what his deepest convictions on the great issues of the day were—"so that if you choose to make me your standard-bearer in the fight you shall make your choice understanding exactly how I feel." If they decided to choose someone else, he would abide by that decision. But he could not alter those convictions; he would do anything for the people "except what my conscience tells me is wrong." It mattered little what happened to those who stood in the forefront of the battle; he hoped that—the people awakened to the struggle—they would win. "But, win or lose, we shall not falter. Whatever fate may at the moment overtake any of us, the movement itself will not stop. Our cause is based on the eternal principle of righteousness. . . ." Calling upon the delegates to stand with him in readiness "to spend and be spent in the endless crusade against wrong," T.R. brought his mesmerized audience back to the promontory to which he had led them seven weeks earlier: "We stand at Armageddon, and we battle for the Lord."

No less than the despised and denounced older parties, the Progressive crusaders assembled at Chicago in August, 1912, found themselves acting like politicians. Despite the ecstatic fervor and elevated harmony of the open sessions, there was the inevitable wrangling and bickering behind closed doors of men who—whether or not they could acknowledge it even to themselves—were working at cross purposes. William Allen White was among those who had come to Chicago a week early to help draft the platform, and he later recalled that the committee worked on it four days and the better part of three nights. The critical issue soon proved to be the plank on trusts.

White, the Pinchots, and other reformers wanted a statement of the specific abuses of trusts that were to be prohibited by a strengthening of the Sherman Act. Perkins was adamant that the plank be phrased in general terms only—and as a former Morgan partner, associated with both U.S. Steel and International Harvester, he was strongly suspect in the eyes of the first group. White, who had a vivid if not always accurate memory, years later described a scene at the Blackstone Hotel in which the Colonel himself acted as intermediary between Perkins and Gifford Pinchot on the matter of the trust plank. "He would toddle out of one room, looking over the tops of his glasses, with the contested plank in his hand, and enter another room—maybe Perkins' room; and then in a few moments, like a faithful retriever, would come popping out, panting across the hall to Pinchot's room, still with the paper in his hand, grinning at me like a dog wagging his tail as he tried to compromise the differences between the pinfeather wings of his new party."

O. K. Davis remembered that the dispute continued through Tuesday night and into Wednesday morning, the day the platform was to be presented to the convention and the nominations made. It was the Colonel himself, Davis claimed, who wrote out the final compromise—one that conformed to the Perkins view. When the convention opened on Wednesday, it was decided to name the candidates first to allow the platform committee additional time to complete its draft. Roosevelt, of course, was nominated for the Presidency by acclamation and, after other candidates for the Vice Presidency had withdrawn, Hiram Johnson was named as T.R.'s running mate.

Roosevelt of New York and Johnson of California were escorted to the platform over which hung an appropriate verse from Kipling:

> For there is neither East nor West,
>   Border nor breed nor birth
> When two strong men stand face to face,
>   Though they come from the ends of the earth.

The Colonel congratulated the Progressive party for picking for the Vice Presidency a man "fit at the moment to be President of the United States," and his acceptance speech, like that of Johnson's, was filled with praise of his running mate.

Not until the speeches were concluded did the chairman of the platform committee, Dean William Draper Lewis of the University of Pennsylvania Law School, appear with the controversial statement. There had not been time to have the platform retyped as one single document, and Lewis was forced to read from a sheaf of loose papers that he had to keep shuffling in his hands. Amos Pinchot remembered a "packed, ecstatic audience" listening to the reading of the platform and frequently bursting into applause. No one listened more intently than George W. Perkins, sitting on the platform and appearing to the pudgy and envious White as "spick-and-span, oiled and curled like an Assyrian bull, and a young one, trim and virile."

The Progressive contract with the people opened with a ritual denunciation of the old parties—the "deliberate betrayal" of the Republicans; the "fatal incapacity" of the Democrats. Among the specific planks were endorsements of a nationwide presidential preference primary, direct primaries for the nomination of state and national officers, the direct election of United States senators, the short ballot, and the adoption by the states of the initiative, referendum, and recall. The party further pledged itself to work for the establishment of minimum safety and health standards in industrial occupations, minimum wage and hour standards for working women, the eight-hour day in twenty-four-hour industries and one day's rest in seven for all workers, and standards of compensation for death and injury in industrial accidents, as well as the prohibition of child labor. Among a host of other specifics, the platform also called for the establishment of a tariff commission to aid Congress and the President in determining fair levies on imports; reform of the national currency system; women's suffrage; a constitutional amendment providing for a federal income tax; limitation of campaign contributions and expenditures and full publicity for both; and, of course, the recall of state judicial decisions.

As for trusts, the platform called for national regulation of interstate corporations. Concentration was described as "inevitable and necessary," but abuses must be curbed. To that end, it was proposed that a strong federal commission be established to regulate corporations—by enforcing the publicity of corporate transactions that are of public interest; by attacking unfair competition, false capitalization, and special privilege; and by informing businessmen of the law so that they could conduct their operations in conformity with that law. "Under such a system of constructive regulation, legitimate business, freed from confusion, uncertainty and fruitless litigation, will develop normally in response to the energy and enterprise of the American business man."

Perkins was leaning forward in his chair as Lewis read this plank. But a look of shock and anger crossed his face as the dean continued: "We favor strengthening the Sherman law by prohibiting agreements to divide territory or limit output; refusing to sell to customers who buy from business rivals; to sell below cost in certain areas while maintaining higher prices in other places; using the power of transportation to aid or injure special business concerns; and other unfair trade practices."

Before Lewis could finish reading this paragraph, Perkins turned to Amos Pinchot and whispered: "Lewis has made a mistake. That doesn't belong in the platform. We cut it out last night." Jumping to his feet and slamming back his chair, Perkins stomped off the platform and left the hall—a one-man bolt by the new party's chief financier. O. K. Davis saw what happened and followed Perkins out of the Coliseum, running into James Garfield as he left. Davis explained the situation to Garfield, who agreed that Lewis had made a mistake in including the paragraph on strengthening the Sherman Act. But others, including White, would not agree that the committee had excised the paragraph.

Back at the hotel, a high-level conference—including Roosevelt and the nervous and exhausted Dean Lewis—was held. Davis was dispatched on an errand to his friends among the press corps. Although some of the reporters remained skeptical, they agreed to send out copies of the platform that omitted the offending paragraph—subjecting Davis to some "joshing" about the committee's disorganization and the herd-like instinct of the convention in accepting whatever was presented to it.

Amos Pinchot conceded that the inclusion or exclusion of the paragraph meant little or nothing to the delegates—or the public at large (it subsequently showed up in most printed editions anyway). For all but a small minority of Bull Moosers that year—of which he and his brother, Gifford, remained the core—Roosevelt alone was the issue. To the bulk of the party it would have made no difference if there had been no platform at all. White felt differently: "This was not the way Christian soldiers marched with the 'cross of Jesus, onward as to war.' It was a detour down a purple primrose path. . . ." But Roosevelt easily talked the Kansas editor out of a defection. In those days at Chicago, White recalled, T.R. was irresistible, he was "indeed the Bull Moose charging about the hotel corridors, stalking down an aisle of the Coliseum while the crowds roared, walking like a gladiator to the lions." The Colonel could be forgiven his defense of Perkins; this was not the time for analysis and questioning, for semantic arguments.

The next day White led a spirited if ineffectual opposition to the selection of Perkins as chairman of the Progressive party's executive committee—in his own words, "a scared but determined, fat and preposterous-looking young man in his early forties trying to overcome his doubts by venting his wrath a little too rancorously. . . ." Because the discussion preceding the vote might become personal, it was suggested that Perkins might want to leave the room. But the financier declined to leave, saying he preferred to answer his challengers to their faces. Finally someone suggested that Perkins be allowed to direct the activities of the executive committee but without any official connection or title. An embarrassed silence followed this proposal, broken at last by the laconic statement of an Arizona delegate: "We believe in toting guns down our way. But we don't carry 'em concealed."

The debate ended and the vote was taken, with no ballots cast against Perkins—though there were a number of abstentions. At the adjournment of the acrimonious meeting Perkins walked over to White, flung his arm around the Kansan's shoulder, and asked that they part friends. White agreed; the two of them, many years later he would see, were but puppets in "the Punch-and-Judy show of the moment. . . . We knocked our heads together for the delectation of the angels who saw far ahead the way the tide was washing. And little we knew about it."

3

One who saw clearly how the tide was washing—though he could never admit it publicly and became increasingly reticent on the subject even in private—was Theodore Roosevelt. On August 10, the day after the Colonel had returned from Chicago, Nicholas Roosevelt came over to Sagamore Hill to play tennis with Ethel. T.R. and Archie appeared, the former looking to Nicholas "younger by ten years than when I had last seen him . . . in such wonderful spirits that he behaved like a boy." A doubles match was quickly organized, an eccentric Roosevelt game that included jokes, songs, laughter, and impromptu dances. At dinner that evening T.R. told his family circle that he was "dumbfounded" at the success of the Bull Moose convention and at the spirit of religious fervor that had taken hold of the movement. Later, as they were sitting on the piazza, George Roosevelt made the observation that whereas Roosevelt used to be the progressive leader of the conservatives, he now was the conservative leader of the progressives. "Yes, yes!" the Colonel agreed. "That's it. I have to hold them in check all the time. I've got to restrain them."

On August 14 Roosevelt confided to his English friend Arthur Lee that he regarded Woodrow Wilson as "an able man" who would make "a creditable President." It was his best judgment that Wilson would win but that he himself would finish ahead of Taft in the three-way contest. (A fourth candidate in the race, Eugene V. Debs of the Socialist party, T.R. regarded as an anarchist, a contemptuous creature beneath acknowledgment or recognition.) There was still the chance that the

Progressive movement would gain enough strength for him to beat Wilson, "but I think this very improbable."

Despite the hopelessness of the cause, Roosevelt was not going to let Wilson win by default. Before the end of August he had made speeches in Providence, Rhode Island, Boston, and Wilkes Barre, Pennsylvania, and had campaigned three days in Vermont. Then, on September 2, he departed on a month-long trip to the Far West, with a return through the South. Prior to leaving, T.R. wrote his sister Corinne that "never was there a fight better worth making, but the exertion is tremendous, and I look forward to Election Day as the end of a battle." Before reaching Seattle on September 10, he had spoken in Illinois, Indiana, Missouri, Iowa, Minnesota, North Dakota, and Montana.

En route to the coast, T.R.'s train had passed through, without stopping in, Idaho—where Senator Borah was running for re-election. The Republican party's most notable fence-straddler, one observer speculated, heaved a sigh of relief and "read tranquilly of the big fuss" the Colonel was making in Washington and Oregon. But then, to Borah's surprise, the special turned east from Portland and made for Boise. The unhappy senator boarded Roosevelt's train as it entered Idaho and agreed to share the platform with the presidential candidate at the state capital on September 12. In a graceful introduction that evening, Borah, a reporter wrote, "steered as adroitly as ever between Taft and Roosevelt, Scylla and Charybdis," concluding with a pious observation that had the Colonel received the Republican nomination he would have swept the country. He then motioned Roosevelt forward with a courtly bow.

Roosevelt started by quoting Borah's last remark and thanking him for it. "So I will explain just why it was that I was *not* nominated," he said. "And I will ask Senator Borah to corroborate me." He thereupon launched into the familiar litany of charges about the stolen convention, ending each accusation of theft with a polite bow to his host and the purely rhetorical question, "Isn't that so, Senator Borah?" Borah, of course, had been in the forefront of the fight over the contested delegates, a role he could not now disclaim; yet, he had refused to follow Roosevelt in his bolt from the G.O.P. Negotiating a largely unsuccessful smile, Borah had to nod in agreement to each charge made by Roosevelt. The crowd was ecstatic, eagerly waiting for each courteous bow of Roosevelt's and each repetition of the question, "Isn't that so, Senator Borah?" Everyone was delighted at seeing the senator thus forced to become party to a thorough arraignment as a pack of thieves of the party in which he was running for re-election. But T.R. reserved a final twist of the knife for his concluding remark: "Any one who is acquainted with the facts and does not condemn them is blinded to the light and has a seared moral sense." Beaming contentedly, T.R. returned to his railroad car, as a reporter asked Borah what he thought of the speech. "It was great," conceded the thoroughly discomfited senator.

Almost to a man, the reporters accompanying T.R. on this swing around the country grew to idolize the man but, by the month's end, as the campaign special was heading up the East Coast on the final lap from Alabama to New York, most of them were weary of the nonstop barnstorming and found that they could repeat almost entire speeches the Colonel was wont to make on certain subjects. To amuse themselves one day the reporters took turns imitating the Colonel—and were discovered in this play by Roosevelt himself. Not the least bit angry, T.R. favored them with a highly exaggerated imitation of himself— elaborate gestures, the cracked falsetto, and a final plea: "Children, don't crowd so close to the car; it might back up, and—we can't afford to lose any little Bull Mooses, you know!"

President Taft, resigned to losing, declined to campaign actively and gave few speeches after his formal acceptance of the nomination on August 1. Later that month he wrote to Elihu Root to say that he had no feeling of enmity toward Roosevelt; "I look upon him as I look upon a freak almost in the Zoological Garden, a kind of animal not often found."

Woodrow Wilson, for very different reasons, had originally decided against an active campaign. "Swings around the circle" he found to be undignified and unproductive—though it would be all right for Bryan to canvass in his behalf. "I intend to discuss principles and not men," he stated loftily at the begnning of August, "and I will make speeches only in such debatable States where I accept invitations from the party leaders." That month he made only a few addresses in his home state of New Jersey. But as September approached, he grew concerned.

The race, Wilson fully realized, was between him and the Colonel; Taft was out of the picture. With party lines so blurred, all was "guesswork," he wrote a friend on August 25. ". . . I am by no means confident. He [Roosevelt] appeals to their imagination; I do not. He is a real, vivid person, whom they have seen and shouted themselves hoarse over and voted for, millions strong; I am a vague, conjectural personality, more made up of opinions and academic prepossessions than of human traits and red corpuscles." And at the beginning of September, the Democratic nominee journeyed to Detroit to give a Labor Day address; it was but the first stop on the long campaign trail he would follow almost without interruption to Election Day.

A few days before he headed west to Michigan, Wilson had a lengthy interview at his summer home on the Jersey shore with the Boston attorney Louis D. Brandeis. A former supporter of La Follette's, Brandeis was now one of the 40,000 members of the Wilson Progressive Republican League—those men who had broken with the G.O.P. Old Guard but yet refused to march behind Colonel Roosevelt in the Bull Moose ranks. At this first meeting with the Democratic candidate, Brandeis outlined his views on monopoly control and, according to Wilson's biographer, easily convinced the governor that he should base his campaign on the issue of restoring competition and free enterprise by means of the regulation and control of corporations. And thus Wilson decided to make trusts the subject of his Labor Day address.

"As to the monopolies, which Mr. Roosevelt proposes to legalize and welcome," Wilson told his Detroit audience, "I know that they are so many cars of juggernaut and I do not look forward with pleasure to the time when the juggernauts are licensed and driven by commissioners of the United States. . . ." Monopolies were created by unregulated competition, Wilson asserted; they could be prevented by remedial legislation that would restrict the wrong use of competition and allow the right use of competiton to destroy monopoly. "Ours is a programme of liberty," he said in comparing the Democratic platform with the Progressive one; "theirs is a programme of regulation." Wilson called his approach the New Freedom, in contrast to T.R.'s New Nationalism. "Between the New Nationalism and the New Freedom," William Allen White solemnly observed, "was that fantastic imaginary gulf that always existed between tweedle-dum and tweedle-dee."

Wilson, Roosevelt later charged, was saying that the states could best control the trusts. Since some 80 per cent of the trusts were organized under the laws of New Jersey, it would be instructive to review Wilson's record of trust regulation as New Jersey governor for the past two years, the Colonel suggested. "The chapter describing what Mr. Wilson has done about the trusts in New Jersey," he concluded, "would read precisely like a chapter describing the snakes in Ireland, which ran: 'There are no snakes in Ireland.' Mr. Wilson has done precisely and exactly nothing about trusts."

Roosevelt came to share at least one opinion with Wilson: that the former history professor—in his own words of August—lacked "human traits and red corpuscles." Midway through the campaign a scandal monger offered first the Republicans, then the Progressives a sheaf of letters from Wilson to a divorced woman, letters that could be made to implicate him in an extramarital affair. Senator Dixon turned down the letters and was congratulated for doing so by the Colonel. "Joe," Roosevelt said, "those letters would be entirely unconvincing. Nothing, no evidence could ever make the American people believe that a man like Woodrow Wilson, cast so perfectly as the apothecary's clerk, could ever play Romeo."

4

"I am profoundly touched," Colonel Roosevelt was heard to say in a jocular mood. "Something tells us that before long George W. Perkins will also be profoundly touched." As T.R. and the other Progressive candidates charged about the country giving speeches, the man insiders referred to as the Dough Moose directed publicity activities from New York. O. K. Davis recalled one example of the intuitive brilliance and decisiveness that had made Perkins such a towering figure in the financial world before he turned to politics as Roosevelt's principal backer. To satisfy the great demand for copies of T.R.'s "Confession of Faith," an edition of three million pamphlets containing the August speech was printed for distribution. Checking the proofs, Davis noticed that the cover photographs—of Roosevelt and Hiram Johnson—were copyrighted by the Moffett Studio in Chicago. To his horror Davis learned that the studio had never been asked its permission to reproduce the photograph; under the copyright law, a fine of one dollar could be levied for every copy printed.

Davis rushed to explain the situation to Perkins. The financier thought but a moment before dictating a telegram to the studio: "WE ARE PLANNING TO ISSUE AN EDITION OF THREE MILLION COPIES OF ROOSEVELT'S SPEECH, WITH PICTURES OF ROOSEVELT AND JOHNSON ON THE FRONT PAGE. THIS WILL BE A GREAT ADVERTISEMENT FOR

THE PHOTOGRAPHER. WHAT WILL YOU GIVE US TO USE YOUR PIC-
TURES. RUSH ANSWER." The reply amazed and delighted Davis: "WE
HAVE NEVER DONE THIS BEFORE, BUT UNDER THE CIRCUMSTANCES WE
WILL GIVE YOU $250." Within ten minutes, Davis said, the issue was
running on the press.

Perkins also edited and published a weekly magazine, beginning in
September, called the *Progressive Bulletin.* The first issue had a circulation of 200,000, but by the end of the campaign a million copies a week
were being distributed, with a cover price of ten cents but generally
given away free. A number of Bull Moosers were less than enchanted
with Perkins's activities, however, and William Allen White complained
of being swamped with pamphlets bearing such provocative titles as
"What Perkins Thinks About the Tariff" and "George W. Perkins'
Views on Labor."

Meanwhile, on October 2 the Colonel had returned to Oyster Bay
from his first major campaign foray. Two days later he was in Washington testifying before a Senate committee on campaign contributions—
his enemies had dredged up the old charges about the Harriman and
Standard Oil contributions in 1904 in order to embarrass his present effort. And on October 7 he departed on another journey, this time to the
Midwest. After barnstorming through Michigan, Minnesota, and Wisconsin, he arrived for a parade and a major address in Chicago on Columbus Day, October 12.

The following week T.R. was to speak in Cincinnati, but to avoid
compromising his son-in-law he had asked Alice and Nick Longworth to
be out of the city on that date. All the other members of the family,
Alice noted bitterly, were "up to their eyebrows in the fight," while she
was forced to take a most unaccustomed seat on the sidelines. Barred
from seeing her father in Cincinnati, she decided on the spur of the moment to meet him in Chicago and was thus in the audience on October
12 when T.R. delivered what she described as "a savage attack on Wilson to a huge and wildly enthusiastic audience." The following day, a
Sunday, Mrs. Longworth joined her father and Ruth and Medill McCormick for dinner. "His voice was showing the strain of such incessant
speechmaking," Alice noted. And although her father seemed "in great
form" as the foursome discussed the campaign to date, the dark cloud of
almost certain defeat in November hung heavily over their dinnertime
conversation.

On Monday morning Roosevelt left for Milwaukee, Wisconsin,

where he was to make another major address. After a dinner that evening in his honor, T.R. stepped out of the Hotel Gilpatrick and crossed the sidewalk toward the open car that was waiting to take him to the hall where he would speak. At his side was Colonel Cecil A. Lyon, a former hunting companion, Texas state chairman of the Progressive party, and the candidate's unofficial bodyguard, who was carrying a loaded automatic in his pocket. The lobby, of course, had been brightly lighted, but the street was dark and Roosevelt barely perceived a crowd, held back by the police, waiting to cheer him. Lyon escorted the Colonel to the automobile and heard the chauffeur start the engine; he then turned to get into his own car, second in the line of official vehicles that was to form a motorcade. As Roosevelt stood up in the car to acknowledge the cheers, a man in the second rank of the crowd raised an old-fashioned pistol and, aiming between two people standing in front of him, fired a shot directly into Roosevelt's chest, at a distance of less than thirty feet.

As the Colonel rocked back from the bullet's impact, the man prepared to fire a second time. Elbert Martin, one of T.R.'s stenographers and a former football player, had seen the glint of the pistol even before the first shot was fired and at this instant leaped across the automobile and flung himself at the assassin. The flying tackle brought them both to the pavement, where Martin got the man under his knee, dug his fingers into his throat, and wrested control of the weapon from him. "I wasn't trying to take him prisoner," Martin later confessed. "I was trying to kill him." It was all the police could do to hold back the surging crowd, but the captain of the detail rushed over and demanded that Martin give him the gun. "I'll be damned if I do," Martin shouted over his shoulder and went back to strangling the assassin. Colonel Lyon—who one eyewitness remembered as "dancing around like a madman with a drawn revolver"—kept back both the police and the crowd. But Roosevelt, still standing in the open car, called out to Martin: "Don't hurt him. Bring him here. I want to look at him." The stenographer released his grip reluctantly and complied with the Colonel's request.

Roosevelt peered intently at the man who just shot him—John F. Schrank, a part-time bartender from New York who had decided to kill the ex-President in defense of the anti-third-term tradition. The obviously demented man later related dreams in which William McKinley had accused his Vice President of assassinating him eleven years earlier and asked Schrank to revenge him. Now T.R. asked him why he had done it and then, without waiting for a reply, told the police to take the man away.

Later the Colonel confessed that he really would not have objected to the man's being killed then and there but had not deemed it "wise or proper" to allow it. Schrank, he charged in a private letter, was no more a madman than Senator La Follette or Eugene Debs. He had shrewdly avoided shooting T.R. in a Southern state, where he probably would have been lynched on the spot, and he had waited until Roosevelt was in a state with no death penalty. He harbored no feeling one way or the other for the man, only ill will "against the people, who, by their cease-less and intemperate abuse, excited him to the action. . . ." Schrank was ultimately judged insane and locked up in a Wisconsin state hospital —living through the election of 1940 that saw the anti-third-term tra-dition at last shattered, by the husband of T.R.'s niece Eleanor.

With the would-be assassin disposed of, Roosevelt could think of his wound. The force of the shot, he subsequently told his son Archie, was no more than the kick of a mule; Archie—having been kicked by a mule—was enormously impressed. The bullet had been slowed by passing through both the manuscript of the speech T.R. was to de-liver and an iron spectacle case in his pocket and had thus only pene-trated three or four inches into the Colonel's chest, breaking his fourth rib and lodging just short of his right lung. The candidate reached inside his coat and dispassionately noted the blood on the hand he withdrew. He then coughed and put his hand to his lips; blood in his mouth would indicate that his lung had been pierced. But there was no blood and he concluded that "the chances were twenty to one" that the bullet was not a fatal one.

A member of the party now stepped forward to suggest that the Colonel's car proceed to a hospital. "You get me to that speech," Roose-velt snapped; "it may be the last I shall deliver, but I am going to de-liver this one." Later he told an English friend that his decision was no more heroic than those of the thirteen men in his Rough Rider regiment who had fought on at San Juan Hill after having been wounded. "In the very unlikely event of the wound being mortal I wished to die with my boots on. . . ." Even if the wound proved slight, "as I deemed overwhelm-ingly probable," it would no doubt curtail his remaining campaign activ-ities—and he wanted to make one more speech "to which under the circumstances it was at least possible that the country would pay some heed."

The caravan drove on to the Milwaukee Auditorium but before Roosevelt was escorted to the platform three doctors were summoned from the audience to examine the wound. None could say how serious the injury was but all three agreed that Roosevelt should be taken to a hospital immediately. Again, the Colonel refused: "I will make this speech, or die; one way or the other." As he strode onto the stage, the audience—still ignorant of the shooting—broke into the prolonged, almost hysterical cheering that greeted all his appearances. At last the chairman quieted the crowd and said: "I have something to tell you and I hope you will receive the news with calmness. Colonel Roosevelt has been shot. He is wounded." Cries of horror and disbelief rose from the throng as T.R. stepped forward. But a mere lifting of his hand brought calm again.

"Friends, I shall ask you to be as quiet as possible," he said. "I don't know whether you fully understand that I have just been shot; but it takes more than that to kill a Bull Moose." He took the manuscript from his pocket and showed his shocked listeners where the sheets had been pierced by the bullet—it was to have been a lengthy address, he joked, and had thus probably saved his life. "The bullet is in me now, so that I cannot make a very long speech, but I will try my best." But he did not ask for pity. He was concerned about too many other things to fear in the least for his own life. "I want you to understand that I am ahead of the game anyway. No man has had a happier life than I have led; a happier life in every way."

He then started to talk about the Progressive movement, a cause he was in "with my whole heart and soul." But before going on, he reverted to the assassination attempt. "He shot to kill," the Colonel said. "He shot—the shot, the bullet went in here—I will show you." The opposition newspapers, he now charged, were responsible; "they cannot, month in and month out and year in and year out, make the kind of untruthful or bitter assault that they have made and not expect that brutal, violent natures . . . will be unaffected by it." Someone on the stage behind him tried to get him to sit down. "I am not sick at all," he said testily. "I am all right." His audience, he again joked, could not escape listening to the speech. When a second attempt to get him off the stage was made, he said: "My friends are a little more nervous than I am. Don't you waste any sympathy on me. I have had an A-1 time in life and I am having it now."

Once in the speech he conceded that he was a little sore in the chest but that he was not yet ready to let the doctors get hold of him. And so he spoke for an hour, though it is doubtful that his audience was able to concentrate on the points he was making. Afterward he confessed to a sensation of heat as he had begun speaking and said that his heart beat unusually fast for the first ten minutes. Thereafter he was forced to take quick, short breaths and found it impossible to get through long sentences without pausing.

His speech at last ended, Roosevelt turned to leave the stage and found his way blocked by scores of well-wishers who—to his amazement and intense disgust—insisted on pumping his hand vigorously and refused to let him go. A member of his entourage said it was as if each greeter wished to be able to say he had been the last person to shake the Colonel's hand before he expired.

It was now decided to take Roosevelt immediately back to Chicago, where he could be treated at Mercy Hospital by the noted specialist Dr. John Benjamin Murphy. (Among the more outrageous campaign slanders was the story later circulated that T.R.—at the moment he was shot and sinking into the arms of an aide—had said: "Take me to Murphy at the Mercy. I need the Catholic vote.") Back in his private railroad car, Roosevelt undressed, shaved, and removed his studs and buttons from the bloody shirt to put them into a fresh one—"as I thought I might be stiff the next morning." When he lay down in his berth, he discovered that his heart was again beating rapidly and his breath was coming in short puffs. Soon he found that he was less uncomfortable lying on his left, unwounded side and in that position he went to sleep. The special train was highballed through on the main line and arrived in Chicago at 3:30 A.M. on October 15. Alongside the tracks an ambulance was waiting. "I'll not go to a hospital lying in that thing," the Colonel insisted when he spied attendants with a stretcher. "I'll walk to it and I'll walk from it to the hospital. I'm no weakling to be crippled by a flesh wound."

An X-ray disclosed that the bullet, which had entered Roosevelt's chest to the right of and just below the right nipple, was embedded in the fourth rib. An examining doctor announced that the Colonel, who had a phenomenal chest development, was "one of the most powerful men I have ever seen laid on an operating table." It was largely due to the fact that he was "a physical marvel" that T.R. was not dangerously wounded, the doctor concluded. The Roosevelt family physician hastened to Chicago and after examining the famous patient said that the folded manuscript and spectacle case had "checked and deflected the bullet so that it passed up at such an angle that it went outside the ribs and in the muscles." If the deflection had not occurred, the bullet would have penetrated the arch of the aorta or auricles of the heart and the Colonel would not have lived sixty seconds. In an official hospital bulletin of October 15, the attending physicians said: "We find him in a magnificent physical condition, due to his regular physical exercise, his habitual abstinence from tobacco and liquor."

On Monday evening Edith Roosevelt was attending the theater in New York with Mrs. J. West Roosevelt and young George Roosevelt. The two ladies were seated on the aisle; between Edith and George was an empty seat, reserved for another young cousin, Oliver Roosevelt, who was working late at Progressive party headquarters. Oliver received a bulletin from Milwaukee about the shooting and went immediately to the theater, arriving in the middle of the performance. He found the ladies and slipped into the empty seat next to Edith. Pleased that the young man was joining them after all, Mrs. Roosevelt reached over to pat Oliver on the knee and found him shaking violently. She grasped his hand and leaned toward him. In a steady voice he whispered that Cousin Theodore had been shot.

Edith let out a gasp and then asked: "You say he wasn't hurt, Oliver?" She sent him back for confirmation and when he reappeared she learned that, though wounded, her husband had been able to finish his speech. Mrs. Roosevelt decided to stay through the performance, but as she left the theater, reporters were already waiting to ask her for a statement. At party headquarters she learned the full story and made plans to leave for Chicago the next day on the Twentieth Century Limited. From Theodore came a reassuring telegram: "Am in excellent shape. . . . The wound is a trivial one. . . . and isn't a particle more serious than one of the injuries any of the boys used continually to be having."

When she arrived at Chicago's Mercy Hospital, Edith set up a command post two doors away from her husband's sickroom. All visitors and messages were directed to her. Reporter Charles Willis Thompson sent *The New York Times* a dispatch about the new boss of the Progressive party—Boss Edith Roosevelt. "That sedate and determined woman, from the moment of her arrival in Chicago, took charge of affairs and reduced the Colonel to pitiable subjection," Thompson wrote. Before her advent, Roosevelt had been "throwing bombshells" at his doctors, directing his own medical campaign. The moment Edith appeared, "a hush fell upon T.R. . . . he became meek as Moses." Whether or not the Colonel really believed in women's rights, as the Progressive platform recorded, there was no doubt that in one household women's rights was the rule, concluded the newsman. "This thing about ours being a campaign against boss rule is a fake," T.R. told Thompson. "I never was so boss-ruled in my life as I am at this moment." But the Colonel smiled fondly at his wife as he made the remark, Thompson reported; it was evident that "the Great Unbossed likes being bossed for once."

Albert Beveridge had been among the early arrivals at Mercy Hospital, and he left with a fighting statement from the Colonel. "If one soldier who happens to carry the flag is stricken, another will take it from his hand and carry it on. . . . it is not important whether one leader lives or dies, it is important only that the cause shall live and win."

Taft and Wilson sent messages of sympathy, and the Democratic candidate offered to cut short his own campaigning until the stricken Bull Moose was well enough to return to the hustings. Yet Wilson first had to make a scheduled tour through Delaware, West Virginia, and Pennsylvania; he promised, however, to speak only on state issues. "I came out to fulfill the engagements of this week with a very great reluctance," he declared at one stop on October 16, "because my thought is constantly of that gallant gentleman lying in the hospital at Chicago." From Chicago Roosevelt issued a statement saying he agreed with Bryan, who had insisted that the discussion of the issues continue. Men such as Johnson, Beveridge, Oscar Straus—running for governor in New York, and Gifford Pinchot would carry on for him. "This is not a contest about any man; it is a contest concerning principles." If his broken rib healed fast enough, he would make one or two more speeches before Election Day.

From Nahant, Massachusetts, Henry Cabot Lodge broke his long silence to wire of his "distress and anxiety" over the news of the shooting. "Our dearest love is with you always," he wrote for himself and Nannie. "I am practically all right again," T.R. replied the following week; "and felt a little like the old maid who, when she at last discovered a man under the bed, seized him and said, 'You're the burglar I have been looking for these last twenty years.'" On October 19, T.R. was sitting up in bed, dictating a letter to his elder sister, Anna Cowles. He was in "great shape" and with Edith and three of the children at hand was having "a positive spree." But Edith had to sign the letter for him and added a postscript: "He is very weak & easily tired."

To reporters, at last admitted to the hospital room, the Colonel described his condition in clinical detail, noting that there were only three possible dangers—pleurisy, pneumonia, and blood poisoning. Through the journalists he expressed gratitude for Wilson's offer to suspend the campaign but reiterated his agreement with Bryan: "I don't ask for quarter." Then he laughed over what he said must be the dilemma of Governor Marshall of Indiana, running for Vice President on the Democratic ticket. Marshall had built his entire campaign on the proposition that Roosevelt had never been at San Juan Hill, T.R. claimed. Now he would have to prove that it was someone else who had been shot in front of the Hotel Gilpatrick on October 14 and that the Bull Moose leader that evening was in Oshkosh, not Milwaukee.

5

On Monday, October 21, just a week after he had been shot, Colonel Roosevelt left Mercy Hospital and the following day was back at Oyster Bay. Although he remained quietly at home, he continued to see reporters and people from his campaign staff, and on October 27 members of the family helped him celebrate his fifty-fourth birthday. Three days later he made a dramatic appearance at New York's Madison Square Garden.

Alice Longworth had been attending occasional political meetings with her husband in Cincinnati but since some speaker or other invariably launched into a furious attack on her father, she had found them "not altogether enjoyable." At last she had permission to break away and attend the New York rally. The streets were jammed for blocks in all directions, and Corinne Robinson was caught in the throng. "Had I lived my whole life only for those fifteen minutes during which I marched toward the garden already full to overflowing with my brother's adoring followers," she later wrote, "I should have been content to do so." For some reason Mrs. Robinson's pass was not acknowledged, and she and her party had to climb a fire escape to gain admittance. Mrs. Longworth described the Garden as packed with a "resounding, enthusiastic" crowd that gave her father forty-five minutes of "ear-splitting racket" when he came to the platform. The ovation, reporter Richard Harding Davis wrote, was one of "congratulation and thanksgiving. . . . a greeting from old friends to one who had nearly escaped them."

Earlier in the campaign Cecil Lyon had marveled at T.R.'s approach to the voters and at the wild, intense reception invariably given him. "Damned if I know how he does it," Lyon remarked. "He doesn't have to make a speech; in fact, half the time he doesn't make one. He says, 'Friends, I'm glad to see you,' and they go off and vote for him." Roosevelt certainly did not need to convert anyone in that partisan audience at Madison Square Garden a week before Election Day and his relatively short speech was one of platitudinous uplift. "The doctrines we preach reach back to the Golden Rule and the Sermon on the Mount," he observed. "They reach back to the commandments delivered at Sinai. All that we are doing is to apply those doctrines in the shape necessary to make them available for meeting the living issues of our own day."

The day after the rally, Alice Longworth went out to Oyster Bay, where Edith and Theodore Roosevelt met her at the foot of Sagamore Hill so that the three of them could walk slowly up to the house. Lunch that day was a rather subdued occasion; the family, Alice reported, was under no illusions about the outcome of the election. "We had the conviction and the vision," she wrote, "but alas, not the votes."

T.R. spoke three more times before the balloting: on November 1 at another Madison Square Garden rally—this time for Oscar Straus and the New York State ticket—and on November 4 at Oyster Bay and Mineola, Long Island. To the second crowd at the Garden, the Colonel said that he wanted not record cheering but a record vote the following Tuesday.

Before Election Day the forlorn Taft candidacy received one more buffeting by fate. On October 30, fifty-seven-year-old James Schoolcraft Sherman, running for re-election as Vice President on the G.O.P. ticket, suddenly died. Nicholas Murray Butler subsequently allowed Republican electoral votes to be cast for him to fill the slot, but that was only for the record.

There was little surprise in the final outcome of the voting on Tuesday, November 5. Wilson, of course, was elected President, with a vote of 6,293,019; Roosevelt was second, with 4,119,507; and Taft, third, with 3,484,956. Eugene V. Debs polled some 900,000 votes on the Socialist line, and a Prohibition candidate attracted more than 200,000 ballots. Although Wilson's popular vote fell far short of a majority, he achieved an electoral total that was the highest in the country's history to that date: 435, with 88 for Roosevelt, and a humiliating 8—Utah and Vermont—for Taft. The President, *The New York Times* later observed, "has been the victim of too much Roosevelt." The Colonel had carried Michigan, Minnesota, Pennsylvania, South Dakota, Washington, and had won eleven of California's thirteen electoral votes. Among the many Republican casualties was Nicholas Longworth, who lost his seat in the House of Representatives by ninety-seven votes.

"The meaning of Mr. Wilson's election is plain," a sour and frustrated La Follette stated in his magazine the following week. "The people have been mere pawns in the political game. They had Roosevelt as President. They had Taft as President. . . . They demanded a change. And they forged their demand into a call for Wilson."

"We have fought the good fight, we have kept the faith, and we have nothing to regret," T.R. wrote to James Garfield three days after the election. "Probably we have put the ideal a little higher than we can expect the people as a whole to take offhand." Historians have generally agreed. It was Roosevelt—pointing to the record of his Presidency and proposing the New Nationalism as a logical yet innovative extension of those achievements—who set the tone for the great debate that year. The excitement, the fervor, the idealism of 1912 can be attributed principally to T.R. In this there was triumph as real as victory.

✧§ Chapter 14 §✧

Into the River
of Doubt

A friend calling on Roosevelt at Sagamore Hill after the defeat of November, 1912, urged him to think ahead, to victory in 1916. "I thought you were a better politician," T.R. shot back. "The fight is over. We are beaten. There is only one thing to do and that is to go back to the Republican party. You can't hold a party like the Progressive party together. There are no loaves and fishes." In the hundreds of contests across the country there had been but a handful of Bull Moose victories. The Democratic-controlled Sixty-third Congress would have only seventeen Progressive representatives and no Progressive senators—though there continued to be lower-case progressives in both the old parties. Nearly everywhere the national ticket had run ahead of the state and local slates. ". . . there is no use disguising the fact that the defeat at the polls is overwhelming," the Colonel wrote to Arthur Lee in England. "I had expected defeat, but I had expected that we would make a better showing." The triumph over Taft, T.R. knew, was merely a tribute to his own enduring popularity with a large segment of the electorate; it did not really signify a permanent shift of voter allegiance from the G.O.P. to the new party.

To Gifford Pinchot—"Mr. Secretary of State that-was-to-have-been"—T.R. wrote the following week that he "was not in the least cast down at my defeat, but I have to struggle hard not to be cast down at the thought of having to go on with the lead now." There was abundant evidence already that, if the new party were to retain even the shadow of an existence, Roosevelt would have to continue his leadership of the unruly coalition.

With the fights first against the Republican Old Guard and then against the Democrats behind them, the Bull Moose chieftains could now devote their considerable energies, talents, and passions to intense and spirited squabbling among themselves. Speaking for the radical wing of the new party, the Pinchots were convinced that George Perkins tainted the purity of the progressive cause and they now insisted that he be ousted as Chairman of the Executive Committee. If the Progressives banished Perkins and men like him from the party leadership, the Colonel wrote "Dear Amos" on December 5, they might gain one or two hundred thousand votes, but they would lose two or three million by appearing to be "engaged in an assault on property, or in wild and foolish radicalism." If the party attempted to act in any more radical fashion than it had already acted, "we should all make ourselves a laughingstock. . . ."

The Pinchots, T.R. wrote a few days later to another friend, were extremists who were trying to break up the Bull Moose party by attacking the moderates within its ranks. After a defeat, he wearily acknowledged, "we must always expect quarreling among the generals." Trying to keep the two sides together, he confided to Kermit, was tiring and irritating; "this whole business of leading a new party should be for an ambitious young colonel, and not for a retired major general." In order to keep himself "fairly good-tempered," he told his youngest son, Quentin, he had to remember that "even although the wild asses of the desert are mainly in our ranks, our opponents have a fairly exclusive monopoly of the swine!" On December 10 Roosevelt spoke at the opening of a major Bull Moose conference in Chicago, a meeting at which the rift in the new party was papered over. But the chasm would never truly be bridged.

The weary, exasperated, and pessimistic Roosevelt showed himself only in private; in public, of course, he had to act and speak as if the struggle had only begun and as if the ultimate triumph was assured. In an open letter to Midwestern Progressive committeemen and state chairmen on January 22, 1913, he proclaimed that the Bull Moose party had come to stay. Any attempt to bring the new party into union with the Republicans was "not merely mischievous but impossible; for in guiding purpose and spirit the Progressive Party and the present Republican Party are as far as the poles asunder."

Curiously William Howard Taft was much less unhappy and troubled in defeat. "The nearer I get to the inauguration of my successor," he wrote in mid-December, "the greater the relief I feel." Before the election he had accepted an invitation to address the New York Lotus Club on November 16, though he was convinced that by that date he would be "shorn of interest as a guest and be changed from an active and virile participant in the day's doings of the nation to merely a dissolving view." Despite their name, the club members, he concluded, were "not merely cold, selfish seekers after pleasures" but rather organized "to furnish consolation to those who mourn, oblivion to those who would forget, a swan song for those about to disappear." In a graceful and well-received address on the Presidency, Taft could not help hitting out at those—it was unnecessary to mention Roosevelt by name— who ignored the limitations of the office. And for ex-presidents, he had a novel suggestion: they be given a dose of chloroform and their bodies set upon a funeral pyre, to "secure the country from the troublesome fear that the occupant could ever come back."

As for himself, Taft first considered returning to Cincinnati to practice law but instead accepted a professorship at the Yale School of Law. His ambition—or rather Nellie Taft's—to occupy the Chief Executive's chair fulfilled, he could now dream of his other goal, a seat on the Supreme Court bench.

Roosevelt remained embittered and caustic toward the onetime trusted lieutenant who had proved to be such a disappointing successor. In mid-December Whitelaw Reid, appointed as ambassador to the Court of St. James's by Roosevelt and retained in office by Taft, died in London. A British cruiser carried his body back to the United States and both President and ex-President attended the funeral services in New York's Cathedral of St. John the Divine. At the conclusion of the service, but before the coffin was carried out, Taft rose and with his entire party made a rather noisy exit. Seated with her father-in-law a few seats back, Mrs. Theodore Roosevelt, Jr., asked if it was customary for a President to leave the church ahead of the coffin. "No, dear, no," T.R. whispered. "It is not customary, but in this case Mr. Taft probably thought there should be precedence even between corpses!"

The "retired major general" now did what public figures who know deep within that the peak has been reached and passed—no matter how brave and optimistic their wishes for the future continue— always seem do; he began to write his *Autobiography*. "I am having my hands full writing certain chapters of my past experiences," he wrote to Edith's sister, Emily Carow, on January 4, 1913. He had neglected

The Outlook "rather scandalously" for a year, he said, and wanted to do something for the magazine. But it was not proving easy, he confessed, "to strike just the happy mean between being too reticent and not reticent enough! I find it difficult both as regards my life when I was a child and my political experiences. I can only hope that I am handling it in a proper way." What Roosevelt called "Chapters of a Possible Autobiography" began appearing in *The Outlook* in February. The chapters were later distributed in forty-six weekly installments by a newspaper syndicate and Macmillan published the book at the end of the year.

"Naturally, there are chapters of my autobiography which cannot now be written," T.R. announced in his foreword to the volume. The incompleteness and lack of candor in his memoirs had earlier been acknowledged to Senator Lodge, who had written to comment on the first chapter when it appeared in *The Outlook.* "The hardest task I have is to keep my temper, and not speak of certain people . . . as they richly deserve." Thus, the Colonel remained uncharacteristically dispassionate and circumspect in writing his life, and the work—though it contains some charming chapters on his early years—is curiously unsatisfying. The presidential years are treated topically rather than chronologically and this section remains a useful index of what Roosevelt himself considered important in his Presidency: publicizing conservation, making the G.O.P. more progressive, settling the 1902 coal strike, negotiating peace in the Russo-Japanese War, stemming the panic of 1907, initiating work on the Panama Canal, sending the Great White Fleet around the world.

And there, almost abruptly, T.R. ended his story, standing on the deck of the fleet's flagship in Hampton Roads on February 22, 1909, and delivering his message of welcome home. Not a word was written about the campaign of 1908 and the election of Roosevelt's designated heir apparent; indeed, among the many men cited for their contributions to his administration, the name of William Howard Taft is not to be found —though T.R. jabbed at his successor for having removed Henry White and Gifford Pinchot. Africa, the triumphal procession through Europe, the ecstatic welcome back to America, the political revolution of 1910–1912 are unmentioned. Ulysses S. Grant ended his celebrated memoirs at Appomattox; about his scandal-ridden two terms as President he remained silent. Roosevelt, it seems, likewise wanted to end on a note of triumph and accomplishment and studiously ignored what he must have then realized was the beginning of a downward curve.

That Roosevelt's *Autobiography* is so truncated and elusive is especially surprising in view of a speech delivered on December 27, 1912, just at the time he was beginning to write it. Two years previously he had been elected a vice president of the American Historical Association, with the suggestion that he later be elevated to the presidency of that distinguished learned society. "I do not want to be churlish, and I do not want to seem to show lack of sensibility of the great honor conferred on me," he wrote to an officer of the association, "but it does seem to me that it would be wiser to take someone else in my place." Nonetheless, he accepted the initial appointment and the month after his defeat for the Presidency of the United States by Woodrow Wilson, Roosevelt went to Boston to be installed as president of the A.H.A. at its annual meeting; it is a distinction, incidentally, that he holds in common with only one other former Chief Executive—Woodrow Wilson, who was chosen president of the association in the year of his death, 1924.

Since Roosevelt's accomplishments as a historian are largely forgotten today, it may seem incongruous that the A.H.A. would have selected the ex-President to head the organization in 1913. But T.R. had published his first historical work in 1882, at the age of twenty-three. It was a scholarly yet lively work, *The Naval War of 1812,* an outgrowth of his undergraduate studies at Harvard and long considered as the definitive account, from the American viewpoint, of that conflict. In the succeeding decade he published biographies of Thomas Hart Benton and Gouverneur Morris that lamentably were mere potboilers, but in 1896 he brought out the fourth and final volume of *The Winning of the West,* a massive work on which he clearly wished to base his reputation as a historian.

Yet none of these works—nor his formal *Autobiography* of 1913—can be compared with the real chapters of his autobiography, the books he wrote on specific phases of his extraordinarily varied career, as he experienced them. Roosevelt's reputation as a writer and a historian would be placed high if it were allowed to rest with these memorable volumes. Indeed, there are few works of American history or literature that can match the youthful exuberance and sense of locale of *Hunting Trips of a Ranchman* (1886) and *Ranch Life and the Hunting Trail* (1888); the smell of saddle leather, sweat, and gunpowder that pervades *The Rough Riders* (1899); the rhapsody and excitement of *African Game Trails* (1909); the high drama and suspense of *Through the Brazilian Wilderness* (1914). Added to these works are the scores of

285

speeches, essays, and reviews that fill another several volumes—to make Theodore Roosevelt the most ambitious and prolific of presidential writers in the nation's history. Before he entered elective politics in 1898, T.R. considered himself principally a historical writer—even if of the gentleman amateur class—and he always felt that he could fall back on writing to support his family should the vagaries of public life leave him unemployed.

Roosevelt, however, was not the man to devote a year to anything so solitary and reflective as writing an autobiography; his calendar for the year 1913 seems uncrowded only when compared with the exceptional year that preceded it. Through mid-May he remained in Oyster Bay with brief trips only to Philadelphia and Detroit to speak before local Progressive party groups. But on one of his near weekly forays into Manhattan he attended the historic and controversial "International Exhibit of Modern Art" in the 69th Regiment Armory at Lexington Avenue and 25th Street.

This first exposure in America of the Post-Impressionists, especially the Cubists, proved even too much for professional art critics, who loudly assailed the revolutionary works. "Why should time be wasted in advertising these 'carpenters' who in a few weeks, when the public has had its laugh, will have to seek places in their real trade?" wrote one observer in *American Art News*. And the magazine offered a ten-dollar prize for the best solution to the exhibit's most famous painting, Marcel Duchamp's "Nude Descending a Staircase," a work that drew "shrieks of laughter from the crowds who gathered about it eight deep, in the eagerness to discover the lady or the stairway." The Colonel was no less wary— and nearly as lacking in prescience—in an article on the exhibit he contributed to *The Outlook*. There was only one note entirely absent from the Armory Show, Roosevelt observed, and that was the commonplace; for this he had hearty praise. As for the works of Whistler, Monet, Augustus John, Cezanne, Redon, "a worthy critic should speak of these." But he charged that most of the artists on display were motivated by "the astute appreciation of the power to make folly lucrative which the late P. T. Barnum showed with his faked mermaid." The Cubists, he continued, "are entitled to the serious attention of all who find enjoyment in the colored puzzle-pictures of the Sunday newspapers." As for the notorious Duchamp painting, he had a Navajo rug in his bathroom that was "a far more satisfactory and decorative picture." The Futurists as they liked to call themselves, he sincerely hoped, would soon come to be known as the "Past-ists."

The day Roosevelt was viewing this provocative art in New York, March 4, Woodrow Wilson was sworn in as Taft's successor. Taft returned from the Capitol to the White House with the new President and, according to one account, stayed on and on at a luncheon to which the Wilsons had only reluctantly invited him—ultimately having to be nearly dragged from the Executive Mansion in time to catch a train out of Washington. The Longworths, who would also soon be leaving, were in the capital so that Nicholas could attend the lame-duck session of the Sixty-second Congress. Alice, who had first come to Washington with her father in 1889 had "only the haziest recollection of the second Cleveland Administration; it was almost impossible to believe that those odd beings called Democrats were actually there in the offing about to take things over." She and Nick would be returning to Cincinnati, to sit out what she later called her husband's two-year sabbatical from Congress; he was returned to office in the congressional elections of 1914.

At the beginning of the next month, on April 4, the family assembled at Oyster Bay for the wedding of twenty-one-year-old Ethel to Dr. Richard Derby. Derby had been among the Harvard students who had attended Vice President Roosevelt's seminar on politics at Sagamore Hill during the summer of 1901; he had later traveled in Alice's Washington circle—his first memory of his future wife would be of a little girl walking on stilts with Archie and Quentin at the White House. The wedding of her younger sister, Alice Longworth reported, was "the prettiest, gayest wedding on a lovely April day." With her flair for the dramatic, she had proposed wearing a gown of "dark blue satin and dingy yellow"; Edith Roosevelt promptly sent her into town for something "light and becoming," something more appropriate for a spring wedding.

"Darling Ethely-bye," T.R. answered his daughter's letter from her wedding trip. "Evidently Dick is even more than all we were sure he was! I really believe you are going to be just as happy as darling mother and I have been." He "capitulated" to her request for one of the picture-letters that had so entranced all his children in their younger days, though he feared Derby would wonder "whether or not he has married an out-patient of bedlam's daughter." But more sober business was to occupy Colonel Roosevelt the following month.

At the outset of his campaign for the Republican nomination in 1912 Roosevelt had been met with renewed charges—intermittently leveled at him throughout his long career in politics—that he was a heavy drinker. His opponents, he had confided to Lodge toward the end of his Presidency, were circulating stories that he had become partially insane through excessive drinking. To one man bold enough to enquire about his drinking habits in 1909, he had written to say that the rumor was a "malignant invention—just as sheer an invention as if they had said that at the age of five I had poisoned my grandmother or had been mixt up in the assassination of Lincoln by Wilkes Booth." But since there was no public charge there could be no public denial. The historian William Roscoe Thayer, who knew Roosevelt well, felt that the "vehemence" of T.R.'s public speaking was to blame for the stories. His staccato, high-pitched delivery "caused in part by a physical difficulty of utterance—the sequel of his early asthmatic trouble—and in part by his extraordinary vigor, created among some of his hearers who did not know him the impression that he must be a hard drinker, or that he drank to stimulate his eloquence." The stories started, T.R. once explained to a reporter, with a joke. In declining a cigar because he did not smoke, Roosevelt would be asked what his bad habits were. "Prize fighting and strong drink," he often replied as a jest. Henry Adams, as usual, had an appropriate wry comment: "Theodore is never sober, only he is drunk with himself and not with rum."

Yet as he once more sought the Presidency, Roosevelt grew sensitive to the rumors. ". . . I only wish we could persuade someone to make such a statement in the open where I could get at them for the heaviest kind of libel damages," he had written to a California supporter in February, 1912. A case might be made that he drank too much coffee and milk and tea, he said, but he had never touched a highball or cocktail in his life, averaged two wine glasses of whisky or brandy a year, "and then only in the form of a mint julep, or about once every four or five years with milk punch." He recounted the story of the six ounces of brandy consumed during his eleven months in Africa, admitted to an occasional glass of madeira or white wine since returning and at big dinners perhaps a glass of champagne.

Toward the end of the primary he had asked Senator Bristow of Kansas whether he should not sue the Salina *Union* for libel in charging that he was drunk on a campaign swing through that state. It turned out, however, that the Salina paper was owned by an old political foe of

Roosevelt's and a suit against the paper might seem like a vendetta. A publication of the Prohibition party next made the charge of drunkenness against Roosevelt but it hardly seemed worth the effort to go after so small a target. It was curious, a reporter in the Colonel's entourage observed, that such a widespread slander did not get into print more often.

On October 12, in the homestretch of his campaign for the Presidency, Roosevelt came to Chicago. The following evening O. K. Davis came in jubilantly waving a letter. "Congratulations, Colonel," he said. "I think we've got them now!" Someone had forwarded to Davis a statement published in *Iron Ore,* a trade paper edited by George A. Newett —a man ironically once appointed postmaster by Roosevelt—and published at Ishpeming, Michigan. "Roosevelt lies and curses in a most disgusting way," Newett had written; "he gets drunk, too, and that not infrequently, and all of his intimates know about it." The next day, of course, the Colonel encountered the would-be assassin at Milwaukee; barely able to finish the campaign, Roosevelt could not consider what to do about the slander in the Michigan paper until after the election. But then he filed suit against Newett and began soliciting depositions from his friends attesting to his sobriety. "I think the intoxication was altogether with his own verbosity," Taft wrote his brother. ". . . I would make an excellent witness in his defense."

The libel trial was held at the end of May, 1913, at Marquette, Michigan. It was probably the most noteworthy event in the history of the little county seat on the shore of Lake Superior in Michigan's remote upper peninsula. Roosevelt's friends and supporters invaded the town and the testimony in his behalf was overwhelming. Newett's lawyers could produce no testimony, other than unallowable hearsay, to support the editor's accusation; and he had no choice but to retract and apologize for the slander. Roosevelt then asked to address the court. "I did not go into this suit for money," he stated; "I did not go into it for any vindictive purpose. I went into it . . . because I wish once and for all during my lifetime thoroughly and comprehensively to deal with these slanders so that never again will it be possible for any man in good faith to repeat them. I have achieved my purpose, and I am content." At the end of his statement he lifted a clenched fist above his head, the judge called a recess, and a crowd of well-wishers surged about the Colonel.

After the recess, the judge directed the jury to return a verdict for the plaintiff and, in view of the Colonel's wishes, award only nominal damages—under Michigan law, six cents. "It would seem incredible that I should have to undertake such a trial," T.R. wrote to Arthur Lee, "and it was intensely distasteful. But it was absolutely necessary, and I have finished that business once for all." To O. K. Davis he gave some homely advice. "Never have a daughter married, get shot, and prosecute a libel suit all in one year," the Colonel said. "They're all very expensive proceedings."

On June 13, nineteen-year-old Archibald Roosevelt graduated from Phillips Academy at Andover, Massachusetts. Early the following month, the Colonel headed west with Archie and Quentin, then fifteen, for a cougar hunt and a camping trip along the Grand Canyon. In Arizona they were met by Nicholas Roosevelt, a year older than Archie, who had driven the horses and the camping outfit from southern Arizona to the north side of the canyon and then crossed back to be at Flagstaff when his cousins got off the train. On July 12 the party reached the Grand Canyon and three days later started down Bright Angel Trail. They reached the Colorado River in a raging thunderstorm and clambered into a caged cable car for the crossing. The cage jerked irregularly across the torrent and once, swaying and dangling unnervingly fifty feet above the water, stopped altogether. On the other side they found a single old man, exhausted from the effort of cranking the cable-car mechanism. He was naturally surprised to see the famous passenger he had reeled in. "I've always been a Democrat, Colonel," he said as the ex-President stepped from the cage, "but I'm an admirer of Roosevelt and I want to shake you by the hand."

Roosevelt let the boys do most of the shooting, so that each could get his cougar. Nicholas later recalled that T.R. was the perfect camping companion, always taking his share of camp chores and always managing to keep clean and neat—in sharp contrast to the three boys who, the Colonel wrote Nicholas's mother, soon became "the very dirtiest objects you have ever seen."

At the beginning of August the campers had left the Grand Canyon and were crossing the Painted Desert of the Navajo Indian Reservation. On the tenth they started on a six-day pack trip into Rainbow Natural Bridge. The spectacular arch had been discovered by white men only four years previously and Roosevelt's was the eleventh party to reach the nearly inaccessible site; Zane Grey had headed the preceding party. The Colonel was properly awed by the natural bridge: "It is a triumphal arch rather than a bridge, and spans the torrent bed in a majesty never shared by any arch ever reared by the mightiest conqueror among the nations of mankind." Through with ruminating on the scenic wonder, T.R. promptly appropriated one of the two pools beneath the arch for a bath and a swim—the three boys shared the other—and later emerged to join the party around a campfire at the foot of the arch. A full moon rose to bathe the cliffs in radiance and when it disappeared the stars in a cloudless sky formed a brilliant backdrop to the arch whenever, during the course of a restless night, T.R. awakened to gaze upward.

On the nineteenth they reached Walpi in the Hopi Indian Reservation, where the ex-Great White Father from Washington was admitted, along with the three boys, to the snake-washing ceremony that precedes the famous Hopi Snake Dance. Nicholas confessed to some apprehension as he, Archie, and Quentin followed T.R. down a ladder into the murky recesses of an Indian kiva. The fifteen-by-twenty-five-foot room was dimly lit and had a raised dais occupying one third the floor space at one end. The visitors were asked to sit on a blanket at the edge of the dais. In back of them, along the wall about eight feet away, was a writhing mass of some hundred snakes, about half rattlers. "To look at them piled against the back of the kiva," Nicholas confessed with some surprise, "slowly creeping about and crawling towards us gave me a sense of utmost security." T.R., however, kept a wary eye on the serpents and when one would glide too near, he motioned silently but emphatically to a priest who brushed it back with a fan made of eagle feathers.

Following some chanting and ceremonial pipe-smoking, the priests "in tranquil, matter-of-fact fashion" picked up handfuls of snakes, doused them in a bowl filled with a dark liquid, and flung them violently against the wall. That the bathing and the throwing did not "upset the nerves of every snake there" astonished the Colonel. At the end of the extraordinary ceremony, he shook hands with the priests and asked if there was anything, as an ex-President, he could do for them. They asked for some cowry shells and he promised to send them two sacks full. The Hopi Snake Dance, held in the open and attended by a horde of tourists, proved almost anticlimactic and the next day T.R. boarded the train for Chicago. But ahead lay new excitement. The Arizona camping trip was but a warm-up exercise for a new great adventure the restless Colonel had already been planning.

2

One day in 1908, during the last year of his Presidency, Roosevelt had been visited at the White House by John Augustine Zahm, a former provincial of the Congregation of the Holy Cross, the Catholic order that runs Notre Dame University in South Bend, Indiana. Since 1905 Father Zahm had devoted himself to scientific studies and writing; Roosevelt especially liked his earlier work *Evolution and Dogma,* which he had often recommended to theologians of various faiths. Zahm—later described by T.R. as "a funny little Catholic priest, who is a friend of mine, a great Dante scholar, and with a thirst for wandering in the wilderness"—had a proposal to make to the retiring President. He had just come back from a trip across the Andes and down the Amazon to the Atlantic Ocean. He now wished to return to South America and traverse the continent from south to north: up the Paraguay River to the Amazon basin and then, via the Rio Negro, through Venezuela on the Orinoco to Trinidad in the West Indies. He hoped Roosevelt could accompany him.

The President was intrigued, but he had already begun to make plans for the African safari and had to tell Father Zahm that he could not make the journey. In the succeeding five years the two kept in touch; the Colonel wrote an introduction to Zahm's 1911 book *Along the Andes and Down the Amazon;* and the idea of a South American expedition was from time to time discussed between them. The project, according to Zahm, "was never abandoned. It was merely deferred." Then, in June, 1913, Roosevelt accepted invitations from the governments of Brazil, Argentina, and Chile to deliver addresses in their capitals, and it occurred to T.R. that—"instead of making the conventional tourist trip by sea round South America"—he would return via the route originally proposed by Father Zahm.

Before writing to the priest, the Colonel decided to pay a call on the officials of the American Musum of Natural History in New York to see if they could be persuaded to send naturalists along to make his excursion an official scientific expedition—much as the Smithsonian had endorsed the African trip. To T.R.'s surprise and delight, Father Zahm turned up at the museum that very day, on an identical mission, and over lunch the two readily decided to join forces. The museum shortly thereafter agreed to assign two naturalists to the project: George K. Cherrie, a Vermont farmer, the father of six, and an ornithologist who had spent twenty-two years collecting bird species in the American tropics; and a young mammalogist named Leo E. Miller, who was then in Guiana.

When Roosevelt left for Arizona at the beginning of July, the job of making concrete arrangements for the expedition—now scheduled to leave New York the first week in October—devolved upon Father Zahm. Visiting the sporting goods department of the Rogers Peet Company in New York, the priest met a former Arctic explorer named Anthony Fiala. "I would give anything in the world to go with you," Fiala told Zahm at the end of their first discussion about equipage for the undertaking. "Come along," Zahm impulsively replied. "I am sure Colonel Roosevelt will be glad to have you as a member of the expedition." Fiala seized the opportunity and agreed to serve as commissary. Two later additions to the company were T.R.'s private secretary Frank Harper, and a young Swiss named Jacob Sigg, who enlisted as general handyman. The eighth member of the party would be the Colonel's "side-partner" in his "great adventure" in Africa, Kermit Roosevelt, soon to be twenty-four.

Upon his graduation from Harvard in 1912, Kermit had accepted a job with the Brazil Railway Company; Alice Longworth remembered a few days at Sagamore Hill, during that most hectic of summers, when all political activities had to be curtailed so that the entire family could get Kermit ready to leave on what was expected to be a two-years' absence in South America. In Brazil Kermit soon switched from railroads to bridge construction and by the summer of 1913 was planning to return to the United States the next year to marry Belle Willard, daughter of Joseph E. Willard of the Washington hotel family, Woodrow Wilson's new ambassador to Spain. T.R. expressed some reservations about his second son's decision to join the expedition on the eve of his marriage, but Kermit was determined to go; he did not wish to be married in his father's absence and told him that "this semi-exploration business was exactly in his line." Edith Roosevelt, along with a young cousin, Miss L. Margaret Roosevelt, would accompany her husband on the speaking tour and return to the United States on a ship from Chile. *Scribner's* magazine would again publish the Colonel's articles about his wanderings.

On Friday evening, October 3, the eve of the Roosevelt party's departure, a farewell dinner for 2,350 Progressive supporters of the Colonel was held on the glass-covered roof of the New York Theatre, Manhattan's "Garden of the Dance." The place was so jammed, reported *The New York Times,* that there were "few indeed who had a chance to partake of each of the five courses in which the meal was served." The speeches would still have been going on the next morning, the newspaper claimed, if toastmaster Gifford Pinchot had not simply banished the waiters halfway through the serving in order to get the program underway. Roosevelt listened attentively to each speaker, enthusiastically applauded each new enunciation of the Progressive doctrine, rose to speak himself on two separate occasions, and assured the crowd that there was no reason for talk that the days of the new party were numbered.

The sailing the next day, from Brooklyn on the liner *Vandyck,* was "much quieter" than the frenzied departure for Africa in 1909, according to the *Times.* T.R. wore a gray suit with a vest, a soft hat of the same color, a tie with a stickpin, and a boutonniere in his lapel. But the decks of the ship, the pier, and even a few surrounding streets were thronged with well-wishers; the Progressive party sent a band; and the ambassadors of the three South American republics T.R. would visit came to see him off. The Roosevelt family contingent included Corinne Robinson, Ethel Derby, and Mr. and Mrs. Theodore Roosevelt, Jr.

En route south T.R. easily proved to be the most popular passenger on board the *Vandyck.* His uninhibited version of the sailor's hornpipe at an evening entertainment brought cries of "Encore," while George Cherrie noted that the Colonel's "two hundred and twenty pounds of avoirdupois were the deciding factor in the 'tug-of-war' between the married men and the bachelors on the ship." A passenger who had originally said he would travel ten thousand miles to vote against Roosevelt was introduced to the ex-President, was charmed by him, and said that the next time he would travel twenty thousand miles to vote *for* him.

The first port of call on the cruise south was Bridgetown, Barbados, where Leo Miller joined the party; and on October 17 the liner put in at Bahia, Brazil, where Kermit came aboard. Four days later the *Vandyck* steamed into Rio de Janeiro. A small fleet of gaily decked craft, flying Brazilian and American flags, welcomed the former President to the breathtakingly beautiful harbor; T.R.'s reception ashore, wrote Father Zahm, had "all the wild enthusiasm of a national holiday." And for the next six weeks Roosevelt made what was in effect a reprise of his triumphal procession through Europe in 1910: from Rio to Sao Paulo, where he celebrated his fifty-fifth birthday on October 27; to Montevideo, Uruguay; to Buenos Aires, Rosario, Tucuman, and Mendoza, Argentina; across the Andes to Santiago and Valparaiso, Chile, from which Edith Roosevelt sailed for the United States; and back to the Argentine capital by early December. Along the way, T.R. had preached the progressive doctrine and endorsed honesty before large, enthusiastic, but perhaps bemused audiences; and he even lectured the Latins on the Monroe Doctrine. ". . . I think I have been able under pressure to state the Monroe Doctrine in a way . . . so as to make it correspond exactly to the facts and to our national needs," he wrote Henry Cabot Lodge on December 12. By that date, the Colonel was steaming up the Paraguay River and the expedition into the Brazilian wilderness was about to get underway.

At Rio, Roosevelt had been met by Lauro Müller, the Brazilian minister of foreign affairs, who had suggested a change in plans for his trip through the interior of the continent, from south to north. At the headwaters of the Paraguay River, at the town of Caceres, Roosevelt would be met by Colonel Candido Mariano da Silva Rondon, an army officer of chiefly Indian blood, who for the past quarter century had been exploring the Brazilian hinterland. Four years earlier, while surveying a route for a government telegraph line through the Mato Grosso, Colonel Rondon had come upon a large, previously unknown river flowing north. To this mysterious stream Rondon gave the name Rio da Dúvida, the River of Doubt. Its course seemed to lie roughly along the parallel of longitude 60 west of Greenwich, with a source between the 12th and 13th parallels south of the equator and perhaps an outlet into the Madeira, a major affluent of the Amazon. It was the largest uncharted river between the Gy-Paraná, another tributary to the Madeira, and the Juruena, which flowed into the Tapajos, yet another affluent of the Amazon. It was now Colonel Rondon's plan to follow the River of Doubt wherever it led, and Roosevelt was invited by the government to join him in this journey into the unknown.

T.R. knew that this was an unrivaled opportunity, a chance for another great adventure, his "last chance to be a boy"—and, of course, he accepted. The undertaking was christened the Expedição Scientifica Roosevelt-Rondon; and while the Colonel completed his speaking tour, Cherrie and Miller went up the Paraguay to begin collecting species of birds and mammals and Fiala and Sigg organized the supplies.

By December 7 Roosevelt was at Asuncion, the sleepy capital of the landlocked republic of Paraguay, and two days later he was journeying upstream on the Paraguay aboard the gunboat-yacht of the president. On the twelfth he reached the Brazilian boundary, where he was met by a shallow draft river steamer carrying Colonel Rondon and his party. The colonel and his companions, "spick and span in their white uniforms," came aboard Roosevelt's boat to introduce themselves. The Brazilian contingent would include four other officers, a doctor, and a geologist. "It was evident," T.R. wrote of this initial meeting with Rondon, "that he knew his business thoroughly, and it was equally evident that he would be a pleasant companion." T.R. spoke no Portuguese and the officers apparently understood little English; but Kermit, after his year and a half in Brazil, could easily bridge the language gap.

During the next three weeks Roosevelt made a number of side trips to visit ranches and hunt jaguar, tapir, and the giant peccary—thus fulfilling his ambition to hunt the major big game of South America and also help complete the American Museum's collection of southern fauna. The indefatigable Colonel spent New Year's Day, January 1, 1914, on an all-day hunt on foot. Hacking their way through the thick jungle with machetes, wading through marshes up to their hips, swimming across two bayous, the members of the party were "drenched with sweat. . . . torn by the spines of the innumerable clusters of small pines with thorns like needles. . . . bitten by the hosts of fire-ants, and by the mosquitoes. . . ." T.R.'s watch, a veteran of Cuba, came to an "indignant halt," but he went on, although there was no breeze, the sun stood overhead in an "undimmed sky," and the "heat beat on us in waves." Ever the observant nauralist, Roosevelt interrupted his account of the hunt for *Scribner's* to write a brief discourse on fire-ants and the effects of being bitten by one. During these weeks of traveling and hunting, Father Zahm described T.R. as being "happy as a schoolboy on a picnic."

En route up the Paraguay, Roosevelt kept finding "so much of interest all along the banks that we were continually longing to stop and spend days where we were." He was fascinated by the infinitely varied flora and fauna of Brazil and wrote knowingly and appreciatively of all he saw—especially the gorgeous birds. But he seemed almost obsessed with the terrifying piranha fish and eagerly collected accounts of their grisly proclivities. Almost every night, as he had done in Africa, he would work at his magazine articles, later published in book form as *Through the Brazilian Wilderness.* When other members of the party would flop wearily into their hammocks, he would sit at his folding table, his head draped in mosquito netting, his hands and arms protected from the insects by thick gloves and gauntlets, slowly writing out the articles in longhand. Until they reached the headwaters of the River of Doubt, the finished pieces could still be sent back to New York for publication. But he continued to work on the articles after the expedition plunged into the unknown, even working when he was tormented with a fever. "This is not written very clearly," he advised his editor at *Scribner's* in the margin of one manuscript; "my temperature is 105."

T.R. had brought no Pigskin Library on this trip and for his reading he had to fall back on Kermit's *Oxford Book of French Verse,* Everyman editions of Gibbon, Marcus Aurelius, and Epictetus, and some translations of Greek plays. Kermit also had brought some Portuguese classics, useless to his father, and a few French novels, which the Colonel disdained.

On January 15 the party reached the outpost of Tapirapuan on an upper tributary of the Paraguay, and there they left their boats. All the specimens thus far gathered, along with excess baggage no longer deemed essential, were sent back down the river, and eventually to New York. Six days later the expedition on horse and muleback left for a month-long trek across the highland wilderness of the Mato Grosso, a "healthy land of dry air, of cool nights, of clear, running brooks," T.R. called it. Father Zahm did not find the terrain quite so enticing; rarely did they see a tree more than twenty feet high and the lack of water became a serious problem for the animals. Soon, along the route they were following, they began to see carcasses and bleaching bones of pack animals from the supply train that had been sent on ahead. Ominously among the bones were abandoned boxes labeled, "Roosevelt South American Expedition." With muleteers, cooks, and other assistants, the expedition now numbered nearly forty persons; there were some two hundred pack animals. So impressive was the train that Fiala recorded its departure from Tapirapuan on motion-picture film. The third day out the expedition crossed the divide separating the basin of the Paraguay from that of the Amazon, and for this part of the journey they could follow the telegraph lines set up along the route surveyed a few years earlier by Colonel Rondon.

By the end of January the expedition was at Utiarity, an Indian settlement and telegraph station on the Rio Papgaio. From this point Father Zahm, who had decided against making the exploration of the

Rio da Dúvida with Roosevelt, and Sigg returned to civilization; while Fiala and one of the Brazilian officers departed for a canoe trip down the Juruena and Tapajos to the Amazon. The main body continued overland to the headwaters of the Dúvida, which was reached on February 26. Here the final separation was made. Miller, with two officers and the geologist, was to march three days to the Gy-Paraná and follow it down to the Madeira and eventually the Amazon, a route previously explored by Rondon. Unless they encountered the others, coming down the Dúvida to its supposed juncture with the Madeira, they were to proceed to Manáos for an eventual rendezvous.

3

Shortly after noon on February 27, the Gy-Paraná group gathered on the fragile wooden bridge that had been flung across the Rio da Dúvida at the telegraph line crossing to wave good-bye and call out "Good Luck" to the Roosevelt-Rondon party. In addition to the two colonels, the exploring team included Kermit, Cherrie, Lieutenant Lyra, Doctor Cajazeira, and sixteen camaradas, the expert rivermen of the tropical forest. The paddlers, T.R. wrote, were "a strapping set. . . . lithe as panthers and brawny as bears." They swam like water dogs, he reported, and "were equally at home with pole and paddle, with axe and machete." The camaradas looked like pirates out of a storybook, he further noted; indeed "one or two of them were pirates, and one worse than a pirate." They were white, black, copper-colored, "and of all intermediate shades"; of Portuguese, Negro, and Indian blood. As a group, they were "hardworking, willing, and cheerful."

The twenty-two man party would travel in seven dugout canoes —one small, one "cranky," two "old, waterlogged, and leaky," three good. Personal baggage had been cut down to the "limit necessary for health and efficiency"; yet in such a voyage it was impossible not to take a large amount of equipment and the canoes, Roosevelt later wrote, were too heavily laden.

The Colonel, Cherrie, and Kermit would share a light tent; the three Brazilian officers would have another tent; and there would be a third for anyone who felt sick. The camaradas would sleep in hammocks slung between trees. All would be armed but shooting would be limited to the collection of species, the procuring of food, and the warning off or repelling of Indian attacks. The food and arms taken "represented all reasonable precautions against suffering and starvation"; there were provisions for fifty days but "not full rations, for we hoped in part to live on the country—on fish, game, nuts, and palm tops." Yet, the Colonel conceded, anything might happen: "We were about to go into the unknown, and no one could say what it held."

The surveying was to be done by Colonel Rondon and Lieutenant Lyra, assisted by Kermit. The younger Roosevelt would go ahead in a light canoe with a sighting rod; finding a point with a good vista up- and downstream, he would land and set up the rod. Upstream, Lyra would estimate the distance while Rondon took directions with a compass and recorded the figures. While they moved on to the place Kermit had been standing, he would move downstream to establish a new point. The first half day Kermit landed nearly a hundred times and the surveyors made but nine and a third kilometers.

T.R. ran ahead in his canoe, through "a lofty and matted forest [that] rose like a green wall on either hand." The trees were "stately and beautiful. . . . looped and twisted vines hung from them like great ropes." Fragrant scents blew from flowers on the banks, and apart from an occasional bird call out of the depths of the forest all was silent. The Colonel only traveled a few hours on February 27, then pulled ashore to make camp and wait for the surveyors. It had rained at intervals during the day—this was toward the end of the rainy season—but after sunset the sky cleared. "The stars were brilliant overhead," Roosevelt wrote, "and the new moon hung in the west. It was a pleasant night, the air almost cool, and we slept soundly." The following morning T.R. stayed on in camp after the surveyors left downstream to wait for Cherrie who was gathering specimens in the nearby forests. It was almost noon before the two embarked again on the Dúvida's "swirling brown current." It seemed as if it were going to be a leisurely and relaxing journey for Roosevelt.

The second day on the river, the party registered an advance of sixteen and a half kilometers, and the third day—in rain that went from showers to "vertical sheets of water"—they traveled and recorded twenty and a half kilometers. For the first time they detected signs of Indian habitation: abandoned palm-leaf shelters, overgrown planting fields, the vine hand-rail of a washed-away pole bridge. Cherrie shot a large monkey, which proved "very good eating." Sunday, March 2, their fourth day, was again almost without rain, and T.R. found it "delightful to drift and paddle slowly down the beautiful tropical river." The current was slow, and "the broad, deep, placid stream bent and curved in every direction, although the general course was northwest." The country through which they were traveling was flat, noted the Colonel, "and more of the land was under than above water. Continually we found ourselves travelling between stretches of marshy forest where for miles the water stood or ran among the trees." In midafternoon the current quickened, became faster and faster "until it began to run like a mill-race, and we heard the roar of rapids ahead." The dugouts were pulled ashore so that a survey could be made.

Stretching for nearly a mile, with many curls and several drops of at least six feet, the rapids proved to be a serious obstacle. At one point the river narrowed to less than two yards between ledges of naked rock. "It seemed extraordinary, almost impossible," the Colonel marveled, "that so broad a river could in so short a space of time contract its dimensions to the width of the strangled channel through which it now poured its entire volume." It took the expedition two and a half days to make a portage of these first rapids. They camped above the rapids on March 2, the next day moved their baggage to the foot of the rapids, and on March 4 and the morning of the fifth dragged the dugouts across a road chopped through the forests. The heavy, cumbersome boats were moved with the aid of several hundred small logs cut to serve as rollers and placed about two yards apart. Two men harnessed to a drag-rope pulled, while a third pried with a lever behind; and thus each canoe, "bumping and sliding, was twitched through the woods."

Not only did the portage cost the party two and a half days of "severe and incessant labor," it also resulted in some damage to the dugouts. In launching the canoes again below the rapids, one of the boats filled with water and went to the bottom, and more hard work was needed to raise it. For the first time, perhaps, the enormity of their undertaking struck the members of the expedition. Gathered around the campfire after dinner, the men discussed what might lie ahead. They realized that they did not know whether they had one hundred or eight hundred kilometers to go; whether the stream would continue smooth and calm or be broken by innumerable rapids such as the ones just encountered; whether hostile Indians lurked in the surrounding darkness. "We had no idea how much time the trip would take," Roosevelt reflected. "We had entered a land of unknown possibilities."

In the half day of March 5 the explorers made twelve kilometers and nineteen by three o'clock the following day. In the lead, T.R. once more noted the quickening of the current that indicated rapids ahead and signaled the party ashore. It took three days to make a second portage, and on a foraging journey downstream Kermit discovered a third set of rapids only five or six kilometers below the second. On the tenth they unloaded the canoes a third time, carried the burdens down, and lowered the boats through the swirling waters of the lesser rapids. Even though it was dangerous to work nearly naked in the river and they were constantly plagued by biting and stinging insects, this was preferable to manhandling the dugouts over land. T.R. found that termites had eaten holes in his sun helmet and in the cover of his cot. During the night the two older canoes filled with water in the rising river, sank, and were broken apart on boulders along the river bottom. Wryly naming the place Broken Canoe Rapids, the expedition halted for four days to make a new dugout.

Resuming their course on March 15, the party made six kilometers before rising ground and "the roar of broken water announced that once more our course was checked by dangerous rapids." Rounding a bend, they saw the new obstacle, "a wide descent of white water, with an island in the middle, at the upper edge." This time Kermit was in the lead canoe, along with two camaradas, a pet dog, and a week's supply of boxed provisions. Reconnoitering the island to see if a descent could be made on the far side, Kermit suddenly found his canoe caught in a shifting whirlpool and carried broadside into the rapids.

The paddlers were unable to head their craft into the current—the only possible way to navigate the rapids—the boat took wave after wave of water, quickly filled, and overturned in the frothy current. One of the camaradas reached shore but the other disappeared beneath the waters—his body was never recovered. The current beat Kermit's helmet down over his face and his 405 Winchester—the gun he had taken through Africa—was torn from his grasp. In swift but quieter water he swam toward shore. Although his jacket hindered his strokes, he knew that he did not have the strength to take it off. An overhanging tree appeared on the shore, and "with the curious calm one feels when death is but a moment away," his father later wrote, "he realized that the utmost his failing strength could do was to reach the branch." Desperately clutching at the limb, Kermit was then barely able to pull himself ashore with his last reserve of energy. Swimming alongside Kermit, the dog also clambered onto dry land.

T.R. was naturally distraught. The fear of some such accident be-falling his second son had been a nightmare all along; "it did not seem to me that I could bear to bring bad tidings to his betrothed and to his mother." A sign was erected: "In These Rapids Died Poor Simplicio." Looking for his lost canoe, Kermit discovered even worse rapids a couple of kilometers downstream.

"The morning of the 16th was dark and gloomy," wrote the Colo-nel. "Through sheets of blinding rain we left our camp of misfortune for another camp where misfortune also awaited us." While another portage was being made that day, Colonel Rondon strolled with a dog into the forest. Running on ahead, the animal was suddenly felled by Indian ar-rows; although the natives were not seen, their hostile presence was cause for new alarm. And during the portage the new dugout was lost when the rope by which it was being lowered through the churning wa-ters broke. With Indians undoubtedly lurking nearby, it was deemed un-wise to tarry long enough to build new canoes. All the baggage, trimmed to the barest necessity, was loaded into the four remaining dug-outs. Roosevelt, Dr. Cajazeira, and six camaradas—three with feet so swollen from insect bites that they could scarcely walk—embarked once more on the stream. Colonel Rondon, Lyra, Cherrie, Kermit, and the nine other camaradas marched in a single file along the bank. The boats had to be halted continually, to allow the slower shore party to catch up. Two more sets of rapids were traversed that day.

The expedition camped at a point where a major stream joined the Dúvida; Colonel Rondon named it the Rio Kermit, and during a cere-mony the next morning to erect a marker on the tributary he pulled from his pocket orders from the Brazilian government formally christen-ing the Dúvida the Rio Roosevelt. T.R. protested; he felt that the River of Doubt was an unusually good name for the stream that was so pla-guing them. "But my kind friends insisted otherwise, and it would have been churlish of me to object longer." Three cheers were given for the United States, for T.R., and for Kermit. Roosevelt proposed three cheers for Brazil, for Colonel Rondon, for Lyra, for the doctor, and finally for all the camaradas. Only Cherrie had not been cheered, an omission soon taken care of, "and the meeting broke up in high good humor."

Just above its juncture with the Dúvida the tributary Rio Kermit plunged over a waterfall six to eight feet in height; in the pool below were a number of fish, two of which were caught and provided delicious eating. One of the camaradas, a Parecís Indian named Antonio, said that fish never came up heavy rapids in which falls had to be jumped. The fish in the Rio Kermit indicated there would be no downstream rapids steep enough to require overland portaging of the dugouts. "But the event showed that he was mistaken," T.R. later noted sadly. "The worst rapids were ahead of us."

On March 19 the party halted for three days to make two new dug-outs. An Indian fishing village, from which the natives had obviously just fled, was discovered in the vicinity; and gifts—an axe, a knife, some strings of red beads—were left to show that the interlopers were friendly. During the pause, the members of the expedition had plenty of time to speculate about the river they were following.

There was no longer any doubt, Roosevelt concluded, that the Dúvida was a big river, one of major importance. It was now judged un-likely that it joined either the Gy-Paraná or the Tapajos; despite its twistings, the river's course was too generally north to enter either of those streams to the west and east of it. It was therefore probable, though still far from certain, that it emptied into the Madeira near that river's juncture with the Amazon; possibly it became the Aripuanan, an-other affluent of the Madeira, although the Aripuanan had never been judged such a big river. In the three weeks since embarking on the River of Doubt, the expedition had covered only about one hundred forty kilometers, traveling two kilometers for every one made northward, with a descent of some one hundred twenty-four meters. A river nor-mally describes a parabola in its course, Roosevelt recalled, with the steepest descent in the upper reaches. This led him to hope that they would not have to encounter so many and such difficult rapids in the future—a hope, he wrote, "destined to failure."

On March 22, once more with six dugouts so that all could ride, the expedition again started down the Dúvida. Twenty minutes out they struck the first rapids of the day and made only ten kilometers before pitching camp. The following day, traveling an additional thirteen kilo-meters, the party spent only one and three-quarters hours traveling but seven hours making a one-kilometer portage. This pattern was to be mo-notonously repeated for the next three weeks, the men counting them-selves fortunate when the rapids were gentle enough to allow them to lower the unloaded boats through the water and they had only to carry the baggage over land. Roosevelt remained cheerful and optimistic; ". . . while we were actually on the river, paddling and floating down-stream along the reaches of swift, smooth water, it was very lovely." The very rapids that were now making their navigation downstream so hazardous, he mused, one day "would drive electric trolleys up and down its whole length and far out on either side, and run mills and factories, and lighten the labor on farms." Such a rich and fertile land should not be permitted "to lie as a tenantless wilderness, while there are such teeming swarms of human beings in the overcrowded, overpeopled countries of the Old World."

All along, the six leaders had been eating only two meals a day, consuming each day the contents of one provision box packed in New York by Fiala (the camaradas carried separate rations); but now they made each box last a day and a half or even two days. Only when some large bird or monkey was shot, or a fish caught, was there really enough food. In the evenings the men from North America would sit around discussing what they would eat when they got home. Cherrie craved griddle cakes and maple syrup; Kermit dreamed of strawberries and cream; T.R. said he would choose a mutton chop "with a tail to it!" In addition to the generally weakened condition of the entire party, caused by the strenuous exertions of repeated portagings on short rations, two men were now down with the fever. For several days Cherrie was too weak to make entries in his diary.

At the end of March they discovered that they were crossing a range of mountains, "about the height of the lower ridges of the Alleghenies." The river here entered a rapids three kilometers long that took them three days to portage; one kilometer below was another set of rapids that cost them an additional day. "We thought we had reduced our baggage before," T.R. wrote; "but now we cut to the bone." Kermit's shoes had finally given out, a casualty of so many hours spent in the water among the sharp rocks; and he took his father's spare pair. In addition to the clothes on his back, the Colonel retained only one set of pajamas, one spare pair each of drawers and socks, half a dozen handkerchiefs, a wash kit, a pocket medicine case, and a little bag containing extra spectacles, needles and thread, gun grease, adhesive plaster, and his purse and a letter of credit to use at Manáos. T.R. still had a cot—the others were all sleeping on hammocks by then—but two tents were abandoned. The six leaders would sleep under one fly henceforth; the camaradas, under netting in the open.

Rondon surveyed and cut a trail for the camaradas to carry their burdens to the foot of the new rapids, while Kermit and Lyra, with four of the best watermen, worked the canoes down the gorge on ropes. Because of the constant fear of hostile natives, someone had to stand guard with a loaded rifle. In four days, T.R. wrote of this effort, the party had "accomplished a work of incredible labor and of the utmost importance; for at the first glance it had seemed an absolute impossibility to avoid abandoning the canoes when we found that the river sank into a cataract-broken torrent at the bottom of a canyon-like gorge between steep mountains." Nonetheless, one dugout was lost.

On April 2 the expedition started out on the river once more, "wondering how soon we should strike other rapids in the mountains ahead, and whether in any reasonable time we should, as the aneroid indicated, be so low down that we should necessarily be in a plain where we could make a journey of at least a few days without rapids." For a month they had been descending an uninterrupted series of rapids. They had lost four of the seven canoes with which they had started and one of the three built en route; one man; and a dog "which by its death had in all probability saved the life of Colonel Rondon." The camaradas were dispirited, occasionally asking one or more of the leaders if they thought they would ever get out of the jungle alive, "and we had to cheer them up as best we could." To his diary Cherrie confided that it was "doubtful if all our party ever reaches Manaos." Reconnoitering ahead, Rondon, Lyra, and Kermit discovered yet another series of "sinister rapids."

"Under such conditions whatever is evil in men's natures comes to the front," T.R. wrote of the situation as they confronted the grueling portage. "On this day a strange and terrible tragedy occurred." One man alone of the original sixteen camaradas had proved worthless; he was a huge, surly man of pure European blood named Julio. He constantly shirked tasks and had been caught stealing food on several occasions. At the outset of this day's portage one of the men accused Julio of stealing some dried meat and a Negro corporal named Paishon rebuked him for lagging behind. Yet no one paid attention when Julio casually picked up a carbine and followed Paishon down the portage trail. A minute later a shot rang out and three or four of the men ran back to say that Julio had killed Paishon and run off into the woods. The Colonel and the doctor tried to find the killer but shortly lost his track in the dense undergrowth; they feared he had gone amuck and would try to wipe out the entire party.

Paishon was simply and quickly buried along the portage trail where he had been slain. The expediton's cook noted that the corporal had fallen forward on his hands and knees, "and when a murdered man falls like that his ghost will follow the slayer as long as the slayer lives." The party could not immediately stop to pursue Julio, but three days later he appeared on the bank and called out that he wished to surrender. Roosevelt feared that, if the murderer were taken, he would prove a menace to the party; they could ill afford to maintain a round-the-clock guard over him and meanwhile he would be but an extra mouth to feed. Rondon, however, felt that it was his duty to bring the man back to civilization and to justice. But meanwhile the canoes had swept on past Julio, he had disappeared once more into the wilderness, and the two men sent back to take the murderer never found him.

In such a tense situation, the party had tried to hurry the dangerous portage and had lost another canoe. Jumping in the water to help with an overturned dugout, T.R. badly bruised his leg; the resulting inflammation, he wrote in deliberate understatement, "was somewhat bothersome." As luck would have it, the bruised leg was the one that had been seriously injured in the carriage accident in 1902, and Roosevelt developed what his son called "a veritable plague of deep abscesses." Doctor Cajazeira lanced the abscesses to relieve the inflammation and inserted a drainage tube. There was "an added charm" to this primitive operation, Roosevelt observed, in the enthusaism with which the numerous insects "took part therein." But T.R.'s condition was not a matter to be taken lightly; concurrently, he had a sharp attack of fever which completely disabled him for the next forty-eight hours.

"The scene is vivid before me," Kermit later wrote of that night, as he and the doctor divided a watch over the delirious Colonel. "The black rushing river with the great trees towering high above along the bank; the sodden earth under foot; for a few moments the stars would be shining, and then the sky would cloud over and the rain would fall in torrents, shutting out sky and trees and river." T.R. started reciting poetry—"In Xanadu did Kubla Khan a stately pleasure dome decree. . . ." Then he would enter into an incoherent monologue, mostly focusing on the lack of supplies; he wondered if Kermit and Cherrie were getting enough food. "I can't work now," Kermit heard him say, "so I don't need much food, but he [Kermit] and Cherrie have worked all day with the canoes; they must have part of mine."

Colonel Rondon himself had nearly given in to despair; only that morning he had proposed that they abandon the canoes rather than attempt another portage and that the party fight its way out of the jungle on foot "every man for himself." When he came out of his fever, T.R.

called Cherrie and Kermit to his bedside. "Cherrie, I want you and Kermit to go ahead. We have reached a point where some of us must stop. I feel I am only a burden to the party." He had morphine in his kit and thought of ending his life there. But, he later told O. K. Davis, he knew that his son would leave neither him nor his body in the Brazilian jungle. "So there was only one thing for me to do, and that was to come out myself."

At this point, Cherrie later claimed, it was twenty-four-year-old Kermit who held the expedition together—working nearly naked in the water with the canoes, his legs cut and bruised and swollen with insect bites, suffering occasionally from attacks of fever himself. They finally got through the "sinister rapids" of the double tragedy and out once more on the broad river, where the relentless sun, Kermit recalled, "hung above us all the day like a molten ball and broiled us as if the river were a grid on which we were made fast." To a sick man like his father, Kermit knew, the heat must have been intolerable.

"How I longed for a big Maine birchbark such as that in which I once went down the Mattawamkeag at high water!" T.R. wrote of his final days on the Dúvida. "It would have slipped down these rapids as a girl trips through a country-dance." But the pattern of brief runs on the wide river and long, laborious portagings around the numerous rapids continued through the first two weeks of April. Easter Sunday, April 12, was passed "in the fashion with which we were altogether too familiar," the Colonel recorded. They enjoyed a grand total of ten minutes in a clear course and then endured eight hours of portaging. The forenoon of the following day was spent in much the same manner, but late in the afternoon "the river began to run in long and quiet reaches." And the day after that they made fifteen kilometers; for the first time in several weeks they camped where they did not hear the sound of rapids. Fish were caught, a monkey and some birds that tasted like turkey were shot, and the camaradas gorged themselves on nuts—which unfortunately made them sick the next day. Thus, it was "a sorry crew" that embarked on the morning of the fifteenth. "But it turned out a red-letter day."

The previous day the party had noted what appeared to be cuttings of rubber trees, perhaps a year old but very likely the work of pioneer rubber men pressing into the wilderness. Two and a half hours out on April 15 they spied a board on a post with the initials "J.A."—evidently marking the farthest point upriver from the Amazon penetrated by a rubber man and claimed as his own. An hour after that they came upon a newly built house in a planted clearing and all cheered heartily. "No one was at home, but the house of palm thatch was clean and cool. A couple of dogs were on watch, and the belongings showed that a man and a woman and a child lived there and had only just left." An hour later a second house was sighted and they were welcomed to it by "an old black man who showed the innate courtesy of the Brazilian peasant." Civilization, however rude, had been reached; and the Dúvida proved to be what these frontier rubber men called the Castanho, an affluent or western branch of the Aripuanan, which eventually flowed into the Madeira and thus led to the Amazon. Henceforth, they would be following a river that, if still not on any maps, was at least one known to men of the wilderness.

"It was time to get out," T.R. concluded. "The wearing work, under very unhealthy conditions, was beginning to tell on every one." Half the camaradas had been down with the fever, and although Kermit and Cherrie had recovered from their attacks of fever, he and Lyra suffered greatly from bleeding sores on their legs, sores that had developed from the bruises incurred during the river work. The Colonel, at last, could admit that he himself was in bad shape—from the fever and from the abscesses on his injured leg. But the worst was past, and the "north was calling strongly. . . ." At nightfall they could see the Big Dipper well above the horizon—"upside down, with the two pointers pointing to a north star below the world's rim; but the Dipper, with all its stars." At Sagamore Hill, he knew, spring had come, "the wonderful northern spring of long glorious days, of brooding twilights, of cool delightful nights." Each of the three North Americans, Cherrie, Kermit, and the Colonel, "was longing for the homely things that were so dear to him, for the home people who were dearer still, and for the one who was dearest of all."

"Our adventures and our troubles alike were over," T.R. wrote of their last two weeks on the Rio da Dúvida. A rubber man was hired as a guide, and even though there were additional rapids to traverse, "It was all child's play compared to what we had gone through." Their guide could tell them what lay ahead, and trails for portaging had been blazed around the worst rapids; soon they were making fifty kilometers a day. On April 27—two full months after embarking on the River of Doubt—the Expedição Scientifica Roosevelt-Rondon reached the hamlet of Sao Joao. A three-day journey downstream aboard a river steamer brought them to Manáos, where they learned that the two other parties had come out safely down the Tapajos and Gy-Paraná rivers. Leo

Miller later recalled that Colonel Roosevelt, by the time of his arrival at the river city, "had wasted to a mere shadow of his former self; but his unbounded enthusiasm remained undiminished." The young naturalist was sorry that Fiala had already left for New York and could not record the arrival at Manáos on motion-picture film—as he had the expedition's departure overland from Tapirapuan three months earlier; "the two pictures side by side would have told an interesting story."

"We have had a hard and somewhat dangerous but very successful trip," T.R. wired the Brazilian minister of foreign affairs, General Müller, from Manáos on April 30. He briefly recounted the expedition's tribulations but then triumphantly recorded that they had "put on the map a river about 1500 kilometers in length running from just south of the 13th degree to north of the 5th degree and the biggest affluent of the Madeira." The river's course was completely traced and Roosevelt concluded, "My dear Sir, I thank you from my heart for the chance to take part in this great work of exploration."

At Manáos, Roosevelt said good-bye to the thirteen remaining camaradas, giving each some gold sovereigns—one of which, he later learned, each man kept as a token of his journey with the famous North American. An Amazon steamer took the rest of the party to Para, or Belem, where final farewells were said between the Brazilians and the Americans. Together with his admiration for the "hardihood, courage, and resolution" of Rondon, Lyra, and Doctor Cajazeira, Roosevelt confessed to a "strong and affectionate friendship for them"; he was glad to have "been their companion in the performance of a feat which possessed a certain lasting importance." The association with Roosevelt, incidentally, made Colonel Rondon something of an international celebrity while his work in behalf of the Brazilian Indians made him a hero at home. He helped create the Service for the Protection of the Indians, was made a marshal of Brazil, lived into his nineties, and at his death in 1958 was accorded a state funeral. The vast, still wild territory stretching northwest of the Rio Roosevelt and reaching to Brazil's border with Bolivia today is called Rondonia.

4

"The Brazilian wilderness," Roosevelt's longtime friend the historian William Roscoe Thayer wrote, "stole away ten years of his life." Corinne Robinson claimed that her brother returned from the trip "a man in whom a secret poison still lurked"; he was never thereafter "wholly free from recurrent attacks of the terrible jungle fever. . . ." Passengers on the liner *Aidan* were shocked at the Colonel's appearance when he came aboard at Belem on May 7; he was thin and gaunt and subject to frequent attacks of fever. But his appetite soon picked up. At Bridgetown, Barbados, where the ship stopped, he purchased fifty books and, sitting in the sun on deck each day, read them all before the *Aidan* reached New York on May 19.

There was no grand and glorious reception for Theodore Roosevelt on this return. When the liner stopped at quarantine shortly before four in the afternoon, a tug pulled up; aboard were Edith, Theodore, Jr., Archie, and T.R.'s cousin Emlen Roosevelt. Two other tugs carried photographers and reporters. Passing in the channel was the *Hamburg,* which had borne the Colonel across the Atlantic in 1909 at the outset of his African adventure; she signaled a greeting with three whistles and disappeared into open waters. The newspapermen were dismayed to see how thin and old the Bull Moose hero looked; "Roosevelt Returns 35 Pounds Lighter," *The New York Times* headlined its story about the arrival. Side by side the paper ran "before" and "after" pictures of the Colonel. The *Times* writer described T.R. as being "thinner and older looking, and there was something lacking in the power of his voice. His face had a hearty color, but there were lines that were not there before." Yet, the reporter concluded, "none of the old time vivacity of manner was lacking." Calling attention himself to the cane he was heavily leaning on, T.R. joked ". . . you see I still have the big stick."

"I was a pretty sick man when I reached Para, but I am much better now," Roosevelt told the newsmen. "I am worth more than several dead men yet." Dudley Field Malone, the Democratic Collector of the Port of New York, personally cleared the Colonel through customs; he only wondered if T.R. had brought the Rio da Dúvida back in his luggage and if he would be able to appraise it. Roosevelt laughed and insisted on declaring some lace he had brought for Edith, two jaguar skins, his old saddle, two silver christening mugs for grandchildren, and a bundle of bows and arrows from a friendly Indian tribe. When porters called for his luggage, T.R. refused to part with one parcel. It contained his final manuscripts for *Scribner's;* having carried the papers through jungle and rapids, he would not risk losing them now.

A reporter asked the inevitable question: would T.R. run for President in 1916. No, he would not speak of 1916 "to any human being," the Colonel answered. Within two weeks he would be leaving for Europe to attend Kermit's wedding to Belle Willard in Madrid. Before then he would go to Washington to lecture the National Geographic Society on the Rio da Dúvida. Upon that occasion he "would be prepared to answer any question that might be put to him by any man of reputation on geography." But that was the only speech or interview he would give in the foreseeable future.

The Roosevelt party transferred from the *Aidan* to a smaller craft that took them up the East River and into Long Island Sound; they arrived at Oyster Bay after eight. A small crowd was waiting at the dock on Emlen Roosevelt's property as a rowboat pulled toward land. A voice that was unmistakably the Colonel's, though the words were indistinguishable, called out in the darkness. Ethel Derby cried out in excitement, ran fifty feet down a wooden walk, and threw herself into her father's arms as he stepped ashore. "Oh, my darling," T.R. said, hugging and kissing his younger daughter and asking about her son, Richard, born only ten weeks earlier. "By George, I am glad to be back," he called to one of the family servants among the welcoming party. He climbed into a car, and as the door slammed shut, Archie called, "I'll see you at the house, Pop." A public welcome to Oyster Bay was planned for two days later but that evening at Sagamore Hill there would be only a very private family dinner.

On Wednesday, May 20, Roosevelt had two callers at Oyster Bay; the first was George W. Perkins, who stayed three hours; the second was Gifford Pinchot. "Not a word about politics," T.R. said to reporters who wanted to know what had been discussed with the two rivals of the Progressive party, "not a word."

A week later the Colonel went to Washington. It was a typical Roosevelt day. On the train down he was surrounded by reporters and politicians whose talk he apparently found only mildly interesting; the ex-President was observed "making frequent surreptitious dives" into Booth Tarkington's latest novel *Penrod*. Arriving at Union Station at 3 P.M., he first went to the National Museum to see the newly mounted exposition of his African trophies; en route, he was told that his old friend Jacob Riis had died and he took time to dictate a thoughtful statement to the press. Next he paid a courtesy call on Woodrow Wilson at the White House.

The President himself met T.R. at the door to the Executive Mansion and the two were alone together for a half hour, sipping lemonade and enjoying the breeze on the South Portico. As he left, the Colonel waved his panama hat to a crowd at the gate, and a young man called out: "Hurrah for Teddy! Hurrah for our next President!" T.R. brought his hat down on the youth's head in a friendly tap and everyone laughed. The Lodges had arranged a reception at their home for the diplomatic corps and following that Roosevelt was the guest of honor at a private dinner party. He next received newspapermen at the New Willard Hotel and finally entered Convention Hall at 8:30 for his address to the National Geographic Society.

An usher stationed at the entrance waved a handkerchief as a signal that the Colonel had arrived, and a great cheer went up from the audience of four thousand. Following his introduction by the society's president, Roosevelt warned the crowd that this was going to be a long and serious scientific discourse. Geographers abroad, especially in England, had deprecated his achievement and were expressing doubt about the River of Doubt. To his old friend Arthur Lee he had written in exasperation the previous week that the river he had helped explore would stay there; any skeptic could go to Brazil and "verify for himself what we have done."

At the outset of his Washington address Roosevelt gave full credit to Colonel Rondon and his associates in the Brazilian Telegraph Commission; without their earlier efforts, the journey down the Dúvida would have been impossible. "All that we did was put the cap on the pyramid of which they had laid deep and broad the foundations." On the platform behind him were maps, a blackboard, and a stereopticon screen; but he could not show what the Roosevelt-Rondon expedition had accomplished on any standard maps because they were "so preposterously wrong." Instead he had on stage that evening what he called "Exhibits A, B, C, and D" in the persons of his fellow explorers. They had put on the map a river as long as the Rhine or the Elbe, a river nearly a thousand miles long. And he wanted to thank the Brazilian government for giving him this opportunity, "a chance that from now on, in the present state of the world's geography, can come to only a limited number of men." Following the lecture, Roosevelt conferred for an hour with party leaders at Progressive headquarters and finally took the 12:15 A.M. train back to New York.

On May 30, accompanied by Alice Longworth and his cousin Philip Roosevelt, the Colonel left for Europe on the White Star liner *Olympic*. Passing through Paris, they arrived in Madrid on June 8 for a stay of four days that later seemed to Alice like "a movie run at several times life speed." Ambassador and Mrs. Willard gave a dinner party the first night at the embassy; the next day the Roosevelt party lunched with the royal family at La Granja—arriving at the country palace on an unusually cold June day nearly frozen after a drive in open cars of several hours. En route back to Madrid, they stopped at El Escorial, which Alice described as a "vast monument of gloom, austerity, and sombre magnificence." On the morning of the third day, T.R. visited the Prado Museum and at eleven o'clock went to the Prefecture of Police for the civil wedding ceremony before a district judge. The bride, the groom, Ambassador Willard, Colonel Roosevelt, and two Spanish noblemen signed the contract at the end of the simple ceremony. Afterward, T.R. and Alice "sped down the ribbon of road to Toledo to lunch and see the Cathedral and El Greco's house, and wander about that city that seems straight out of a fairy book." At noon on the eleventh there was a religious ceremony at the English church, followed by a reception at the embassy—during which the ex-President danced a Virginia reel with the wife of the Spanish premier. That evening the Colonel and Alice left for Paris and London.

T.R. spent a week in England, renewing old friendships, visiting museums, and giving essentially the same lecture on the Rio da Dúvida that he had delivered in Washington to the Royal Geographic Society in London. On June 18 he sailed for home aboard the *Imperator,* but Alice "managed to miss two or three boats" before returning late in July.

When he had emerged from the Brazilian wilderness at the end of April, Roosevelt learned that the Wilson administration had just signed a treaty with Colombia containing an apology for the United States's role in the Panama revolution of 1903 and agreeing to pay that country an indemnity of $25,000,000 for loss of its Isthmian territory. He immediately had denounced the treaty as "dishonorable"; paying Colombia that sum would be "nothing but blackmail." En route home from Europe in June, T.R. encountered the diplomat who had served Taft as minister to Colombia, an apparently fearless individual who urged the Colonel to take a favorable view of the treaty. The ensuing conversation, recalled Lawrence Abbott, another passenger aboard the *Imperator,* "was a thoroughly lively one."

Arriving in New York on June 24, Roosevelt expressed great interest in the news that he might be called to testify before the Senate committee considering the treaty. If the treaty were right, he told reporters, then Panama should be awarded to Colombia and work on the canal should cease. But the pact, he again charged, was "merely the belated payment of blackmail with an apology to the blackmailers." Wilson's conduct of foreign affairs had made the United States "a figure of fun in the international world"; the treaty was the climax and, if ratified, would "render us an object of contemptuous derision to every great nation." Roosevelt, however, was not asked to testify and, led by Henry Cabot Lodge, the Senate later in the year defeated ratification.

"Moose Herd Has Colonel Cornered," a headline in *The New York Times* of June 27 read; Roosevelt, whether or not he wanted to, might be forced to run as the Progressive candidate for Governor of New York that fall, the paper speculated. T.R. had already said, while still on board ship, that he would not seek the governorship; but Perkins and his nephew Theodore Douglas Robinson, Progressive State Chairman, said that they would wait to hear the denial from his own lips. Dr. Alexander Lambert, the Roosevelt family physician, examined the Colonel upon his arrival home and promptly urged a four-month rest; the ex-President was suffering from an enlargement of the spleen and recurrent attacks of fever. "I think Dr. Lambert took a gloomy view," T.R. told reporters on June 27, "but I shall take care of myself, and I'll see that the malaria does not get settled in my system." As for the long rest, it was "impossible"; by that time the campaign for the fall congressional elections would be nearly over. Although he emphatically would not run for office himself, he did plan to tour New York State in behalf of the Progressive ticket and would also make several appearances elsewhere across the country.

On June 30 Roosevelt delivered his first major political address since 1912, speaking at a dinner of the Progressive League in Pittsburgh. "Was it a swan song—was it the plea of a broken man —what was the character of the gathering? Was it a congregation of saddened and disheartened people, come to pay a kindly tribute to a passing leader?" asked the Philadelphia *North American* in an editorial entitled "The Amazing Roosevelt." "It was none of these things," the editorialist answered his own question. The demonstration for the Colonel "surpassed anything in the 1912 campaign, and the Roosevelt who greeted this demonstration was the vigorous, fighting Roosevelt who so long had led the people's battles." "The Colonel enjoyed every minute," wrote the *World;* malaria and other physical weaknesses were forgotten "as he stood at the vortex of the night's enthusiasm." Swinging out at both Democrats and Republicans, Roosevelt announced to the country that the Bull Moose was still alive, aggressive, and ambitious.

He did not speak, that evening, of an event two days earlier, a story that received substantial if uncomprehending coverage in the newspapers on June 29. Like millions of others around the world, T.R. had read the surprising but scarcely alarming news that in the remote Bosnian town of Sarajevo, the heir to the throne of Austria-Hungary had been assassinated by a Serbian nationalist.

◆§ Chapter 15 ◆◆

Unanswered Trumpet

"*It would* be the irony of fate," Woodrow Wilson told a friend at Princeton as he was about to leave for Washington to assume the Presidency, "if my administration had to deal chiefly with foreign affairs." A scholarly authority on American government, he had made his debut in politics as a domestic reformer; he had demonstrated no great interest in or concern with what went on beyond the country's shores. Fate, however, was to provide that very irony but not before the new Chief Executive was able to chalk up some very substantial accomplishments during his first two years in office.

Wilson's initial act following his inauguration on March 4, 1913, was to call a special session of Congress to eliminate the high tariff system that the Republican party had so carefully constructed over the past two decades. And on April 8, shattering the tradition of merely sending written messages to Congress set by Thomas Jefferson in 1801, he appeared in person before both houses to deliver his tariff message. He wanted the assembled legislators to see that he was a real person, "not a mere department of the Government hailing Congress from some isolated island of jealous power." It must have irritated Roosevelt, so anxious to enhance the office of the President during his two terms, to think that he had not made use of such a dramatic gesture. The resulting tariff bill—named for Oscar W. Underwood, Chairman of the House Ways and Means Committee—was indeed a genuine downward revision of protective duties. More important, to offset anticipated reductions in customs receipts, the Underwood Act provided for the nation's first progressive income tax—constitutional then under the Sixteenth Amendment adopted earlier that year.

In May, 1913, the Seventeenth Amendment, proposed a year earlier, was also declared adopted; it provided for the direct election of United States senators. At the end of the year Congress gave its assent to the Federal Reserve Act, Wilson's proposal for a government controlled, decentralized banking system. And in October, 1914, the Clayton Antitrust Act was passed. In addition to strengthening the Sherman Act, much along the lines suggested in the disputed Progressive party plank of 1912, and providing specific remedies for parties injured by illegal combinations, the Clayton bill forbade the use of injunctions in labor disputes and made strikes, peaceful picketing, and boycotts legal. Organized labor hailed the measure as its Magna Carta. Another accomplishment of late 1914 was the establishment of the Federal Trade Commission, a regulatory body again very much of the kind sought by the Progressives.

By the end of 1914 Woodrow Wilson had come to believe that the New Freedom he had preached in his campaign for the Presidency was achieved. But such an advanced progressive as Robert M. La Follette predictably broke ranks with the new President after his first year in office. The atmosphere in Washington, the discontented Wisconsin senator wrote in April, 1914, reminded him "of the beginning of the second year of the reign of one William Howard Taft." Wilson allowed his Cabinet officers to segregate Negro workers in the Post Office and Treasury departments, refused to support a child labor act, and told suffragettes that he could not support their plea for the vote. Yet, one of the ladies in a delegation visiting the White House said, he had spoken in favor of women's suffrage during the 1912 campaign. "But, you see," said the President, "I was speaking as an individual then, and now I am speaking as a representative of the party to which I belong." "Of course," one of the ladies angrily retorted, "you were gunning for votes then."

During a good part of Wilson's first year and a half in office, Colonel Roosevelt was out of the country, in South America and in Europe, and made few public comments on the policies of the man who had defeated him for the Presidency. But as he warmed up for the campaign of 1914, he felt free to deal with what he considered the spectacular inadequacies of Woodrow Wilson to sit in the chair he had once occupied. Already in the President's dealings with Mexico, and soon because of his reaction to the outbreak of war in Europe, T.R. was finding ample grounds for private anguish and public condemnation of the man in the White House.

Among the important decisions the new President had had to make in March, 1913, was America's attitude toward revolutionary Mexico. Two years earlier the rank and tottering dictatorship of Porfirio Diaz had been swept away in a revolt led by Francisco I. Madero. On February 11, 1913, Madero's liberal government was, in turn, overthrown in a coup d'etat organized by General Victoriano Huerta, who coolly saw to it that his predecessor was murdered. In the closing days of his administration, Taft declined to recognize the reactionary Huerta regime as the legitimate government of Mexico. A week after his inaugural Wilson, saying that the United States could have no sympathy with those who seized power to advance "their own personal interests or ambition," likewise refused to acknowledge Huerta's rule. "I will not recognize a government of butchers," Wilson said in private.

Inexperienced and perhaps even disinterested in diplomacy, Wilson should have picked a knowledgeable and forceful man as Secretary of State. Party politics, however, made it necessary for him to offer the top Cabinet post to William Jennings Bryan, then only fifty-two and obviously a has-been but nonetheless a man with a still large and loyal following of Democrats. Only one consideration had made Bryan hesitate: he and his wife were teetotalers; they could not serve wine or spiritous liquors at diplomatic functions. Wilson agreed that the Bryans should be allowed to follow the dictates of their own consciences and Washington entered an era of what contemptuous and thirsty critics called "grape-juice diplomacy."

Wilson and Bryan had some reason for withholding recognition from Huerta. The day after the general's coup, a flag of revolt against the new central government had been raised by Venustiano Carranza, the governor of Coahuila in northern Mexico. Proclaiming himself First Chief of the Constitutionalists, Carranza pledged to fight until Huerta was ousted and legal government reestablished. Wilson asked Huerta to hold free elections in which he would not be a candidate for the presidency. When the general refused, Wilson announced that the United States would adopt a policy of "watchful waiting." After Huerta dissolved the Mexican Chamber of Deputies in October and set himself up as military dictator, Wilson lifted the embargo against the supplying of American arms to Mexico—an act that favored Carranza—and stationed ships off Vera Cruz to block shipments of European arms to Huerta.

In April, 1914, an incident involving a shore party of American sailors at Tampico led to the United States bombardment of Vera Cruz and the occupation of that city. With Mexico and the United States on the brink of war, Argentina, Brazil, and Chile stepped in to mediate the dispute and in July Huerta was forced out of office. Carranza marched into Mexico City the next month and was subsequently recognized by Wilson as de facto president. By year's end the American occupation forces were withdrawn.

Theodore Roosevelt had watched the unfolding drama in Mexico with shocked dismay. At the outset he had written in confidence to a Tennessee editor that he felt the United States should join the major Latin American powers in restoring order in Mexico but he did "not want to seem to be advising Mr. Wilson." By September, 1913, he was writing to Lodge that Bryan—because of what T.R. considered his bungled handling of the Mexican problem—was "the most contemptible figure we have ever had as Secretary of State, and of course Wilson must accept full responsibility for him." Upon the occupation of Vera Cruz, the Colonel wrote another friend that, although he would like to lead a cavalry division in a serious war, he was doubtful about taking part in a "mere war with Mexico." Finally, in December, 1914, Roosevelt spoke out in public on Wilson's Mexico policy.

In a long article published in *The New York Times,* the Colonel charged that only "wordsplitters" could deny that Wilson had intervened in Mexican affairs; such defenders of the President "would be obliged to make a fine discrimination between intervention and officious and mischievous intermeddling." Because of the President's action— "and at times his inaction has been the most effective and vicious form of action"—the nation had become partially responsible for "some of the worst acts ever committed even in the civil wars of Mexico." In a subsequent magazine essay, T.R. recounted numerous Mexican atrocity stories and put the blame for them at Wilson's doorstep. "A weakling who fears to stand up manfully for the right may work as much mischief as any strong-armed wrong-doer," he charged.

Wilson chose to ignore T.R.'s intemperate criticism, advising political supporters to do likewise. "The very extravagance and unrestrained ill feeling of what he is now writing serve to nullify any influence that his utterances could have," the President wrote. "He cannot possibly in his present situation or temper cause any embarrassment which need give us a second thought. I am sincerely sorry that he should have so forgotten the dignity and responsibility of a man placed as he is who might exercise so great an influence for good if he only saw and chose the way."

Still hammering away at Wilson's Mexican policy early in 1916, Roosevelt wrote that the President had made war on America's neighbor "in the interest of some bandit chief whom at the moment he liked, in order to harm some other bandit chief whom at the moment he disliked." The President's methods and his defense of his actions had not been those of "an American statesman who is true to the traditions of Washington and Lincoln" but rather those of—and T.R. here set thousands of readers leafing through their unabridged dictionaries—"a Byzantine logothete." General Francisco Villa by then was in full revolt against Carranza and Villa's raids across the border into Texas and New Mexico at last resulted in the dispatch of an American punitive expedition under Brigadier General John J. Pershing into Mexico on March 15—an intervention that was to last nearly a year. By the time Pershing's force was withdrawn from Mexico, the United States stood on the brink of a much larger conflict, one that had already led Roosevelt into near-apoplectic denunciation of Wilson.

2

With fascinated horror Americans had watched the inexplicable, inevitable chain of events that had followed the assassination of the Austrian archduke at Sarajevo on June 28, 1914. Ultimatums were exchanged, armies were mobilized, troops were dispatched to frontiers on predetermined schedules. Then, in a decisive, climactic maneuver, Germany wheeled her armies westward through neutral Belgium and flung them against her historic enemy, France. England called Germany's attention to the international guarantee of Belgium neutrality; "a scrap of paper," sneered the German chancellor. Britain hesitated only momentarily before plunging into the vortex.

Theodore Roosevelt was at Sagamore Hill on August 4, 1914, the day England declared war on Germany. "You've got to go in! You've got to go in!" T.R. exclaimed to one of his visitors that day, the English reformer Charles Booth. The Colonel and his other visitors Herbert Croly and Felix Frankfurter, a future Supreme Court justice, agreed that German militarism should be checked but that the German nation itself should not be destroyed. Nor could America watch unconcernedly if

Germany triumphed. Roosevelt was a man of large vision in the field of foreign relations, one who saw far ahead of his times. An unashamed Anglophile, he had helped build a very real though informal and publicly unacknowledged alliance between the United States and England. A German victory now, he felt, would upset the balance and order imposed by the hegemony of Anglo-American power.

Sometime during that first week of war T.R. had a visitor at Progressive party headquarters in New York—a German count bearing letters from both the German embassy in Washington and from the head of the German steamship line on which he had often traveled. The count bowed and said that he was the bearer of a message from Kaiser Wilhelm; his Majesty wished Roosevelt to know that he treasured the memory of the ex-President's visit to Berlin and Potsdam in 1910 and felt assured that he could count on Roosevelt's "sympathetic understanding of Germany's position and action" in the war. T.R. bowed back, looked the count straight in the eye, and said: "Pray thank his Imperial Majesty from me for his very courteous message; and inform him that I was deeply conscious of the honors done me in Germany and that I shall never forget the way in which his Majesty the Emperor received me in Berlin, *nor the way in which his Majesty King Albert of Belgium received me in Brussels.*"

Publicly, Roosevelt adopted the neutrality that was the nation's official policy, as enunciated by Woodrow Wilson. Between August 4 and November 6 the President was to issue no fewer than ten proclamations of neutrality, in that of August 19 calling upon his fellow citizens to be "impartial in thought as well as in action. . . ." On August 6, *The New York Times* quoted T.R. as saying that it was not the time to criticize the President and that he would work "hand in hand" with any man to see that the country came "through this crisis unharmed." T.R.'s first major public statement on the war appeared in *The Outlook* on August 22. "I am not now taking sides one way or the other as concerns the violation or disregard of these treaties," he wrote. "When giants are engaged in a death wrestle, as they reel to and fro they are certain to trample on whomever gets in the way of either of the huge straining combatants." But in private he was writing that very day to Arthur Lee in England that if he were President he would register "a very emphatic protest" to Germany for her violation of Belgium's neutrality. "Even from the standpoint of brutal self-interest, I think Germany's invasion of Belgium was a mistake."

The Colonel continued to maintain his ambivalent stand on the war into October. In a second *Outlook* article, published on September 23, he said that "every circumstance of national honor and interest forced England to act precisely as she did act" in response to the invasion of Belgium. "She could not have held up her head among nations had she acted otherwise." On the other hand, he did not know what action his own country could or would take, although it had been announced that nothing would be done to interfere with American neutrality. The United States could maintain that neutrality only by refusing to aid such "unoffending weak powers [as Belgium] which are dragged into the gulf of bloodshed and misery through no fault of their own. Of course it would be folly to jump into the gulf ourselves to no good purpose; and very probably nothing that we could have done would have helped Belgium." The United States had "not the slightest responsibility for what has befallen her. . . ." American sympathy for the invaded nation was "compatible with the full knowledge of the unwisdom of uttering a single word of official protest unless we are prepared to make that protest effective; and only the clearest and most urgent National duty would ever justify us in deviating from our rule of neutrality and noninterference."

Later Lawrence Abbott would attempt to take the blame for the apparent contradictions in this article. Although not a Wilson man, Abbott had felt that it was important to support the President in time of national crisis and had urged T.R. to put into his article certain equivocations and qualifications that Abbott was certain the Colonel— though he never alluded to it—came to regret. Indeed, when Roosevelt was preparing a collection of his magazine and newspaper articles on the war for publication in book form early in 1915, he excised some of these expressions of apparent indifference about Belgium's fate. He substituted instead a ringing denunciation of Wilson's neutrality.

At any rate, the September article was to be one of T.R.'s last contributions to *The Outlook.* The preceding June he had resigned from the magazine's editorial staff, ending his five-year association with sincere regret. His continuing involvement in political affairs, he claimed, made it impossible to devote sufficient time to his editorial duties. Through 1914 he continued to contribute special articles, such as the two on the war, to *The Outlook* but in December he signed a three-year contract with *Metropolitan* magazine. For an annual retainer of $25,000—more than double his *Outlook* salary—he would publish exclusively in that monthly his views on political, international, and social affairs.

Only four days after his second *Outlook* article was published, Roosevelt held a secret conference—in Cleveland, where he was campaigning for the Progressive state ticket in the fall elections—with a Belgian commission come to the United States to publicize that country's sufferings. The conference lasted two or three hours, recalled O. K. Davis, but since the conversations were in French, Roosevelt and James Garfield later had to tell him what the Belgians had said of German atrocities committed against their country. "It was not so very long after," Davis wrote, "that the Colonel was making vigorous public use of the information thus brought to him." Whether or not he was actually swayed by the Belgian commissioners, the Colonel soon dropped his neutrality.

For the first sixty days of the war, Roosevelt later wrote, he had supported Wilson's neutrality on the assumption that the President "was speaking the truth, had examined the facts, and was correct in his statement that we had no responsibility for what had been done in Belgium." Later, he reexamined the Hague conventions, signed during his own administration, and concluded that the United States did indeed have an obligation toward Belgium. ". . . if I made any error whatever, it was standing by . . . [Wilson] just sixty days too long."

Even before the outbreak of war, Roosevelt had been privately caustic on the subject of Wilson and Bryan's conduct of foreign affairs. As the storm clouds gathered over Europe on August 1, T.R. wrote to Arthur Lee that the Secretary of State and "his ridiculous and insincere chief" were "prattling pleasantly" about the arbitration treaties Bryan had negotiated with twenty-one nations, treaties that called for one-year cooling-off periods while an international commission deliberated over any disputes between two signatories. The treaties promised the impossible, Roosevelt charged, and "would not be worth the paper on which they are written in any serious crisis." It was unfortunate, he concluded, "to have a professional yodeler, a human trombone like Mr. Bryan as Secretary of State, . . . [and] a college president with an astute and shifty mind, a hypocritical ability to deceive plain people . . . as head of the nation." Wilson, he wrote in a subsequent letter to Lee, "is almost as much of a prize jackass as Bryan."

Early in August, however, there was a compelling reason for not attacking the President in public. On August 6, after an illness only shortly before diagnosed as serious, Ellen Axson Wilson had died in the White House, with the President, her husband of twenty-nine years, holding her hand. "Oh, my God, what am I to do?" the distraught Wilson had exclaimed to the attending physician. "I never understood before what a broken heart meant, and did for a man," the President wrote a confidant at the end of the month. "Business, the business of a great country that must be done and cannot wait, the problems that it would be deep unfaithfulness not to give my best powers to because a great people has trusted me, have been my salvation; but, oh! how hard, how desperately hard, it has been to face them, and to face them worthily."

Three months later, Wilson was still oppressed by the tragedy of his loss. The Chief Executive's friend Colonel Edward M. House recorded in his diary on November 6 that Wilson had told him he "was broken in spirit by Mrs. Wilson's death, and was not fit to be President because he did not think straight any longer, and had no heart in the things he was doing." A week later, visiting House in New York, Wilson actually told his friend that he wished someone would kill him, he no longer cared to live.

From Canada where he was vacationing, William Howard Taft had immediately sent a message of condolence. "I know . . . something of the strain and responsibility of office with private anxiety and sorrow," Taft wrote an old friend a few days later. ". . . The White House will seem very solitary to him without her, for . . . there is a splendid isolation about it that makes sorrow keener." Taft had maintained cordial relations with his successor, writing as early as January, 1914, that "[I] very much prefer to have him [Wilson] continue and be re-elected, than to incur any danger at all of Roosevelt's success."

Roosevelt actually gave Wilson's neutrality more than the sixty-day public support he later admitted, but by early October he was at least in private fully committed to the Allied side. T.R.'s old friend Cecil Spring Rice was the British ambassador in Washington; although a public show of their intimacy might have compromised the diplomat's relationship with Wilson and Bryan, Roosevelt continued to correspond with Spring Rice. "If I had been President," the Colonel wrote on October 3, "I should have acted on the thirtieth or thirty-first of July, as head of a signatory power of the Hague treaties, calling attention to the guaranty of Belgium's neutrality and saying that I accepted the treaties as imposing a serious obligation which I expected not only the United States but all other neutral nations to join in enforcing." He would not have made such a statement, he added, unless "I was willing to back it up." If, as President, he had taken such a stand, T.R. continued in his letter to Spring Rice, the American people would have supported him. On the other hand, he was certain that the majority now supported Wilson's neutrality. Few people could be expected to make up their own minds in a crisis; they tended to follow the lead of the President. "It would be worse than folly for me to clamor now about what ought to be done or ought to have been done, when it would be mere clamor and nothing else."

Roosevelt had just published the first two of a series of articles on the war that he had written for the Wheeler Syndicate; the articles, appearing on successive Sundays through October and November in *The New York Times* and other newspapers across the country, took an increasingly strong position on the war. The first four articles, he wrote to Rudyard Kipling on November 4, were but leading up to the two prepared for publication on the first two Sundays of the current month. At last he was coming out publicly on America's duty to interfere on behalf of Belgium. "I purposefully abstained from saying the form this interference should take," he told Kipling. "If I should advocate all that I myself believe, I would do no good among our people, because they would not follow me. Our people are shortsighted, and they do not understand international matters." The British had been shortsighted too, he added, but not as much as the Americans. "The difference, I think, is to be found in the comparative widths of the Channel and the Atlantic Ocean. . . ."

The Wheeler Syndicate articles marked Roosevelt's definitive abandonment of neutrality in the European war and the launching of his emotional and futile crusade in behalf of preparedness for what he considered America's inevitable intervention in behalf of the Allies. In January, 1915, he gathered these, and a few other articles on the war, for publication as a book, *America and the World War*. At Sagamore Hill on New Year's Day, he wrote a foreword to the volume. "The kind of 'neutrality' which seeks to preserve 'peace' by timidly refusing to live up to our plighted word and to denounce and take action against such wrong as that committed in the case of Belgium, is unworthy of an honorable and powerful people," he declared. ". . . Peace is ardently to be desired, but only as the handmaid of righteousness." It was essential to put "the combined power of civilization back of the collective purpose of civilization to secure justice."

A worldwide league to secure peace and justice, T.R. concluded, was presently unrealizable. Until it was created, "the prime necessity for each free and liberty-loving nation is to keep itself in such a state of efficient preparedness as to be able to defend by its own strength both its honor and its vital interest." Preparedness did not avert war any more than the existence of a fire department averted a fire. "But it was the only insurance against war and the only insurance against overwhelming disgrace and disaster in war."

The articles, revised and strengthened for publication in book form, pulled no punches; indeed, they contained numerous harsh and offensive denunciations of Wilson, Bryan, and their supporters. T.R. rejoiced in such phrases as "these shivering apostles of the gospel of national abjectness," "the loquacious impotence . . . which has recently marked our own international policy," "the prattling feebleness that dares not rebuke any concrete wrong, and whose proposals for right are marked by sheer fatuity." He spoke of "the shrill clamor of eunuchs, [who] preach the gospel of the milk and water of virtue"; "the unspeakable silliness of the . . . all-inclusive arbitration treaties of Messrs. Wilson and Bryan"; and of the President's "queer infirmity of purpose" and his use of "verbal adroitness to cover mental hesitancy." Wilson's "cleverness of style and his entire refusal to face facts apparently make him believe that he really has dismissed and done away with ugly realities whenever he has uttered some pretty phrase about them."

Visiting Sagamore Hill, the novelist Owen Wister remarked that, in a democracy, a leader could do nothing unless the people were behind him; equally the people could do nothing unless they had a man to get behind. "Yessss," Roosevelt drew out his agreement. "And just now they've got behind a dictionary."

As for Bryan, T.R. had long come to feel that he was beneath contempt. In support of the President's neutrality, a neutrality that ruled out any preparation for even the possibility of taking sides, Bryan had said that a million men would spring to arms in a day, if Wilson gave the call; a sympathetic senator had raised the figure to ten million. If the ten million sprang to arms, T.R. claimed, they would have about four hundred thousand modern arms to which to spring. "Perhaps six hundred thousand more could spring to squirrel pieces and fairly good shotguns. The remaining nine million men would have to 'spring' to axes, scythes, hand-saws, gimlets, and similar arms."

In one long and thoughtful essay, T.R. reviewed Switzerland's system of universal military training and advocated a similar program for the United States. There were also "small sections of our population out of which it is possible to improvise soldiers in a short time." The volunteers he was speaking of would be no substitute for regulars but they could be used to strengthen the Regular Army much as the Rough Riders had done in the Spanish-American War.

"I kept silence as long as silence was compatible with regard for the national honor and welfare," he wrote in the last syndicated article, published on November 29, 1914. "I spoke only when it became imperative to speak under penalty of tame acquiescence in tame failure to perform national duty." Roosevelt had sounded the unequivocal clarion call of the bugle; he was not to cease making repeated and ever more insistent blasts in behalf of intervention and preparedness for intervention during the next two years of a frustrating, often lonely campaign.

3

"The kaleidoscope has been shaken," Roosevelt wrote to an old Washington friend at the end of February, 1915. "All the combinations are new and I am out of sympathy with what seems to be the predominant political thought in this country." Despite the intensity of his campaign for preparedness, he knew that the people were listening to Wilson and not to him. Moreover, he had just come through another long and fruitless campaign in behalf of the Progressive party.

Although he had successfully resisted pressure to head the party's New York State ticket, T.R. had agreed to campaign actively in New York and in several other states. But he had been reluctant even to do this. To Cal O'Laughlin he wrote in late August, after his first campaign swing, that he had concluded the feeling in the country was "thoroughly hostile" to him. "I believe that my usefulness in public life is about at an end, that the prejudice against me is such that I harm rather than help the cause for which I stand." Nonetheless, between August and November, 1914, he had traveled through New England to Maine, south to Louisiana, and west as far as Kansas and Nebraska. This time there was no private car, though the Colonel had the faithful and efficient O. K.

Davis along to make arrangements. T.R., a hostile journalist wrote toward the end of the campaign, was "rapidly becoming the rank and file of the Recessive Party."

"Oh Lord," he wrote William Allen White in mid-September as he rested at Oyster Bay between campaign trips, "I wish you could be in my place for a little while!" At the end of October he broke away from the New York campaign to spend most of the last week before election barnstorming through Pennsylvania in behalf of Gifford Pinchot's race for the Senate. On the train back to New York he suddenly slapped Davis on the knee and said "Well, O.K., I've got only a few hours more of this campaign, and then I shall be through. I'll be out of politics then for good and all, and I'll be a free man." He had paid every political obligation, though a great deal of the campaigning had been "foolish and useless work." Yet he had done everything that everybody had wanted of him. "This election makes me an absolutely free man," he concluded. "Thereafter I am going to say and do just what I damned please." It was one of the very few times the ex-newspaperman had ever heard his hero "use the big D, and the emphasis with which he uttered it showed how thoroughly he meant it."

"As of course I expected the Progressives went down to utter and hopeless defeat," T.R. wrote his daughter Ethel Derby the day after the election; "I do'n't think they can much longer be kept as a party." Commenting on the returns, he sent his sister Corinne to the Bible— II Timothy 4: 3–4. "For the time will come when they will not endure sound doctrine; but after their own lusts shall they heap to themselves teachers, having itching ears"; "And they shall turn away their ears from the truth, and shall be turned unto fables."

The only two bright spots, he wrote to Hiram Johnson on November 6, were California—where Johnson had been reelected governor and three Progressives sent to the House of Representatives—and Louisiana, which had elected one Progressive congressman. "Lord, how I wish the Republican party would come to its senses, adopt the Progressive platform, and nominate you next time!" T.R. ended his letter to Johnson. East of Indiana, he wrote William Allen White the next day, the party was dead; where the Progressive vote was too small even to hold the balance of power between the two old parties, it would be foolish to run tickets in the future. From Election Night of 1912 he had felt that "the chances were overwhelming against the permanence of the Progressive party." At present there was room in the country for only two parties: Wilson's and the one in opposition to him. The election just concluded demonstrated that the average American considered the Republican and not the Progressive party to be the party of opposition. Two months later, hearing that White wanted to write the history of Roosevelt and the Progressive party, T.R. told the Kansan it would be an "obituary—for I am more like a corpse. . . ."

The results, however, were none too comforting to Woodrow Wilson. Although the Democrats had picked up five seats in the Senate, they had dropped sixty-one in the House of Representatives. With the Progressives slipping to nine House seats, the Republican gain was sixty-nine. "We have squeezed Roosevelt out, and we can attend to the Democrats in two years," Taft crowed. "He is a gone-gosling." Henry Adams wrote a friend in Europe to say that T.R. and his followers were disposed of; "I suspect he is busted and done."

Early in the New Year, 1915, T.R. was agreeing with his former Attorney General Charles J. Bonaparte who had said he would have to hold his nose and swallow "the nauseous dose" of return to the Republican party in 1916. ". . . I will vote to substitute for him [Wilson] even an escaped criminal," he told Bonaparte. ". . . But this does not mean any cordial feeling on my part toward the criminal."

There was at least one major obstacle to Roosevelt's return to the G.O.P., however, and that was the deep and unremitting hostility toward the Colonel on the part of the Republican Old Guard, the party leaders who had never really embraced him, even as President, and who bitterly blamed him for the rift of 1912 that had brought humiliating defeat to the G.O.P. Foremost among the Colonel's political enemies was William Barnes, Jr., of Albany, Republican State Chairman of New York. In 1912 Barnes had remained loyal to Taft and had thus been a prime target of Roosevelt's at the Chicago convention.

In July of 1914, T.R. had suggested that the Progressives also nominate Harvey D. Hinman, a man seeking the Republican nomination for Governor of New York. He also urged Empire State Progressives to consider the support of anti-Tammany Hall Democrats in a nonpartisan crusade against the bosses of both parties. "The interests of Mr. Barnes and Mr. Murphy [Charles F. Murphy, Tammany Hall leader] are fundamentally identical," Roosevelt said in his statement supporting Hinman, "and when the issue between popular rights and corrupt and machine ruled government is clearly drawn, the two bosses will always be found on the same side openly or covertly, giving one another such support as can with safety be rendered. . . . It is idle for a man to pretend that he is against machine politics unless he will . . . openly and by name attack Mr. Barnes and Mr. Murphy." Barnes the next day brought suit against Roosevelt charging libel.

The Colonel at first was fairly confident about the outcome of the trial. Under oath in court, he wrote Hiram Johnson the next week, he would be able to produce testimony ten times stronger than anything he had ever used on the stump. He hoped for, and eventually got, a change of venue from Albany, "where Barnes has, I believe, the courts and all the court officers who control the selection of jurymen completely in his hands." Still with his record of attack on the courts and with the hostility of so many lawyers and newspapers toward him, T.R. could not really be sure of the result. Nonetheless, he welcomed the opportunity to get in the court record "a description of boss rule such as has not hitherto appeared even in campaign speeches." After the election, he was less sanguine about the trial. "The feeling against me in New York State," he told White, "amounts to a mania."

The Colonel was in Syracuse for the Barnes libel trial almost continuously from April 18 through May 22, when the verdict was announced. "I am going to nail Roosevelt's hide to the fence," Barnes's chief counsel remarked to Elihu Root on the eve of the trial. "Let me give you a piece of advice," Root replied. "I know Roosevelt and you want to be very sure that it is Roosevelt's hide that you get on the fence."

Barnes's attorneys had not counted on T.R.'s irrepressible energy, his instant rapport with almost any audience. The Colonel's testimony became so vivid and dramatic that the discomfited lawyers asked the court to rule that the witness "must confine himself to words, and must not answer with his whole body"; his testimony was making what they considered an unfavorable impression on the jury. The judge denied this motion, but he did rule out a good deal of testimony, introduced by Roosevelt's attorneys, that apparently linked Barnes to public printing frauds in Albany—testimony that would have proved the G.O.P. boss to be corrupt and therefore not libeled by T.R.'s charge of the previous summer. "The rulings of the Judge have been such that he has refused to let the jury take into account all my most important evidence, evidence which, to my mind, showed Barnes's guilt beyond a shadow of doubt," the Colonel wrote his son Archie on May 19.

Barnes, however, lost the suit. The jurors deliberated forty-two and a half hours before reaching their unanimous decision exonerating the Colonel of the libel charge. The announcement, reporters said, created a scene in the courtroom resembling the headquarters of a successful candidate on Election Night. T.R. thanked all the jurors warmly and asked them to visist him at Sagamore Hill. His victory, T.R. wrote the Chicago Progressive Raymond Robins early the next month, was "really as much for those who have fought with me during the last three years as for myself." It had justified, by legal evidence submitted in court, all that had been said in the Bull Moose campaign of 1912 about boss rule and political corruption in the older parties. George Perkins was going to have the transcript of the trial printed; he himself could never have afforded to do so. His defense had cost him between thirty and forty thousand dollars.

The Colonel was undoubtedly the propaganda victor as well. Later in the year George Meyer, the ex-Secretary of the Navy, was visiting T.R. at Sagamore Hill. Talk turned to the trial. "By the way," Meyer said almost apologetically, "it's funny, but I've forgotten how that case came out." "Why, I won it," Roosevelt replied with surprise. "Oh, I know that," Meyer answered, "but I can't remember how much damages you got." Artfully concealing a smile, T.R. asked Meyer to repeat the question. A little uneasily, he did so. The Colonel walked over to his friend, patted him gently on the shoulder, and said, "My dear fel-low, *I* was the de-*fend*-ant."

4

For Theodore Roosevelt, the dramatic high point of the Barnes libel trial occurred on May 7. But the event that so gripped his attention that day had nothing to do with the charges of corruption he had leveled against the New York boss and took place far from the Syracuse courtroom—three thousand miles across the Atlantic Ocean off the coast of Ireland.

On May 1 two notices had appeared on an inside page of *The New York Times.* One was a routine advertisement placed by Cunard, the British steamship line, announcing the May and June departures of its ocean-going vessels. The first sailing was to be that of the *Lusitania,* the "Fastest and Largest Steamer now in Atlantic Service"; she would leave for Europe via Liverpool that day at 10 A.M. The other newspaper notice, far from routine, was a boxed announcement from the Imperial German Embassy in Washington, dated April 22; it reminded travelers that a state of war existed between Germany and Great Britain and that the war zone included the waters around the British Isles. Vessels flying the flag of Great Britain or any of her allies were liable to destruction in those waters; "travellers sailing in the war zone on ships of Great Britain or her allies do so at their own risk," the announcement ominously concluded. The British liner, "Undisturbed by German Warning," according to a headline the next day, departed on schedule for England. (He knew what he would have done about the German announcement, had he been President, the Colonel later told William Roscoe Thayer. He would have summoned the German ambassador, given him his passports—thus breaking off diplomatic relations with Germany— and marched him under guard aboard the *Lusitania* upon its departure for Europe.)

Within its first few weeks the European war had reached a virtual stalemate, the huge armies of the contending powers bogged down along a trench line that snaked across the Continent from Belgium to Switzerland. A victory on land seemingly beyond achievement, the opponents had next looked to the high seas as an arena where the deadlock might possibly be broken. Ignoring the protests of the American government, Britain had declared the North Sea a military area, heavily mined its waters, and proclaimed a blockade of all German ports in the hope of starving her enemy into submission. Germany's response was submarine warfare.

In a note of February 10, 1915, drafted by Robert Lansing, Counselor of the State Department, but emended by Wilson himself, the United States protested Germany's action. If American vessels were destroyed on the high seas or if American lives were lost, the United States would view the act as "an indefensible violation of neutral rights"; Germany would be held to "a strict accountability" for such losses; and the United States would take necessary measures to defend her rights. The comparatively weak protest said nothing about Americans traveling or working on vessels of the belligerent powers—an issue the President would soon have to face.

On March 28 a German submarine sank the British steamship *Falaba,* without giving a warning that would have allowed the passengers and crew to abandon ship; among the dead was one American. The discussion over the proper American response to the sinking revealed a major rift in the Wilson administration. Lansing felt that the United States should ask Germany to disavow the act, rebuke the submarine commander, and pay damages—even if such demands led to war. Bryan, Lansing's superior in the State Department, wished to avoid war at all costs and argued that America must give Germany the same right to violate international law as she had given England by not pressing the protest of Britain's blockade. Through April Wilson procrastinated, writing toward the end of the month to Bryan that he had decided to "put the whole note on very high grounds,—not on the loss of this single man's life, but on the interests of mankind which are involved and which Germany has always stood for. . . ." On April 28, however, he again wrote to his Secretary of State, saying this time that "Perhaps it is not necessary to make formal representations in the matter at all."

The President still had not made up his mind what to do about the *Falaba* incident when he received news that an American tanker named the *Gulflight* had been struck by a torpedo off the Scilly Isles during a fight between a German submarine and a British naval patrol; two more Americans were dead. Far worse news came the next week. A German submarine without warning had sunk the *Lusitania* off the coast of Ireland on May 7. Nearly 1,200 people, including 128 Americans, were dead.

Colonel Roosevelt received news of the tragedy in a telegram delivered to him that afternoon in the Syracuse courtroom. When court recessed for the day, he went to the home of Horace S. Wilkinson, a Syracuse friend with whom he had been staying. He knew that he would be called upon to make some statement; he also knew that there were two men of German origin on the jury and that any condemnation of the sinking might cause them to vote against him and in favor of Barnes. "Well," he said to Wilkinson, "it doesn't make any difference. It is more important that I be right than that I win the suit. I've got to be right in this matter."

T.R. retired early in the evening of May 7 but was awakened in the middle of the night by the telephone call of a New York editor who wished to give him the latest details on the *Lusitania* sinking. "That's murder!" Roosevelt bellowed. Would he make a statement? "Yes, yes, I'll make it now. Just take this." Germany's sinking of the *Lusitania,* the Colonel said in the statement dictated over the telephone, "represents not merely piracy, but piracy on a vaster scale of murder than old-time pirates ever practiced. . . . It is warfare against innocent men, women, and children, traveling on the ocean, and our own fellow-countrymen and countrywomen, who are among the sufferers. It seems inconceivable that we can refrain from taking action in this matter, for we owe it not only to humanity but to our own national self-respect."

"Gentlemen," T.R. told his lawyers the following morning, "I am afraid I have made the winning of this case impossible." He revealed his fears that the statement would unalterably alienate the two German-American jurors. "But I cannot help it if we have lost the case," he added. "There is a principle at stake here which is more vital to the American people than my personal welfare is to me." Of course, he proved wrong; the two jurors obviously acted on the evidence and ignored the Colonel's *Lusitania* statement.

That evening, May 8, Roosevelt called the editor of the *Metropolitan* to learn what Wilson had done about the *Lusitania*. "Has he seized the ships? Do you mean to say he hasn't seized the German ships in our harbors," T.R. shouted into the telephone. The next day he drafted an enraged editorial "Murder on the High Seas," which the *Metropolitan* issued as a special broadside on May 11. After a thorough condemnation of Germany, the Colonel demanded that the administration take action. The United States would "earn as a nation measureless scorn and contempt if we follow the lead of those who exalt peace above righteousness, if we heed the voices of those feeble folk who bleat to high heaven that there is peace when there is no peace." For months, he charged, the government had "preserved between right and wrong a neutrality which would have excited the emulous admiration of Pontius Pilate—the archetypical neutral of all time." The nation had failed to do its duty in Mexico; would it now fail to do its duty in the World War?

The newspapers of May 11 carried a statement made by Wilson the previous day in Philadelphia in the course of an address welcoming newly naturalized citizens. There was such a thing, the President had said, "as a man being too proud to fight. There is such a thing as a nation being so right that it does not need to convince others by force that it is right." Wilson and his advisers in the State Department were carefully considering the form their protest to Germany over the *Lusitania* would take; in view of the President's Philadelphia statement, it appeared unlikely it would be an ultimatum leading to war.

The first American protest over the *Lusitania* sinking, drafted by Wilson and reluctantly signed by Bryan, was delivered on May 13. The note was a virtual demand that Germany abandon submarine warfare against unarmed merchant vessels—but it was followed by a statement, released to the press but later recalled, suggesting arbitration of the dispute. The German government's response was considered evasive and Wilson prepared a second, sterner note, delivered on June 9. But the signature on this document was that of Robert Lansing, the new Secretary of State. Sincerely believing that no issue was worth risking war, the tortured Bryan had resigned rather than continue pressing Germany on the *Lusitania* case. The *Lusitania's* cargo, it had been discovered, consisted almost solely of military supplies. "England has been using our citizens to protect her ammunition," Bryan said in anger and sorrow. Germany's second reply was also considered unsatisfactory by Wilson and on July 21 a third and final *Lusitania* note was dispatched. This was as close as the President would come to an ultimatum and it ended with a warning that further such ruthless sinkings would be considered as "deliberately unfriendly" acts that could lead to a rupture of diplomatic relations and even war.

The President's conduct of foreign affairs, T.R. wrote George Perkins, "has been precisely that of a man whose wife's face is slapped by another man, who thinks it over and writes a note telling the other man he must not do it, and when the other man repeats the insult and slaps the wife's face again, writes him another note of protest, and then another and another and another, and lets it go on for a year."

The President's policy, nevertheless, had bought time with Germany. The Kaiser's government had already secretly instructed submarine commanders not to sink liners of the enemy without adequate warning. And when two Americans died in the sinking of the British steamer *Arabic* on August 19, the German ambassador in Washington gave the so-called *Arabic* pledge: Henceforth liners would not be sunk without warning and without providing for the safety of noncombatants, as long as the liners did not try to escape or offer resistance. In October Germany offered apologies and indemnity for the loss of lives in the *Arabic* sinking, and the Wilson administration could close out the year on this diplomatic triumph.

Alice Longworth was visiting Sagamore Hill when news of another Wilson note to Germany was published, and she asked her father if he had read the new protest. "Did you notice what its serial number was?" he asked sarcastically. "I fear I have lost track myself; but I am inclined to think it is No. 11,765, Series B."

5

By the summer of 1915 Roosevelt had thrown himself wholeheartedly into the campaign for preparedness, a campaign in which he had a strong and important ally. Leonard Wood, an army doctor who had won the Congressional Medal of Honor for his part in the capture of the Indian chief Geronimo, had later been T.R.'s commander in the Rough Rider campaign. Elevated to the rank of major-general by Roosevelt in 1903, Wood, seven years later, had been appointed Army Chief of Staff by Taft. At the expiration of his four-year term, he had become commander of the Department of the East with headquarters at New York's Governor's Island.

During his Washington years Wood had made a number of enemies by his blunt efforts to reform the army's bureaucracy. Among the fights Wood waged as Chief of Staff was his campaign for a short enlistment of two years, with seven or eight years in the reserves. When army traditionalists had scoffed that two years was too brief a time to make a soldier, Wood had said he could do it in six months. As early as 1911 he had proposed taking high school and college graduates and giving them six months of concentrated instruction after which they could be returned to civilian life. It would be "a splendid thing," he wrote, thus to train 20,000 to 30,000 men each year; they would never forget what they learned and would be a ready reserve upon which the nation could draw in times of emergency. The general did not get his 20,000 to 30,000 youths but two years later he organized a modest program of summer military training for young men.

In a five-week program during the summer of 1913, Wood saw 63 students from 29 institutions trained at Monterey and 159 from another 61 institutions at Gettysburg. Each youth paid for his own transportation, uniforms, and board. He learned how to fire a rifle and care for his weapon, the manual of arms and close and open order drill, how to dig entrenchments and go on patrol, and was instructed in army organization and camp sanitation. There were maneuvers on the Gettysburg battlefield, a week on the rifle range, and a sixty-five mile forced march to end the training. "I think we have opened up a field of wonderful possibilities," Wood exulted to T.R. at the end of the first summer camps; the program was sure to "result in a far better understanding than has ever before existed of what the country needs and what the true purposes of the army are." With the blessing of President Wilson, Wood organized summer camps at four locations in the summer of 1914; the number of volunteers rose threefold to 667.

Wilson, however, regarded Wood—an avowed Republican and a known partisan of Roosevelt's—with suspicious caution. At the outbreak of war in August, 1914, Wood had asked permission to go to Europe as a military observer but had been told that, because of the uncertainty of the situation in Mexico, no American officers would be permitted to leave the country. Through the fall the general had continued to criticize the army's unreadiness for a big war and preach preparedness. But Bryan's pacifism was then the dominant mood of the administration.

Meanwhile, Admiral Bradley A. Fiske, the Naval Aide for Operations—a position equivalent to Army Chief of Staff—was complaining to his chief, Secretary of the Navy Josephus Daniels, that the United States Navy was likewise unprepared for war. Josephus transformed this information into a December report to the President that it had been "a proud and solemn year for the American navy. . . ." Wilson could be congratulated "upon the record it [the Navy] had made, upon its preparedness for duty, upon the reliance you can place upon it in any time of national need." T.R. backed up Admiral Fiske. There had been no fleet maneuvering for nearly two years, Roosevelt pointed out in a newspaper article. "In spite of fleet maneuvering the navy may be unprepared. But it is an absolute certainty that without fleet maneuvering it cannot possibly be prepared." Who, he asked, would go to a Harvard-Yale football game if either university fielded a team that had not practiced during the preceding sixty days?

In his annual message to Congress on December 8, 1914, the President loftily dismissed such prophets of preparedness as Roosevelt and Wood. "We shall not alter our attitude because some amongst us are nervous and excited," Wilson declaimed. The nation had always found means to defend itself against attack; ". . . if asked, are you ready to defend yourself? we reply, most assuredly, to the utmost," the President continued. ". . . Let there be no misconception. The country has been misinformed. We have not been negligent of national defense."

Speaking in New York a week later, Wood quoted the Revolutionary General "Light Horse" Harry Lee: " 'The nation is a murderer of its people which sends them unprepared to meet those mechanized and disciplined by training.' That statement was absolutely true at that time and it is just as true today." Secretary of War Lindley M. Garrison rebuked the general for so flatly contradicting the President and seeming to make national defense a partisan issue, but Wood, like Roosevelt, could not be silenced.

In the wake of the *Lusitania* crisis, Wood organized a special businessman's training camp, in addition to the student camp, to be held at Plattsburg, New York, in the summer of 1915. Bernard Baruch donated ten thousand dollars and got others to contribute; among those who enrolled for the camp were former Secretary of State and ambassador to France Robert Bacon, New York Mayor John Purroy Mitchel, the war correspondent Richard Harding Davis, and the socialite Regis Post who, Wood noted wryly, "forgot he had insomnia and had to struggle to keep awake" after a day of strenuous drilling. Three of Roosevelt's sons, as well as his son-in-law Richard Derby went to Plattsburg that summer. Quentin and Archie attended the student camp, and Archie did so well that he was allowed to stay over for the businessmen's camp where—to T.R.'s delight he was put over his older brother, Ted. Kermit, back in South America, learned of his brothers' achievements from a proud father; ". . . if this infernal skunk in the White House can be kicked into war a Captain Archie shall be. Ted has already been promoted to be a Sergeant." The Plattsburg camps, being held in other parts of the country as well, were "very successful," the Colonel continued in his letter to Kermit; but they were "nothing whatever but makeshifts. We ought to have universal military service."

On August 25 Roosevelt, at the invitation of General Wood, came to speak at Plattsburg. He had wired his old friend with a cryptic request that the speech be made after duty hours, out of camp, and to men dressed in civilian clothes. "Will explain in full tomorrow morning." Upon his arrival, T.R. readily agreed to submit his speech to Wood for editing. "Theodore," Wood remarked, "as an ex-President, you have presidential prerogatives on a military reservation. You may say what you want. But I suspect that some of the things you are planning to say are likely to stir up a lot of trouble." Roosevelt agreed to eliminate passages Wood considered too inflammatory.

A crowd of several thousand—twelve hundred trainees, six hundred regulars, and three or four thousand visitors—gathered to hear Roosevelt speak late that afternoon. He stood with his back to Lake Champlain and the Green Mountains across the water in Vermont, fac-

ing a western sky in which the sun was slowly sinking. As darkness settled over the land, only the lantern on a photographer's tripod served to
distinguish the speaker. A lost dog, looking for his master, ran up to the
Colonel, rolled over on his back and raised his legs in pleading. "That's
a very nice dog," T.R. said interrupting his speech, "and I like him. His
present attitude is strictly one of neutrality." In his remarks, T.R. attacked pacifists, hyphenated Americans, and those who favored "a policy
of supine inaction." Roosevelt, Wood later maintained, cast no asper-
sions on the Wilson administration and was warmly applauded by prominent Democrats in the audience; his friend's talk was "absolutely
beyond criticism."

Boarding a train for New York later that evening, however, T.R.
had some fairly explicit statements to make to reporters about the President. And these remarks, along with the unedited version of the speech,
were carried in the newspapers the next day. "We have had a terrific
jamboree over my visit to Plattsburg," the Colonel wrote Archie a week
later. ". . . The Administration took ferocious umbrage; and ever since
my speech I have been in an intricate row." Nevertheless, he told his
son, he was glad he had spoken out. "It was worth while to have one
man state the things that ought to be stated." Secretary Garrison reprimanded Wood for allowing Roosevelt to speak, but Wood refused to
give an explanation. And T.R. claimed sole responsibility for his address.
Having made no objection to his visit after three weeks' notice, the
War Department was "disqualified from criticizing General Wood because I went, and because he did not submit my speech to the Administration for approval."

The writer Julian Street visited T.R. at the *Metropolitan* offices the
day after the Plattsburg speech and observed him dictating the reply to
Garrison. He began calmly enough, seated at his desk with the reporters
gathered around him. But as he warmed to the subject, he rose and
paced back and forth. And when he was finished with the formal statement, he seated himself again and launched into a frank discussion of
the incident that was clearly off the record. The reporters were plainly in
the Colonel's camp, Street wrote. Watching their faces was like watching an audience at a play—"when the hero was indignant they became indignant; when he sneered they sneered; and when he was
amused they seemed almost to quiver with rapturous merriment." A
friend of Roosevelt's had previously explained to Street T.R.'s attitude
about swearing. He did not need to swear "because he can say 'Pacifist'

or 'Woodrow Wilson' or 'William Jennings Bryan' in tones which must make the Recording Angel shudder." The only Roosevelt Dam, the friend said, was the one named for him in Arizona.

Street was meeting the Colonel for the first time and thought the word "aged" as applied to T.R. was bizarre. "True, his mustache is now quite gray, but he has not aged and will not age. He has simply ripened, matured." Two months short of his fifty-seventh birthday, Roosevelt "looks forty-seven, and evidently feels as men of thirty-seven wish they felt." A week later the former Bull Moose leader turned his back on the preparedness controversy and headed for Quebec, for a month of moose hunting.

Toward the end of the year, T.R. gathered together his additional writings on the war for publication early in 1916 in a new volume, to which he gave the hortatory title *Fear God and Take Your Own Part.* The ex-President's "fanaticism no longer knows any bounds," the irritated German ambassador wrote the chancellor in Berlin about the time the book was published. "The question now is whether Mr. Roosevelt can still be considered sane. Madness seems to have enveloped his mind." Speculating on the coming presidential election, the ambassador predicted that the Colonel would lead the Republican party to a second defeat by Wilson.

T.R. with the co-leader of the Brazilian expedition, Colonel Rondon

In a dugout, about to descend the River of Doubt
(Theodore Roosevelt Collection, Harvard College Library)

Writing the articles for *Scribner's,*
with gauntlets and netting as protection against insects
(Theodore Roosevelt Collection, Harvard College Library)

One of the laborious portages on the River of Doubt, dragging the dugouts past a rapids

Back from Brazil
in May, 1914—
50 pounds lighter

A family stroll at Sagamore Hill, June, 1914

Apostles of preparedness: Roosevelt and General Leonard Wood

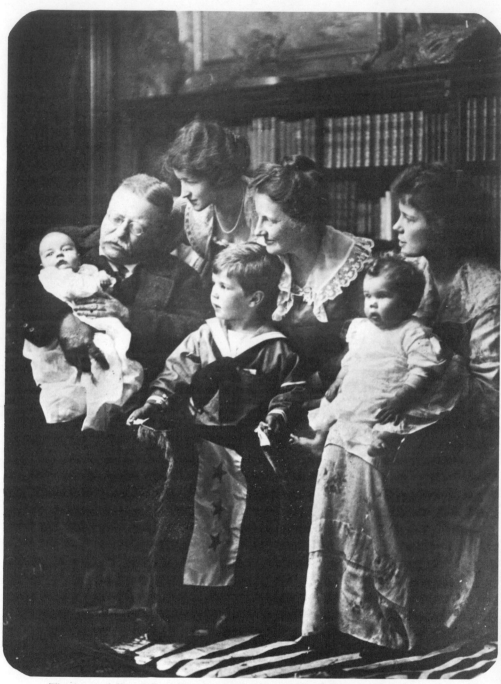

The home folks: T.R. with his newest grandchild, Archie, Jr.; Archie's wife, Grace; Edith and Ethel, with the two Derby children, Richard and Edie

(Theodore Roosevelt Birthplace)

The young airman, Quentin Roosevelt
(Theodore Roosevelt Birthplace)

Colonel Roosevelt boosting a wartime scrap drive of the Girl Scouts
(Theodore Roosevelt Collection, Harvard College Library)

January, 1919: Burial at Oyster Bay

Chapter 16

Return to the Fold

" *I* *most earnestly* hope the Republicans will *not* nominate me," the Colonel wrote to his sister Bamie on February 3, 1916; "for my belief is that the country is not in heroic mood; and unless it *is* in heroic mood and willing to put honor and duty ahead of safety, I would be beaten if nominated." As the presidential year opened, Roosevelt had but one thought: Woodrow Wilson must be defeated for re-election.

T.R. had known since the disastrous congressional elections of 1914 that the Progressive party was moribund; another third-party ticket in the coming presidential contest, he realized, would inevitably give Wilson a second term. There was already considerable sentiment that he, as the leading critic of the administration's policy of neutrality, should oppose the President—possibly on a ticket reuniting the Republican and Progressive parties. To this end the Progressive National Committee had recently announced that the Bull Moose convention would open in Chicago on June 7, the same date the Republicans planned to gather there for their own nominating convention.

Roosevelt clearly wanted to be President again, especially at a time of crisis that called for firm leadership. The only way he could reach the elusive goal was as the G.O.P. standard bearer, but he was enough of a realist to know that the Old Guard had neither forgotten nor forgiven 1912. An endorsement from the Bull Moose, no matter how close the poor creature was to the grave, would give him something to bargain with at Chicago.

The Colonel's motives and methods were far from obscure and had already been perceived by political observers. "It is very evident," William Howard Taft had written to his wife in the spring of 1915, "that

T.R. is taking a running jump back into the party." The two had a stiff, awkward encounter at Yale on April 13, both serving as pallbearers at the funeral of a professor of English there. Ex-Senator Beveridge, in a letter to George Perkins of May 6, had accused Roosevelt of "flirting with the Republicans." Three months later he claimed that there was "a widespread and growing feeling among our rank and file . . . that the design of Colonel Roosevelt . . . was to abandon the [Progressive] party."

Roosevelt, perhaps even to himself, was denying his ambition. Word had reached him, late in the summer of 1915, that Perkins was promoting a fusion ticket. To "my dear George," T.R. wrote on September 3 that "any such effort will not only be useless from the public standpoint but will be exceedingly detrimental to me. It is perfectly evident that this people have made up their minds not only against the policies in which I believe but finally against me personally." If he could disregard the salary paid him by the *Metropolitan* and also— "abruptly in the middle of the war"—afford to abandon preaching the doctrines in which he believed, he would "cease all comment in speech or writing on public affairs, because I am in grave doubt as to what I accomplish thereby."

To Arthur Lee, the day before, he had outlined the four divisions of public opinion. First, there were the German-Americans, "quite willing to drag the honor and interest of the United States in the dust if it will help Germany." Next were the "professional pacificists, the mere materialists, and the mollycoddles, the people who are timid or sordid or utterly selfish and utterly shortsighted." The majority of Americans belonged to a third element, T.R. claimed; these were "good, decent men and women who know very little about international affairs." Although horrified by the war, they were compelled by self-interest to avoid taking any action and were relieved when the President gave them "excellent excuses, excellent justifications for nonaction." Wilson had rendered this majority "the dreadful service of furnishing lofty names to cloak ignoble acts." What T.R. was saying and writing made these people angry "because they have an uncomfortable feeling that maybe I am right and that action should be taken." The fourth and final element was composed of men "who have such initiative, such self-reliance and such a high spirit that they do not need to be roused." These last were the people that were with Roosevelt in his crusade for preparedness and the abandonment of neutrality if necessary, but they comprised "an almost negligible element," less than 5 per cent of the population, he speculated.

By February, 1916, Roosevelt had come to feel that the tide of public opinion was changing. Charles G. Washburn, a Harvard classmate of the Colonel's and a former Republican congressman from Massachusetts, was about to publish a biography of his lifelong friend, *Theodore Roosevelt: The Logic of His Career.* T.R. now wrote to "Dear Charley" that he was greatly amused that "there is a momentary revival of my popularity or notoriety or whatever you choose to call it. . . ." just at the time Washburn's book was to be issued. When his friend had started work on the volume, Roosevelt confessed to being at the "very nadir" of his popularity; only a very devoted friendship—"others would call it a very blind friendship"—could have led Washburn to embark on the project. From "a practically solid public opinion against me," he wrote Senator Lodge, "I believe I now have an appreciable public opinion with me. It is, however, merely an appreciable minority." That minority he put as high as 15 per cent. His wish was that the Republicans—he had written "we" but crossed it out—"would take the right stand, hoist the flag for national honor and national duty and sink or swim as the issue of the battle might determine and without regret." His own nomination still perhaps impossible, he predicted that the Republicans would pick Charles Evans Hughes.

When Hughes had accepted a seat on the Supreme Court in 1910, it was assumed he had also abandoned any further political ambitions. Nonetheless, the reputation for strong progressive leadership he had won in his two terms as Governor of New York still clung to him; stern, upright and self-righteous, respected but unloved, the "bearded lady" came to be everybody's second choice for the G.O.P. nomination in 1916. Among those now championing Hughes was William Howard Taft, who had withdrawn his own name from consideration. Urging the justice to run, Taft wrote in April that "the exigency presented to you is whether you will save the party from Roosevelt and the country from Wilson."

The Republican Old Guard would have preferred one of their own—even Elihu Root at age seventy-one had belatedly developed presidential fever. But, like the Colonel, they realized that their candidate must appeal to a broader political spectrum; he must be a man who could bring together the two wings of the once-dominant party. Although T.R. had told reporters it would be "proper" for Progressives to support the Republican nomination of Hughes, he wrote Lodge that taking a candidate from the Supreme Court would "establish a very bad precedent." Moreover, he was concerned because Hughes—aloof and isolated on the high tribunal—had not taken any position on the Wilson administration's conduct of foreign affairs. Those who were urging the candidacy of Hughes, the Colonel maintained, should demand that the justice "unequivocally, and fully, and with emphasis" declare himself on the issues of the day. "We do not want to find that we have merely swapped Wilson for another Wilson with whiskers," he wrote George Meyer.

On February 11, Theodore and Edith Roosevelt left New York for a six-week-long cruise to the West Indies, with Port of Spain, Trinidad, as their principal destination. The trip would be good for his wife, T.R. had written Bamie, "and it will save me just so much pointless fussing and resultless worry." But there was not distance great enough to keep Roosevelt out of politics, and from Trinidad, on March 9, he made a statement that was at once a withdrawal from the contest for the G.O.P. nomination and a broad hint of availability.

He first insisted that his name not be entered in the forthcoming Massachusetts presidential primary; "I emphatically decline to be a candidate in the primaries of that or any other State." He did not wish the nomination, nor was he interested in his own or any other man's political fortunes. He was interested solely in "awakening my fellow countrymen to the need of facing unpleasant facts" and "in the triumph of the great principles for which with all my heart and soul I have striven and shall continue to strive." He would not himself fight for the nomination nor permit a factional fight to be made in his behalf. Indeed, repeating now for the public the phrase he had earlier used in writing to his sister, to Lodge, and to others, "it would be a mistake to nominate me unless the country has in its mood something of the heroic—unless it feels not only devotion to ideals but the purpose measurably to realize those ideals in action."

Nothing was to be hoped for from the Wilson administration, Roosevelt continued; all the President and his party offered was a choice "between degrees of hypocrisy and degrees of infamy." Thus, the nation's future rested with the forthcoming Republican and Progressive conventions. But "disgust with the unmanly failure" of the Wilson administration should not lead the people to vote "in a spirit of mere protest." They should not be content to exchange the present administration for one "equally timid, equally vacillating, equally lacking in vision, in moral integrity and in high resolve." What the people should desire, "and I believe they do desire," was a candidate "whose one great mission should be to declare in unequivocal terms for a programme of clean-cut, straight-out, national Americanism, in deeds not less than in words, and in internal and international matters alike. . . ."

June was a long way off, T.R. concluded; it was too early to say who should be nominated at Chicago. He only asked that the delegates to the two conventions "approach their task unhampered by any pledge except to bring to its accomplishment every ounce of courage, intelligence and integrity they possess."

A New York *World* cartoon depicted the Colonel, draped in an American flag, his sword drawn, under the legend: "Wilson is *not* heroic; Hughes is *not* heroic; Root is *not* heroic; *I* am heroic." "Are you heroic?" T.R. asked George Perkins in another *World* cartoon, as the uneasy financier lifted pen to checkbook. "Without moving the hat" was the comment of the *Brooklyn Eagle's* cartoonist, who showed the famous Rough Rider headgear circled by lines labeled 1904 and 1912 as the candidate with his Big Stick drew a third circle marked 1916.

On March 31, a week after his return from Trinidad, the Colonel took lunch at the New York home of Robert Bacon. The other guests were Senator Lodge, General Wood, and Elihu Root. It was the first time the ex-President had met his Secretary of State since the steamroller convention of 1912. "All passed off well," Wood wrote in his diary, "Roosevelt and Root seemed to be glad to be together again, really so. Roosevelt cussed out Wilson as did Root and Lodge. Opinion that the country never so low in standing before."

"As you have doubtless seen in the papers," T.R. wrote to Hiram Johnson on April 3, "I have seen Root." The Colonel had arranged immediately afterward to go to Perkins's house and report to various Progressives gathered there about the encounter with the archenemy. "We talked only of preparedness and of the necessity from the public standpoint of doing something that would enable us to get rid of Wilson," Roosevelt reassured Johnson. Nevertheless, the *World* that day published a cartoon showing Roosevelt and Root, in mourning clothes, shaking hands over the tombstone of "B. Moose." A wreath on the fresh grave was "From Perkins." Taft claimed that Root had been "inveigled" into the luncheon and Roosevelt had "used the opportunity unconscionably to give the impression that Root favored him for the nomination."

But Root's friends countered with the launching on April 7 of a campaign to nominate the man they called "the ablest living American."

Taft was among those who still considered Root "the best equipped man for the Presidency" but who nonetheless felt that he could not win. William Allen White was outraged. ". . . to make a fight under a man like Root is hopeless," he wrote T.R.; all over the Midwest there was "a deep abiding revulsion to Root. . . ." Roosevelt agreed with White and with another correspondent who wrote that the movement to nominate Root was "a movement to cut the throat of the Republican Party from ear to ear."

In public, as the opening of the two conventions approached, Roosevelt continued to refuse an endorsement of any man's candidacy. Among the rank and file Republican voters, he confided to a friend early in May, he thought that there was more sentiment for him than for any other candidate; the convention, he feared, would be "in the hands of a very sordid set of machine masters associated with rather well-meaning and rather timid citizens of the ordinary type without strong convictions." But on May 11 he endorsed the Theodore Roosevelt Non-Partisan League, a group devoted to the Colonel's principles and supporting his nomination for the Presidency. He was especially touched to learn that the league had been blessed by Thomas Alva Edison. Meanwhile George Meyer was working with a Roosevelt Republican League to affect a reconciliation with the Old Guard. Finally, on May 29, T.R. wrote to Charles J. Bonaparte, asking that "my friends in the Progressive Convention no more proceed upon the assumption that I will run, than my friends in the Republican Convention proceed upon the assumption that I will not run." There could no longer be any doubt; T.R.'s hat was indeed once more in the ring.

Hiram Johnson, set to lead California's delegation to the Progressive conclave, wrote George Perkins that the Bull Moose party should counter the Old Guard refrain of "anybody but Roosevelt" with its own slogan "nobody but Roosevelt." The Progressive Executive Committee had already announced that the party was ready to consider compromise but not surrender—a declaration the New York *Herald* compared to extending an olive branch on the end of the big stick. Entering Chicago's Blackstone Hotel on June 1, Perkins encountered Charles D. Hilles, the Republican National Chairman. The two men shook hands and chatted together in friendly fashion. Afterward, Hilles told reporters that the two parties "would get together."

2

Somehow, T.R. had convinced himself that he could win both nominations, and he entrusted Perkins with the task of pulling off this improbable coup. The New York financier was set to maintain a rigid control over the Progressive gathering unmatched by the leadership over the rival convention of any single Republican. With one party thus apparently in his vest pocket, he considered his major assignment was to secure the G.O.P. nomination for Roosevelt. Unlike 1912, the Colonel would remain home, but a private telephone line connected Sagamore Hill with Perkins's rooms at the Blackstone.

On June 6, the day before the two conventions were to open, Senator Lodge sat down with William Draper Lewis to compare the platforms each was drafting for his party. Lodge used the private telephone that night to report to Roosevelt that the two party statements "will not clash at all." It was amusing, he remarked, to think that the two platforms were being drafted together. "I think it is one of the funniest things I have ever known," came the voice from Oyster Bay.

A cold rain fell over Chicago on Wednesday, June 7, as the two conventions assembled—the Republicans again at the Coliseum; the Progressives at the Auditorium. Making the keynote speech at the Bull Moose gathering, Raymond Robins mentioned Roosevelt's name and touched off a ninety-three-minute demonstration. It was going to be difficult for Perkins to keep the party rank-and-file from rising up to nominate T.R. by acclamation; yet, he knew that a premature endorsement by the Progressives would ruin the Colonel's chances at the other convention. Nevertheless, he succeeded in pushing through the platform and quickly had the meeting adjourned. The 1916 Bull Moose convention, Amos Pinchot bitterly observed, was going to be every bit as much a steamroller affair as the 1912 Republican conclave.

On the following day James Garfield rose to move that the convention approve the naming of a committee to seek a compromise with the Republicans. Again the delegates called for an immediate endorsement of the Colonel's candidacy. From among all those now rising to put T.R.'s name before the convention, the chairman recognized a Missouri delegate who read a letter from Roosevelt asking the Bull Moosers to cooperate with the Republicans. Silence descended upon the convention hall, and Garfield's motion was carried. Perkins, Hiram Johnson, Horace S. Wilkinson, Charles J. Bonaparte, and John M. Parker of Louisiana were named to the special committee.

That evening the Progressive committee met a similar group appointed by the G.O.P. convention; the Republican contingent included senators Murray Crane, Reed Smoot, and William E. Borah, A. R. Johnson, and Nicholas Murray Butler—of whom only Borah could be considered anything but a standpatter. Senator Smoot reportedly opened the conference with the remark, "We will take anyone you want but Roosevelt." Nonetheless the Progressive conferees gave a two-hour argument in behalf of T.R. The Republicans asked for their second choice; there was none. The Progressives then asked who the Republicans favored but the G.O.P. committee members refused to name anyone before balloting at their convention began. The meeting ended inconclusively at 3 A.M. Friday morning.

Alice Longworth had come to Chicago with her husband and was at the G.O.P. convention with a "sad little prayer" that the Old Guard would relent and name her father. The nominations got underway at the third session, on June 9. In the roll call of states, Alabama passed and Arizona yielded to New York. "We bring you today," Governor Charles S. Whitman declaimed, "the name of a man trained for the battle for the truth. . . . We have seen him the man of action, the champion of the people, the idol of the electorate, the faithful public servant, the profound thinker on national affairs. . . . The great State of New York offers you . . . her son—her noblest and best." But the Empire State's "noblest and best" this time was Charles Evans Hughes, not Theodore Roosevelt.

It was left to Senator Albert B. Fall of New Mexico to place the Colonel's name in nomination—in a speech that led to the G.O.P. convention's longest demonstration, thirty-six minutes, but also to hisses and cries of "Throw him out." Hughes led the first ballot with 253½ votes; T.R. with only 65 votes was seventh in a pack of favorite sons that trailed the justice. At the end of the second ballot, Hughes had 328½ votes—170 short of a majority—to Roosevelt's 81; and the convention was adjourned for the day.

Across town the Progressives had merely been going through the motions of holding a convention session on Friday afternoon; their attention was constantly distracted by reports from the G.O.P. gathering. The news was indeed discouraging and after a dinner adjournment, the

Bull Moose delegates started a chant: "Why not, Why not, Why not nominate now?" It took the firm intervention of Johnson to quiet the throng and win its approval for another adjournment. And again the conference committees met until three in the morning.

The Bull Moose conferees once more stated that Roosevelt was their only choice. Reluctantly, the Republicans suggested Hughes, admitting that three of the five committee members were opposed to his nomination. After the meeting Nicholas Murray Butler went to Perkins's suite at the Blackstone and talked to Roosevelt over the private line. He told the Colonel flatly that he had no chance at the G.O.P. convention and suggested Root, Philander C. Knox, and Charles W. Fairbanks, in that order, as compromise candidates. T.R. objected to each and suggested in turn Leonard Wood and Henry Cabot Lodge. As a military man, Wood was unacceptable to a large part of the country, Butler said, but he would discuss Lodge with Perkins and the others. Perkins felt that Roosevelt's suggestion of Lodge was ridiculous but in a still later telephone conversation agreed to consider him. Pulled out of bed at five in the morning, Lodge gave Perkins approval to put his name before the Bull Moose convention.

The conference committees held a final meeting at nine on Saturday morning—but without Johnson and Parker who had bowed out of what they considered futile negotiations. The Republicans had decided that they could not stop the nomination of Hughes at their convention that morning and again offered him as the compromise candidate. Perkins countered with Lodge's name and the two groups parted for the last time without reaching a consensus.

It was Perkins's unpleasant duty, on Saturday morning, to present to the astonished Progressive delegates T.R.'s suggestion of Henry Cabot Lodge as the compromise candidate. A chorus of unbelieving noes rang through the hall. Roosevelt, Amos Pinchot felt, had done something "not merely fantastic but grossly insulting" in making such a suggestion. To him Lodge was "a staunch old-school reactionary who, as a representative of New England's industrial interests, had been fighting progressivism for thirty years." John Parker rose to demand T.R.'s immediate nomination despite Perkins's plea that they await news of the renewed Republican balloting. Losing control of the gathering, the financier angrily left the rostrum.

Bainbridge Colby made a nominating speech of less than a hundred words in which, Pinchot recalled, "there was a touch of irony"; Johnson

349

seconded the nomination; and at 12:37 P.M. the Bull Moose party by acclamation again nominated T.R. for the Presidency. Three minutes earlier, across the city, the Republicans had named Hughes on their third ballot. Charles W. Fairbanks was nominated for Vice President, the position he had held under Roosevelt from 1905 to 1909.

Hughes received news of his nomination during lunch with his family at their home on Washington's Sixteenth Street. Almost immediately he sent a messenger to the White House, only a mile away, with a terse, sixteen-word letter of resignation from the Supreme Court. Wilson, in a no less succinct reply, accepted the resignation.

Saturday afternoon, just after the Progressives had selected Parker as their candidate for Vice President, a telegram was received from Oyster Bay. "I am very grateful for the honor you confer upon me by nominating me as President," the Colonel stated. "I cannot accept it at this time. I do not know the attitude of the candidate of the Republican Party toward the vital questions of the day. Therefore, if you desire an immediate decision, I must decline the nomination. But if you prefer it, I suggest that my conditional refusal to run be placed in the hands of the Progressive National Committee." If Hughes's statements satisfied the committee that the justice's election "is for the interest of the country," his own refusal to run on a third-party ticket should be definitely accepted.

For a second time, the delegates had been stunned by a pronouncement from their beloved leader, but numbly they agreed to leave the decision to the National Committee, as T.R. had requested, and adjourned, one delegate claimed, "with the conviction that they had been betrayed."

The delegates leaving the Auditorium, Amos Pinchot wrote, were in a sullen mood; they were "a crowd without a leader." William Allen White later described the scene in a melodramatic metaphor: "We looked out across the stark ugly stretches of the dirty marsh where once our current flowed so strong, and in the agony of disillusion and despair we saw the dark rocks and the crawling things that had been underneath the ebbing tide."

3

Corinne Robinson, who had attended the Bull Moose convention in Chicago, went to see her brother in Oyster Bay as soon as she returned to New York. "Theodore—the people wanted you," she exclaimed. "It seems terrible to me that they could not have you." T.R. smiled ironically and answered, "Do not say that; if they had wanted me *hard* enough, they could have had me." William Draper Lewis and James Garfield also went directly from Chicago to Sagamore Hill, to report on the Progressive party conclave; they found the Colonel and his wife seated on the piazza on a lovely June morning. Lewis later wrote that he had never seen T.R. more serene. "There was not a trace of disappointment. We had not been with him ten minutes before our own overstrained nerves were relaxed." What sympathy there was for Roosevelt's rejection by the Republicans was, curiously enough, best expressed by William Howard Taft. "No one with any pity will wish him the agony of spirit that has been his for the last week. . . ." the ex-President wrote shortly after the conventions adjourned. "Ultimately he must cease to occupy the front pages of the newspapers. Then his cup will be full of the bitter draught."

There was never any doubt, of course, that Roosevelt would endorse Hughes. "Well, the country was'n't in heroic mood!" T.R. wrote Bamie on June 16. "We are passing through a thick streak of yellow in our national life." He told his sister that he would indeed support the Republican nominee, "with how much heartiness, his own attitude must decide." There was no alternative to Hughes, the Colonel confided in a letter to James Bryce three days later. "At his worst he will do better than Wilson, and there is always the chance that he will do very well indeed." After a week of intensive conferences, with Old Guard and Bull Moosers alike, he made it official, with a long letter to the Progressive National Committee dated June 22.

It was evident, he told the men who had once stood with him at Armageddon that the people were not prepared to accept a new party; the Progressive organization no longer offered the means to make their convictions effective in national life. "Under such circumstances," he stated, "our duty is to do the best we can, and not to sulk because our leadership is rejected." They must face the situation "good humoredly and with common sense." Hughes's public record had convinced T.R. that he was the sort of man who—as he had called for in his Trinidad statement—"will not merely stand for a programme of clean-cut straightout Americanism before election, but will resolutely and in good faith put it through if elected." The ex-justice was "beyond all comparison" better fitted than Wilson to be President and he urged his fellow Progressives to give Hughes "their ungrudging support."

The following week T.R. had dinner in New York with Hughes and on July 31 he appeared at Carnegie Hall for the ceremony notifying the former justice that he had been nominated and for Hughes's acceptance speech; it was the first Republican meeting Roosevelt had attended in more than four years and, noted Hughes's biographer, the "sweltering crowd divided its enthusiasm" between the two men.

Most Progressives followed the Colonel back into the G.O.P. fold; Perkins was one of six former Bull Moosers named to Hughes's seventeen-man campaign committee. Gifford Pinchot, James Garfield, Raymond Robins, William Allen White, Charles J. Bonaparte all eventually endorsed the Republican candidate. But there were a number of irreconcilables; and to these the isolated vice-presidential candidate, John M. Parker appealed. At a rump convention, held at Indianapolis in August, his candidacy was endorsed, although the group failed to find a presidential nominee. In the half dozen states where his name was entered on the ballot, Parker spoke in behalf of Wilson. Amos Pinchot was among a group who sought an interview with Hughes in July but came away from the chilly encounter feeling that they had made "a grave mistake in not wearing our midwinter suits." When he came out for Wilson, charging that Perkins and Roosevelt had corrupted the progressive movement, the Colonel sent him a withering note. "When I spoke of the Progressive Party as having a lunatic fringe," he wrote Amos on the eve of the election, "I specifically had you in mind."

Woodrow Wilson, of course, had been renominated by the Democrats, meeting at St. Louis in mid-June. Vice President Thomas R. Marshall would again be his running mate. Martin H. Glynn, a former Governor of New York, made his keynote address to the convention a resounding defense of the President's policy of neutrality. "This policy does not satisfy those who revel in destruction and find pleasure in despair," he stated. "It may not satisfy the fire-eater or the swashbuckler. But it does satisfy those who worship at the altar of the God of Peace." With unfeigned passion, the assembled Democrats endorsed Wilson's "splendid diplomatic victories," which had preserved the nation's vital interests and "kept us out of war."

The St. Louis convention, T.R. wrote Bamie, "was one of the most degrading spectacles we have ever seen." As much as he despised Wilson, he despised even more "our foolish, foolish people who, partly from ignorance and partly from sheer timidity and partly from lack of imagination and of sensitive national feeling, support him."

Urged by his secretary Joseph P. Tumulty and his confidential adviser Colonel House, the President had become a devout if tardy convert to preparedness. "Of one thing I am certain," Tumulty wrote his chief in the summer of 1915, "that the whole country wishes effective preparedness and will ruthlessly cast aside any man or party who stands in the way of the carrying out of this programme." The news that the President was studying the problems of national defense was published in September. Wilson, Lodge charged in a letter to T.R., had concluded that "there is a rising popular feeling for preparedness and, seeing votes in it, is prepared to take it up." In November the President announced plans for a $500 million expansion of the Navy, for a substantial increase in the Regular Army, and for the virtual elimination of the National Guard in favor of a reserve force, to be called the Continental Army, of 400,000 men. He made these plans the central theme of his annual message to Congress at the beginning of December—but then put down the reins of leadership for his marriage to Edith Bolling Galt, the fascinating Washington widow he had met and fallen in love with only seven months after the death of his first wife.

"I cannot impress upon you too forcibly the importance of an appeal to the country at this time on the question of preparedness," Tumulty wrote Wilson on January 17, 1916. ". . . Our all is staked upon a successful issue in this matter." Ten days later the President embarked on a speaking tour in behalf of his military program, a swing around the country that took him from New York to St. Louis, where—in an apparently spontaneous burst of rhetoric—he said that the United States should have "incomparably the greatest navy in the world." Even T.R. had been assuming that the American fleet need be no more than second to Britain's, just as the American land forces would doubtless be second to Germany's.

Congress proved to be a jealous defender of the National Guard, however, and Wilson was soon forced to give up his scheme for a Continental Army in favor of federalization of the state troops. Disagreeing with the President on this issue, Secretary of War Garrison—the one man in the administration at all palatable to Roosevelt—resigned and was replaced by the reform mayor of Cleveland, Newton D. Baker, an avowed foe of preparedness.

The compromise army bill that finally emerged from Congress in May was denounced by Leonard Wood as "a menace to public safety in that it purports to provide a military force of value" but did no such thing. The Regular Army was doubled, to more than 200,000 men; the National Guard, to be integrated into a system of national defense, was authorized to increase its strength to 450,000 men. On the other hand, a "big navy" bill, originally introduced by Republicans and ultimately championed by Wilson, was finally passed in August. Meanwhile, the President had agreed to lead a preparedness parade in Washington and later one in New York. As soon as motion pictures throughout the country began to show Wilson in the line of march, Joe Tumulty later wrote, the President's opponents dropped these demonstrations. "By getting into the 'front line,' " Tumulty claimed, "the President had cleverly outwitted his enemies and took command of the forces in the country demanding preparedness."

By the time of the Democratic convention Wilson could thus be depicted not only as a righteous champion of neutrality but also as a stern defender of American honor. He had both protected neutrality and upheld the freedom of the seas, said Senator Ollie M. James of Kentucky in his address as permanent chairman, "without orphaning a single American child, without widowing a single American mother, without firing a single shot, without the shedding of a single drop of blood. . . ." Woodrow Wilson in 1916 would run on the unbeatable slogan "He kept us out of war." The choice presented to the electorate was ultimately simplified as one between "Wilson and Peace with Honor" and "Hughes with Roosevelt and War."

Early in the campaign a Republican committee prepared a motion picture on the candidate. After sitting through a private screening, Hughes said that if he really looked like he did in the film his place was not in the White House but in a morgue; it had convinced *him* to vote for Wilson. The former justice realized that he would have a hard time selling his reserved and thoughtful personality to the electorate and so he determined on an extensive campaign tour—introducing the novelty of taking along his attractive wife.

Perhaps nettled by Hughes's speeches—in one, the ex-justice said *he* was not too proud to fight in defense of American rights—Wilson attempted to brush off the threat of his candidacy. "If you give that gentleman rope enough he will hang himself," the President remarked to a newspaperman. "He has forgotten many things since he closeted himself on the bench, and he will soon find himself out of touch with the spirit of the nation." His opponent's campaign addresses, he added, "are nothing more or less than blank cartridges. . . ." To Bernard Baruch he wrote that he did not believe in murdering a man who was already committing suicide, "and clearly this misdirected gentleman [Hughes] is committing suicide slowly but surely." Meanwhile, Wilson confined his campaigning to addresses before delegations invited to his summer home on the New Jersey shore, Shadow Lawn.

4

The outcome of the election, though no one perceived it at the time, was virtually predetermined by an incident that occurred in mid-August. Reaching California on his swing around the country, Hughes disdained taking a position on the Republican-Progressive quarrel that was still raging fiercely in the Golden State. "I come as the spokesman of a reunited Republican Party to talk to you of national issues—with local differences I have no concern," he told a crowd of 14,000 at San Francisco's Civic Auditorium on August 18. Hiram Johnson was seeking both the Republican and Progressive nominations for United States Senator and leaders of the two parties had urged Hughes to announce his support of the powerful but testy governor. But somehow no plans had been made in advance for the two to meet in California, even though it was probable that, with both men stumping the state, their paths would cross.

Sunday, August 20, was to be a day of rest in Los Angeles for the G.O.P. nominee and his wife. Nonetheless, Hughes began the day with a round of handshaking at the Alexandria Hotel and next attended services at the Temple Baptist Church, where he shook an additional two thousand hands. A casual drive to Pasadena brought Mr. and Mrs. Hughes to a surprise luncheon for two hundred staged by that city's Republican committee. Afterwards he shook the hands of what he later claimed was the entire population of Pasadena. And when someone suggested a side trip to Long Beach before returning to Los Angeles— "It's a lovely drive," Hughes was told—he readily assented.

Some five thousand people were waiting in front of the Virginia Hotel in Long Beach when Hughes's eight-car caravan pulled up at 5:00 P.M. The candidate and his wife briefly retired to a suite made available to them but were soon called out to shake hands again. They had chance for but a glimpse of the sun setting over the Pacific before getting back in their car for the return to Los Angeles. At least it appeared that the two would have the evening to themselves. But then a delegation materialized to invite Hughes, who had not even had dinner, to a meeting being held in his honor at the First Methodist Church and of course he had to go. Exhausted, he returned to the hotel at 10 P.M. and received some stunning news from a campaign aide. That afternoon the Virginia Hotel in Long Beach had had another famous visitor: Governor Hiram Johnson.

Hughes demanded to know why he had not been told of the governor's presence. "If I had known that Johnson was in the hotel," Hughes exclaimed, "I would have seen him if I had been obliged to kick the door down." The Republican candidate immediately dispatched an emissary to Long Beach but Johnson's feelings apparently were injured beyond remedy. As the crowds eddied about the G.O.P. candidate, the governor had waited impatiently in his hotel room for the invitation to join Hughes that had never come. Now, Hughes had to leave on a midnight train for San Diego; Johnson resumed his own campaign; and the two never met in California. Johnson later endorsed the Hughes candidacy but, according to some sources, advised his Progressive supporters to do nothing to aid the Republican national ticket.

Roosevelt, whether Hughes actually wanted such active support from him or not, made his own strenuous contribution to the Republican effort. One of his first appearances back in the orthodox fold was at a reception for Hughes on October 3 at the Union League Club in New York. Among the other guests that evening was Taft.

The two met in the club's library. "We shook hands with a Howdy Do and that was all," Taft wrote to his wife. Chauncey Depew stood between the two former presidents in the reception line; Root, Hughes, and Roosevelt all addressed the meeting—T.R. speaking six minutes longer than the G.O.P. nominee, Taft maliciously noted; and all the leading participants descended to the street floor in the same elevator. Taft joked that they were going to elect Wilson to the ex-presidents' club; Roosevelt answered, "Yes, we'll not blackball him for that." Taft waited until T.R. had left the elevator and the two went out into the night without any further exchanges. A week later when he heard that the Colonel was going to campaign as far west as Arizona, Taft sourly noted, "I am glad of it. The further he goes away the better." The four-year-old wound was definitely not healed.

"I am now being worked to the limit by the Hughes people," T.R. wrote his sister Corinne at the beginning of October; these were the very people, he added, "who four months ago were explaining that I had 'no strength.' " But he wanted Hughes to win; he would not sulk and would put his time entirely at the disposal of the Republican National Committee.

Only three reporters accompanied the Colonel on his trip west; one of them, Edwin N. Lewis, noted in a letter to his mother that T.R.— who would turn fifty-eight en route home—looked older than he used to. "At times, in the thick of the excitement, an expression of fatigue flashes across his features. There is a touch of sadness too, I believe, in his face, as he looks out over these crowds of people who have come for miles just to see him." Roosevelt, the irrepressible candidate, was no longer running himself nor supporting someone he warmly believed in. This for him was the most negative of all his campaigns, one directed simply and forcefully against the hated Wilson. Out West, concluded young Lewis in another letter to his mother, the crowds were for *Roosevelt,* not for the Republican party. ". . . if Mr. Hughes is elected on November 7th," T.R. confidentially told the reporters on his campaign train, "I shall never be seen in politics again. I am through." To another reporter, who called later at Sagamore Hill, he repeated the prediction. After Hughes's inauguration, if that should occur, he would "just be an elderly literary gentleman of quiet tastes and an interesting group of grandchildren."

The Colonel spoke at the Brooklyn Academy of Music on October 28, the day he returned to New York; four days later he was in Ohio; and on November 3—four days before Election Day—he gave the climactic address of his campaign in behalf of Charles Evans Hughes. The setting was New York's Cooper Union, the hall from which in 1860 Abraham Lincoln had launched his drive to the Presidency.

The title of Roosevelt's address was "The Soul of the Nation," and near the end of the speech he put aside his manuscript and spoke extemporaneously and passionately to the hushed assembly. Wilson, he noted, was dwelling at Shadow Lawn. "There should be shadows enough at Shadow Lawn," he charged; "the shadows of men, women, and children who have risen from the ooze of the ocean bottom and from graves in foreign lands; the shadows of the helpless whom Mr. Wilson did not dare protect lest he might have to face danger; the shadows of babies gasping pitifully as they sank under the waves; the shadows of women outraged and slain by bandits; the shadows of . . . [American] troopers who lay in the Mexican desert, the black blood crusted round their

357

mouths, and their dim eyes looking upward. . . . Those are the shadows proper for Shadow Lawn; the shadows of deeds that were never done; the shadows of lofty words that were followed by no action; the shadows of the tortured dead." In place of the man in the White House, "who has wrought such shame on our people," he urged his listeners, "let us put in the Presidential chair the clean and upright justice of the Supreme Court, the fearless governor of New York . . . who will do what is right no matter what influences may be brought against him."

It is an oft-told tale that Charles Evans Hughes went to bed on Election Night, November 7, thinking that he had been elected President; the returns from the East were overwhelmingly in his favor. Actually, according to his biographer, Hughes retired that night, thinking only that his election "seemed probable." Earlier in the evening, the pro-Wilson New York *World* had put out a special bulletin conceding the election to Hughes. "Well, Tumulty," Wilson said over the telephone to his secretary, "it begins to look as if we have been badly licked."

It was actually Wilson who retired thinking that *he* had been defeated. But while he was shaving the next morning, his daughter Margaret knocked on the door to say that *The New York Times* in an extra was claiming the election was in doubt. The electoral count stood: Wilson, 251; Hughes, 247. Four states, including California, were still to be heard from. Not until Friday morning would the count be completed to reveal that Hughes had a final total of 254 electoral votes to Wilson's 277. The Republican nominee had lost California by only 3,806 votes; while Hiram Johnson was being elected senator by 300,000 votes.

Not everyone blamed the G.O.P. defeat on Hughes's failure to shake hands with Johnson in Long Beach. A group of dissident New York Democrats, who had been supporting Hughes, wired ironic congratulations to Roosevelt. T.R., they claimed, had "contributed more than any other person in America" to Wilson's victory; he had given the President a million votes and should be rewarded with a Cabinet post.

"This was my year—1916 was my high twelve," the Colonel is supposed to have remarked to newspaperman John J. Leary two days after the election, when news of Wilson's victory came. "In four years I will be out of it. This was my year to run. I did not want to run in 1912. Circumstances compelled me to run then. This year it was different." Taft did not agree that his great rival was out of contention for the Presidency, as he would have been if Hughes had been elected. He would be sixty-one when the next G.O.P. convention was held. Already, Taft wrote a friend on November 19, T.R. was "planning again for 1920. . . . He is like an old man of the sea on the back of the Republican party."

Four years of apparent inactivity lay ahead, far too long a span of time for the restless Colonel. To Henry Fairfield Osborn of the American Museum of Natural History he wrote on December 5 about "a Polynesian trip which I would greatly like to take next year." Edith Roosevelt would go to the South Seas with him and he wanted the voyage to be a scientific expedition like his trips to Africa and Brazil, this time to gather marine specimens. He would be gone six to eight months and write again for *Scribner's.* "I believe I could make a trip that would be worth while. . . ."

⇜❧ *Chapter 17* ❧⇝

Services to Render

T *he man* who tracked grizzly bears in the Rockies, caught cattle thieves in the Dakotas, bagged his lion in Africa, and explored an unknown river in Brazil; the man who quarreled with the pope, lectured the Kaiser, and advised kings; the man who added new dimensions to the Presidency during his seven and a half years in office—that man always felt that the dramatic highpoint of his life had been reached on a blistering July afternoon in the summer of 1898. For Theodore Roosevelt his "crowded hour" took place outside Santiago, Cuba, as he led his Rough Riders up San Juan Hill. It was indeed a spirited fight, the most hotly contested land engagement of that splendid little war—the only war in America's half century of peace between the Civil War and World War I. And Colonel Roosevelt had rallied his men for the charge with fearless if not almost reckless courage.

Visiting the battlefield some years later, Edith Roosevelt drily remarked that San Juan Hill did not appear nearly as large and steep as she had been led to believe; and the humorist Finley Peter Dunne claimed that the Colonel's book on the Rough Rider campaign should have been entitled *Alone in Cubia.* T.R., nonetheless, was convinced that his had been an exploit of true heroism. Self-righteously and utterly shamelessly he lobbied, first in private then in public, for the Congressional Medal of Honor he so earnestly believed he merited. The nation's highest military award was denied him—purely for political reasons, Roosevelt remained convinced; for he had dared to criticize the War Department for unpreparedness in peacetime and for inefficiency and mismanagement of the ultimate war effort. T.R. always maintained that he had no regrets in his life but this applied only to the actions he had taken; his failure to win the Medal of Honor rankled deep within him ever after.

"The trumpet call is the most inspiring of all sounds," he wrote in October, 1908, to a youth leader who had requested an inspirational statement, "because it summons men to spurn ease and self-indulgence and timidity, and bids them forth to the field where they must dare and do and die at need." Martial metaphors crackled through much of Roosevelt's speeches and writings; his political campaigns were figuratively waged with rifle and bayonet, as if the spilling of blood was inevitable if not actually desirable. In the last decade of his life, T.R. sounded many a trumpet blast—and mostly waited in vain for a response. As 1917 opened, it was Roosevelt who waited for the summons.

Following his election to a second term on the slogan "He kept us out of war," Woodrow Wilson—in T.R.'s jaundiced view and colorful phrase—allowed the nation "to drift stern foremost" into World War I. In December, 1916, the President attempted to get the belligerents to state their war aims, as a possible first step to mediation of the dispute by the United States. Rebuffed by both sides, Wilson went before Congress on January 22, 1917, to call for a "peace without victory" in Europe and a concert of powers, in which America would join, to keep the peace. Germany's answer, delivered a week later, was that she would resume unrestricted submarine warfare on February 1. On February 3, Wilson announced that he was breaking diplomatic relations with Germany. Although hostilities between the two countries were not declared until two months later, Roosevelt considered the nation already at war —a war in which he must be permitted to serve.

In December, 1908, T.R. had written to Kaiser Wilhelm II, whom he had not yet met, about some of his feelings as he prepared to leave the Presidency. It was unlikely that he would ever hold office again, he told the German emperor; but if the United States should ever be engaged in a big war, "while I am still in bodily vigor," he would try to get permission to raise a division of mounted rifles—a force "such as the one I commanded in the war with Spain." He hoped, however, that the chance would never come.

Two years after he had left office, in March, 1911, during one of America's recurring crises with Mexico, the Colonel had asked his successor, Taft, for permission to raise a cavalry division to fight south of the border. And three years later, after the Tampico and Vera Cruz incidents of April, 1914, once more brought the United States to the brink of war with Mexico, the Colonel again thought of raising his division but again only in the case of a "serious war." The attitude of the Wilson administration, he confided to an old friend, made it doubtful that he would ever get to the front. Finally in July, 1916, following yet new disturbances along the border, T.R. wrote to Wilson's Secretary of War, Newton D. Baker, asking permission to raise and command a division in the event of war with Mexico. When news of Roosevelt's offer was published, he was so deluged with offers to serve under him that he had to ask Regis Post to undertake the full-time job of answering this correspondence.

To Roosevelt, however, Mexico was but a secondary theater; the real front by that time, of course, was in Europe. As early as the summer of 1915, he had already formulated the composition of the cavalry division that he hoped to take across the Atlantic. It would consist of four cavalry brigades, of two regiments each; a brigade of horse artillery of two regiments; a regiment or battalion of machine guns; one or two pioneer battalions; and a field battalion of signal troops in addition to motorized supply and ammunition trains and a sanitary train. Captain Frank R. McCoy of the Regular Army would be his chief of staff with the rank of colonel. He also had in mind the names of most other staff and line officers for the division. "Probably we wouldn't fight with horses, but in trenches," he conceded. In September, 1915, he wrote Arthur Lee, by then his closest confidant in England, he had "the whole skeleton of my Division worked out; and I would guarantee to bring it over in ninety days if I were given the chance; and I would guarantee that it would do its duty when brought over. . . ."

A year passed and there was still no war in which Roosevelt could serve. Lee joined by David Lloyd George urged T.R. to visit England and write a series of articles on the British war effort. The Colonel replied to the suggestion on November 10, 1916. Since it looked as if Wilson had been re-elected, it would be "deception" to represent to the English people that his own words carried any weight. Moreover, it was useless to give any advice or express any opinion as to what America's conduct toward the war should be; the President would "certainly endeavor to do exactly the opposite of what he thought I had indicated. . . ." He would like to come to Europe at the head of his cavalry division, he wrote Lee—"but not otherwise."

On February 2, 1917, T.R. took lunch with Oscar Straus at the Hotel Langdon in New York. Discussing Germany's announcement of the resumption of unrestricted submarine warfare, the Colonel said he thought that Wilson would find a way to avoid war. He had just booked passage, for himself and Edith, on a United Fruit Company steamer to Jamaica; the two needed a change, he told Straus. Meanwhile, Roosevelt had sent to Secretary of War Baker a reminder that he had on file in the War Department his application to raise a division. He was ready to cancel his trip to the Caribbean; but even if he sailed the following week, he was ready to return immediately "if and when it becomes certain that we will have war, and that there will be a call for volunteers to go to war. . . ." Baker replied the next day—the day Wilson broke relations with Germany—stating that no situation had arisen justifying a request that Roosevelt cancel his trip. "Your letter and its suggestion will be filed for consideration should occasion arise." T.R. nonetheless canceled the voyage to Jamaica and so informed Baker on February 7. If allowed to raise his division, the Colonel pledged, "I should of course strain every nerve to have it ready for efficient action at the earliest moment, so that it could be sent across with the first expeditionary force, if the Department were willing." He asked Baker to appoint Captain McCoy as his chief of staff and send him to Oyster Bay to confer on the formation of the division.

Reading of his predecessor's request, Taft wrote to an English friend that he doubted Roosevelt's ability to command, though Wilson might think it wise to unite public opinion by giving T.R. what he wanted. But he concluded that the "Presbyterian hater in the White House will have to see more clearly than he does now before yielding and giving to Theodore the stage of the world for the building of another presidential campaign."

Wilson's Secretary of War was now drawn into a protracted and what he must have considered an unpleasant and unnecessary correspondence with Roosevelt. On February 9 Baker told the ex-President that the War Department could not act on his request "without the express sanction of Congress." In the event of war, he added, Congress would doubtlessly complete legislation relating to volunteer forces.

Sensing that his route to the front was to be blocked, the Colonel tried a new tack. On February 16 he wrote to Jules Jusserand and Cecil Spring Rice, the French and British ambassadors to the United States and both old friends of his. In cooperation with the two allies, he offered to raise a division of Americans to fight under either the French or British flag; he could hoist his standard in Canada. "As for myself," he told

Jusserand, "at this time I think I could do this country most good by dying in a reasonably honorable fashion, at the head of my division in the European War." However, he did not intend to die, he added, "if it can be legitimately avoided. . . ." He was going to have his hands full in getting to the front at all, he confided to the French ambassador, "with the dreadful creatures we have at Washington." To Hiram Johnson he wrote that he anticipated "heartbreaking experiences" over his request to raise a division.

The United States Senate, in which Johnson was soon to represent California, was engaged in a final struggle with the President over American neutrality. On February 26 Wilson asked Congress for authority to arm merchant vessels, as a deterrent against attack by German submarines. The House of Representatives promptly and overwhelmingly passed the Armed Ship Bill but a determined group of pacifist senators—seven Republicans and five Democrats—filibustered until the bill expired with the second session of the Sixty-fourth Congress on March 4. Frustrated and infuriated, Wilson gave the press an uncharacteristically intemperate statement: "A little group of willful men, representing no opinion but their own, have rendered the great Government of the United States helpless and contemptible."

The senators, T.R. complained to Cal O'Laughlin, had "reached a lower depth than the President has reached—but it is only a little lower—because he is so low that there isn't much room to get lower." To Senator Lodge he wrote that he regarded Wilson as "far more blameworthy than the 'willful' Senators. . . ." If the President did not soon go to war with Germany, T.R. threatened, "I shall skin him alive." Striking out at a convenient target, he raged against Hughes "and the folly of those who nominated Hughes, having cursed this country with the really hideous misfortune of four years more of Wilson in this great and terrible world crisis!"

Wilson almost immediately determined that he did not need congressional authority to arm merchantmen sailing through war zones and on March 13, through the Navy Department, authorized such vessels to defend themselves against submarine attack. But the President's "armed neutrality" was never to have an opportunity of being tested. On Sunday, March 18, news was published that German submarines had sunk three American vessels, with the loss of fifteen lives on one ship. Roosevelt demanded that war be declared, and Wilson heard from his

Cabinet two days later a unanimous recommendation that the United States at last fight.

Appearing before a special session of Congress on April 2, the President asked for a declaration of war. "There is one choice we cannot make, we are incapable of making," Wilson told the legislators; "we will not choose the path of submission and suffer the most sacred rights of our Nation and our people to be ignored or violated." The recent acts of Germany, he continued, were nothing less than war against the United States; the nation must now "formally accept the status of belligerent which has thus been thrust upon it. . . ." The nation would be glad, Wilson said in winding up to his peroration, "to fight thus for the ultimate peace of the world. . . . The world must be made safe for democracy." At the end of his thirty-six minute speech, Wilson was greeted with a standing ovation, the senators, congressmen, and other assembled dignitaries cheering wildly and waving tiny flags. The exhilarated but emotionally drained President returned to the White House. "Think of what it was they were applauding," Joe Tumulty remembered his chief as saying. "My message to-day was a message of death for our young men. How strange it seems to applaud that."

At news of the three submarine sinkings in mid-March, T.R. had wired Baker that "In view of the fact that Germany is now actually engaged in war with us, I again earnestly ask permission to be allowed to raise a division for immediate service at the front." After some six weeks of preliminary training in America, he proposed to take his division directly to France for more intensive training before being assigned to the front. He asked permission to assemble his men at Fort Sill, Oklahoma, and offered to raise money himself to bear the costs of arming and maintaining the men until Congress could act. He requested by name a chief of staff (McCoy was no longer available) and three brigade commanders and one additional regular officer for every eight hundred to one thousand men in the division. Baker wired a terse reply the next day, March 20. No additional armies could be raised without specific authorization by Congress. No obligations for future expenditures in excess of appropriations could be entered into unless authorized by law. A much larger army than the force Roosevelt suggested was under consideration. General officers for all volunteer forces were to be drawn from the Regular Army.

That evening the Colonel was among those speaking in favor of immediate war at a meeting held at New York's Union League Club. After the speeches were over, a small group including Charles Evans Hughes and Elihu Root gathered in the club's grill room. Roosevelt elaborated on his plans for the division and asked each man present to help him win Wilson's approval. If he were sent to the front, T.R. claimed, he did not expect to return; most probably he would be buried in France. Root assumed a serious expression and asked Roosevelt to repeat the assertion. He did so, with great feeling. "Theodore," Root declared, "if you can convince Wilson of that I am sure he will give you a commission."

2

Patiently but with some urgency, T.R. wrote once more to Baker, on March 23. He understood that a force far larger than a division would be called out; he merely wished to raise his division "for immediate use in the first expeditionary force sent over." Respectfully, he pointed out to the secretary that he was a retired Commander in Chief of the United States Army; as for his fitness to command troops, he referred Baker to his superiors in the Spanish-American War, Leonard Wood and two other generals, now retired. Baker replied that Roosevelt's military record was, of course, on file in the War Department. "The patriotic spirit of your suggestion is cordially appreciated."

En route home from a fishing trip to Florida, Roosevelt stopped in the capital on April 2, the day Wilson delivered his war message. Before returning to New York, the Colonel made an unscheduled appearance at the White House, found that the President was in a Cabinet meeting, and issued a statement hailing the message as "a great state paper . . . of which Americans in future years will be proud." It would be necessary to send troops abroad as soon as possible, he continued. "Defensive war is hopeless. We must by vigorous offensive warfare win the right to have our voice count for civilization and justice when the time for peace comes." He concluded by stating his earnest hope that he be allowed to raise the division "for immediate service at the front."

Back home in Oyster Bay, T.R. began to fret about the administration's failure to accept his offer. "I am making no headway, and I won't so long as I try to do business with Mr. Wilson by letter," he told newspaperman John J. Leary. "It's too easy to shunt me [to] one side. He won't find it so easy talking to me face to face." He still was not certain the President would give in to him, he added, "but I'll give him an argument anyway." Roosevelt was back in the capital on the evening of April 9, again with no appointment to see Wilson, according to Leary, but convinced that the President would not dare to snub him. Nonetheless, he had told the reporter that he wanted to avoid any appearance of storming the White House.

The Colonel made the Longworth home his campaign headquarters. Joe Tumulty telephoned on the morning of the tenth to say that Wilson would see his predecessor at noon. Alice drove him there and returned home to await news of the interview.

The President and the ex-President both must have drawn upon whatever reserves of impassivity they possessed to avoid acknowledging the rivers of ill will that flowed between them. It was the first time the two had met since the Colonel visited the White House upon his return from Brazil in the spring of 1914—before war had erupted in Europe and before the Colonel had begun to criticize the administration so vociferously and so persistently. T.R., as usual, had the vivid metaphor: "Mr. President," he began, "what I have said and thought . . . is all dust in a windy street. . . ." Wilson, Roosevelt later reported, received him pleasantly enough, and the two had an hour's talk. The Colonel again congratulated him on his war message and said that he only "wanted a chance to help him make it good." He found it necessary, however, to explain in detail his plans for the division; although he had written "plainly enough" about it, he found "some confusion" in Wilson's mind as to what it was he wanted to do.

Before leaving, Roosevelt reminded the President that reporters were waiting outside and that he would be "bombarded with questions"; he would say only what Wilson allowed him to say and asked that Tumulty be called in to witness the statement. When the President's secretary arrived, T.R. slapped him heartily on the back, complimented him on having six sons, and asked him to join the division—he promised a safe berth at headquarters. Wilson later confided to Tumulty that he had been charmed by the Roosevelt personality. "There is a sweetness about him that is very compelling," he said. "You can't resist the man."

Outside the White House, T.R. spoke to reporters. "The President received me with the utmost courtesy and consideration," he said, "and, doubtless, in his own good time will come to a decision. . . ." In private, he was not so cheerful. "If any other man in the world had talked to me as Mr. Wilson did," he remarked to Leary, "I would say I was sure to go. But it was Mr. Wilson who was talking and I am not at all confident."

Later in the day Baker called on Roosevelt at the Longworth home, and the Colonel took him upstairs for a private conversation. Among the callers that day were Lodge, Jusserand, Spring Rice, and the chairmen of the Senate and House military affairs committees. The following morning, before returning to New York, he breakfasted with General Joseph E. Kuhn, one of the three Regular Army officers—the others being Wood and John J. Pershing—he proposed as commander of the expeditionary force to which his division would be attached.

On the twelfth Roosevelt wrote to Baker to say how greatly he had enjoyed their conversation and appreciated the secretary's courtesy in calling upon him. If he were a younger man, he told Baker, he would be willing to go to the front in any position, "as a second lieutenant, or as a private"; at his age, however, he could do good service only as a general officer. He had nearly been rejected for service in the Spanish-American War because of his poor eyesight, which would have been "nonsense." As for the position he now sought, "the physical examination does not apply, so long as I am fit to do the work, which I certainly can do—that is enlisting the best type of fighting men, and putting into them the spirit which will enable me to get the best possible results out of them in the actual fight." The German commander in chief, Field Marshal von Hindenburg, he reminded Baker, was a retired officer who had not passed a physical examination. He did not claim to be a Hindenburg, but he knew he could raise and lead the division "in a way that will do credit to the American people, and to you, and to the President." With his letter to Baker, he enclosed copies of letters sent that day to House and Senate committee chairmen in which he supported the administration's draft bill and urged additional legislation to permit the raising of volunteer forces—legislation under which he would ask to be allowed to raise his division.

Baker also followed up his conversation with Roosevelt by writing a letter, dated April 13. He had thought earnestly about their talk and had reached some conclusions "which, I think, in frankness, I ought to indicate to you." The War College Division of the General Staff had recommended that no American troops be sent to the front until adequately trained. All Regular Army and National Guard officers would be needed to train the levies called out by the draft. The national policy should be "to devote all our energies to raising troops in sufficient numbers to exert a substantial influence in a later stage of the war." Partially trained troops would be unfit for such duty. The recommended policy, Baker continued, did not "undertake to estimate what, if any, sentimental value would attach to a representation of the United States in France by a former President. . . ." There were "doubtless other ways in which that value could be contributed apart from a military expedition." The composition of any expeditionary force sent to Europe should be determined by "military considerations alone." The secretary, therefore, would be "obliged to withhold my approval from an expedition of the sort you propose." Baker, unquestionably speaking for Wilson, had said no; but Roosevelt was not going to accept the decision gracefully.

In two long letters, dated April 23 and May 8, Roosevelt elaborated upon his reasons for wanting to raise the division and poured forth his longing to join the fight in Europe. He had not asked the secretary to consider any "sentimental value" in granting his request; he was speaking of moral effect, not of sentimental value. "Sentimentality is as different from morality as Rousseau's life from Abraham Lincoln's." If the nation had begun preparing for war two and a half years ago—it was needless to say as he had urged—there would be no need for a volunteer force now. "Nine tenths of wisdom is being wise in time. But we were not wise in time. . . . Let us not advance our unwisdom in the past as a justification for fresh unwisdom in the present." A town without a fire department should be willing to fight a fire with any means at hand.

The cautious, time consuming policy Baker outlined, the Colonel bluntly stated, came from "doubtless well-meaning military men, of the red-tape and pipe-clay school, who are hidebound in the pedantry of that kind of wooden militarism which is only one degree worse than its extreme opposite, the folly which believes that an army can be improvised between sunrise and sunset."

Once more, he reviewed his own war record and said that he was "best fitted" to be a division commander in an expeditionary corps. If the secretary desired, he would accept a lesser position, brigade commander. He renewed his request to raise the division not only because he desired to serve the country under the President and under Baker, "but because I am certain that in this way I can render the best service." In his reply, Baker said that, "stripped of personal considerations," the questions raised by Roosevelt were simple ones to answer; and the answer again must be no. Roosevelt's next letter was an even more detailed outline of his plan for a division, as if there were still some hope for it. And Roosevelt now had some encouragement, from an impartial source, that did indeed appear to offer a faint hope that he would be going to France.

Jusserand had responded promptly and favorably to his offer of February 16 to fight under the flag of France. Although greatly pleased, Roosevelt replied that he could not do so until his country was actually a belligerent. Shortly after the declaration of war, both France and England sent special missions to the United States to urge that an American expeditionary force be dispatched to Europe at once. Speaking for France, as strongly as diplomacy allowed, Marshal Joseph Joffre joined Jusserand in urging that Roosevelt lead that force. Corinne Robinson recalled tea one afternoon at her home in New York, during which her brother spoke poignantly to his old friend the French ambassador of his desire to lead the division. The President need not fear him politically, T.R. affirmed. "If I am allowed to go, I could not last; I am too old to last long under such circumstances. I should *crack* but I *could* arouse the belief that America was coming. . . . That is what I am good for now, and what difference would it make if I cracked or not!"

Roosevelt, moreover, still had political allies in Washington. To the administration's draft bill Senator Warren Harding of Ohio proposed an amendment—promptly dubbed the Roosevelt Amendment —providing for the enlistment of four volunteer divisions. Hiram Johnson rose to support Harding's amendment and answer another senator who had spoken contemptuously of "the Roosevelt division." "What is it that is asked for . . . ? It is asked only by a man who is now really in the twilight of life that he may finally lay down his life for the country that is his." Roosevelt, Johnson continued, "has red blood in his veins and he has the ability to fight and he has the tenacity to win when he fights, and that is the sort of an American that is needed and required in this war."

Applications to serve under Roosevelt were soon coming in at such a rate that a special office was set up on Fifth Avenue to handle the correspondence. By May 7, T.R. reported that he was receiving up to two thousand applicants per day; he was confident he could raise a quarter million troops. Among those Roosevelt claimed for his division were Henry Stimson, James Garfield, Raymond Robins; descendants of Phil Sheridan, Stonewall Jackson, and Nathan Bedford Forest; Jonathan M. Wainwright and William J. Donovan, who would win fame in World

War II; T.R.'s cousin George Roosevelt and his son-in-law Richard Derby. "I ask only that I be given a chance to render a service which I know I can render. . . ." he told a Brooklyn gathering on the eighth. In private Roosevelt was pessimistic. "I wish there was a chance of my going with a division," he wrote Owen Wister on May 10, "but this Administration is playing the dirtiest and smallest politics, and I don't think they have the slightest intention of letting me go."

Meanwhile, the draft bill had passed both houses of Congress, the Senate version including Harding's amendment. Despite pressure from the administration, the conference committee recommended adoption of the amendment and the House concurred. "The vote," T.R. told Leary, "does not mean that I am commissioned, not by a jugful. It does open the door, but that might have been opened any time Mr. Wilson wished it opened." He still hoped for the best, Roosevelt remarked to the reporter a few days later, and he was still exchanging letters with Baker. The secretary had changed his mind so rapidly, T.R. stated, that he "reminds one of the fly wheel of an engine." The "dear little fellow" was not to blame; he was trying to defend a bad case.

On May 16 Governor Charles S. Whitman of New York offered to make Roosevelt a major general in the National Guard. If the state troops were nationalized, T.R. would have a chance to get to Europe that way. The Colonel went to Albany to talk it over with the governor but declined the proposition.

John M. Parker of Louisiana, the candidate for Vice President on the aborted Progressive ticket in 1916 and another volunteer for the Roosevelt division, called at the White House on May 17. He came to criticize the President, "because you are my hired man, just as you are the hired man of the people." In the whole world, Parker claimed, there was "no greater autocrat or more arbitrary ruler" than Wilson. He begged him not to play politics with Roosevelt's request. The President barely contained his anger. He was not playing politics, but he had made up his mind. Roosevelt was "an admirable man and a patriotic citizen, but he is not a military leader."

The next day Wilson signed the draft bill and T.R. promptly wired a request directly to the President requesting permission to raise a volunteer division under terms of Harding's amendment. "I very much regret that I cannot comply with the request in your telegram of yesterday," the President replied, and referred Roosevelt to a statement given out that morning, the nineteenth. It would be "very agreeable" the President said, to pay Roosevelt the compliment, "and the Allies the compliment of sending to their aid one of our most distinguished public men, an ex-President who has rendered many conspicuous public services and proved his gallantry in many striking ways." This was not the time, Wilson continued, to pay compliments. "The business now in hand is undramatic, practical, and of scientific definiteness and precision."

Stimson later described Roosevelt as being surprised, dumbfounded, astonished by the refusal; he believed that it had never really entered T.R.'s head that he would not eventually be able to serve. Seth Bullock said he felt "like hell about the whole thing" and so did the rest of the volunteers. The Colonel felt worst of all, the Dakotan said, but he was too proud to let on. "I did want to ride a spotted cayuse into Berlin, but it don't look now as if I would," Bullock sadly concluded. In all his years of service, Roosevelt's valet James Amos had only twice before seen the Colonel really angry. But this decision, Amos wrote, "wounded him to the quick." His idolized master "was really in a state of great depression such as I seldom saw him in." O. K. Davis, meeting Roosevelt at the Harvard Club shortly after Wilson's refusal had been made known, wrote that he had never seen the Colonel "in a blacker mood." His offer, he told Davis, had been one of his very life and had not received the courteous consideration to which it had been entitled. "He was angered to the core."

On May 21 T.R. issued a bitter statement in the form of an open letter to all those who had volunteered to serve in his division. The President's decision left him with no course but to "disband and abandon all further effort . . . thereby leaving each man free to get into the military service in some other way, if that is possible. . . ." To the various men who had helped in his recruiting efforts he wrote four days later, thanking them for their assistance. From the standpoint of the country, he regretted that their services were not to be utilized. "But the country has every reason to be proud of the zeal, patriotism and businesslike efficiency with which you came forward."

As for his personal ambitions, he next prepared an application to be submitted directly to the President. His "training, experience and qualifications" fitted him for a line and not staff position, especially "for the work at the front." He understood that his age, fifty-eight, barred him from serving in any rank below that of brigadier general. If this were not so, or if the President could waive the regulation, he would serve in any position available for the duration of the war. "After much thought, and considerable irresolution," he wrote a friend on June 6, the petition was shelved. Although the Colonel still wished to render service, he did not want to be in a position where Wilson "would treat me as an importunate and self-seeking beggar." There would be no war for Theodore Roosevelt.

Roosevelt later published his complete correspondence with Baker and Wilson in the *Metropolitan.* The President's reasons for refusing his offer, he concluded, "had nothing to do either with military considerations or with the public needs." As for Wilson, he remained adamant against Roosevelt's participation in the war effort. It was suggested that the former President be added to the special commission being sent to investigate conditions in revolutionary Russia. He could not "in any circumstances," Wilson declared, consider sending Roosevelt anywhere to represent the administration.

A final word came from across the seas. Georges Clemenceau, soon to become French Prime Minister, published an open letter to Wilson. In all candor, he told the President, there was in France "one name which summons up the beauty of American intervention. It is the name of Roosevelt, your predecessor, even your rival but with whom there can now be no other rivalry than heartening success. . . ." The soldiers of France needed "something approaching a miracle." It was in Wilson's power to give them at least the promised reward—"send them Roosevelt," Clemenceau begged. Wilson was unmoved.

Less than two months later, on July 4, the first troops of John J. Pershing's American Expeditionary Force, having arrived in France, paraded through the streets of Paris. Ecstatically, Frenchmen cheered the boys in khaki who held the promise of turning the tide against Germany and called out to them—the nickname "doughboys" not yet having gained currency—"Vive les Teddies!"

3

"My four sons will be with me," Roosevelt told an English friend in the summer of 1915, if "Wilson makes up his mind at last that we must fight Germany. . . ." The Roosevelt division, as the Colonel envisioned it, was to be something of a family affair. That summer Theodore, Jr., Archibald, and Quentin trained at Plattsburg. Kermit had returned to

South America with his bride, Belle Willard, the year before but promised to come straight home if war were declared.

He had always explained to his boys, T.R. had written Rudyard Kipling late in 1914, that if there was a war in their lifetime, he wanted them to be able to explain to their children why they did fight, rather than why they did not. ". . . I should be ashamed of my sons if they shirked war," he wrote on another occasion, "just as I should be ashamed of my daughters if they shirked motherhood."

On April 14, 1917, the week after the United States entered the war, the Roosevelt family gathered at Boston for the wedding of Archie to Grace Lockwood. Quentin was best man; Ted, Kermit, and Ethel's husband, Dick Derby, were ushers. Somehow they sensed that this was the last time they would all be together; at least until the war was over. "We were all as cheerful as might be," Alice Longworth recalled; "but there was little of the gaiety of the other family weddings."

As hope of being able to raise and lead his own division faded, the Colonel stepped up his campaign to get his boys to the front as soon as possible. For a time he feared that politics would block these efforts as well. "His bitterness at that was inexpressible," wrote O. K. Davis. As the result of his Plattsburg training, Ted, twenty-nine and the father of three children, had a major's commission in the Officers' Reserve Corps; twenty-three-year-old Archie was a captain. On May 20 T.R. wrote to congratulate John J. Pershing on his appointment to command the American Expeditionary Force; as President, he had advanced Pershing's promotion to brigadier general over many of his seniors and was thus in a position to ask a favor.

A third summer at Plattsburg would do the two young men little good, Roosevelt told Pershing. Since the President had announced that only officers of the Regular Army were to go with the A.E.F. initially, he asked that his first and third sons be allowed to enlist as privates. They were "keenly desirous" to serve; if they did get to the front and were not killed, they would be able to return in the fall to help train the draft army. "If I were physically fit, instead of old and heavy," Roosevelt added in a postscript, "I should myself ask to go under you in any capacity down to and including a sergeant. . . ." At his age and condition, he sadly acknowledged, he could not be considered capable of any worthwhile service in the fighting line—"my only line"—below the grade of brigade commander. Pershing and his chief of staff, James G. Harbord—a man formerly slated for the Roosevelt division and to whom T.R. had also appealed in behalf of his sons—felt that it would be a waste for Ted and Archie to resign their reserve commissions and enlist. In his farewell conversation with Baker at the War Department, Pershing asked the secretary if he would grant his request should Pershing cable from France for the two Roosevelt boys. "Certainly," Baker replied. By July, both were in France as officers in combat units.

"The big bear was not, down at the bottom of his heart, any too happy at striving to get the two little bears where the danger is," Roosevelt acknowledged to Ted before he and Archie left; "elderly bears whose teeth and claws are blunted by age can far better be spared. . . ."

Quentin was nineteen in 1917, Edith and Theodore Roosevelt's youngest, a fey and clever lad who received all the attention the baby of any family does. At first he planned to join the Canadian air force in order to get overseas quicker. But his father, when there was some delay over waiving the oath of allegiance that might have jeopardized his son's citizenship, had him enlist in the United States Army Signal Corps. The corps' small aviation section was the nation's only air force at the time. T.R. wrote to Baker about his son's assignment to Fortress Monroe, and the secretary—in the midst of his controversy with the ex-President—replied that "it will give me great pleasure to think that your boy is there and a part of our establishment." Quentin was later transferred to the army flying field at Mineola, Long Island, where he completed his training in July. He could get over some evenings to Sagamore Hill, bringing with him his fiancée, Flora Payne Whitney.

Kermit, twenty-seven and the father of one son, went to Plattsburg in the spring of 1917. But the Colonel feared that this would be too slow a route to the front for his second son, the beloved and faithful companion of his African and Brazilian adventures. On June 18 he wrote to Arthur Lee, asking his closest English friend a special favor. Kermit's hunting and exploring activities and his construction and bridge-building work in South America "fits him for work in the open, in such a campaign as that in Mesopotamia." Yet he might be kept in the United States training conscripts "if I cannot get him sent by you to the Tigris land." He asked for Kermit a second lieutenant's commission in the British Army and that he not be asked to forswear his allegiance to the United States. ". . . I ask that he be permitted to render service to your flag as well as to my own. Will you try to help me, old friend?" A formal request was forwarded through British Ambassador Spring Rice "to avoid all chance of miscarriage."

With the assistance of Lee and David Lloyd George, Kermit was given a British commission, as captain in the motorized machine gun corps in Mesopotamia. The answer came to the Colonel and he accepted in behalf of his son "eagerly and gratefully." "Like Artemus Ward [the Civil War humorist] I am straining every nerve to get all my wife's relations to the front!" the Colonel wrote Ted, explaining that his sons were, after all, his wife's relations.

Alice Longworth remembered the summer of 1917 as one of constant excitement and suspense, with the family getting reports almost daily as to when each of the boys would sail for Europe. First to go were Ted and Archie on June 20. The family had lunch at Sherry's and then went to the pier "to say the casual good-bys that one says at times like that."

The next to leave was Eleanor, Ted's wife. She had tried to be gay when her husband sailed and "not show him what I was feeling." It was the couple's seventh wedding anniversary. The next month she volunteered to serve with the Y.M.C.A., which was in charge of recreational work for the A.E.F., sailing on July 24 just before a regulation forbidding soldiers' wives to go to France went into effect. Ted had advised her against coming and her father-in-law had "emphatically" declared that no women in the Roosevelt family were to follow their husbands abroad. Sitting on the piazza at Sagamore Hill one evening after Ted left, Eleanor finally summoned the courage to tell T.R. of her plans. "Darling, I see you have made up your mind," he said. "I don't know of anything I can do to help you, but if you can think of something you must let me know."

Shortly afterward, it was announced that President Wilson's son-in-law was joining the Y.M.C.A. in France. "How very nice," the Colonel told reporters who had asked for a comment. "We are sending our *daughter-in-law* to France in the Y.M.C.A!" Eleanor and Ted's three children—five-year-old Grace and two younger boys—would be left with Eleanor's mother; but the toddlers would make Sagamore Hill a second home for much of the next year and a half.

When Kermit left for England, to accept his commission before going out to the Near East, he took his wife, Belle, and their eighteen-month-old son, Kermit, Jr. (Kim), with him. Belle later took the baby to Madrid, where her father was still serving as ambassador. Alice's farewell present was castor oil, baby food, and a tiny life preserver for Kim;

she recalled them all jammed into a taxi on the way to the pier and the lid of the baby's training seat dropping off when they got out.

Finally it was Quentin's turn to leave—and there was only Edith, Theodore, and Alice to say good-bye. All her brothers were now gone, Alice reflected, and she knew how "bitterly hard" it was for her father not to be with them. Often she would repeat to herself a couplet: "The old Lion perisheth for lack of prey, and the stout Lion's whelps are scattered abroad."

At Sagamore Hill the Roosevelts hung a flag with four stars in the window—and to it soon added a fifth. In September, 1914, a month after the outbreak of war, Ethel's husband, Dr. Richard Derby, had gone to France to serve in the American Ambulance Hospital in Paris. Ethel joined him and worked as a nurse before they returned in December. Derby had trained two summers at Plattsburg and had also been slated for the Roosevelt division. Now, in the summer of 1917, he received his commission and went to Fort Oglethorpe, Georgia, for training; Ethel left their two children—three-year-old Richard, Jr., and an infant daughter, Edith, with her parents and joined her husband. Derby sailed for France in November and became division surgeon of the A.E.F.'s Second Division. Ethel brought her children to Sagamore Hill, where, T.R. wrote his son-in-law, she thoroughly enjoyed seeing them grow up in the home where she had grown up.

"Well, I am *very* proud of you—and of all my boys," T.R. wrote Ted in August. "And my only personal consolation is that I was in the only war I had a chance at, even altho it was only a small one." Faithfully and cheerfully, he kept sending a steady stream of letters to his far-flung family—although he admitted to Ted that it was difficult to find anything to write of; ". . . all seems trivial compared to the real work, the work of all of you at the front." And later he reminded his eldest son that he was having his "crowded hours of glorious life; you have seized the great chance. . . ." Eagerly he awaited letters from the boys; he could not get enough news of their activities. "Lord, what a good time we'll have when we are all together again! " he wrote Archie in September. There would be all kinds of things that would have to wait the telling, he wrote Ted two months later, "until the young vikings come back and gather around the old hearthstone."

377

Chapter 18

Another Part of the Great Adventure

Early in 1915 an old friend in a sentimental and reflective mood had written to the Colonel, reminding him of the good old days. T.R. commented on the man's attitude in a letter to Spring Rice. His friend, it was evident, was thinking too often of those days "when, even if we were not all of us completely carefree, we all of us had youth and the power of looking forward that gives youth its unconquerable spirit." The true way to look at things, Roosevelt declared, was to realize how fortunate one had been in life: ". . . we have encountered troubles and at times disaster and we cannot expect to escape a certain grayness in the afternoon of life—for it is not often that life ends in the splendor of a golden sunset."

Wilson's refusal to let him fight in the war, Roosevelt was convinced, denied him that splendor of a golden sunset; after May, 1917, he was forced to walk through a gray afternoon—his vision perhaps somewhat impaired by the gloom but his courage in facing the uncertain and the unknown by no means daunted.

Roosevelt's calendar of activities for the rest of 1917 was certainly not that of a man in retirement. He continued to be sought out by the various allied missions visiting the United States and he accepted invitations to address such groups as the American Medical Association, the Railroad Brotherhood and Order of Railway Telegraphers, the Red Cross, the Loyal Order of Moose, the National Security League, the Columbia County (New York) Fair, and the American Friends of Russian Freedom. He not only addressed gatherings held to promote the successive Liberty Loans, he invested heavily in them himself. In October he took out $60,000 worth of bonds, a substantial dip into his own capital. ". . . I putter round like . . . the other old frumps, trying to help with the Liberty Loan & Red Cross and such like," he wrote Quentin. Saturdays, later in the war, became open-house day at Sagamore Hill for visiting soldiers and sailors, whom the Roosevelts delighted in entertaining.

The ex-President toured the Great Lakes Naval Training Station in Illinois and visited various army training camps; at the Mineola, Long Island, field where Quentin had received his initial instruction, he went up in a Liberty motor airplane. And wherever he spoke and whatever he wrote, he continued to criticize the Wilson administration—a continuation of the relentless barrage that had been lifted only momentarily when he was seeking permission to raise his division. Attempts were eventually made, early in 1918, to curb Roosevelt. Included in a bill reported out of the Senate Judiciary Committee was a provision for imprisoning anyone who used "contemptuous or slurring language about the President." The lower house of the Delaware legislature came within one vote of passing a resolution calling for T.R.'s arrest because he had "severely criticized the conduct of our National Government."

The general theme of his criticism was expressed in an address delivered on June 14, 1917, at the semi-centennial celebration of Nebraska statehood held at Lincoln. For two and a half years, the Colonel charged, fine phrases had been used to cover ugly facts. The nation had "unctuously protested" its devotion to liberty in the abstract while failing to come out against German brutality or even daring to act when its own innocent women and children were murdered on the high seas. The national policy had been swayed by traitors who prostituted their citizenship to the interests of Germany or to their hatred of England. The moral fiber of the country had been damaged by the professional pacifist and peace-at-any-price propaganda. "At last, thank Heaven, we came to our senses, realized our shortcomings, and tardily did our duty. At last we spurned the mean counsels of timidity and folly. At last we showed that we were not too proud to fight. . . ."

Yet America, "utterly unprepared" for war, would now be forced to fight without adequate preparation. The country must prepare as well as it could at this late date; "and the most important of all forms of preparedness is spiritual preparedness."

This brought T.R. to the vanguard of a new crusade, one in behalf of 100 per cent Americanism—a crusade that seems in retrospect unfortunate at best, not for its underlying justification but rather for the intemperance with which it was waged. "In this country," Roosevelt affirmed at Lincoln, "we must have but one flag, the American flag, but one language, the English language; and above all, but one loyalty, an exclusive and undivided loyalty to the United States. . . ." Patriotism under stress, alas, often becomes heedless and undiluted chauvinism. In the months to come T.R. would call for simultaneous publication in English of all articles in the German-language press and then for the suppression of German periodicals altogether; for the prohibition of the teaching of German in public schools; for the forced repatriation of immigrants who did not learn English within five years; for the dismissal of teachers who refused to sign a loyalty oath. He did draw the line, however, at barring from Red Cross service abroad Americans born in Germany or Austria-Hungary and those whose parents were born there. The Colonel's scorn for hyphenated Americanism was not a pose assumed for the occasion but rather a magnification and an articulation of long-held views. He had argued against a divided loyalty even in the years before he became President. It was his undeviating opinion that a man had to be either German or American, Irish or American—never a German-American or an Irish-American.

The American people, Roosevelt claimed in a newspaper article published early in September, were the children of the crucible. "The crucible does not do its work unless it turns out those cast into it in one national mould. . . ." In October he gathered together a number of his recent speeches and articles for publication in book form, a volume for which Edith supplied the title, *The Foes of Our Own Household*. The book was dedicated by Edith and Theodore "To Our Sons and Daughters"; the dedications embraced daughters-in-law and a copy went to Flora Whitney to indicate that she too was included. "In the long run," the Colonel wrote in the foreword, "we have less to fear from foes without than from foes within; for the former will be formidable only as the latter break our strength."

On a swing through the Midwest in late September, T.R. had come to Kansas City, Missouri, where he visited the offices of the Kansas City *Star*. The late founder and editor of the *Star*, William Rockhill Nelson, had been "for Roosevelt, first, last, and all the time" from the day they met when T.R. was running for Vice President in 1900 until Nelson's death in April, 1915; and he made his influential newspaper one of the staunchest and most insistent supporters of Roosevelt in the nation. Nelson's successor had approached the Colonel earlier in the year with a proposition. T.R. was continuing to contribute his monthly articles to the *Metropolitan,* but the pressing daily problems created by the war demanded the more immediate comment that only newspaper publication offered. The columns of the *Star* were his, for as frequent and as uninhibited comment as he wished to make.

"You, of course, know what you're doing," T.R. said of the offer. "Many people do not like my ideas and probably many of your subscribers will be perfectly furious at The Star for printing my editorials." The *Star* was not worried about this problem and it was shortly agreed that Roosevelt would contribute at least two signed editorials per week, of about five hundred words each—a limitation the Colonel felt it might be difficult for him to accept. No contract was signed but it was decided that the arrangement should run from October, 1917, to October, 1919, the eve of another presidential year. He would telegraph his editorials from Oyster Bay, or wherever he might be traveling, to Kansas City, and the *Star* would set them in type for simultaneous publication in about fifty additional papers.

Roosevelt's three-year contract with the *Metropolitan* was about to expire but he agreed to continue contributing short monthly articles for an annual fee of $5,000. The *Star* would pay him $25,000 per year. "About all I can do now is to earn what money I can for Archie, & perhaps Quentin, during the war, and have things ready for them to start after the war," T.R. wrote Ted.

Appearing at the *Star* offices on September 22, T.R. was shown a desk reserved for him and immediately sat down to write out in longhand, "with much scratching and interlining," his first editorial for the newspaper. During his Midwestern tour, he visited Camp Funston, Kansas, and was horrified to observe that recruits were being trained with mock cannon made of wood and broomsticks in place of rifles. In an early *Star* editorial he lashed out at "broomstick preparedness" and later at "broomstick apologists" when the War Department attempted to brush off his criticism and spoke of "perfectly endurable delay." The nation had been at war six months by early October; six months was a "perfectly endurable delay" only if the nation were content to accept the speed standards of Pharaoh Necho, T.R. thundered. "The United States must learn to adopt the war speed standards of the Twentieth Century, A.D., instead of those of the Seventh Century, B.C."

The editorials were printed just as he had written them; any changes in copy were made only after consulting with the author. On two occasions, however, the *Star* considered it inadvisable to publish Roosevelt's contributions, although it did agree to transmit them to other papers. "I am not dead sure that the prophet business can be combined with keeping up circulation," he wrote the editor of another paper subscribing to his editorials; a man with such strong feelings as his was "apt to get cater-cornered as regards the surrounding world. . . ." Now approaching sixty, he should perhaps cease being a prophet "and become that far pleasanter and more innocuous person, a sage." But Roosevelt, of course, would never be a sage. After reading a *Star* editorial, the mayor of Abilene, Texas, wrote that T.R. was "a seditious conspirator who should be shot dead"; the editor of the paper who published his articles should be tarred and feathered.

A favorite target of Roosevelt's, not unexpectedly, was Newton D. Baker. On June 7, the Secretary of War was quoted in an official bulletin as saying that there was "difficulty . . . disorder and confusion . . . in getting things started." And, most unfortunately, he added: "But it is a happy confusion. I delight in the fact that when we entered this war we were not, like our adversary, ready for it, anxious for it, prepared for it, and inviting it. Accustomed to peace, we were not ready." Meanwhile, Wilson's Secretary of the Navy, Josephus Daniels, said that the Navy was not doing anything about new weapons "until we know whether we are going to fight an offensive or a defensive war." T.R.'s scorn knew no bounds. "Apparently, it is proposed to continue our policy of unpreparedness in the future because it has not brought us to destruction in the past," he wrote in the *Metropolitan*. A half year after entering the war, the United States was still relying for its own protection on the British fleet and on the French and British armies. "No American worth his salt can look these facts in the face without shame and alarm." To his fellow Americans, Roosevelt preached the sword of the Lord and of Gideon in a great war for righteousness. "The test of our worth now is the service we render. Sacrifice? Yes, as an incident of service; but let us think only of the service, not of the sacrifice. There never yet was a service worth rendering that did not entail sacrifice; and no man renders the highest service if he thinks overmuch of the sacrifice."

"Why cry over spilt milk you say?" he asked in a lecture delivered at Princeton in November. "Because now is the time to provide that it shall not be spilt in the future; and we never shall so provide if we complacently ignore the fact that it has been spilt in the past." Baker had just said that in another six months the United States would "show a record of preparedness and achievement that will challenge the world's admiration." "Perhaps!" T.R. replied. "It depends upon what the world feels like admiring." Brag is a good dog, he was fond of quoting, but Holdfast is a better.

Other favorite targets of Roosevelt's were the Milwaukee socialist Victor Berger, radical labor leaders such as Big Bill Haywood, the new Bolshevist leaders of Russia and their American supporters, William Randolph Hearst, and Robert M. La Follette. Anything the Wisconsin senator now proposed, T.R. regarded with deepest distrust, he told Senator Frank B. Kellogg of Minnesota; but he hoped that neither of them would let such distrust "warp our judgment if we found that for some doubtless bad reason he happened on some one point to advocate something good." The Colonel later supported a move to have La Follette expelled from the Senate because of his opposition to the war effort.

In October T.R. went to Jack Cooper's training camp at Stamford, Connecticut, to "lose a little weight and get a little wind." He returned to Sagamore Hill to celebrate his fifty-ninth birthday on October 27 and to revel in a visit from the three children of Ted and Eleanor. He wrote to his daughter-in-law of taking the three "to that haven of delight, the pig pen" and sliding them down a hay rick "until I finally rebelled."

Alice and Nick Longworth came to Sagamore Hill for Christmas, arriving in time for Christmas Eve services at the little Oyster Bay Episcopal church. T.R. joined the family in decorating a tree, principally for the benefit of Ethel's three-year-old son, Richard. "We did not have a gloomy Christmas," Alice recalled, "—it simply was not Christmas at all."

As winter settled in over Long Island, the huge North Room at Sagamore Hill was closed off; logs kept blazing in the small library made that room a cosy place for Edith and Theodore to sit and read or write. "I am kept very busy writing, and occasionally speaking, always on behalf of the war," the Colonel wrote Quentin; "so long as we are still in the talky-talky stage some one has to do the talky-talky on the right side." His "modest function," he told Kermit, was to tell "disagreeable truths which ought to be told but which it is very unpopular to tell and which nobody else will tell." His only wish, he added, was to keep going "until all of you get back and take up your own lives, and until Quentin marries Flora. . . ." Only then would he retire. ". . . it is not wise to linger superfluous on the stage; and it is worse to be sour and gloomy and forecast all kinds of evil. . . ." Moreover, he lamented to Archie, he was no longer in sympathy with the bulk of his fellow countrymen, "and therefore am no longer fit to lead. . . ."

At the end of January, 1918, Edith and Theodore Roosevelt spent four days in Washington. "I was kept on the jump," T.R. wrote Quentin upon his return to Oyster Bay, "literally without a minute's intermission, seeing Senators, Congressmen, publicists, army officers and the like, and had no time to be melancholy. . . ." They stayed at the Longworths, where Alice, leaning over the banisters from upstairs, counted thirty-three newspapermen in her small front hall at one time. "The house was a rallying point for all those Republicans, and some Democrats, who were dissatisfied with Wilson's conduct of the war," she wrote. Nick held a stag dinner for his father-in-law; one of the guests reported to Alice that "many backbones were stiffened."

Suddenly, there was talk of 1920 and the need for T.R. once more to take up leadership of the G.O.P. To all who asked if he wanted their support, Roosevelt informed William Allen White, he replied that he was not seeking any support "either now or at any future time; all I am concerned with is that you should so act that *I* can support *you*."

2

The euphoria of the Washington trip evaporated almost immediately. At the beginning of February T.R. once again suffered an attack of the fever that he had originally contracted in Cuba and which had brought him near death on the perilous journey down the Rio da Dúvida in 1914. While in bed at Sagamore Hill he developed abscesses in his thigh and ear. On the sixth he was admitted to Roosevelt Hospital in New York for an emergency operation. Although the operation was judged successful, complications made his illness a serious one. Rumors spread that T.R. was dying and the New York *Tribune* published a brief editorial: "Theodore Roosevelt—listen! You must be up and well again; we cannot have it otherwise; we could not run this world without you."

Edith, Ethel, Alice, T.R.'s secretary Josephine Stricker, and a private nurse were all required to handle a deluge of letters, telephone calls, and visitors that threatened to engulf the hospital. Messages of sympathy and cheer poured in from around the world, from George V of England, from Clemenceau of France, and from William Howard Taft. Corinne Robinson was at his bedside at a particularly dark moment as her brother asked her to lean close so he could whisper a final message: "I am so glad that it is not one of my boys who is dying here," he said, "for *they* can die for their country."

The Colonel soon rallied, however, and by February 15 was receiving visitors and dictating long personal and political letters. His trouble had been "entirely trivial," he told Kermit. "I have taken a somewhat sardonic amusement in the real panic that affected a great many people when for a moment it looked as if I might not pull through." Those who had been bitterly opposed to him for the past three-and-a-half years, he claimed, suddenly realized that "maybe I represented what down at the bottom of their hearts they really believed to be right. . . ." To Lord Bryce he later wrote that he "never did care a rap for being sick"; at a time when so many young men were dying, "the fate of a retired, elderly civilian seems to me singularly unimportant." The illness, nonetheless, left him permanently deaf in the left ear, an impairment not as serious, of course, as the earlier loss of sight in his left eye.

On March 4 the Colonel was moved to the Hotel Langdon and three days later he returned to Sagamore Hill. And once more he became thoroughly enmeshed in political affairs. Just before going into surgery T.R. had written a letter of support to Will H. Hays of Indiana who was seeking the chairmanship of the Republican National Committee. When Hays was elected, George Perkins—insinuating himself back into the party—claimed that this was a victory for progressives and that the G.O.P. would be forced to nominate a progressive for President in 1920. Furthermore, he led reporters to believe he was Roosevelt's official spokesman. *The New York Times* then claimed that Perkins was already organizing an effort "to draft the Colonel for the big national contest." T.R. immediately wrote "Dear George" to remind him that "I speak for myself."

T.R.'s emergence from the hospital, he later complained to reporter John J. Leary, was "the signal to pile invitations to work on me. Really it seems as though one half of the letters congratulating me on my recovery conclude with an invitation to speak here, there, anywhere. There are hundreds of them." One invitation he accepted with alacrity, that of the Republican National Committee to address the Maine party convention in Portland on March 28. He sent drafts of the speech to Lodge, to Root, and to Taft. Once more, it was "Dear Will" and "My dear Theodore," as the friends-turned-enemies came together in their opposition to Wilson's conduct of the war. "We have strongly agreed as to the President," Taft told his brother, "and that I think is the chief bond between us. . . . Life is too short to preserve these personal attitudes of enmity, and I am glad to have the normal status resumed."

Roosevelt's speech in Maine, "Speed Up the War and Take Thought for After the War," was widely distributed as the first major campaign document of the 1918 congressional elections. And before long the Colonel was once more on the campaign trail. On May 24 he left Oyster Bay for a week's speaking tour of the Midwest; two days later he was at Chicago's Blackstone Hotel, dining alone.

Entirely by coincidence, Taft arrived to check in at the hotel and learned that his predecessor was in the dining room. He asked to be shown to the Colonel's table, shook hands with Roosevelt, and sat down at his table. A cheer broke out from other guests and people rushed from the lobby to the dining room entrance to see what it was all about. Taft later reported that T.R. looked well but was forced to listen with great intensity in order to hear well. Roosevelt told Leary that he "never felt happier over anything in my life." The news of the cordial meeting would be in all the morning papers, the reporter reminded the Colonel; it would be notice that the Republican party was reunited. "I believe you are right," T.R. said with a laugh. "It is too bad to spoil Mr. Wilson's breakfast!"

By this time Roosevelt had yet another cause to resent and scorn the President and his Secretary of War. In March, 1917, on the eve of the declaration of war against Germany, Leonard Wood's Eastern Department of the Army had been broken into three commands and he had been transferred to a new, lesser post at Charleston, South Carolina. It soon became apparent that the Democratic administration had no intention of using the Army's senior general in the war. Roosevelt considered that his old friend had been found quilty by association.

"The failure to use Leonard Wood has been due to Wilson's steady and inflexible purpose to carry this war out on the narrowest political grounds," he wrote Lord Bryce early in May, 1918. Worse was to come. On the twenty-fourth of that month, en route to New York to embark for Europe with the division he had been training, Wood was relieved of his command and posted to San Francisco. T.R. promptly wrote in the *Star* of the "cruel injustice" done to the general. Wilson and Baker contended that Pershing did not want Wood in his command, but the public protest was so great that the general was eventually allowed to train another division—though he never did get to the front with it. In a wry reference to Wilson's 1916 campaign slogan, a cartoonist depicted Roosevelt and Wood with the legend: "Well, he kept *us* out of war." "There isn't a man in this country," T.R. would write his friend later in the year, ". . . who has been treated as unjustly; all I beg is that you hold your horses and don't let these creatures have any excuse for putting you in wrong."

Roosevelt made another extensive speaking tour in early June and then settled down for the summer of 1918 at Oyster Bay. As absorbed as he had been in his renewed political activity that spring, T.R. continued to live vicariously with his four sons overseas. A heckler had interrupted T.R.'s speech the previous year before a patriotic rally at Madison Square Garden, asking the Colonel what he was doing for the war effort. Roosevelt quieted the storm of boos and shouts to put the man out. Looking into the darkness of the auditorium, in the direction from which the voice had come, he answered. "What am I doing for my country in this war? I have sent my four boys over there. I have sent my four boys, for each of whose lives I care a thousand times more than I care for my own, if you can understand that. . . ." A hush fell over the vast throng and then came the ovation for the proud but sad and lonely figure on the platform.

Early in 1918 news arrived that Kermit had taken part the previous November in the British capture of Tekrit, Iraq. "Three cheers!" T.R. wrote his old side-partner. "You have proved yourself; you have made good. . . . It *is* better than to be drilling drafted men with wooden cannon here at home, isn't it?" With the winter campaign in Mesopotamia ended, Roosevelt pulled strings to get Kermit transferred to the A.E.F. in France, "foxily" arranging to have him report to Madrid so that he could briefly be reunited with his wife, Belle, their son, Kim, and a second boy just born. Awarded the British Military Cross for his service in the Near East, Kermit eventually was assigned to the same infantry regiment in which Ted served.

Roosevelt had earlier expressed his concern when Archie was transferred to his older brother's unit, writing of the "inadvisability, other things being equal, of one brother being in immediate command of another." There was the risk that any achievement of the younger one would be set down to favoritism. Happily, the Colonel had nothing to fear as Archie—commanding a company in Major Ted Roosevelt's battalion—soon proved his worth. Preparing to lead an attack in March, Roosevelt's third son was severely wounded by shrapnel in his left leg and his left arm. News reached Sagamore Hill that Archie had been awarded the *croix de guerre* by the French. At lunch Edith ordered some madeira and then, "her eyes shining, her cheeks flushed, as pretty as a picture, and as spirited as any heroine of romance," the Colonel wrote Archie, dashed her glass to the floor and the others at the table followed suit. He and Archie's mother, T.R. added, were "divided between pride and anxiety, beloved fellow."

At first it was feared that Archie's leg would have to be amputated; next it was discovered that a nerve in his broken arm was severed and shrunken. He was moved from a front line hospital to Paris, operated on again in July, and sent back to the United States in September. Upon his return, he was introduced to Archibald, Jr., born the preceding February—the eighth Roosevelt grandchild.

In Paris Eleanor was serving as mother hen to the Roosevelt brood. She had a steady stream of visitors—her husband Ted, Archie, Quentin, later Kermit; Dick Derby and his brother Lloyd; three Roosevelt cousins, George, Philip, and Nicholas Roosevelt. At a dinner party she met General Pershing. "How do you happen to be here anyhow?" snapped the American commander. No wives were allowed to come overseas; her place was home with her children. Eleanor left the party feeling as if she had been spanked, but later the general, hearing of her good work with the Y.M.C.A., apologized and asked to be friends.

An unexpected visitor to Eleanor's Paris apartment on June 2 was Ted. She had never seen anyone look so ghastly, Eleanor later wrote. "His face was scorched and inflamed, the whites of his eyes an angry red. He was thickly covered with dust and shaken by a racking cough." At Cantigny a few days earlier he had been gassed. He had only come to Paris to see that his wife was safe; there were rumors that the Germans —in their last great drive of the war—were about to take the French capital. The two visited Archie in the hospital, Ted got a restless night's sleep—propped up in bed with pillows to keep from choking —and returned to the front the next morning. Three weeks later, Eleanor read in the Paris *Herald* that her husband had been cited for gallantry.

Speaking at St. Louis on June 10, T.R. told his delighted audience of a remark recently made to him about his sons by Finley Peter Dunne. "Colonel, you want to watch out," the humorist had said. "The first thing you know they'll be putting the name Roosevelt on the map."

On July 19 Ted was back at his wife's apartment, cheerily announcing that he had been shot in the leg at Soissons that morning and wearing on his shirt a tag reading "Gunshot Wound Severe." He insisted the wound was nothing but Dick Derby, walking in by chance shortly thereafter, thought otherwise. He and Eleanor took Ted in a taxi to a military hospital where he was operated on that evening. Serious damage to his leg had been avoided but T.R.'s eldest son never again had feeling in that heel. He was soon walking about on crutches, however, and in September was assigned to the General Staff College at Langres.

Quentin was the last of the Roosevelt boys to get into combat. His training as a flyer was slow and had its own hazards. In December, 1917, he came down with pneumonia. Given a three weeks' sick leave, he went first to the Riviera, found it cold and wet, and returned to Paris to be with his sister-in-law.

At Sagamore Hill they did not yet know of Quentin's illness. "Mother, the adamantine," T.R. wrote his youngest son on December 24, "has stopped writing to you because you have not written to her— or to any of us—for a long time." This was perhaps not so important but what was important, the Colonel lectured, was Quentin's failure to write to his fiancée, Flora Whitney. If he wanted to keep Flora, he must write her "interesting letters, love letters" at least three times a week. "Write no matter how tired you are, no matter how inconvenient it is; write if you're smashed up in a hospital; write when you are doing your most dangerous stunts; write when your work is most irksome and disheartening; write all the time! Write enough letters to allow for half being lost." The letter was signed, "A hardened and wary old father." By the end of January T.R. could tell Quentin that his letters were "more than satisfactory," but he still urged his son to write first to his fiancée. In March he suggested that Quentin ask permission of the Whitneys for Flora to go to France to marry him; "even if he were killed," the Colonel explained to his sister Bamie, "she and he would have known their white hour. . . ." It proved impossible to cut through red tape, however, and Flora remained at home.

Early in July Quentin finally saw his first combat, brought down a German airplane, and went to Paris to celebrate with Eleanor. They dined together and attended the theater. The next morning Quentin returned to the front. "Well, Quentin too is at least at the front," the Colonel told Dick Derby; "and his part is one of peculiar honor and peril."

And to Ethel, vacationing with her children in Maine, he wrote, "Whatever now befalls Quentin he has now had his crowded hour, and his day of honor and triumph."

3

Toward evening on July 16 the resident correspondent of the Associated Press at Oyster Bay, Phil Thompson, appeared at Sagamore Hill. The New York *Sun* had received a cryptic message from a reporter at the front; heavily censored, the cable read only, "Watch Oyster Bay for. . . ." "Have you any idea what it means?" Thompson asked the Colonel. "Something has happened to one of the boys," T.R. replied. It could be neither Ted nor Archie, he speculated; both were recovering from wounds. Kermit, en route from Mesopotamia to France, had not yet reached the front. It must be Quentin. He did not want to say anything that night to Edith, however.

The next morning Thompson was back at the Roosevelt doorstep, tears in his eyes. Quentin was dead, shot down behind enemy lines. The Germans had buried him with full military honors. "I must tell his mother," the Colonel said grimly. Only a few minutes later he emerged and handed the correspondent a simple statement: "Quentin's mother and I are very glad that he got to the front and had a chance to render some service to his country and to show the stuff there was in him before his fate befell him." Later Edith expressed concern for her husband to a sympathetic Thompson. "We must do everything we can to help him," she said. "The burden must not rest entirely on his shoulders."

A short time earlier the editor of the Paris *Matin* had paid a call on the Colonel before returning to France from his visit to the United States. He asked Roosevelt for a message he could take back across the Atlantic. "I have no message for France," Roosevelt said; "I have already given her the best I had. But if, over there, they speak of me, tell them that my only regret is that I could not give myself." In 1915 T.R. had written William Allen White that he must continue to make his living by his pen. "I don't care to go into any work that will take me beyond the time when Quentin, my youngest son, is launched into the world. . . ." Quentin would have been twenty-one on November 19, 1918.

Messages of sympathy came from Wilson, George V, Clemenceau, Pershing. When he and Mrs. Roosevelt saw the four boys sail from their native shores, Roosevelt told the king, they did not expect them all to return. "It is a very sad thing to see the young die," he wrote Clemenceau, "when the old who are doing nothing, as I am doing nothing, are left alive." "I would not for all the world have had him fail fearlessly to do his duty, and to tread his allotted path, high of heart, even altho it led to the gates of death," T.R. wrote his daughter-in-law Belle. "But it is useless for me to pretend that it is not very bitter to see that good, gallant, tenderhearted boy, leave life at its crest. . . ."

The boy's mother would carry the heartache to her death, he knew. The last night Quentin had slept at Sagamore Hill, she had gone upstairs to tuck him into bed; he was still her baby. His great dread now was the arrival of letters Quentin had written before his death. Later he vetoed plans to publish Quentin's letters home and to raise a monument in Oyster Bay. His youngest son's letters were "only such letters as many, many other gallant, clever, manly and gentle boys wrote home—just as our loss is merely like countless other such losses," he told Corinne. To the man who proposed a monument, he said that "our loss is irreparable but to the country he is simply one among many gallant boys who gave their lives for the Cause."

At the end of July the Roosevelts joined Ethel in Maine. The only person capable of making her husband merry after Quentin's death, Edith later recalled, was Ethel's year-old daughter Edie. From Maine T.R. replied to a message from the novelist Edith Wharton: "There is no use of my writing about Quentin; for I should break down if I tried." But he had Quentin very much in mind when he wrote an article for the October, 1918, *Metropolitan,* an article that later served as the first chapter of his fourth and final book of wartime writings, *The Great Adventure.* "Only those are fit to live who do not fear to die," he began "and none are fit to die who have shrunk from the joy of life and the duty of life. Both life and death are part of the same Great Adventure." Learning of the War Department's plan to return to the United States all the American dead in France, the Colonel entered a "most respectful, but a most emphatic" protest. He and Edith agreed with the clergyman they had once known, who was fond of saying, "where the tree falls, there let it lie." After the war, he and Mrs. Roosevelt planned to visit the gravesite in France, put up a small stone, and leave funds for local people to maintain the grave.

On July 18, the day after he received news of Quentin's death, T.R. was scheduled to speak at the Republican state convention at Saratoga Springs. Corinne and Douglas Robinson had planned to meet him there, but his sister called now to see if she should instead come to Sagamore Hill. "Of course not—I will meet you in Saratoga as planned," he fairly snapped over the telephone. "It is more than ever my duty to be there." A group of dissident Republicans, including Corinne's son Theodore Douglas Robinson, then a state senator, was opposed to the renomination for a third term of Governor Charles S. Whitman. Their candidate: Theodore Roosevelt—a suggestion endorsed by Root, Taft, and Hughes, among others. The Colonel spoke at Saratoga, but on the train back to New York he confided to Corinne that he had only one more fight left in him; ". . . I think I should reserve my strength in case I am needed in 1920." In a telegram published in *The New York Times* on July 22 he stated that he could not be a candidate for nor accept the nomination for governor.

Despite his refusal to run for governor, T.R. was inevitably drawn into the fall campaign. He endorsed a number of candidates around the country and accepted several speaking engagements. Emerging from the hall in Columbus, Ohio, where he had just endorsed the Fourth Liberty Loan, Roosevelt was surrounded by an emotional group of gold star mothers. "We must not weep," he told the women. "Though I too have lost a dear one, I think only of victory. We must carry on no matter what the cost." On the train back to New York an attendant saw him sitting with an open book on his lap. But he was not reading. Staring out the window, as if in a trance, he muttered under his breath, "Poor Quinikins!"

Owen Wister visited Sagamore Hill in October and found himself speaking mostly of the past with his old friends. T.R. often lapsed into uncharacteristic silence. "When I went to South America," he told the novelist, "I had only one captain's job left in me. Now I am good only for a major's." To John J. Leary the Colonel complained about the pace of campaigning that year. "The usual committee idea is to pass me along to the next town as nearly dead as possible, always taking pains to see that I do not die on their hands."

At the height of the campaign Wilson issued a call for the return of Democratic majorities to both houses of Congress. The election of a Republican majority to either house would "certainly be interpreted on the other side of the water as a repudiation of my leadership." Roosevelt exploded. "I hope every citizen," he said in a public telegram, "will vote in such fashion that never again in a great war will a President of the United States try to turn his high office into an electioneering rostrum for one party without regard to the interests of the country." A Democratic newspaper called for a Congress that would see eye to eye with Wilson. "But only a Congress of whirling dervishes could see eye to eye with Mr. Wilson for more than twenty-four hours at a time," the Colonel wrote in the *Star;* it was impossible to keep up with what he considered the President's rapid changes of policy.

Forgotten were his own speeches, twenty years earlier, in behalf of Republican candidates at the end of the Spanish-American War. A refusal to sustain President McKinley, he had then claimed, would be viewed by Europe "as a refusal to sustain the war and sustain the efforts of our peace commission to secure the fruit of war." The end of a war was not time "for divided councils," Roosevelt had said in 1898.

What angered the Colonel most about Wilson's call in 1918 was the President's failure to distinguish between prowar and antiwar candidates; he was asking for the election of senators and congressmen merely on the basis of their party affiliation. At the same time, however, T.R. was supporting for re-election Senator John W. Weeks of Massachusetts, whom he admitted was "a reactionary by conviction." Weeks, he confided, was "a good deal like an Egyptian mummy; but after all he is a mummy who loves his country, and he will fight the cold-blooded, selfish, and tricky creature now at the head of the nation, who does *not* give a rap for the country." For Theodore Roosevelt there were still no shades of gray.

Wilson, to Roosevelt's further rage, had been exchanging notes with Germany concerning an end to the war based on the "fourteen points" outlined in the President's speech of the preceding January. "Let us dictate peace by the hammering guns and not chat about peace to the accompaniment of the clicking of typewriters," T.R. exclaimed in a statement for publication on October 24. Wilson's fourteen points were "thoroly mischievous and if made the basis of a peace, such peace would represent not the unconditional surrender of Germany but the conditional surrender of the United States." They were nothing more than "fourteen scraps of paper," he charged in the *Star.* Why was Wilson negotiating separately with Germany? Roosevelt asked. Why was he not consulting with the Allies, whom Wilson, incidentally, referred to merely as "associates" of the United States?

The results of the election of November 5 were a signal triumph for Roosevelt; in the new Congress the Republicans would control the Senate by two votes and the House by fifty. "Under these circumstances our allies and our enemies, and Mr. Wilson himself, should all understand that Mr. Wilson has no authority whatever to speak for the American people at this time," he wrote in the Kansas City *Star.* The election had been a "stinging rebuke," he said in a letter to Ted a few days later. In any parliamentary system of government the President would have been forced to resign. It was a victory, he noted in the *Star,* for all those who "put loyalty to the Nation above servility to a political leader." T.R.'s reaction to the outcome was typically excessive—as unfair as Wilson's call for a Democratic Congress had been unwise. Whatever the makeup of the new Congress, Wilson was still President; other chief executives had managed to govern with the opposition in control of the legislative branch. And such joyful vituperation from so prominent a rival as the Colonel would weaken Wilson's bargaining power in the peace negotiations to come. Yet Roosevelt clearly saw that the President's defeat provided the Republican party—and perhaps him as well—with a great opportunity.

Even before the congressional elections there had been renewed talk of Roosevelt in 1920. Boies Penrose of Pennsylvania, admitting that he had once despised T.R., now said that the Colonel was the leading candidate for the Republican presidential nomination two years hence. Senator Weeks told Alice Longworth that her father was "the only man in sight"; campaign funds were already pledged, a Republican politician informed her.

The former Progressive leader Raymond Robins encountered two G.O.P. politicians in an Albany hotel lobby shortly after the elections, and the three men started to discuss the 1920 nomination. One suggested Roosevelt. "Of course, it's going to be Roosevelt," said the second man. "I shouldn't wonder if we nominated him by acclamation," the first man continued. "Acclamation, hell!" interjected the second man. "We'll nominate him by assault." The Colonel's enthusiastic champion was none other than William Barnes, Jr., who had charged T.R. with libel four years earlier.

"I am indifferent on the subject," the Colonel told his future biographer Joseph Bucklin Bishop. He would not lift a finger to get the nomination. Since Quentin's death, his world seemed to have "shut down" on him. If the other boys did not come back, what would the

Presidency mean? He could think of no greater joy than to spend his remaining years with his family. Yet, if the party leaders wanted him, "by George . . . they will take me without a single reservation or modification of the things I have always stood for!"

A week before the election, on October 27, the Colonel had celebrated his sixtieth birthday. "I am glad to be sixty," he wrote Kermit, "for it somehow gives me the right to be titularly as old as I feel." He only hoped that, when his second son was sixty, he would "have as much happiness to look back upon as I have had, and be as proud of your sons and daughters as I am of mine . . . [and] still be as much in love with Belle as I am with your Mother. . . ."

4

Armistice brought quiet to the Western Front on November 11, 1918. That day, in New York, the Colonel re-entered Roosevelt Hospital, suffering from a new attack of inflammatory rheumatism.

"Events tread on one another's heels now," he had written Ted a day earlier, "but I should scarcely expect the German armed resistance to continue much longer." He speculated on whether American troops would soon be brought home or kept in Europe for "police work, especially if Germany turns Bolshevist." However, he expected that Wilson, because of his defeat in the congressional elections, would now be forced to work in closer agreement with the Allies and "with less partiality towards either Germanism or Bolshevism." The letter had been dictated to Edith Roosevelt, who added a postcript: "Father is flat on his back with his gout. . . . He is having a horrid suffering time."

The family was "not seriously apprehensive" about this latest illness, Corinne Robinson later recalled, although she had been surprised to learn that her brother was back in the hospital. "Darling Pussie," a widow for two months, had permission to visit the hospital daily. There were generally lines of people "of the most varied kind" waiting to see T.R. Hamlin Garland stopped by to discuss literature; Senator Lodge came to talk about the peace treaty and Wilson's proposed League of Nations. En route to Paris with a Red Cross mission, William Allen White called at the hospital but was told that the Colonel was resting under the influence of a narcotic and could not be disturbed. Awakening and learning that he had missed the Kansas newspaper editor, Roosevelt "turned the hospital upside down for three hours" until White could be located and brought to his bedside.

White found the Colonel "propped up in bed, sweet as a cherub, reading." Leonard Wood, White told Roosevelt, was going to be a serious contender for the 1920 Republican nomination. Sooner or later, he would have to reach an agreement with his old friend. "Well, probably I shall have to get in this thing in June," T.R. remarked. White left, convinced that the Colonel would be a candidate in 1920.

To his enormous circle of personal and political correspondents, Roosevelt continued to send long, thoughtful, and entertaining letters. And he continued writing editorials for publication in the *Star*. His criticism of Wilson was unrelenting; more and more, he was acting like the leader of a not-so-loyal opposition. "Well, we have seen the mighty days," he wrote Arthur Lee on November 19, "and you, at least, have done your full share in them." His own service, he was convinced, had been in preventing Wilson "from doing what he fully intended to do, double-cross the allies, appear as an umpire between them and the Central Powers and get a negotiated peace which would put him on a pinnacle of glory in the sight of every sinister pro-German and every vapid and fatuous doctrinaire sentimentalist throughout the world." But the nation had not been prepared to follow the President "in another somersault"; the election results showed that they wanted an unconditional surrender. In closing, Roosevelt told Lee that Ted and Kermit had taken part in the last fighting and were even then walking toward the Rhine to establish an occupation force in Germany, and that both Ted and Dick Derby had been promoted to lieutenant colonel. "This is Quentin's birthday," he added.

To Rudyard Kipling, next to Lee his closest English friend, T.R. wrote that he was strongly in favor of a "working agreement" in peacetime between the British Empire and the United States; "indeed, I am now content to call it an alliance." News that Henry White had been named as the only Republican to Wilson's peace commission was greeted with joy in a letter to Lodge. He supported the efforts of George Haven Putnam to create an American branch of the English-Speaking Union. And when Wilson urged, in his annual message to Congress on December 2, that the Senate once more take up the treaty with Colombia providing for an indemnity and an apology for taking Panama, T.R.

wrote to Philander Knox, offering to testify before his Senate committee and promising "an entertaining morning."

Roosevelt was a great favorite with the doctors and nurses at the hospital, "a model patient and good in obeying orders," newspaperman John J. Leary recalled. But he had "a strong man's objections to being 'waited on.' In his sickest hours he always insisted on trying to help himself." The staff did not give the Colonel orders, a surgeon observed; they just thought they did. "He's just come in, captivated everybody in the place, and comes pretty near to running things. It's what I suspect he does everywhere."

At one point the doctors told Roosevelt that he might leave the hospital as an invalid, confined to a wheelchair. Well, the Colonel remarked grimly, he could learn to live with that too. "I feel like a faker," he wrote to his older sister, Bamie, long an invalid, "because my troubles are not to be mentioned in the same breath with all you have gone through." His illness was just "a severe attack of inflammatory rheumatism and a little sciatica. . . ." While he would probably not be able to do much for a few months, "I have every reason to think I shall in the end recover completely." Oscar Straus saw him on December 22 and found him "neither enfeebled nor emaciated, though he showed signs of illness."

Sitting quietly with Mrs. Robinson one day, the Colonel alluded to his recently celebrated sixtieth birthday. "Well, anyway, no matter what comes, I have kept the promise I made to myself when I was twenty-one," he said to his sister. Corinne asked what that promise was. "I promised myself," she recalled him saying with a bang of his fist on the arm of his chair, "that I would work *up to the hilt* until I was sixty, and I have done it." Even if he should now be an invalid, or if he should die—he snapped his finger and thumb in a gesture of contempt— "what difference would it make?" His only regret was that he had been unable, like Quentin, to have died for his country. Her brother, Corinne quietly observed, was not only willing and anxious to die for his country, he lived for his country every day of his life.

On December 16, Ted's wife, Eleanor, arrived home from France. T.R. had sent word that she must go immediately to see her children but she insisted on coming to the hospital first. "The darling girl looks very well and is pretty as a picture," the Colonel wrote his eldest son. That Friday, "as I probably won't be able to get out to Oyster Bay," Archie was going to take his place in the annual Cove School Christmas pageant—a local event the ex-President tried never to miss.

On Christmas Day Theodore Roosevelt returned to Sagamore Hill, expecting to go back to the hospital after the holidays. Eleanor came to visit him again. "You know, Father," she said, "Ted has always worried for fear he would not be worthy of you." She wrote down his reply immediately afterward, only to learn that T.R. had said virtually the same thing in a letter to his first son. "Worthy of me? Darling, I'm so very proud of him. He has won high honor not only for his children but, like the Chinese, he has ennobled his ancestors. I walk with my head higher because of him."

In the week after Christmas Roosevelt drove down to the village in an automobile once and took several walks about his property. At night he slept in Ethel's old bedroom, on the southwest corner of the second floor, a room with a connecting door to the master bedroom where Edith remained. The family physician, Dr. George W. Faller, made two calls daily on his famous patient. The Colonel had a ruddy complexion and appeared as sturdy as ever, the physician later recalled, but he would not discuss his illness. "He talked about almost everything except himself and his condition of health," Dr. Faller said.

On Friday, January 3, Roosevelt dictated several letters to his secretary, Josephine Stricker. In one he told a man in Iowa that, as far as his criticism of Wilson was concerned, he made only one error and that was when he supported Wilson's neutrality for the first sixty days after the outbreak of war. "I have never erred when I opposed him." He sent a message to a benefit concert of the American Defense League, scheduled for the following Sunday evening at the Hippodrome in New York. In the United States, he repeated, there was room for but one flag, one language; "and we have room for but one soul loyalty, and that loyalty is to the American people." He dictated an editorial for the Kansas City *Star,* urging a cautious approach to the League of Nations that Wilson was promoting, and asked Miss Stricker to return on Monday with a typed copy for correction. He penciled a memorandum for Will Hays, urging the Chairman of the Republican National Committee to go to Washington and see Senate and House leaders in order to prevent a split in the party on domestic policies.

Corinne Robinson had planned to visit her brother that Friday but received a message that he was not feeling so well. Could she postpone her arrival until the following Monday? On Saturday morning Edith telephoned James Amos, the Colonel's former valet then working for a detective agency, and asked him to come to Sagamore Hill. T.R. needed a man servant and would not have anyone else. Amos arrived that evening and was saddened at Roosevelt's appearance. "His face bore a tired expression. There was a look of weariness in his eyes. It was perfectly plain that he had suffered deeply." To Amos, it seemed unnatural for the Colonel, "always so full of vigor and life, to be thus brought down." He bathed him, dressed him in clean pajamas, and put him in a chair where he could look out the window toward the water. After the early darkness fell, Amos put Roosevelt in bed and sat next to him through the night.

On Sunday, for the first time since returning from the hospital, Roosevelt did not dress and come downstairs. Instead he remained in the little corner bedroom, Edith sitting by his bedside and the two of them taking turns reading aloud to each other. "He had a happy day," Mrs. Roosevelt later wrote Ted. ". . . as it got dusk he watched the dancing flames and spoke of the happiness of being home, and made little plans for me. I think he had made up his mind that he would have to suffer for some time to come and with his high courage had adjusted himself to bear it." As his wife rose to leave the room, T.R. put down a book he had been reading and said, "I wonder if you will ever know how I love Sagamore Hill."

Dr. Faller called at 8 P.M. and James Amos returned to his vigil at the bedside. The Colonel did not go to sleep, however, and Edith continued to look in from time to time. At 11, when he complained that he was having trouble getting his breath, Dr. Faller was again summoned. The doctor gave him some medication and left. "James," Roosevelt said to his valet, "will you please put out the light." A small lamp on the dresser, which had cast a dim yellow light about the room, was turned off and Amos took a chair near the bed. Soon his eyes got used to the darkness and he could see that the Colonel was now breathing regularly.

About 4 A.M. James Amos was startled awake by the sound of very irregular breathing from the patient. He hastened to a room next door, in which a trained nurse was sleeping, but when the two returned, the breathing had stopped altogether. They called Mrs. Roosevelt who came to her husband's bed, leaned over him, and said softly, "Theodore, darling!" There was no answer. Dr. Faller arrived shortly thereafter to pronounce him dead. The cause of death was a pulmonary embolism, a blood clot in his lungs, the result it was said not only of his recent illness but of a lifetime of too strenuous living. Roosevelt was less than three months into his sixty-first year.

5

Two extra telegraphers were put to work at Oyster Bay to receive incoming messages of condolences on the death of the former President. He was shocked to hear the news, Taft wired Edith Roosevelt. "My heart goes out to you and yours in your very great sorrow. The country can ill afford in this critical period of history to lose one who has done and could in the next decade have done so much for it and humanity. We have lost . . . the most commanding personality in our public life since Lincoln." In Washington both houses of Congress adjourned after paying a brief tribute to Roosevelt.

Woodrow Wilson was traveling in Italy, on his great triumphal journey before going to Paris for the opening of the peace conference. Reporters outside his train saw the President handed a message and noticed an expression of surprise and then almost a smile flicker across his lips. The message, they learned, had been of the death of his great adversary. Wilson sent a perfunctory note of sympathy to Mrs. Roosevelt and ordered flags at half mast on all federal buildings for thirty days. Vice President Marshall was more generous. "Death had to take him sleeping," he was quoted as saying, "for if Roosevelt had been awake, there would have been a fight." "Roosevelt's death left a great gap," Tumulty wired a Wilson aide in Paris. "We must from now on make the people not only admire but love the President." William Allen White read the news in the Paris edition of the New York *Herald* and ever after remembered standing in a hotel lobby with the paper, "dumb, speechless, probably tearful." Later he and the journalists Ray Stannard Baker and Ida Tarbell sat down "to talk it all over, and get used to a world without Roosevelt in it."

Ted and Kermit received news of their father's death in a little town in Germany. The lines of Kipling kept running through Kermit's mind "with monotonous insistency":

> He scarce had need to doff his pride,
> Or slough the dress of earth,
> E'en as he trod that day to God

> So walked he from his birth,
> In simpleness and gentleness and honor and
> clean mirth.

Edith called Corinne Robinson at six on Monday morning and T.R.'s younger sister came immediately to Sagamore Hill. The two women walked in silence along the shore and through the woodlands that Roosevelt had loved so well. At twilight they saw airplanes circling the big rambling house. They had been sent from the field where Quentin trained and now were dropping laurel wreaths in honor of the dead youth's father.

The secretary of Harvard's class of 1880 sent out an announcement of Roosevelt's death to his classmates, concluding with the speech of Valiant-for-truth in John Bunyan's *Pilgrim's Progress:* "I am going to my Father's, and though with great difficulty I have got hither, yet now I do not repent me of all the trouble I have been at to arrive where I am. My sword I give to him that shall succeed me in my pilgrimage, and my courage and skill to him that can get it. My marks and scars I carry with me, to be a witness for me that I have fought His battles who now will be my rewarder."

The funeral for the ex-President was held on Wednesday, January 8, at Oyster Bay's Christ Episcopal Church. There had been talk of national services in the capital but the family vetoed such proposals. Instead four to five hundred mourners crowded into the simple wooden chapel for the short service. There was to be no music, no elegy.

The delegation from Washington was headed by Vice President Marshall, and among the dignitaries on hand were senators Lodge and Knox, Uncle Joe Cannon and Champ Clark, New York Governor Alfred E. Smith, Elihu Root, Charles Evans Hughes, Henry Stimson, James Garfield, Oscar Straus, and Joseph Murray, the former G.O.P. leader who had started Roosevelt on his political career in 1881. Alice and Ethel attended the service but Edith Roosevelt remained at Sagamore Hill, alone with her memories and thoughts. Archie, his arm and hand still heavily bandaged, served as an usher. Arriving late, Taft was put in a pew with the family servants but Archie rescued him: "You're a dear personal friend and you must come up further," he whispered to the former President.

At the conclusion of the service the rector pronounced the benediction: "Theodore, the Lord bless thee, and keep thee. The Lord make his face to shine upon thee, and be gracious unto thee. The Lord lift up his countenance upon thee, and give thee peace, both now and evermore. Amen." It had been snowing earlier in the morning but the sun had broken through as the simple oak coffin, covered with an American flag, was brought into the church, and now the sunlight poured through the stained-glass windows.

The funeral party followed the pallbearers outside and through the bare trees of a snow-dusted hill to the nearby cemetery. Roosevelt and his wife had previously picked a burial site, a wooded knoll overlooking Oyster Bay and the waters of Long Island Sound beyond; through the trees to the east was Sagamore Hill. The coffin was lowered into the earth and the onlookers drifted away. Among the last to depart was William Howard Taft. He stood a long time, looking at the grave, before turning to leave; that night, he went to the theater in New York.

Upon hearing of the death of John Hay in 1905, T.R. had written Lodge that he "should esteem any man happy who lived till 65 . . . who saw his children marry, his grandchildren born, who was happy in his home life, who wrote his name clearly in the record of our times, who rendered great and durable services to the nation. . . . and died in the harness in the zenith of his fame. When it comes our turn to go out into the blackness, I only hope the circumstances will be as favorable." Hay, he subsequently reiterated, died at that zenith and had not yet been thrown aside as useless. Four years later, from Africa, Roosevelt had written each of his sisters on the subject of death. "As our lives draw towards the end," he told Corinne, "we are sure to meet bitter sorrow, and we must meet it undauntedly." He wrote Bamie that if he were about to die, he would be sorry not to feel that those who loved him would mourn; "but I should be still more sorry to feel that they would be broken and beaten down by grief, and would not cherish tenderly the memories of the dead; but all that can be done for anyone must be done while he or she is living; grief in no way helps the dead. . . ." Finally, he had written to Dick Derby, to tell him of the death of Corinne's husband, Douglas Robinson, in September, 1918: ". . . my sorrow is so keen for the young of your generation, who die, that the edge of my grief is blunted when death comes to the old, of my own generation; for in the nature of things we must soon die anyhow—and we have warmed both hands before the fire of life."

Epilogue

In June, 1920, the Republicans once more gathered in Chicago to nominate a candidate for President. With Roosevelt dead and with both Taft and Hughes having taken themselves out of contention, the G.O.P. had no clear leader. The three principal candidates for the nomination were Hiram Johnson and Leonard Wood, both draping about themselves the mantle of the Colonel, and the young reform governor of Illinois, Frank O. Lowden. By the end of four ballots, it appeared that the convention had reached a deadlock. In an effort to find a compromise candidate, Will Hays, Chairman of the Republican National Committee, summoned to his suite in the Blackstone Hotel a progression of party leaders. The name that emerged from what was later called "the smoke-filled room" was that of Warren G. Harding, the first term United States Senator from Ohio.

Harding was told of his designation by the party elders and asked if there was anything in his past that might cloud his candidacy. Choosing to ignore a long, drawn-out affair with a friend's wife and the existence of an illegitimate daughter in that very city, Harding said no. And thus was nominated and ultimately elected the man perhaps least qualified in the nation's history to hold the high office of President.

In the ensuing election Harding and his running mate, Governor Calvin Coolidge of Massachusetts, easily triumphed over the Democratic ticket. Wilson, though broken in body by a paralyzing stroke he had suffered late in 1919 and broken in spirit by the Senate's defeat of his cherished League of Nations, had pathetically clung to the hope that the Democrats might name him for a third term. Instead, his party designated the Governor of Ohio, James M. Cox, and for Vice President,

Franklin D. Roosevelt. The young man, having served in the Wilson administration as Assistant Secretary of the Navy—a post once held by his wife's uncle—seemed destined for a larger, national career, and the defeat that year proved only a momentary setback.

As President, the guileless, indolent, and overwhelmed Harding let the nation drift into what he called "normalcy." Fortunately, he died suddenly in the summer of 1923 before the deep corruption of his administration was revealed. His most noteworthy act, perhaps, was the appointment of William Howard Taft as Chief Justice of the Supreme Court—Taft's ambition thus being fulfilled more happily than had his wife's thirteen years earlier. After Harding came Coolidge, elected to his own term in 1924, and then Herbert Hoover, who helplessly watched the nation sink into the Great Depression.

In 1925 the Philadelphia newspaperman and Bull Moose leader E. A. Van Valkenburg wrote a preface to one of the volumes being published in a new edition of Theodore Roosevelt's works. "Already he has taken a rank of which history will not deprive him," Van Valkenburg wrote of his old hero, "standing with Washington and Lincoln as one of the trinity of great Americans." But then came 1932. After twelve years of Republican rule, it was time for a change. The people turned to a Democratic Roosevelt, F.D.R.

Trusts, tariffs, recall of judicial decisions, the Panama Canal, the League of Nations—all were forgotten issues of a bygone day. The image of Theodore Roosevelt faded, in time being reduced to little more than bared teeth, flashing eyeglasses, a cowboy hat, and the Big Stick. To a new generation of Americans the name Roosevelt conjured up that affable patrician and masterful politician from Hyde Park—and not the gifted, ambitious, exasperating and controversial, but always interesting and generally well-meaning man who had so dominated the American political scene back in those days when the century was young.

Notes on Sources

Unfortunately, there is no definitive life of Theodore Roosevelt nor, to my knowledge, is any such work under preparation at present. Two full-length studies are Henry F. Pringle's Pulitzer Prize-winning *Theodore Roosevelt, A Biography* and William Henry Harbaugh's *Power and Responsibility, The Life and Times of Theodore Roosevelt.* Although Pringle is more lively and provocative, Harbaugh's work is scholarly, dependable, and boasts a helpful essay on sources; both are available in revised editions in paperback. Carleton Putnam published only one volume of his projected multivolume biography, *Theodore Roosevelt: The Formative Years.* John Morton Blum's *The Republican Roosevelt* provides an incisive, thought-provoking interpretation, while Edward Wagenknecht's *The Seven Worlds of Theodore Roosevelt* offers a novel way of looking at the man and boasts a comprehensive bibliography. *Theodore Roosevelt Cyclopedia,* edited by Albert Bushnell Hart and Herbert Ronald Ferleger, is a unique reference work.

A number of Roosevelt's contemporaries attempted biographies; all suffer from being too close to their subject. In this category I would place works by Joseph Bucklin Bishop, Lord Charnwood, Lewis Einstein, William Draper Lewis, Jacob Riis, William Roscoe Thayer, and Charles G. Washburn. More interesting are the reminiscences of T.R.'s family, friends, and political associates—notably Alice Roosevelt Longworth, Corinne Roosevelt Robinson, Eleanor Alexander Roosevelt, Kermit Roosevelt, Nicholas Roosevelt, Theodore Roosevelt, Jr., Oscar S. Straus, and Owen Wister. Especially helpful and revealing are works by the journalists Lawrence Abbott, O. K. Davis, John J. Leary, Jr., H. H. Kohlsaat, Julian Street, Charles Willis Thompson, and William Allen White. The six volumes of Mark Sullivan's *Our Times* are rich with anecdotal material. The three volumes of Archie Butt's letters, as acknowledged below, are in a class by themselves.

Biographies of T.R.'s contemporaries allow one to look at the subject from other perspectives. Among these should be mentioned Claude G. Bowers's *Beveridge,* John A. Garraty's *Lodge* and *Perkins,* Hermann Hagedorn's *Wood,* Philip Jessup's *Root,* Margaret Leech's *McKinley,* Arthur S. Link's *Wilson,* Elting E. Morison's *Stimson,* Allan Nevins's *White,* Henry F. Pringle's *Taft,* Merlo J. Pusey's *Hughes,* Francis Russell's *Harding,* and W. A. Swanberg's *Hearst* and *Pulitzer.*

The best source of information on Theodore Roosevelt is, of course, T.R. himself. Hermann Hagedorn was editor of *The Works of Theodore Roosevelt, Memorial Edition* (24 vols., 1923–26), the most comprehensive and attractive edition of T.R.'s writings. In writing the present study, it should be obvious to the reader, the author has relied most heavily on the letters of Theodore Roosevelt. The Theodore Roosevelt Papers in the Library of Congress is a collection of 250,000 documents, with about 100,000 letters written by T.R. himself; from this and other collections a team of scholars at Harvard, under the direction of Elting E. Morison, produced *The Letters of Theodore Roosevelt* (8 vols., 1951–54). The intent behind this publishing venture, it is stated in the introduction to the first volume, was "to make easily accessible all the available letters of Theodore Roosevelt that seem necessary to reveal, insofar as letters can, his thought and action in all the major and many of the minor undertakings of his public and private life." The goal is quite remarkably achieved; the some seven thousand letters presented are really the best "biography" of Roosevelt in print. The footnotes, especially in the later volumes, provide an unusual wealth of information; appendixes in the form of essays shed light on a number of subjects; a chronology of T.R.'s life—virtually day-by-day from August, 1898, to his death—is of enormous assistance to the writer; and the volumes have superlative indexes. Only occasionally was it necessary to supplement the Morison edition by quotations from the other published collections of letters cited in the following bibliography.

In these notes I have listed only the principal sources for each chapter; some books, as indicated, were used for several successive chapters. *The Letters* were used for every chapter.

MR. PRESIDENT

Chapter 1. Hour of Triumph

Since it was such a pivotal event in his career, nearly everyone who has written on T.R. has something to say about the no-third-term statement issued on Election Night, 1904. For the President's activities that day I have followed accounts in the New York *Tribune* and *Sun* and in Corinne Robinson's *My Brother*. Election statistics given here and in other chapters are drawn from *History of American Presidential Elections, 1789–1968*, Volume III, edited by Arthur M. Schlesinger, Jr.

Chapter 2. The Reluctant Candidate

Major sources for this and the following chapter include Margaret Leech's *In the Days of McKinley,* Thomas Beer's and Herbert Croly's biographies of Mark Hanna, *The Autobiography of Thomas Collier Platt,* Worthington C. Ford's *Letters of Henry Adams* and William Roscoe Thayer's *The Life and Letters of John Hay.*

Chapter 3. A Fateful Bullet

A. Wesley Johns's *The Man Who Shot McKinley* supplements Leech's account of the assassination. T.R.'s journey from Mount Marcy to Buffalo is most dramatically recounted in Jacob Riis's *Theodore Roosevelt, The Citizen,* a 1904 campaign biography. The parallel with the 1881 succession is drawn from Jessup's *Root.* H. H. Kohlsaat, in *From McKinley to Harding,* recalled the train trip to Washington. The Nicholas Murray Butler quote is from his *Across the Busy Years.*

Chapter 4. Serving McKinley's Term

For the presidential years, covered in this and the following two chapters, I have used Harbaugh and Pringle, Joseph Bucklin Bishop's *Theodore Roosevelt and His Time* (Volumes XXIII and XXIV of *The Works*), T.R.'s *Autobiography* (Volume XXII of *The Works*), Howard K. Beale's *Theodore Roosevelt and the Rise of America to World Power,* and George E. Mowry's *The Era of Theodore Roosevelt, 1900–1912.* The New York *Tribune* and *Sun* were consulted for the 1904 conventions and campaigns.

Chapter 5. In His Own Right

John D. Weaver's *The Brownsville Raid* is a meticulous study of that regrettable incident; its publication in 1970 was instrumental in posthu-
mously clearing the record of the black soldiers. Arthur Wallace Dunn's
Gridiron Nights recounts a number of those famous dinners; Joseph B.
Foraker's *Notes of a Busy Life* has the story of the one in January, 1907.

Chapter 6. Choosing a Successor

Henry F. Pringle's *The Life and Times of William Howard Taft* is far
too uncritical of its subject but is a valuable source of quotations from
Taft letters. The happiest event of T.R.'s last year in office, from the historian's viewpoint, was the appointment in the spring of 1908 of Archie
Butt as military aide to the President; *The Letters of Archie Butt* covers
the period to March, 1909. The New York *Tribune* and *Sun* provided
details about the election of 1908 and Taft's inaugural. Both Alice
Longworth, in *Crowded Hours,* and Helen Herron Taft, in *Recollections
of Full Years,* left accounts of the dinner party preceding Taft's inaugural. Corinne Robinson's *My Brother* and Oscar S. Straus's *Under Four
Administrations* contain information on the last days of T.R.'s second
term.

COLONEL ROOSEVELT

Chapter 7. Through Darkest Africa

The account of T.R.'s sailing on March 23 is based mainly on the New
York *Tribune.* The Colonel's article on the Pigskin Library, originally
published in *The Outlook* for April 30, 1910, is reprinted in *Literary Essays* (Volume XIV of *The Works*). The safari is superbly recounted in
Roosevelt's *African Game Trails* (Volume V of *The Works,* with an introduction by Carl Akeley). T.R. collaborated with Edmund Heller on a
two-volume study, *Life-Histories of African Game Animals.* Kermit Roosevelt wrote about the great adventure with his father in *The Happy-
Hunting Grounds.* His son Kermit took his two boys—T.R.'s great-
grandsons—to East Africa in 1960 to retrace the safari route for *Life*
magazine; their experiences were recounted in *A Sentimental Safari.*
Warrington Dawson, *Opportunity and Theodore Roosevelt,* and John T.
McCutcheon, *In Africa,* wrote about their encounters with the Colonel.
W. Robert Foran's article "With Roosevelt in Africa" appeared in the

October, 1912, issue of *Field and Stream*. Archie Butt's incomparable letters continue in *Taft and Roosevelt,* covering the period from March, 1909, to February, 1912. Pringle's *Taft* remained a helpful source, while the entire story of the split in the G.O.P.—from Taft's succession through the election of 1916—is best presented in George E. Mowry's detailed work *Theodore Roosevelt and the Progressive Movement.*

Chapter 8. In the Presence of Kings

Roosevelt described his trip through Europe in two long and delightful letters, to George Otto Trevelyan (October 1, 1911) and to David Gray (October 5, 1911); both are reprinted in *The Letters* (Volume 7) and in *Cowboys and Kings*. T.R.'s speeches are in *African and European Addresses;* Lawrence Abbott's introduction to this volume provides information about the trip, as does his *Impressions of Theodore Roosevelt*. John Callan O'Laughlin's account appears in *From the Jungle Through Europe with Roosevelt*. The Ballinger-Pinchot controversy, greatly compressed here, is treated in Pringle's *Taft,* Gifford Pinchot's *Breaking New Ground,* Alpheus Thomas Mason's *Bureaucracy Convicts Itself,* and Elmo E. Richardson's *The Politics of Conservation,* which attempts to be the final word. Also consulted for this chapter were Nevins's *White,* Straus's *Under Four Administrations,* and Jessup's *Root.*

Chapter 9. Return of the Hunter

The description of T.R.'s triumphal return to the United States is based on accounts in *The New York Times*. The best source of the Republican split remains Mowry's *Theodore Roosevelt and the Progressive Movement,* though Arthur S. Link's *Woodrow Wilson and the Progressive Era* is also helpful. Herbert Croly's seminal work of 1909, *The Promise of American Life,* is available in a 1965 edition with a penetrating introduction by Arthur M. Schlesinger, Jr. T.R.'s 1910 speeches are reprinted in *The New Nationalism,* while his two meetings with his successor—June 30 and September 19—are described vividly by Archie Butt in *Taft and Roosevelt*. Further information on the 1910 campaign was gleaned from Owen Wister's *Roosevelt, The Story of a Friendship,* Corinne Robinson's *My Brother,* Morison's *Stimson,* Pringle's *Taft,* Sullivan's *Our Times,* and Dunn's *Gridiron Nights*. I am indebted to Marvin W. McFarland of the Library of Congress for the story of T.R.'s airplane ride with Arch Hoxsey.

Chapter 10. A Fissure in the G.O.P.

To the sources cited for the preceding chapter should be added, in particular, Oscar King Davis's *Released for Publication* and the autobiographies of Robert M. La Follette and William Allen White. A number of T.R.'s 1911 *Outlook* articles are reprinted in *Social Justice and Popular Rule* (Volume XIX of *The Works*). The Earl Lectures, *Realizable Ideals*, are reprinted in *Citizenship, Politics and the Elemental Virtues* (Volume XV of *The Works*, with an introduction by William Allen White). A defense of his 1907 dealings with U.S. Steel, originally written for *The Outlook*, was reprinted as an appendix to the first (1913) edition of his *Autobiography*. Owen Wister was a pained guest at the Periodical Publishers' dinner in Philadelphia that proved a fatal blow to La Follette's presidential ambitions. The Colonel's letter to the "seven little governors" is reprinted in *The Letters* (Volume 7).

Chapter 11. When Friends Become Enemies

The most detailed account of the 1912 primaries is in Mowry's *Theodore Roosevelt and the Progressive Movement*. Also useful are Norman Wilensky's *Conservatives in the Progressive Era* and Claude G. Bowers's *Beveridge and the Progressive Era*. The dinner at Judge Grant's home on February 25 is described in a letter of Grant's to the historian James Ford Rhodes, dated March 22, 1912, and reprinted as an appendix to Volume 8 of *The Letters*, and in White's *Autobiography* and William Roscoe Thayer's *Roosevelt*. White's description of T.R. appears in *Masks in a Pageant*. Speeches and articles of the primary campaign are reprinted in *Social Justice and Popular Rule*.

Chapter 12. Standing at Armageddon

Nicholas Roosevelt generously allowed me to consult a typescript of his unpublished diary of the 1912 Republican convention; I also have used Mr. Roosevelt's *A Front Row Seat* and *Theodore Roosevelt, The Man As I Knew Him*. Most of the works cited for the preceding three chapters continued to prove helpful for this and the following chapter, but to these sources should be added John A. Garraty's *Right-Hand Man, The Life of George W. Perkins* and Amos Pinchot's *History of the Progressive Party*. Alice Longworth's *Crowded Hours* contains her colorful and highly colored account of the convention and the ensuing campaign. Nicholas Murray Butler's version of the seventy-two challenged votes appears in his *Across the Busy Years.* The drunk who would have shot Victor Rosewater is described by James Amos in *Theodore Roosevelt, Hero to his Valet;* Rosewater's own story is in *Back Stage in 1912.* The Armageddon speech is in *Social Justice and Popular Rule,* as are subsequent addresses of the 1912 campaign.

Chapter 13. A Bull Moose at Large

I have relied heavily on Arthur S. Link's *Wilson: The Road to the White House* for my account of the 1912 Democratic convention and for Wilson's role in the campaign. Melvin I. Urofsky's *A Mind of One Piece, Brandeis and American Reform* supplements Link on the Wilson-Brandeis relationship. Especially helpful for the Bull Moose convention are Garraty's *Perkins,* Amos Pinchot's *History of the Progressive Party,* and William Draper Lewis's *Roosevelt.* The disputed platform was reprinted as an appendix to *Progressive Principles,* a collection of T.R.'s campaign speeches. Charles Willis Thompson's *Presidents I've Known* contains the encounter in Boise with Senator Borah and a vivid account of the assassination attempt. Corinne Robinson was a closely involved observer of her brother's 1912 race for the Presidency.

Chapter 14. Into the River of Doubt

T.R.'s address as president of the American Historical Association and his review of the 1913 Armory Show are reprinted in *Literary Essays.* The camping trip in the Southwest is recounted by T.R. in *A Book-Lover's Holidays in the Open* (Volume IV of *The Works*) and also by Nicholas Roosevelt in *Theodore Roosevelt, The Man As I Knew Him. Through the Brazilian Wilderness* matches T.R.'s earlier *African Game Trails* for excitement and literary style and is all the more remarkable for having been written under such adverse circumstances; it appears as Volume VI of *The Works,* with an introduction by Frank M. Chapman of the American Museum of Natural History. The members of the Expedição-Scientifica Roosevelt-Rondon who left accounts of the perilous journey include George K. Cherrie, *Dark Trails;* Leo E. Miller, *In the Wilds of South America;* Kermit Roosevelt, *The Happy-Hunting Grounds;* and J. A. Zahm, *Through South America's Southland.* Lucien Bodard's *Green Hell* contains information about Colonel Rondon's later career. T.R.'s return and subsequent trip to Washington are from *The New York Times.* Alice Longworth wrote of Kermit's wedding.

Chapter 15. Unanswered Trumpet

Succeeding volumes in Arthur S. Link's monumental *Wilson* proved helpful in writing this and the following chapter; these are *The New Freedom, The Struggle for Neutrality, 1914–1915,* and *Confusions and Crises, 1915–1916.* Ray Stannard Baker's volumes on Wilson, though lacking Link's scholarly objectivity, contain much interesting information. Other works that shed light on Wilson's first term include Link's *Woodrow Wilson and the Progressive Era,* Joseph P. Tumulty's *Woodrow Wilson As I Know Him,* and John Morton Blum's *Joe Tumulty and the Wilson Era.* O. K. Davis's *Released for Publication* covers T.R.'s 1914 political activities. *Talks With T.R.* by the newspaperman John J. Leary, Jr., was an indispensable source of anecdotal material for the final four chapters of this work. Hermann Hagedorn detailed T.R.'s wartime activities in *The Bugle That Woke America;* the same author's *Leonard Wood* proved a valuable source for this chapter. The story of Roosevelt's message to the Kaiser is in Eleanor Alexander Roosevelt's *Day Before Yesterday;* the Meyer anecdote is from Thompson's *Presidents I've Known.* Owen Wister's *Roosevelt* has information about the Barnes trial. Julian Street titled his brief study of T.R. *The Most Interesting American.* T.R.'s *America and the World War* and *Fear God and Take Your Own Part* constitute Volume XX of *The Works.*

Chapter 16. Return to the Fold

Merlo J. Pusey's *Hughes* and Garraty's *Perkins* are important sources for the 1916 campaign. Link's *Wilson* continues with *Campaigns for Progressivism and Peace, 1916–1917.* T.R.'s Trinidad statement is reprinted in Volume 8 of *The Letters.*

Chapter 17. Services to Render

Since Link has not yet reached the war years, it is necessary to rely on Ray Stannard Baker's *Wilson,* especially Volume 6, *War Leader.* Another pro-Wilson view is found in Frederick Palmer's *Newton D. Baker.* Joe Tumulty and Alice Longworth, as well as T.R. himself in a letter to Cal O'Laughlin on April 13, 1917, wrote of the interview with Wilson; John J. Leary reported a conversation with T.R. on the subject. The complete Roosevelt-Baker correspondence, as originally published in the *Metropolitan* for August, 1917, appears as an appendix to *The Foes of Our Own Household* (Volume XXI of *The Works*). The "Vive les Teddies!" anecdote is from S.L.A. Marshall's *The American Heritage History of World War I*. The best source for T.R.'s sons at war, other than *The Letters*, is Eleanor Alexander Roosevelt's *Day Before Yesterday*.

Chapter 18.   Another Part of the Great Adventure

T.R.'s Nebraska speech is published in *The Foes of Our Own Household; The Great Adventure* is also reprinted in Volume XXI of *The Works*. The Stafford Little Lectures T.R. delivered at Princeton in 1917 were published as *National Strength and International Duty*. *Roosevelt in the Kansas City Star* contains more than a hundred of his contributions to that newspaper; Ralph Stout's introduction tells how they came to be written. Facts about T.R.'s final illnesses and death are taken from Hagedorn's *The Bugle That Woke America*, Wister's *Roosevelt*, Corinne Robinson's *My Brother*, Straus's *Under Four Administrations*, White's *Autobiography*, Leary's *Talks With T.R.*, and Bishop's *Theodore Roosevelt and His Time*. The record of his last days has been reconstructed principally from Amos's *Hero to His Valet* and *The New York Times*. Pringle describes Taft at the funeral. The message to T.R.'s Harvard classmates is reprinted at the end of Thayer's *Roosevelt*. T.R.'s thoughts on death are taken from *The Letters* (Volume 4: 1279, 1286–87; Volume 7: 35, 37; Volume 8: 1370).

Bibliography

Abbott, Lawrence F. *Impressions of Theodore Roosevelt*. Garden City, N.Y.: Doubleday, Page, 1919.

Adams, Henry. *Letters of Henry Adams*. 2 vols. Edited by Worthington Chauncey Ford. Boston and New York: Houghton Mifflin, 1938.

Amos, James E. *Theodore Roosevelt: Hero to His Valet*. New York: John Day, 1927.

Baker, Ray Stannard. *Woodrow Wilson*, 8 vols. Garden City, N.Y.: Doubleday, Page, 1927–39.

Beer, Thomas. *Hanna*. New York: Alfred A. Knopf, 1929.

Beisner, Robert L. *Twelve Against Empire, The Anti-Imperialists. 1898–1900*. New York: McGraw-Hill, 1968.

Beale, Howard K. *Theodore Roosevelt and the Rise of America to World Power*. Baltimore: The Johns Hopkins Press, 1956.

Bishop, Joseph Bucklin. *Theodore Roosevelt and His Time, Shown in His Own Letters*, 2 vols. New York: Charles Scribner's Sons, 1920.

Blum, John Morton. *Joe Tumulty and the Wilson Era*. Boston: Houghton Mifflin, 1951.

———. *The Republican Roosevelt*. Cambridge, Mass.: Harvard University Press, 1954. (Paperback edition—New York: Atheneum, 1962.)

Bodard, Lucien. *Green Hell, Massacre of the Brazilian Indians*. Translated by Jennifer Monaghan. New York: Outerbridge & Dienstfrey, 1971.

Bowers, Claude G. *Beveridge and the Progressive Era*. Cambridge, Mass.: Houghton Mifflin, 1932.

Butler, Nicholas Murray. *Across the Busy Years, Recollections and Reflections*. 2 vols. New York: Charles Scribner's Sons, 1939.

Butt, Archibald. *The Letters of Archie Butt*. Edited by Lawrence F. Abbott. Garden City, N.Y.: Doubleday, Page, 1924.

———. *Taft and Roosevelt, The Intimate Letters of Archie Butt, Military Aide*. Garden City, N.Y.: Doubleday, Doran, 1930.

Charnwood, Lord. *Theodore Roosevelt*. Boston: Atlantic Monthly Press, 1923.

Cherrie, George K. *Dark Trails, Adventures of a Naturalist.* New York: G. P. Putnam's Sons, 1930.

Chessman, G. Wallace. *Governor Theodore Roosevelt: The Albany Apprenticeship, 1898–1900.* Cambridge, Mass.: Harvard University Press, 1965.

———. *Theodore Roosevelt and the Politics of Power.* Boston: Little, Brown, 1969.

Cotton, Edward H. *The Ideals of Theodore Roosevelt.* New York: Appleton, 1923.

Cowles, Virginia. *The Kaiser.* New York: Harper, 1963.

Croly, Herbert. *Marcus Alonzo Hanna, His Life and Work.* New York: Macmillan, 1912.

———. *The Promise of American Life.* Introduction by Arthur M. Schlesinger, Jr. Cambridge, Mass.: Harvard University Press, 1965.

Davis, Oscar King. *Released for Publication, Some Inside Political History of Theodore Roosevelt and His Times, 1898–1918.* Boston: Houghton Mifflin, 1925.

Dawson, Warrington. *Opportunity and Theodore Roosevelt.* No publisher given, 1923?

Dulles, Foster Rhea. *America's Rise to World Power, 1898–1954.* New York: Harper, 1955.

Dunn, Arthur Wallace. *From Harrison to Harding.* 2 vols. New York: G. P. Putnam's Sons, 1922.

———. *Gridiron Nights.* New York: Frederick A. Stokes, 1915.

Einstein, Lewis. *Roosevelt, His Mind in Action.* Boston: Houghton Mifflin, 1930.

Foraker, Joseph B. *Notes of a Busy Life.* 2 vols. New York: Stewart & Kidd, 1916.

Foraker, Julia B. *I Would Live It Again, Memories of a Vivid Life.* New York: Harper, 1932.

Garraty, John A. *Henry Cabot Lodge, A Biography.* New York: Alfred A. Knopf, 1953.

———. *Right-Hand Man, The Life of George W. Perkins.* New York: Harper, 1960.

George, Alexander L. and Juliette L. *Woodrow Wilson and Colonel House, A Personality Study.* New York: John Day, 1956.

Hart, Albert Bushnell and Ferleger, Herbert Ronald, eds. *Theodore Roosevelt Cyclopedia.* New York: Roosevelt Memorial Association, 1941.

Hagedorn, Hermann. *The Bugle That Woke America, The Saga of Theodore Roosevelt's Last Battle for His Country.* New York: John Day, 1940.

———. *Leonard Wood, A Biography.* 2 vols. New York: Harper, 1931.

———. *The Roosevelt Family of Sagamore Hill.* New York: Macmillan, 1954.

———. *Roosevelt, Prophet of Unity.* New York: Charles Scribner's Sons, 1924.

Harbaugh, William Henry. *Power and Responsibility, The Life and Times of*

Theodore Roosevelt. New York: Farrar, Straus and Cudahy, 1961. (Paperback edition—New York: Collier Books, 1963).

Hobbs, William Herbert. *Leonard Wood, Administrator, Soldier, Citizen.* New York: G. P. Putnam's Sons, 1920.

Hofstadter, Richard. *The Age of Reform.* New York: Alfred A. Knopf, 1955.

Jessup, Philip C. *Elihu Root.* 2 vols. New York: Dodd, Mead, 1938.

Johns, A. Wesley. *The Man Who Shot McKinley.* South Brunswick and New York: A. S. Barnes, 1970.

Kelly, Frank K. *The Fight for the White House, The Story of 1912.* New York: Crowell, 1961.

Kohlsaat, H. H. *From McKinley to Harding, Personal Recollections of Our Presidents.* New York: Charles Scribner's Sons, 1923.

La Follette, Robert M. *La Follette's Autobiography, A Personal Narrative of Political Experiences.* Madison, Wisc.: Robert M. La Follette Co., 1913.

Leary, John J., Jr. *Talks with T.R., From the Diaries of John J. Leary, Jr.* Boston and New York: Houghton Mifflin, 1920.

Leech, Margaret. *In the Days of McKinley.* New York: Harper, 1959.

Lewis, William Draper. *The Life of Theodore Roosevelt.* No city listed: United Publishers, 1919.

Link, Arthur S. *Wilson: The Road to the White House.* Princeton, N.J.: Princeton University Press, 1947.

———. *Wilson: The New Freedom.* Princeton, N.J.: Princeton University Press, 1956.

———. *Wilson: The Struggle for Neutrality, 1914–1915.* Princeton, N.J.: Princeton University Press, 1960.

———. *Wilson: Confusions and Crises, 1915–1916.* Princeton, N.J.: Princeton University Press, 1964.

———. *Wilson: Campaigns for Progressivism and Peace, 1916–1917.* Princeton, N.J.: Princeton University Press, 1965.

———. *Woodrow Wilson and the Progressive Era.* New York: Harper, 1954.

Lodge, Henry Cabot. *Theodore Roosevelt.* Boston: Houghton Mifflin, 1919.

Looker, Eugene. *Colonel Roosevelt, Private Citizen.* New York: Fleming H. Revell, 1932.

Longworth, Alice Roosevelt. *Crowded Hours, Reminiscences of Alice Roosevelt Longworth.* New York: Charles Scribner's Sons, 1933.

McCutcheon, John T. *In Africa, Hunting Adventures in the Big Game Country.* Indianapolis: Bobbs-Merrill, 1910.

MacIntyre, Niel. *Great-Heart, The Life of Theodore Roosevelt.* New York: Rudge, 1919.

Mason, Alpheus Thomas. *Bureaucracy Convicts Itself, The Ballinger-Pinchot Controversy of 1910.* New York: Viking, 1941.

Miller, Leo E. *In the Wilds of South America.* New York: Charles Scribner's Sons, 1918.

Morison, Elting E. *Turmoil and Tradition, A Study of the Life and Times of Henry L. Stimson.* Boston: Houghton Mifflin, 1960.

Mowry, George E. *The Era of Theodore Roosevelt, 1900–1912*. New York: Harper, 1958.

———. *Theodore Roosevelt and the Progressive Movement*. Madison, Wisc.: University of Wisconsin Press, 1946.

Nevins, Allan. *Henry White, Thirty Years of American Diplomacy*. New York: Harper, 1930.

O'Laughlin, John Callan. *From the Jungle Through Europe with Roosevelt*. Boston: Chapple, 1910.

Palmer, Frederick. *Newton D. Baker, America at War*. 2 vols. New York: Dodd, Mead, 1931.

Pinchot, Amos. *History of the Progressive Party, 1912–1916*. Edited by Helene Maxwell Hooker. New York: New York University Press, 1958.

Pinchot, Gifford. *Breaking New Ground*. New York: Harcourt, Brace, 1947.

———. *The Fight for Conservation*. New York: Doubleday, Page, 1910.

Platt, Thomas Collier. *The Autobiography of Thomas Collier Platt*. Compiled and edited by Louis J. Lang. New York: Dodge, 1910.

Pringle, Henry F. *The Life and Times of William Howard Taft*. 2 vols. New York: Farrar & Rinehart, 1939.

———. *Theodore Roosevelt, A Biography*. New York: Harcourt, Brace, 1931. (Paperback edition—New York, Harcourt, Brace, 1956.)

Pusey, Merlo J. *Charles Evans Hughes*. 2 vols. New York: Macmillan, 1951.

Putnam, Carleton. *Theodore Roosevelt, The Formative Years, 1858–1866*. Charles Scribner's Sons, 1958.

Richardson, Elmo R. *The Politics of Conservation, Crusades and Controversies, 1897–1913*. Berkeley and Los Angeles: University of California Press, 1962.

Riis, Jacob A. *Theodore Roosevelt, The Citizen*. New York: The Outlook, 1904.

Rixey, Lilian. *Bamie, Theodore Roosevelt's Remarkable Sister*. New York, David McKay, 1963.

Robinson, Corinne Roosevelt. *My Brother Theodore Roosevelt*. New York: Charles Scribner's Sons, 1921.

Roosevelt, Eleanor Alexander. *Day Before Yesterday, The Reminiscences of Mrs. Theodore Roosevelt, Jr.* Garden City, N.Y.: Doubleday, 1959.

Roosevelt, Kermit. *The Happy-Hunting Grounds*. New York: Charles Scribner's Sons, 1920.

Roosevelt, Kermit (Jr.). *A Sentimental Safari*. New York: Alfred A. Knopf, 1963.

Roosevelt, Nicholas. *A Front Row Seat*. Norman, Okla.: University of Oklahoma Press, 1953.

———. *Theodore Roosevelt, The Man As I Knew Him*. New York: Dodd, Mead, 1967.

Roosevelt, Theodore. *African and European Addresses*. New York: G. P. Putnam's Sons, 1910.

———. *An Autobiography*. New York: Macmillan, 1913.

————. *A Book-Lover's Holidays in the Open.* New York: Charles Scribner's Sons, 1916.

————. *Cowboys and Kings, Three Great Letters by Theodore Roosevelt.* Cambridge, Mass.: Harvard University Press, 1954.

————. *History as Literature and Other Essays.* New York: Charles Scribner's Sons, 1913.

————. *Letters from Theodore Roosevelt to Anna Roosevelt Cowles.* New York: Charles Scribner's Sons, 1924.

————. *The Letters of Theodore Roosevelt.* 8 vols. Edited by Elting E. Morison and others. Cambridge, Mass.: Harvard University Press, 1951–54.

————. *Letters to Kermit from Theodore Roosevelt, 1902–1908.* Edited by Will Irvin. New York: Charles Scribner's Sons, 1946.

————. With Edmund Heller. *Life-Histories of African Game Animals.* 2 vols. New York: Charles Scribner's Sons, 1914.

————. *National Strength and International Duty.* Princeton, N.J.: Princeton University Press, 1917.

————. *The New Nationalism.* New York: The Outlook, 1910.

————. *Progressive Principles, Selections from Addresses Made During the Presidential Campaign of 1912.* Edited by Elmer H. Youngman. New York: Progressive National Service, 1913.

————. *Theodore Roosevelt's Letters to His Children.* New York: Charles Scribner's Sons, 1919.

————. *Roosevelt in the Kansas City Star. War-Time Editorials By Theodore Roosevelt.* Boston and New York: Houghton Mifflin, 1921.

————. *Selections from the Correspondence of Theodore Roosevelt and Henry Cabot Lodge, 1884–1918.* 2 vols. Edited by Henry Cabot Lodge. New York: Charles Scribner's Sons, 1925.

————. *The Works of Theodore Roosevelt, Memorial Edition.* 24 vols. Edited by Hermann Hagedorn. New York: Charles Scribner's Sons, 1923–26.

Roosevelt, Theodore, Jr. *All in the Family,* New York, G. P. Putnam's Sons, 1929.

Rosewater, Victor. *Back Stage in 1912.* Philadelphia: Dorrance, 1932.

Russell, Francis. *The Shadow of Blooming Grove, Warren G. Harding and His Times.* New York: McGraw-Hill, 1925.

Schlesinger, Arthur M., Jr., ed. *History of American Presidential Elections, 1789–1968.* Volume III, 1900–1936. New York: Chelsea House-McGraw Hill, 1971.

Straus, Oscar S. *Under Four Administrations, From Cleveland to Taft.* Boston and New York: Houghton Mifflin, 1922.

Street, Julian. *The Most Interesting American.* New York: Century, 1915.

Sullivan, Mark. *Our Times, 1900–1925.* 6 vols. New York: Charles Scribner's Sons, 1926–35.

Swanberg, W. A. *Citizen Hearst.* New York: Charles Scribner's Sons, 1961.

————. *Pulitzer.* New York: Charles Scribner's Sons, 1967.

Taft, Helen Herron. *Recollections of Full Years.* New York: Dodd, Mead, 1914.

Thayer, William Roscoe. *The Life and Letters of John Hay.* 2 vols. Boston and New York: Houghton Mifflin, 1915.

————. *Theodore Roosevelt, An Intimate Biography.* Boston and New York: Houghton Mifflin, 1919.

Thompson, Charles Willis. *Presidents I've Known and Two Near Presidents.* Indianapolis: Bobbs-Merrill, 1929.

Tumulty, Joseph P. *Woodrow Wilson As I Know Him.* Garden City, N.Y.: Doubleday, Page, 1921.

Wagenknecht, Edward. *The Seven Worlds of Theodore Roosevelt.* New York: Longmans, Green, 1958.

Washburn, Charles G. *Theodore Roosevelt, The Logic of His Career.* Boston and New York: Houghton Mifflin, 1916.

Weaver, John D. *The Brownsville Raid.* New York: Norton, 1970.

White, William Allen. *The Autobiography of William Allen White.* New York, Macmillan, 1946.

————. *Masks in a Pageant.* New York: Macmillan, 1929.

Wiebe, Robert H. *The Search for Order, 1877–1920.* New York: Hill and Wang, 1967.

Wilensky, Norman M. *Conservatives in the Progressive Era, The Taft Republicans of 1912.* Gainesville, Fla.: University of Florida Press, 1965.

Wister, Owen. *Roosevelt, The Story of a Friendship.* New York: Macmillan, 1930.

Urofsky, Melvin I. *A Mind of One Piece, Brandeis and American Reform.* New York: Charles Scribner's Sons, 1971.

Zahm, J. A. *Through South America's Southland, With an Account of the Roosevelt Scientific Expedition to South America.* New York: Appleton, 1916.

Index

SADAKO GARDNER

A former editor at American Heritage, Joseph L. Gardner is now Editor of Newsweek Books. He is the author of a juvenile history of the American labor movement and was a Woodrow Wilson Fellow at the University of Wisconsin. He now lives in Hartsdale, New York, with his wife and two small children.